INDUSTRIAL BIOTECHNOLOGY

"...Beginners guide to industry & healthcare"

Second Edition

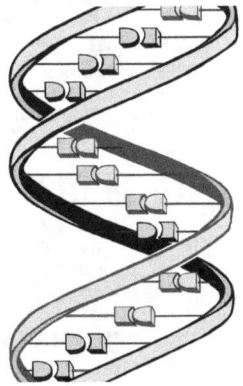

Dr. N. N. Bandela
Ph.D
Dr. Jitendra Ambulge
Ph.D
Dr. Rahul Mayee
M.Pharm, Ph.D
D. A. Savant
B.Pharm, M.S. (Pharmatechology)

Price ₹ : 300.00

NIRALI PRAKASHAN

INDUSTRIAL BIOTECHNOLOGY

ISBN 978-93-82448-98-3

Second Edition : January 2015

© : Authors

The text of this publication, or any part thereof, should not be reproduced or transmitted in any form or stored in any computer storage system or device for distribution including photocopy, recording, taping or information retrieval system or reproduced on any disc, tape, perforated media or other information storage device etc., without the written permission of Authors with whom the rights are reserved. Breach of this condition is liable for legal action.

Every effort has been made to avoid errors or omissions in this publication. In spite of this, errors may have crept in. Any mistake, error or discrepancy so noted and shall be brought to our notice shall be taken care of in the next edition. It is notified that neither the publisher nor the authors or seller shall be responsible for any damage or loss of action to any one, of any kind, in any manner, therefrom.

Published By :
NIRALI PRAKASHAN
Abhyudaya Pragati, 1312, Shivaji Nagar,
Off J.M. Road, PUNE – 411005
Tel - (020) 25512336/37/39, Fax - (020) 25511379
Email : niralipune@pragationline.com

Printed By :
REPRO INDIA LTD,
Mumbai.

DISTRIBUTION CENTRES
PUNE

Nirali Prakashan
119, Budhwar Peth, Jogeshwari Mandir Lane
Pune 411002, Maharashtra
Tel : (020) 2445 2044, 66022708, Fax : (020) 2445 1538
Email : bookorder@pragationline.com

Nirali Prakashan
S. No. 28/27, Dhyari,
Near Pari Company, Pune 411041
Tel : (020) 24690204 Fax : (020) 24690316
Email : dhyari@pragationline.com
bookorder@pragationline.com

MUMBAI
Nirali Prakashan
385, S.V.P. Road, Rasdhara Co-op. Hsg. Society Ltd.,
Girgaum, Mumbai 400004, Maharashtra
Tel : (022) 2385 6339 / 2386 9976, Fax : (022) 2386 9976
Email : niralimumbai@pragationline.com

DISTRIBUTION BRANCHES

NAGPUR
Pratibha Book Distributors
Above Maratha Mandir, Shop No. 3, First Floor,
Rani Jhanshi Square, Sitabuldi, Nagpur 440012,
Maharashtra, Tel : (0712) 254 7129

BENGALURU
Pragati Book House
House No. 1, Sanjeevappa Lane, Avenue Road Cross,
Opp. Rice Church, Bengaluru – 560002.
Tel : (080) 64513344, 64513355,
Mob : 9880582331, 9845021552
Email:bharatsavla@yahoo.com

JALGAON
Nirali Prakashan
34, V. V. Golani Market, Navi Peth, Jalgaon 425001,
Maharashtra, Tel : (0257) 222 0395
Mob : 94234 91860

KOLHAPUR
Nirali Prakashan
New Mahadvar Road,
Kedar Plaza, 1st Floor Opp. IDBI Bank
Kolhapur 416 012, Maharashtra. Mob : 9855046155

CHENNAI
Pragati Books
9/1, Montieth Road, Behind Taas Mahal, Egmore,
Chennai 600008 Tamil Nadu, Tel : (044) 6518 3535,
Mob : 94440 01782 / 98450 21552 / 98805 82331, Email : bharatsavla@yahoo.com

RETAIL OUTLETS
PUNE

Pragati Book Centre
157, Budhwar Peth, Opp. Ratan Talkies,
Pune 411002, Maharashtra
Tel : (020) 2445 8887 / 6602 2707, Fax : (020) 2445 8887

Pragati Book Centre
Amber Chamber, 28/A, Budhwar Peth,
Appa Balwant Chowk, Pune : 411002, Maharashtra,
Tel : (020) 20240335 / 66281669
Email : pbcpune@pragationline.com

Pragati Book Centre
676/B, Budhwar Peth, Opp. Jogeshwari Mandir,
Pune 411002, Maharashtra
Tel : (020) 6601 7784 / 6602 0855

PBC Book Sellers & Stationers
152, Budhwar Peth, Pune 411002, Maharashtra
Tel : (020) 2445 2254 / 6609 2463

MUMBAI
Pragati Book Corner
Indira Niwas, 111 - A, Bhavani Shankar Road, Dadar (W), Mumbai 400028, Maharashtra
Tel : (022) 2422 3526 / 6662 5254, Email : pbcmumbai@pragationline.com

"THIS BOOK IS DEDICATED TO ALL THOSE SCIENTISTS WHO DEVOTED THEIR LIVES TO UNREVEL THE MYSTRIES OF BIOTECHNOLOGY"

PREFACE

Dear Readers,

We have entered the 21st millennium with new hopes. Liberalisation and Globalisation of biotechnology trade, has sprung millions of new challenges in the new millennium. This is the IT/BT (Information Technology/Biotechnology) Era. In this era survival is possible by upgrading our business, and our self with the requirement of international genetic information. For international business we have to comply with regulatory as well as non-regulatory requirements. For pharmaceutical and genetically engineered products, manufacturing certifications such as WHO GMP, USFDA, ICH, MCA-UK, MCC, TGA, ISO 9001-2000 etc. are of prime importance.

The content of this book is focused on practical biotechnology industry setup. This book will serve as a guide for the industrialist and researches to set up new biotechnology industry and provide basic information about industrial biotechnology ,microorganisms and their applications for biotechnology. Biotechnology industrial setup is also incorporated in this book. In the chapter biotechnology for healthcare various topics such as vaccines, neutraceuticals, gene replacement, genetic treatment, cellular therapy, tissue engineering are explained. Procedures for regulatory licenses for biotechnology industry, patent procedures, financial supports and schemes from government of India for biotechnology industry are also given in this book.

The second section of this book is full of information on pharmaceutical and biotechnology Industry. Various definitions, calibrations, validations, equipments qualifications, WHO GMP related information, some focus on Drug and Cosmetic Act all are included in this book. ICH Guidelines, Good laboratory practices, clean room classes, sterilisation process design is included in this book. Quality risk management protocol and report, quality system documents ,important abbreviations, colour coding of service pipelines and information on water system is given in detail.

Over all this book is helpful not only to all pharmacy, biotechnology and medical professionals but also to the all students and professors

We are thankful to Dr M. K. Sahib for his valuable contribution and encouragement for writing this book especially for the biotechnology section,

We are also thankful to Shri. S.K. Dhas, and all Wockhardians for their continuous support, valuable guidance and encouragement.

It is very difficult to mention a long list, but we all are grateful and thankful to all our friends, colleagues for their help and encouragement.

The lion's share of my success goes to Mr. M. P. Munde - Sales Executive, Pragati Books Pvt. Ltd. I am also thankful to the publisher **Shri. Dineshbhai Furia and Shri Jigneshbhai Furia** for publishing this book in a short period, with very nice get-up.

We are indebted to our wives, sons, daughters, brothers, parents for their moral support through out our career.

Suggestions to improve the quality of this book are most welcome.

Dr. Bandela N.
Dr. Ambulge J.
Dr. Rahul Mayee
Datta Savant

READERSHIP

This Book is helpful to:

1. Students: Diploma, Degree or PG Students of all Academic Years of Pharmacy and biotechnology science graduates. (Regular and Ex-Students).

2. Lecturers, Professors, Technicians and Non-teaching staff.

3. Employees of Pharmaceutical Companies and Biotechnology companies.

4. Biotechnology and Pharmaceutical Consultants and Service Agencies.

5. Food and Drug Administration (Govt.) Technical and Non-Technical Employees.

6. Drug Testing Laboratories.

7. Medical Stores and Hospital Pharmacists.

8. Physicians, Nurses and Hospitals.

9. Bulk Drug Manufacturers and Employees.

10. As a gift to their Customers: Suppliers of Raw Material, Packing Material and Pharmaceuticals Suppliers can purchase it in bulk.

11. Biotechnology Research Institutes.

12. Biotechnology, Microbiology Organizations and Institutions.

13. People Related to Pharmaceuticals and Biotechnology.

14. All Pharma Marketing People and Research Laboratories.

CONTENTS

SECTION I
BEGINNERS GUIDE FOR BIOTECHNOLOGY INDUSTRY — I.1 – I.168

1.	Biotechnology : Introduction and Basics	I.2 – I.21
2.	Microscopy	I.22 – I.39
3.	Microorganisms in Biotechnology	I.40 – I.68
4.	Biotechnology Industry set up	I.69 – I.84
5.	Biotechnology For Healthcare – Preventive Management	I.85 – I.97

- Biotechnology for Healthcare – Preventive Management
- Biotechnology in Production of Proteins
- siRNA
- Gene
- Cellular Therapy
- Tissue Engineering

6.	Regulatory Approval	I.98 – I.108
7.	Financial Support from Government of India and Other Countries	I.109 – I.118
8.	List of Biotech Industries in India and Their Products	I.119 – I.122
9.	Classification of Insulin Preparations Based on Duration of Action	I.123 – I.123
10.	Operational Excellence and Six Sigma in Pharma Industry	I.124 – I.168

SECTION II
DOCUMENTATION AND cGMP FOR BIOTECHNOLOGY AND PHARMACEUTICAL INDUSTRY. — II.1 – II.222

1.	Definitions of GMP, cGMP, QA, QC and IPQC	II.2 – II.3
2.	Certifications for Pharmaceutical Industries	II.4 – II.7
3.	Classification and Definitions of Various Dosage Forms	II.8 – II.12
4.	Detergents and their Concentration used in Pharmaceuticals and Hospitals	II.13 – II.13
5.	Disinfectants and their Concentrations used in Pharmaceuticals and Hospitals	II.14 – II.14
6.	US Federal Standard 209 E: Classification, Testing and Monitoring Reports	II.15 – II.16
7.	Fumigation Technology for Industry and Hospitals	II.17 – II.18
8.	Calibrations	II.19 – II.19
9.	Validations	II.20 – II.20
10.	URS, FAT, DQ, SAT, IQ, OQ, PQ of Machine and Equipments	II.21 – II.28

11.	WHO GMP Minimum Document Check List	II.29 – II.29
12.	Schedules from Drug and Cosmetic Act 1940	II.30 – II.30
13.	Schedules from Drug and Cosmetic Rules 1945	II.31 – II.32
14.	Food and Drug Administration (FDA) Licensing Forms	II.33 – II.35
15.	List of Machineries and Equipments for pharmaceutical Plant with Advanced Technology	II.36 – II.41
16.	Accelerated Stability Testing and Shelf Life Calculation	II.42 – II.42
17.	International Conference on Harmonization (ICH, CTD) and ECTD	II.43 – II.59
18.	WHO-GMP and ICH Stability Testing Guideline for Drug Products	II.60 – II.68
19.	Good Laboratory Practices	II.69 – II.79
20.	US-FDA Drug Master files (DMF)	II.80 – II.81
21.	Cleanroom Standards for Different Countries and Names	II.82 – II.82
22.	Guidance for Preparation of Site Master File (SMF) (MHRA)	II.83 – II.96
23.	Sterilization Methods	II.97 – II.99
24.	Sterilization Indicators : Including ISO and EN	II.100 – II.103
25.	Definitions of Pharmaceutical Standard and Normal Values	II.104 – II.106
26.	Commonly used Pharmaceutical Words	II.107 – II.109
27.	List of Important SOP in Pharmaceuticals	II.110 – II.115
28.	Bowie Dick Test for Autoclave Validation	II.116 – II.118
29.	Sterilization Values: F_0, F_H, D and Z Values	II.119 – II.121
30.	Calculation of ideal Sterilization Cycle Time and Overkill Approach	II.122 – II.123
31.	Filtration Basic Concept	II.124 – II.126
32.	Intellectual Property Right: Patents, Copyright and Trade Marks	II.127 – II.147
33.	Quality Risk management with Protocol and Report	II.148 – II.182
34.	Quality Management System (GMP) Documentation	II.183 – II.192
35.	Solubility : Definitions as per IP 2007	II.193 – II.193
36.	Microorganisms and Nutrient Medias	II.194 – II.194
37.	Validation of Air Sampler used in Microbiology	II.195 – II.199
38.	Analytical Method Technologies	II.200 – II.200
39.	Important Terms used in Microbiological Testing	II.201 – II.203
40.	Frequently used Abbreviations in Pharmaceuticals	II.204 – II.213
41.	Light Illumination (LUX) for Pharmaceutical Plant	II.214 – II.214
42.	Clean Room Lighting	II.215 – II.216
43.	Colour coding for Pipelines and Gaslines	II.217 – II.219
44.	Pure Steam Quality	II.220 – II.221
45.	Water Pipeline – Slope Measurement and Limit	II.222 – II.222
	Bibliography	B.1 – B.4

SECTION-I

BEGINNERS GUIDE FOR BIOTECHNOLOGY INDUSTRY

1. BIOTECHNOLOGY: INTRODUCTION AND BASIC

INTRODUCTION AND APPLICATIONS:

Biotechnology is the word familiar to people. But very few people know the application and meaning of biotechnology. We are using products manufactured using this technology in our day to today life. Biotechnology has made human life simple, easy and comfortable due to low cost production. By using this technology one can create animal, plant and their product as per our desire.

Biotechnology is defined as a collection of technologies that uses living systems, or materials derived from living systems, to make products of desire. By this definition, biotechnology is one of the oldest industries – for thousands of years, humans have used organisms to make help, make products such as wine, cheese, and bread. However, when people use the term "biotechnology", they are usually referring not to bread and cheese production, but rather to the more dazzling products of "modern biotechnology", such as cloned sheep, gene therapies, and DNA fingerprints.

Modern biotechnology is rooted in hundreds of years of basic biological research into the intricacies of living systems. In the early 1970s, Dr. Herbert Boyer and Dr. Stanley Cohen published the results of basic scientific research demonstrating that genetic information could be intentionally transferred from one organism to another. In 1976, venture capitalist Robert A. Swanson and Dr. Boyer founded a company, Genentech Inc., to apply this genetic methodology for the production of commercial products. In 1977, Genentech Inc. reported production of the first human protein manufactured in bacteria, *Somatostatin,* a hormone that has many effects in the human body. Genentech is generally considered to be the first "modern" biotechnology company, but many others were quickly founded. There are now hundreds of biotechnology products such as: human growth hormone, used to treat dwarfism; Interferon α-2b, used to treat a variety of viral diseases and cancers; and Hepatitis B vaccine, used to immunize people against the Hepatitis B agent. **Gene therapy** is a promising application of biotechnology that *involves replacing a gene that is missing, or correcting the function of a faulty gene, in order to cure an illness.*

Biotechnology is also called as Genetic Engineering or Recombinant DNA Technology or Gene cloning. The fundamental techniques for accomplishing this have been mutagenesis, Gene transfer, and genetic recombination followed by selection of desired characteristic. Recently, a new term has been developed by which the Genotype of an organism can be modified in a directed and predetermined way. In this way, "Technique which is alternatively called Biotechnology, Recombinant DNA technology or gene cloning, a purified DNA fragments are isolated and recombined by in vitro manipulation. The recombinant DNA technique has generally enhanced our ability to manipulate organism and has revolutionised the study of gene structure. In order to understand Biotechnology we have to know some basic terminology and Structure of DNA.

Roughly construction, presence of DNA and other components of cells and body:

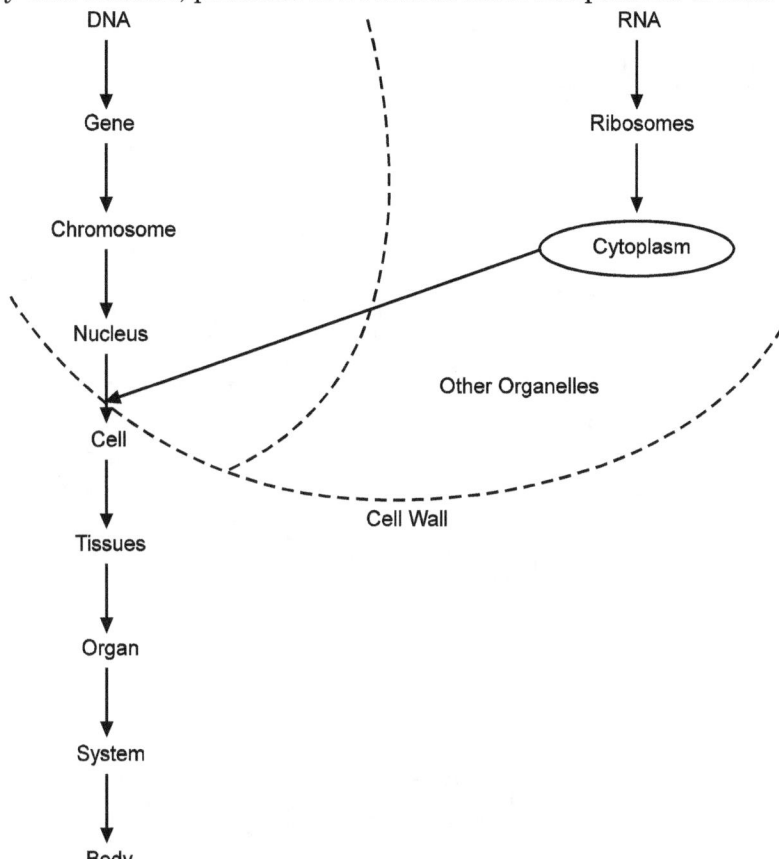

Fig. 1.1: Composition of the body

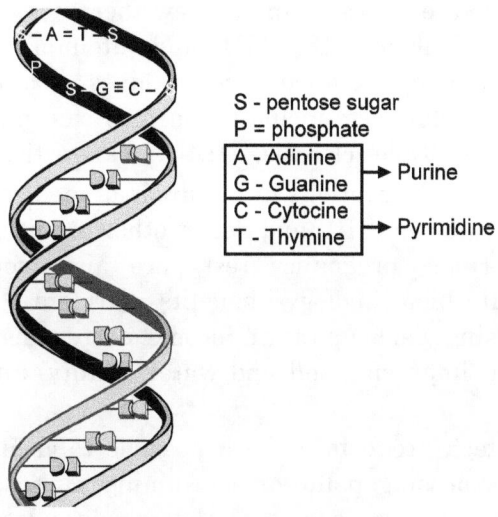

Fig.1.2: Double Helix DNA

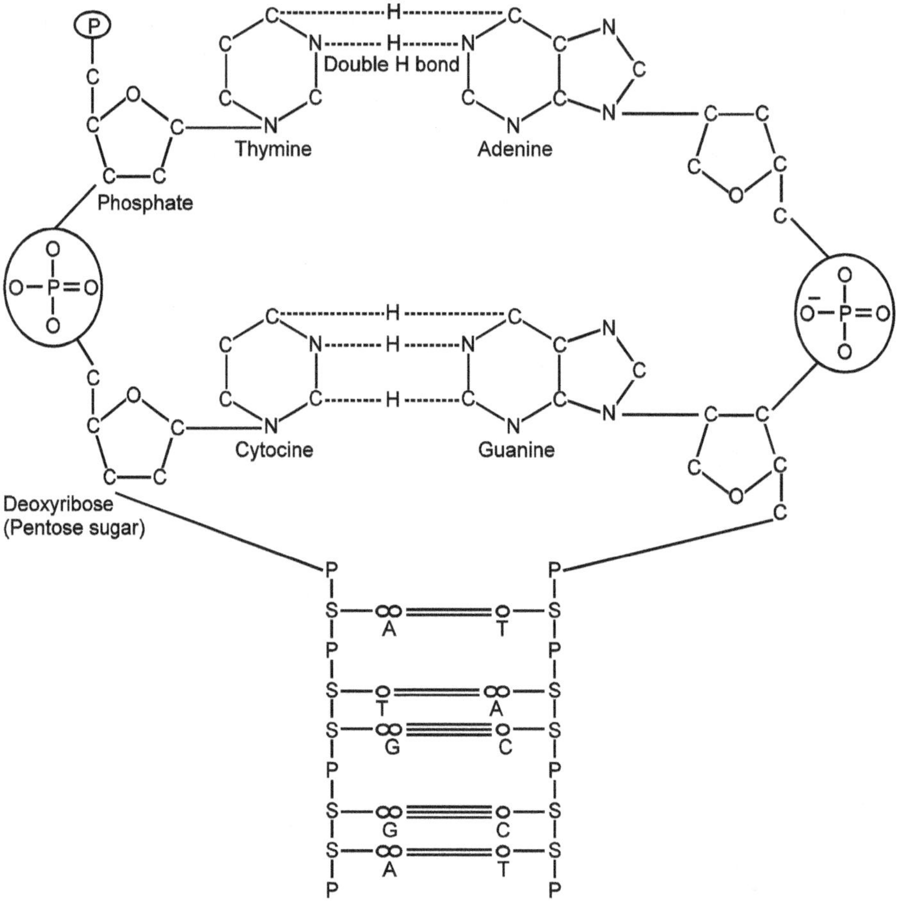

Fig. 1.3: DNA Structure

Biotechnology has created more than 200 new therapies and vaccines, including products to treat cancer, diabetes, HIV/ AIDS and autoimmune disorders. There are more than 400 biotech drug products and vaccines currently in clinical trials targeting more than 200 diseases, including various cancers, Alzheimer's disease, heart disease, diabetes, multiple sclerosis, AIDS and arthritis.

Biotechnology finds its applications in hundreds of medical diagnostic tests that keep the blood supply safe from HIV and detect other conditions early enough to be successfully treated. Home pregnancy tests are also biotechnology diagnostic products. Agricultural biotechnology benefits farmers, consumers and the environment by increasing yields and farm income, decreasing pesticide applications and operation cost and improving soil and water quality, and providing healthful foods for human life.

Environmental biotech products make it possible to clean up hazardous waste more efficiently by harnessing pollution consuming microbes. Industrial biotech applications have led to cleaner processes that produce less waste and use less energy and water in such industrial sectors as chemicals, pulp and paper, textiles, food, energy, and metals and minerals. For example, most laundry detergents produced in the United States contain biotechnology-based enzymes to protect the environment.

DNA fingerprinting, a biotech process, has dramatically improved criminal investigation and forensic medicine. It has also led to significant advances in anthropology and wildlife management.

INDIAN BIOTECH INDUSTRY

The Department of Biotechnology (DBT) was set up by the Government of India under the Ministry of Science and Technology in 1986, to give a boost to the Biotech industry in India. Since then there has been no looking back. The funding and initiatives of DBT have been successful in generating a rich pool of academicians and scientists. India has become a hub of Biotechnology activity in the last decade. It is an ideal ground to set up biotech companies not only by Indian ventures, but also MNCs. India provides a sound knowledge base combined with skilled manpower. It is also a great place to set up manufacturing units, not to mention research laboratories.

Success didn't come early to the biotech industry in India. Due to the prolonged period of research involved in the development of the processes and products, it was difficult for the industry to sustain itself in the face of scant funding. The high initial investment required and the uncertain nature of research made investors wary of funding activities, till a developed and tested product was available. But India could not afford to lag behind in the face of the huge benefits of Biotechnology. The science of biotechnology is a dynamic one, adopting the principles of various disciplines such as Biology, Biochemistry, Genetics, Cytology, Chemistry, Pharmacology, Bioinformatics and impacting important areas such as medicine, agriculture and environment. The applications of biotech research are many, some of which are cited below.

The field of medicine is making rapid progress and breakthroughs, thanks to new biotechnological processes and products. Traditional medicine cured the symptoms of various diseases. But biotechnological processes, in combination with pharmacology have the capability to develop proteins or molecules, which target the pathway of the disease and provide a permanent cure. Microorganisms can be manipulated to produce insulin, human growth factors, blood clotting factors, fertility drugs, antibiotics, vaccines and enzymes, which can be used to cure many human disorders. Gene therapy, a gift of biotechnology can cure genetically acquired diseases. It involves replacing defective genes, which may (somatic treatment) or may not (germline treatment) be transmitted to the next generation, as the need may be. Genetic testing can confirm paternity in the case of disputed parentage or help in solving a crime using DNA manipulative techniques available. A whole range of diseases like AIDS, cancer, sickle cell anemia, hemophilia, cystic fibrosis, diabetes, etc., can be detected and treated using biotechnological procedures which can detect mutations and address them at a genetic level.

The production of high yielding and disease resistant crops through biotechnological means is a real boon to agriculture. Plants can be engineered with new genes for a favorable trait. They can be induced to form more nutritious fruits and/or vegetables. Their color and size too can be manipulated by altering their genetic constitution, viz. replacing defective genes or incorporating new genes. Banana and tomato plants have been engineered to produce vaccines. If clinical trials are successful, we are in for a revolution in biopharmaceuticals. Disease resistance crop varieties can be produced by incorporating Bt (*Bacillus thuringiensis*) gene in the crops, which when expressed produces the Bt toxin. When the insect feeds on the plant, the toxin acts on its metabolism and causes the death of the pest. Crops can also be engineered to tolerate biotic and abiotic stress conditions. Biotechnology has erased the divide of the seasons, allowing us to enjoy our favorite fruits, vegetables and flowers all through the year.

The environment around us is undergoing a lot of change due to increased amounts of pollutants and climatic changes around the globe. To maintain a sustainable environment, it is necessary to cleanse our habitat. Biotechnology helps us to study the existing degradation pathways and improvise on them. For example, the oil spills in coastal regions and petroleum seepage into water bodies, can be controlled by bioengineered microorganisms, which can degrade these harmful pollutants. Biotechnology in conjunction with environmental sciences provides valuable insights into the different pathways and networks of important elements in nature, thereby helping in bioremediation.

The Government of India is going all out to embrace the biotech industry and its products. Funds are flowing through Venture Capitalists (VCs) to biotech startups. Rebate on R&D, 100% foreign direct investment, excise and customs duty waiver on certain products, etc., are some of the incentives introduced by the government. India has made great strides in all the above biotechnological applications. The Indian biotech industry today encompasses 325 companies, some of them including Biocon, Serum Institute of India and Panacea Biotec alone, contributing to 27% of revenues. According to the 5th BioSpectrum-ABLE (Association of Biotechnology Led Enterprises) Biotech Industry Survey, of April-May 2007, the industry has grown by 30.9% in 2006-2007 alone. The contract research industry in India could reach as high as US $ 270 million by 2009 (Asia Specific Biotechnology Market 2007-2010, June 2007).

The top ten biotech companies of India listed below have broken new grounds and given new products and technologies to the world.

1. Biocon
2. Serum Institute of India
3. Panacea Biotec

4. Nicholas Piramal
5. Wockhadrt Limited
6. GlaxoSmithKline
7. Bharat Serum
8. Krebs Biochemicals and Industries Limited
9. Zydus Cadila
10. Indian Immunologicals

Close on the heels of the companies listed above, are Shantha Biotechnics, Biological E, Mahyco Monsanto, Bharat Biotech, Ranbaxy and Novozymes to name a few. Biocon is the first and presently the leading biotech company in India. Initially it brought in revenues by manufacturing enzymes. But it has gradually become more research oriented with the goal of introducing new drugs in to the market. Its manufacturing capabilities include microbial and mammalian cell culture fermentation, synthetic chemistry and therapeutic drugs for the treatment of cancer, autoimmune and metabolic diseases. Serum Institute of India, Indian Immunologicals and Bharat Biotech specialise in the production of vaccines. Serum Institute of India is the world's largest producer of measles and DTP vaccines. Panacea Biotec has recently set up a plant in Himachal Pradesh, India, for production of bacterial and viral vaccines. Wockhardt is a biopharma powerhouse with 11 world class manufacturing plants in India. Shantha Biotechnics is located in Hyderabad and its products include Hepatitis B vaccine, Streptokinase drug and Interferon alpha-2b. The big player in agro-biotech, MAHYCO Monsanto has released a number of Bt cotton hybrids, which have been approved for commercial cultivation. The significant reduction in the use of pesticides and higher and better quality yields will result in increased income to farmers. Genetically modified field crops like rice, mustard, groundnut, maize, tubers like potato, vegetables like tomato, cabbage, okra, etc., are also under various stages of field trial led by Indian biotech companies. Development of products tailored to the needs of the Indian agricultural sector, will go a long way in making the country self-sufficient.

The above-mentioned achievements of Indian biotech companies have started attracting overseas partners and investors. Indian biotech firms have started scaling up their capabilities to become global players. With proactive government schemes, VC funding, new products and groundbreaking research, India is fast emerging as a biotech leader in the Pacific, alongside Singapore, Japan, Taiwan, Korea and China.

The biotech industry is regulated by the U.S. Food and Drug Administration (FDA), the Environmental Protection Agency (EPA) and the Department of Agriculture (USDA).

As of Dec. 31, 2006, there were 1,452 biotechnology companies in the United States. Market capitalization, the total value of publicly traded biotech companies

(U.S.) at market prices, was $360 billion as of late April 2008 (based on stocks tracked by BioWorld). The biotechnology industry has mushroomed since 1992, with U.S. health care biotech revenues from publicly traded companies rising from $8 billion in 1992 to $58.8 billion in 2006. Biotechnology is one of the most research-intensive industries in the world. U.S. publicly traded biotech companies spent $27.1 billion on research and development in 2006. There were 180,000 employed in U.S. biotech companies in 2006. The top five biotech companies invested an average of $170,000 per employee in R&D in 2007.

In 1982, recombinant human insulin became the first biotech therapy to earn FDA approval. The product was developed by Genentech and Eli Lilly and Co. Corporate partnering has been critical to biotech success. According to BioWorld, in 2007 biotechnology companies struck 417 new partnerships with pharmaceutical companies and 473 deals with fellow biotech companies. The industry also saw 126 mergers and acquisitions. Most biotechnology companies are young companies developing their first products and depend on investor capital for survival. According to BioWorld, biotechnology attracted more than $24.8 billion in financing in 2007 and raised more than $100 billion in the five-year span of 2003-2007.

The biosciences - including all life-sciences activities - employed 1.3 million people in the United States in 2006 and generated an additional 7.5 million related jobs.

The average annual wage of U.S. bioscience workers was $71,000 in 2006, more than $29,000 greater than the average private-sector annual wage.

The Biotechnology Industry Organization (BIO) was founded in 1993 to represent biotechnology companies at the local, state, federal and international levels. BIO comprises more than 1,200 members, including biotech companies, academic centers, state and local associations, and related enterprises.

Some important terminologies used in biotechnology:

1) **DNA:** Deoxyribonucleic Acid is carrier of genetic information, a type of nucleic acid occurring in cell.

2) **Gene:** A segment of chromosome, definable in operational terms as the **repository** of a unit of genetic information. Gene will undergo duplication when DNA molecule replicate

3) **Genome:** A complete set of genetic material, that is complete set of genes.

4) **Chromosomes:** A gene containing filamentous structure in cell nucleus. The number of Chromosomes per cell nucleus is constant for each species.

5) **Nucleoside:** A pentose sugar links to a purine and Pyrimidine bases in DNA. (Pentose Sugar + Nitrogen bases)

6) **Nucleotide:** The basic building block of nucleic acids (DNA and RNA), consists of a purine or pyrimidine base, Ribose or deoxyribose and Phosphate. (Pentose sugar + Nitrogen bases + Phosphate.)

7) **Phenotype:** That part of genetic material of an organism which is actually expressed.
8) **Genotype:** Particular set of gene present in an organisms cell; an organisms genetic constitution.
9) **Codon:** A sequence of three nucleotide bases (in mRNA) that codes for an amino acid or the initiation or termination of a polypeptide chain.
10) **Anti Codon:** A sequence of three nucleotide (in tRNA) complementary to a codon triplet in mRNA.
11) **Replication:** Production of a Stranded DNA from original DNA.
12) **Transcription:** Process in which a complementary single stranded mRNA is synthesized from one of the DNA strand.
13) **Translation:** The Process in which genetic information in mRNA directs the order of assembly of the specific amino acids during Protein synthesis.

DNA

It is Deoxyribonucleic acid, present mainly in chromosome. Most of DNA are double stranded, but bacteriophase DNA is single stranded. The size of *E.Coli* DNA is 1,000 micron in length.

Structure of DNA is double helix, (see fig). Each strand consists of alternating molecule of deoxyribose (pentose sugar) and Phosphate groups. Each step is made up of double ring purine base and a single ring purimidine nitrogen base.

Adenine and Guanine are Purine base pairs. Thymine and Cytosine are Pyrimidine base pairs. Purine and Pyrimidine bases are connected to deoxyribose sugar molecule. DNA molecule is a polymer consisting of several thousand pairs of nucleotide monomers. Each Nucleotide consists of Sugar (Deoxyribose), a Phosphate and a Nitrogen bases (Purine and Pyrimidine). Deoxyribose and nitrogen base together forms Nucleoside. Nucleoside and Phosphate forms Nucleotide.

Some Normal Values:
1. One human Cell = 5 picogram of DNA = 5 Billion Base pairs.
2. In one Human cell = 5 millions of Genes.
3. Each base pair molecular weight = About 600 Da.
4. One Gene contains average about 2000 nitrogen base pairs.
5. Human: 1 Gene = 1000 Nitrogen base pairs.
   1 Cell = 5 million gene.
   1 Cell = 5 billion Base pairs.

Protein (Building Block) Synthesis:

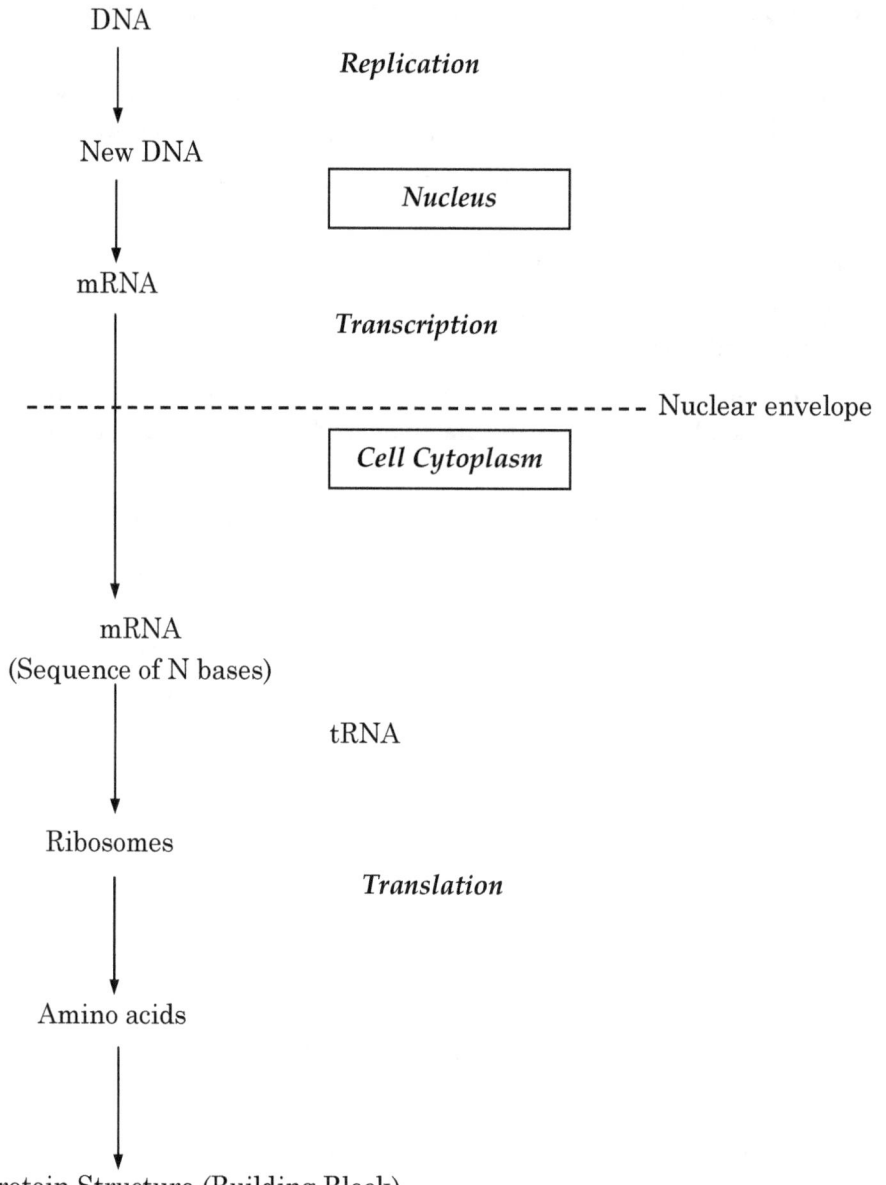

The amino acid produced depends on the sequence of 3 nitrogen bases in mRNA.

There are only 4 kinds of nucleotide bases present on each strand viz, Adenine, Guanine, Thymine and Cytosine. Both old and new DNA Stands are complementary.

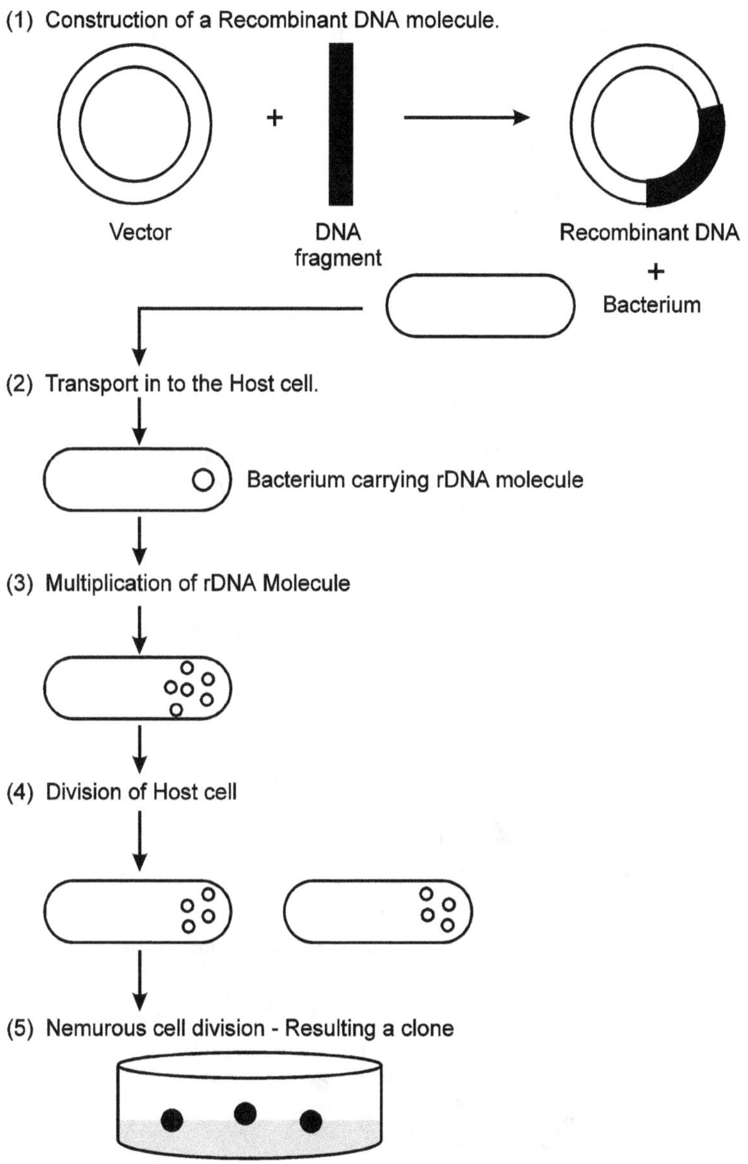

(1) Construction of a Recombinant DNA molecule.

Vector + DNA fragment → Recombinant DNA + Bacterium

(2) Transport in to the Host cell.

Bacterium carrying rDNA molecule

(3) Multiplication of rDNA Molecule

(4) Division of Host cell

(5) Nemurous cell division - Resulting a clone

Fig. 1.4: Steps in rDNA Technology

BIOTECHNOLOGY (rDNA TECHNOLOGY)

From above basic information it is easy to understand the biotechnology. The basic Technique are quite simple - Two DNA molecule are isolated and cut in to the fragments by one or more specialised enzymes and has then, these fragments are joined together in a desired combination.

In rDNA technology, foreign gene is introduced in bacteria or yeast. This foreign DNA should get replicated and faithfully passes on to the next generation, otherwise it will be lost and there after the foreign protein will not be synthesized by the bacterium or yeast.

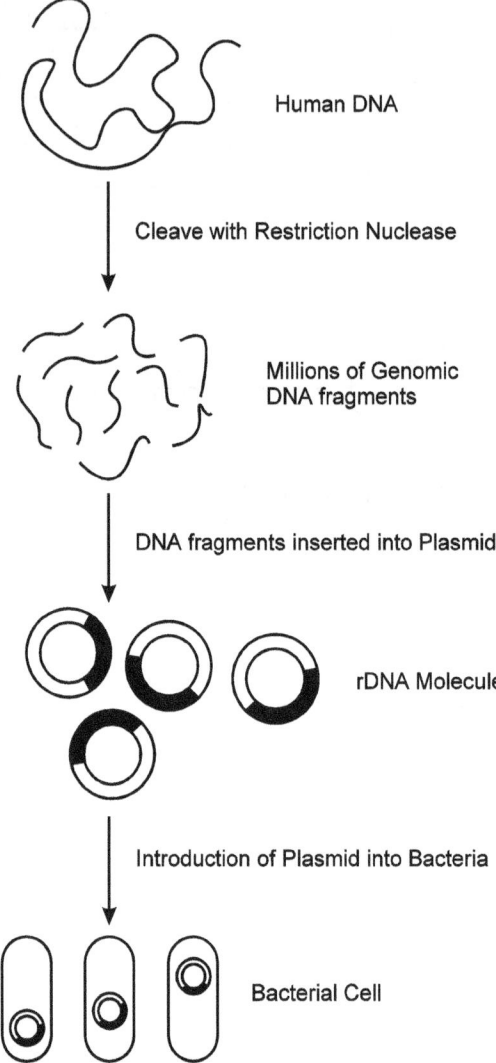

Fig. 1.5: Preparation of rDNA Molecule

Following are the steps in rDNA technology:

1. ISOLATION OF GENE:

There are three methods for gene isolation:

A) Creation of Genomic Library:

Genes are present on the chromosomes. Total genome content present on chromosome is cut using Restriction Endonuclease into manageable length of DNA fragments. These individual DNA fragments may contain the desired gene.

Hence each DNA fragment is inserted into a vector and introduced into host cell like *E.Coli*. Thus, all the DNA fragments are introduced into the different *E.Coli* cells, creating a library of gene.

B) Creation of Complimentary DNA Library:

Messenger RNA for the desired gene is isolated from organism or tissue. The enzyme Reverse Transcriptage can use mRNA as a template and synthesize complementary DNA (cDNA). These cDNA fragments containing respective gene are incorporated into vectors and introduced into host cell.

C) Chemical Synthesis of DNA:

If amino acid sequence of the protein is known. The corresponding nucleotide sequence can be determined using codon dictionary of the life. Once this is known, the corresponding gene can be synthesized in the laboratory by incorporating nucleotide bases one by one in the predetermined order.

2. INSERTION OF FOREIGN GENE INTO VECTOR:

Plasmid or any vector is treated with restriction endonuclease enzyme which has only one recognition sequence or restriction site or cutting site on the vector. This results in the opening of the circular plasmid, creating a linear molecule with sticky ends at both the termini. DNA fragment containing foreign gene is treated with the same restriction Endonuclease, leading to the formation of similar sticky ends at both the termini. Linear plasmid and foreign gene are mixed together and the enzyme DNA ligase is added. Because of the sticky ends, Foreign gene gets incorporated into the plasmid and the two DNA species are joined together by DNA Ligase. This is like cutting and pasting of DNA molecules, Leading to creation of recombinant DNA molecule that is cell called a Chemeric or Hybrid Plasmid.

3. INTRODUCTION OF FOREIGN GENE INTO THE HOST:

Chemeric or Hybrid Plasmid can be transported in to the host cell like E.Coli. For this purpose, E.Coli cells have to treated with calcium Chloride. These treatments render cell wall and cell membrane of E.Coli permeable to free DNA. This Process is called **Transformation.** Foreign gene can be transported into host cell like E.Coli by other route also that is by using bacteriophase as a vector. This process is called **Transduction.**

4. SELECTION OF CELLS CONTAINING FOREIGN GENES.

Introduction of gene into the host is not the end of the process. This gene should replicate faithfully and pass from one generation to the next. When the host cells are grown in large numbers. At the same time that is, it should instruct the synthesis of the corresponding protein. Various methods can be used to find out whether the foreign gene is really transported to the host cell and is expressing the desired protein.

A) Vectors containing Gene for Antibiotic Resistance are Used as Makers for Selection:

Vectors are used containing two selectable makers that is, resistance to two antibiotics, for example, Ampicillin and Tetracycline. If the foreign Gene gets integrated into the Ampicillin resistance gene, then activity of this gene gets lost and the host cell containing hybrid plasmid will be resistant to tetracycline and sensitive to Ampicilline. These cells will be able to grow in a nutrient medium containing tetracycline. The same cells, when transferred to nutrient medium containing Ampicilline, will not grow at all.

B) Single Stranded Radioactive Gene Probe can be Used to Detect Corresponding Foreign Gene in Host Cell:

The DNA from host cell is denaturated that is two strands are separated. Radioactive gene probes are added into this mixture. If the complementary strand of the foreign gene is present in sample, then radioactive hybrid molecule will be produced, Which can be detected by auto-radiography. If foreign gene is not present in the host cell, hybridization will not occur and hence, will not be seen in the autoradiography.

C) Immunological Method can be Used to Find Out the Production of Foreign Protein by Recombinant Host Cell:

Antibody against foreign protein, coupled with radio isotope or enzyme, can be used to detect the protein expressed by foreign gene. Radio - Immuno assay, ELISA are examples of this Technique. Various hosts are used for the expression of foreign gene. Bacteria such as E.Coli, Bacillus Subtillis; Yeasts such as Saccharomyces cerevisiae, Pichia pastoris or mammalian cells such as Chinese Hamster Ovary Cells are used hosts in rDNA technology. Vectors used for transportation foreign genes into each of these systems are different. E.Coli is extensively used as host cell because it's genetic has been studied in great detail.

Yeasts also can be grown on large scale in fermentor. Fermentation using Yeasts is a fairly well studied and established process. These organism do not produce endotoxin. They are capable of glycosylating proteins up to a certain extent like mammalian cells. Hence, now-a-days organisms from class yeasts are being tried extensively for commercial production of rDNA products. Mammalian cells can also be an ideal choice for production of human therapeutic proteins.

ENZYMES USED IN BIOTECHNOLOGY

Several kinds of specific enzymes are employed in genetic engineering. These include lysing enzymes, cleaving enzymes, synthesizing enzymes, joining enzymes and alkaline phosphates.

Lysing enzyme: These are enzymes used to extract DNA from a cell for genetic experiments. Lysozyme is commonly used to dissolve the bacterial cell wall.

Cleaving enzyme: These are used to break DNA molecule into fragments. They are further of three kinds,

Exonucleases: It release nucleotides from 5 or 3 ends of a DNA molecule;

Endonucleases: It cleave DNA helix at any point except the at the terminal ends.

Restriction endonucleases: which cleave DNA molecule at specific points in such a way that single-stranded free ends project from each fragment of the DNA molecule. These single-stranded free ends are called "sticky ends" because they join with similar complementary ends of DNA fragment from some other source. Restriction endonuclease was discovered by Arber in 1962 in bacteria. Restriction endonuclease 1 (ECOR-1) is found in the colon bacterium Escherichia coli. It recognizes the base sequence GAATTC in DNA duplex and cleaves its strands between G and A as shown below. The arrows indicate the sites where the enzyme cleaves the sequence.

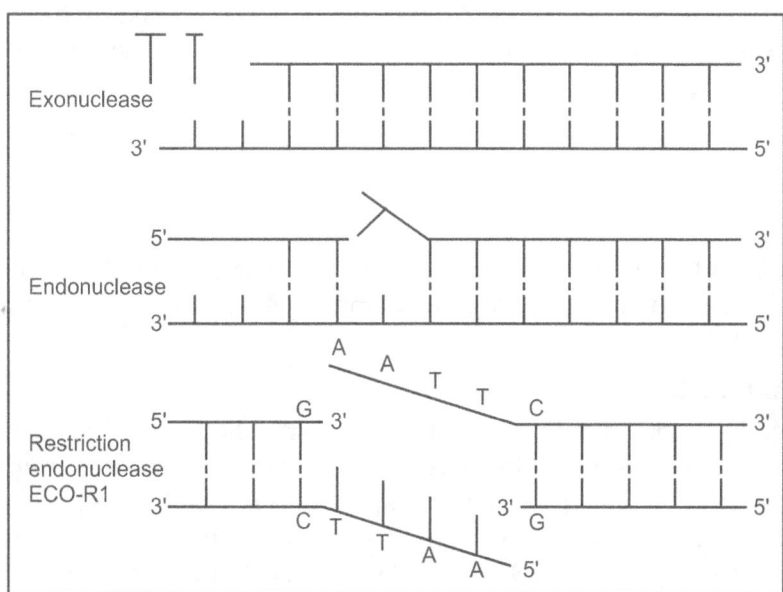

Fig. 1.6.: The action of DNA cleaving enzymes

Synthesising Enzymes: These enzymes play a role in the synthesis of DNA strands on suitable templates. They are of two type:

1. **Reverse transcriptases:** which help in the synthesis of complementary DNA strands on RNA templates, DNA polymerase, which aid in the synthesis of complementary DNA strands on DNA templates.

2. **Joining Enzymes:** These enzymes, also called as ligases, help in sealing gaps in DNA fragments joined by complementary base pairing. e.g. Tuligases.

Alkaline phosphotase:

These enzymes release phosphate group from the 5 end of linearised circular DNA to check its recircularization.

VEHICLE OR VECTOR DNA USED IN GENETIC ENGINEERING

The DNA used as a carrier for transferring a fragment of foreign DNA into a suitable host is called vehicle DNA. Two types of DNA are used as vehicles: plasmid DNA and bacteriophage DNA.

Plasmids:

The plasmids are small, circular DNA molecules present in bacterial cells in addition to the chromosomal DNA. Genes from one organism may be added to the plasmids of a bacterium and transfer them to another. They retain their characters after combining with the DNA of another organisms. Not being a part of the main genome, they can be easily isolated and transferred. These features make the plasmids most suitable for use as a vehicle DNA. A plasmid having DNA of another organism integrated with it is known as cosmid, also recombinant plasmid or hybrid plasmid. Cosmids are picked up by or can be introduced into plasmid free bacteria.

Bacteriophage DNA:

The bacteriophages (or phages), are viruses that infect and kill bacteria. Their circular DNA is also suitable for use as a vehicle DNA.

Passenger DNA:

It is the DNA that is transferred from one organism into another by combining it with the vehicle DNA. Three types of DNA are used as passengers: complimentary, synthetic and random

Complementary DNA (cDNA):

It is the DNA synthesised on RNA template with the help of the enzyme reverse transcriptase and necessary nucleotides. The DNA strand is isolated from the hybrid RNA-DNA complex by using alkaline phosphatase enzyme. A complementary DNA strand is then synthesized on the isolated single-stranded DNA template with the help of DNA polymerase. The cDNA double helix so obtained can be joined with the vehicle DNA for introduction into a new host cell.

Synthetic DNA (sDNA):

It is the DNA synthesised with the help of DNA polymerases on the DNA template or from free deoxybironucleotides without a template.

BLOTTING TECHNIQUES

Blots are techniques for transferring DNA,RNA and proteins onto a carrier so they can be separated, and often follows the use of a gel electrophoresis. The Southern blot is used for transferring DNA, the Northern blot for RNA and the western blot for PROTEIN.

Blotting technique: There are three methods of blotting technique.
1) Southern blot: It is used to detect DNA.
2) Northern blot: It is used to detect RNS.
3) Western blot: It is used to detect Protein.

1) **Southern Blot:** This method Involves separation, transfer and hybridization. The Southern blot is used to detect the presence of a particular piece of DNA in a sample. The DNA detected can be a single gene, or it can be part of a larger piece of DNA such as a viral genome. The key to this method is Hybridization. Hybridization- Process of forming a double-stranded DNA molecule between a single-stranded DNA probe and a single-stranded target patient DNA.

   Applications:

   Southern blots are used in gene discovery, mapping, evolution and development studies, diagnostics and forensics. In regards to genetically modified organisms, Southern blotting is used for testing to ensure that a particular section of DNA of known genetic sequence has been successfully incorporated into the genome of the host organism. Southern blots allow investigators to determine the molecular weight of are striction fragment and to measure relative amounts in different samples. Southern blot is used to detect the presence of a particular bit of DNA in a sample. Also sued to analyze the genetic patterns which appear in a person's DNA and to analyze restriction digestion fragmentation of DNA or a biological sample.

2) **Northern blot:** Northern blotting is a technique for detection of specific RNA sequences. Northern blotting was developed by James Alwine and George Stark at Stanford University and was named such by analogy to Southern blotting. A standard for the direct study of gene expression at the level of mRNA (messenger RNA transcripts).

   Application:

   (a) Detection of mRNA transcript size.

   (b) Study RNA degradation.

   (c) Study RNA splicing - can detect alternatively spliced transcripts.

   (d) Study RNA half-life.

   (d) Study IRES (internal ribosomal entry site) – to remove possibility of RNA digestion vs. 2nd cistrontranslation.

   (f) Often used to confirm and check transgenic /knockout mice (animals).

3) **Western blot:** Western blotting is an Immuno-blotting technique which rely on the specificity of binding between a molecule of interest and aprobe to allow detection of the molecule of interest in a mixture of many other similar molecules. In Western blotting, the molecule of interest is a protein and the probe is typically an antibody raised against that particular protein. The SDS PAGE technique is a prerequisite for Western blotting.

Applications:

The confirmatory HIV test employs a Western blot to detect anti-HIV antibody in a human serum sample. Proteins from known HIV-infected cells are separated and blotted on a membrane then, the serum to be tested is applied in the primary antibody incubation step; free antibody is washed away, and a secondary anti-human antibody linked to an enzyme signal is added. The stained bands then indicate the proteins to which the patient's serum contains antibody.

A Western blot is also used as the definitive testfor Bovine spongiform encephalopathy (BSE,commonly referred to as 'mad cow disease').Some forms of Lyme disease testing employ Western blotting.

OTHER TECHNIQUES USED IN BIOTECHNOLOGY

PCR (Polymerase Chain Reaction)

It is a revolutionary method developed by Kary Mullis in the 1980s. PCR is based on using the ability of DNA polymerase to synthesize new strand of DNA complementary to the offered template strand. Because DNA polymerase can add a nucleotide only onto a preexisting 3'-OH group, it needs a primer to which it can add the first nucleotide. This requirement makes it possible to delineate a specific region of template sequence that the researcher wants to amplify. At the end of the PCR reaction, the specific sequence will be accumulated in billions of copies (amplicons).

The PCR reaction requires the following components:

DNA template - the sample DNA that contains the target sequence. At the beginning of the reaction, high temperature is applied to the original double-stranded DNA molecule to separate the strands from each other.

DNA polymerase - a type of enzyme that synthesizes new strands of DNA complementary to the target sequence. The first and most commonly used of these enzymes is *Taq* DNA polymerase (from *Thermis aquaticus*), whereas *Pfu* DNA polymerase (from *Pyrococcus furiosus*) is used widely because of its higher fidelity when copying DNA. Although these enzymes are subtly different, they both have two capabilities that make them suitable for PCR: 1) they can generate new strands of DNA using a DNA template and primers, and 2) they are heat resistant. Primers short pieces of single-stranded DNA that are complementary to the target sequence. The polymerase begins synthesizing new DNA from the end of the primer. Nucleotides (dNTPs or deoxynucleotide triphosphates) - single units of the bases A, T, G, and C, which are essentially "building blocks" for new DNA strands.RT-PCR (Reverse Transcription PCR) is PCR preceded with conversion of sample RNA into cDNA with enzyme reverse transcriptase .

Applications of PCR:

Cloning, genetic engineering, sequencing.

Limitations of PCR and RT-PCR:

The PCR reaction starts to generate copies of the target sequence exponentially. Only during the exponential phase of the PCR reaction is it possible to extrapolate back to determine the starting quantity of the target sequence contained in the sample. Because of inhibitors of the polymerase reaction found in the sample, reagent limitation, accumulation of pyrophosphate molecules, and self-annealing of the accumulating product, the PCR reaction eventually ceases to amplify target sequence at an exponential rate and a "plateau effect" occurs, making the end point quantification of PCR products unreliable. This is the attribute of PCR that makes Real-Time Quantitative RT-PCRso necessary.

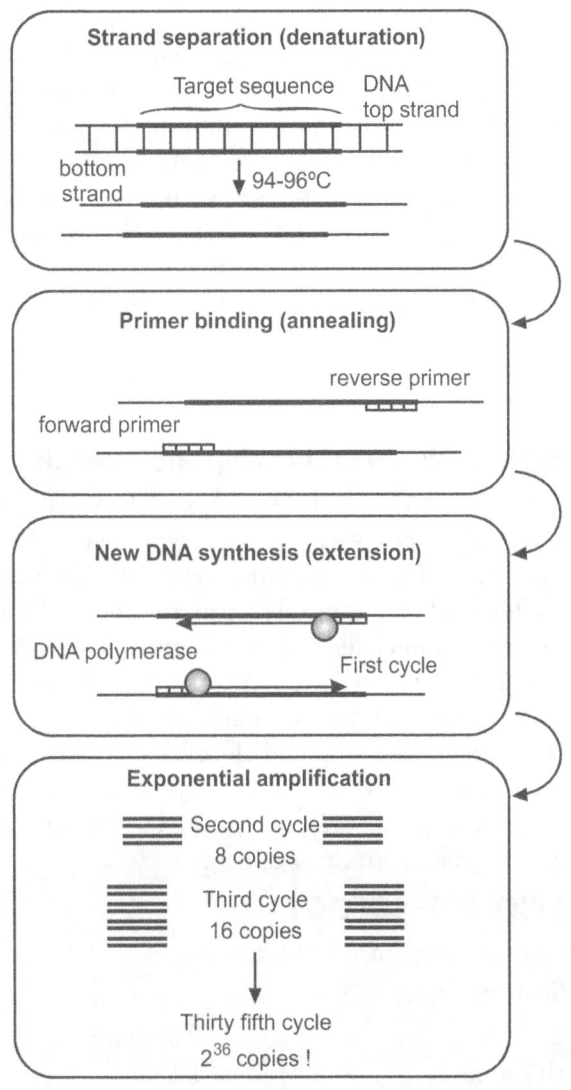

Fig. 1.7: Polymerase Chain reaction: Working Principle.

RESTRICTION FRAGMENT LENGTH POLYMORPHISM, (RFLP) ANALYSIS:

RFLP methodology involves cutting a particular region of DNA with known variability, with restriction enzymes, then separating the DNA fragments by agarose gel electrophoresis and determining the number of fragments and relative sizes. The pattern of fragment sizes will differ for each individual tested.

RFLP is one technique used by forensic scientists in DNA fingerprinting. It is also used for tracing ancestry, studying evolution and migration of wildlife, and detection and diagnosis of certain diseases. It is also known as Restriction Fragment Length Polymorphism, RFLP Analysis. Developed by Alec Jeffreys in England, in the beginning of the 1980s, this technique is based on the distance between restriction sites in the DNA. The RFLP technique uses special enzymes called *restriction enzymes* to cut DNA into fragments. These enzymes recognize short, specific sequences of DNA and cut the DNA at those sites. After the DNA is treated with a restriction enzyme, it is cut into fragments of various sizes. The number and size of the fragments is unique to each individual. The restriction (cut) sites of a person, a corn variety, or a sheep are as unique as a finger print, allowing unequivocal identification of the individual. If the DNA of two individuals are cut with the same enzyme, *Eco*R V for example, two patterns of DNA fragments are produced, making it possible to distinguish them on the basis of the variation in the length of the fragments because each pattern of fragments is unique to each individual. The occurrence of many patterns of fragments with different lengths is called RFLP.

AMPLIFIED FRAGMENT LENGTH POLYMORPHISM (AFLP ANALYSIS):

Amplified Fragment Length Polymorphism is a PCR based genetic fingerprinting technique developed by KeyGene. AFLP technology has the capability to detect various polymorphisms in different genomic regions simultaneously, is highly sensitive and reproducible and can generate large numbers of marker fragments for any organism, without prior knowledge of the genomic sequence. As a result, AFLP has become widely used for the identification of genetic variation in strains or closely related species of plants, fungi, animals, and bacteria; has been used in population genetics to determine slight differences within populations, and in linkage studies to generate maps for QTL analysis. Unique sizing and pattern recognition technologies significantly improve analysis accuracy, requires less user intervention and provides greater analysis speed.

APPLICATIONS OF BIOTECHNOLOGY

1. Production of Human Therapeutic Proteins:
   Products and indication are as follows:

Erythropoietin	Anaemia.
Epidermal Growth Factor	Ulcer.
Factor VIII	Haemophilia.

Factor IX	Christmas Disease.
Granulocyte colony stimulating factor	Cancer.
Hepatitis B surface antigen	Hepatitis B (Vaccination).
Human serum albumin	Plasma supplements.
Human Insulin	Diabetes.
Human Somatotropin	Dwarfism.
Interleukin	Cancer.
Interferon - Alpha	Leukaemia and other cancer.
Interferon - Beta	Cancer.
Relaxin	Child Birth.
Tissue Plasminogen Activator (tPA)	Heart Attack.
Vascular Endothelial growth factor	CVS Disorders.

2. Production of citric acid.
3. Production of desired plants seeds.
4. Production of desired characteristic organisms.
5. In the treatment of diseases.
6. Various drugs and pharmaceutical.

The medical/pharmaceutical industry is not the only one impacted by the methods of modern biotechnology. For example, farmers commonly plant crops that are genetically modified to be resistant to herbicides. Genetically modified microorganisms are sometimes used to detoxify contaminated soil or water. Crime investigators use DNA methods to link a suspect to a crime scene. Biotechnology is thus a collection of technologies that have profoundly impacted many human enterprises.

❖❖❖

2. MICROSCOPY

The object which is not seen by the healthy normal naked eyes are called micron sized object. Microscope is the instrument which is used to see the object which are not visible to the healthy human naked eyes.

A microscope is term derived from Greek word *Micros* means "small" and *Skopein* means "to see" or "to look".

The first microscope to be developed was the optical microscope in which light is used to image the sample. The original inventor of the microscope is not yet identified. An early microscope is made in 1590 in Middelburg, Netherland. Giovanni Faber coined the name for Galileo Galilei's microscope in 1625.The great contribution come from Antonie Van Leeuwenhoek and helped to popularizes the microscopy as technology. On 9th October 1676 Van Leeuwenhoek reported the discovery of microorganism.

In the early 1900 s a significant alternative to light microscopy was developed, using electron in place of light to generate the image. Ernst Ruska started development of first electron microscope in 1931, which was the transmission electron microscope. Transmission electron microscope works on the principles as an optical microscope but uses electron in place of glass lenses. Use of electron instead of light allows a much better resolution and clear image of the object.

After this in 1935 "Scanning Electron Microscope was developed. In 1980 third type of microscope "Scanning Probe Microscope" was developed. The first was the Scanning Tunneling microscope in 1981 developed by Gerd Binnigand Heinrich Roher. This was closely followed in 1986 with Gerd, Quate and Gerber's invention of the atomic force microscope.

The most recent development in the light microscope largely center on the rise of fluorescence microscopy in biology. During the last decade of the 20th century,particularly in the post genomic era, many technique for fluorescent labeling of cellular structures were developed. In this way there are 3 to 4 main branches of microscopy.

1) Optical microscopy.
2) Electron microscopy.
3) Scanning probe microscopy.
4) Fluorescent microscopy

Optical and electron microscopy involve the diffraction, reflection, or refraction of electromagnetic radiation/electron beams interacting with the specimen, and the subsequent collection of this scattered radiation or another signal in order to create an image. This process may be carried out by wide-field irradiation of the sample (for example standard light microscopy and transmission electron microscopy) or by scanning of a fine beam over the sample (for example confocal laser scanning microscopy and scanning electron microscopy). Scanning probe microscopy involves the interaction of a scanning probe with the surface of the object of interest. The development of microscopy revolutionized biology and remains an essential technique in the life and physical sciences.

PARTS AND MAGNIFICATION POWERS OF THE MICROSCOPE

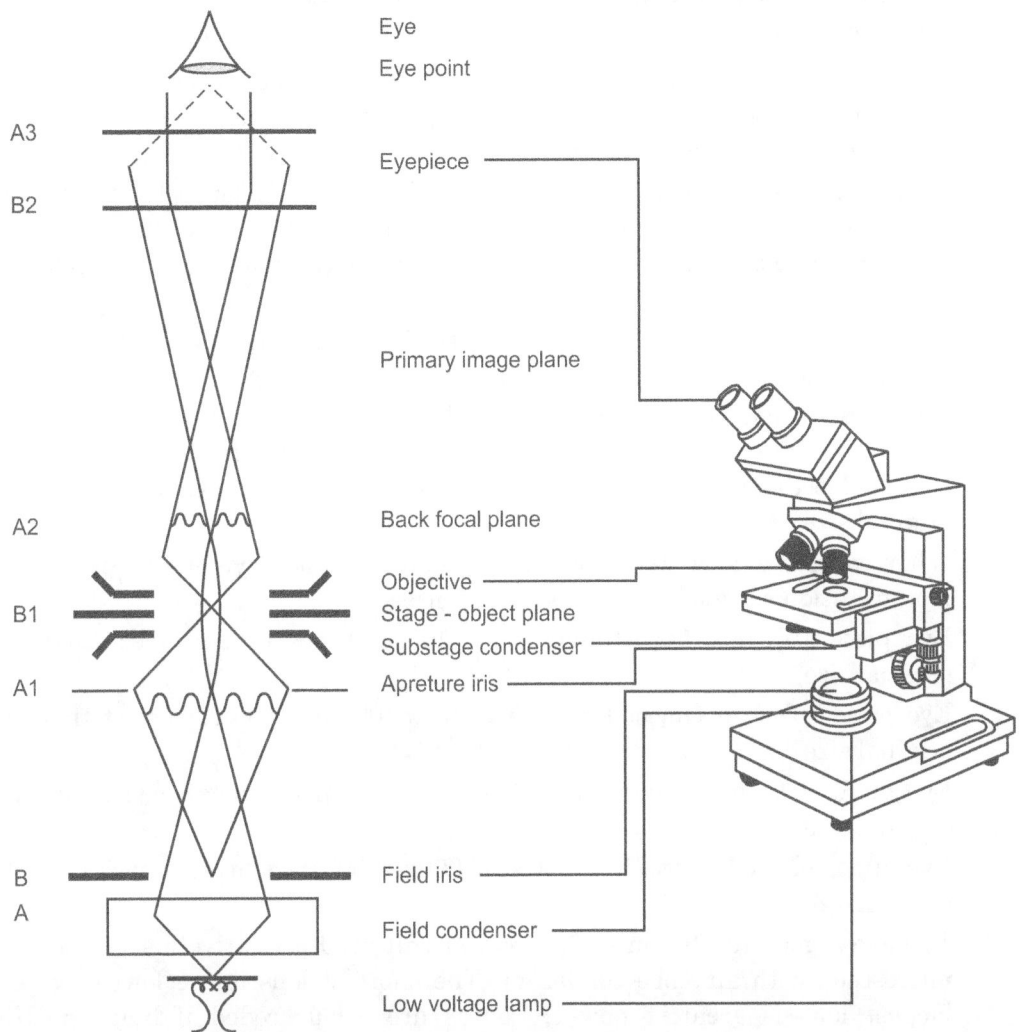

Fig. 2.1: Parts of a compound microscope

The compound microscope has two systems of lenses for greater magnification.
1) The Ocular or eye piece lens: That we look in to it.
2) The Objective Lens or lens closet to the object.

Before purchase or use of microscope we must know the function of each part of microscope. These are as follows:

A) Eye piece lens: It is the lens of the top that we look through. They are usually 10X or 15X power. It means object will be magnified 10 to 15 times bigger than its original shape and size.

B) Tube: Tube is the connection to eye piece and objective lens.

C) Arm: It support the tube and connects it to support.

3) Base: IT is the bottom of microscope, used for bottom support.

4) Illuminator: It is a steady light source (110 volt) used in place of a mirror .Some microscope have mirror which is used to reflect from an external source up through the bottom of the stage.

5) Stage: This is flat platform where you place slides. Stage clips holds the slides in place .If your microscope has mechanical stage, you will be able to move the slide around, by turning two knobs. We can make it left or right, up and down.

6) Revolving nose piece or turret: This is the part that holds two or more objective lenses and can be rotated to easily change the power of lens.

7) Object lens: Generally we find 3 to 4 objective lenses on a microscope nose piece. They almost always consists of 4X,10X,40X,and 100 X powers. That means object can be magnified and viewed up to 10 time bigger size than its original size.

8) When coupled with a 10 X power lens (almost common eye piece lens) we get magnification as below with nose piece lenses.

Eye piece 10X and Object lens 4X = 40x,40 times bigger object than its original size

Eye piece 10X and Object lens 10X = 100x,100 times bigger object than its original size

Eye piece 10X and Object lens 40X = 400x,400 times bigger object than its original size

Eye piece 10X and Object lens 100X = 1000x,1000 times bigger object than its original size.

To have a good resolution at 1000x, you will need a relatively sophisticated microscope with an Abbe condenser. The shortest lens is the lowest power, longest lens is greatest power. Lenses are colour coded if built to DIN standard are interchangeable between microscopes. The high power objective lenses are retractable (i.e. 40 × R). This means that if they hit or touch the slide, the end of the lens will push inside, this will protect the lens as well as slide. All quality microscopes have achromatic par centered par focal lenses.

Magnification factor 400 means the object will be magnified 400 times larger than it can view it with the naked eye. Sometime we may have question, why can you not have a 100x Eye piece and 100x objective lenses. But if we use this it will give magnification of 100,000 times, The problem is resolution. the way your eyes see the image. A compound light microscope is limited to about 2000x magnification. Beyond that limit you could magnify it, but neither your eyes nor your brain recognize the image with a limit of around 2000x magnification you can view bacteria, algeae, protozoa and variety of human and animal cells, viruses,molecules and atoms are beyond the capabilities of today's compound microscope. And we need to use

9) Rack stop: This is an adjustment that determines how close the objective lens can et to the slide. It is set at the factory and keeps student away from cracking the high power objective lenses down up to the slide and breaking things. You would only need to adjust . This if you were using very thin slide and you were not able to focus on the specimen at high power .

10) Condenser lens: The purpose of the condenser lens is to focus the light on to the specimen. Condenser lenses are most useful at the highest powers(400x and above). Microscopes with in stage condenser lenses render a sharper image than those with no lenses (at 400x) . if your microscope has maximum power of 400 x, you will get the maximum benefits by using a condenser lenses read at 0.65 NA or greater . 0,65 NA condenser lenses may be mounted in the stage and work quite well. A big advantage to a stage mounted lens is that there is one less focusing item to deal with. If you go to 1000x then you should have a focusable condenser lens with an NA of 1.25 or greater. Most 1000x microscope uses 1.25 Abbe condenser lense system. The Abbe's condenser lens can be moved up and down . It is very close to slide at 1000X and moved further away at the lower powers.

11) Diaphragm or Iris: Many microscopes have a rotation disc under the stage. This diaphragm has different sized holes and is used to vary the intensity and size of the cone of light that is particular power. Rather, the setting is a function of the transparency, the specimen, the degree of contrast you desire other particular objective lens in sue.

12) The numerical aperture (NA) of an optical system is a dimensionless number that characterizes the range of angles over which the system can accept or emit light. By incorporating index of refraction in its definition, NA has the property that it is constant for a beam as it goes from one material to another provided there is no optical power at the interface. The exact definition of the term varies slightly between different areas of optics. Numerical aperture is commonly used in microscopy to describe the acceptance cone of an objective (and hence its light-gathering ability and resolution), and in fiber optics, in which it describes the cone of light accepted into the fiber or exiting it. Numerical aperture refers to the maximum angle at which the light incident on the fiber & is totally internally reflected and it can be transmitted properly along the fiber.

13) **Resolving power** is the ability of an imaging device to separate (i.e., to see as distinct) points of an object that are located at a small angular distance. The term resolution or minimum resolvable distance is the minimum distance between distinguishable objects in an image, although the term is loosely used by many users of microscopes and telescopes to describe resolving power. In scientific analysis, in general, the term "resolution" is used to describe the precision with which any instrument measures and records (in an image or spectrum) any variable in the specimen or sample under study.

HOW TO USE MICROSCOPE

1. Start the lowest power objective lens first.
2. While looking from the side, crank the lens down as close to the specimen as possible, do not touch the object lens to slide.
3. Look through the eye lens and focus up word only until the image is sharp.
4. If you cannot get it in focus, repeat the process again.
5. once the image is sharpen with the low power lens, you should be able to simply click in the next high power lens.
6. If required do minor adjustment with the focus knob.
7. If your microscope has fine focus adjustment, turning it a bit should be all that's necessary.

ELECTRON MICROSCOPE

Beam of electrons are used in the electron microscope to illuminate a specimen and produce a magnified image .electron microscope has greater resolution power than a high powered optical microscope. This is because of wavelength of electron is about 100,000 times shorter than visible light (photon). Electrons can achieves better than 50 picometer (1 meter divided by 1000000000000 or 10^{12} picometer) resolution and magnification of up to about 10,000,000x, where as ordinary non-confocal light microscope are limited by diffraction to about 200 nm resolution. Resolution is helpful for enlarge the image.

Electrostatic or electromagnetic lenses are used in electron microscope. Electron microscope are used to observe wide range of biological and inorganic specimens including microorganisms, cells, large molecules, biopsy sample and metals and crystals.

Types of Microscopes:
1. Bright field
2. Oblique illumination
3. Dark field
4. Dispersion staining
5. Phase contrast

6. Differential interference contrast microscopy.
7. Interference reflection microscopy
8. Fluorescence

1. **Bright field microscopy:** this microscopic field is brightly lighted and microorganism appears dark because they absorb light. The name "brightfield" is derived from the fact that the specimen is dark and contrasted by the surrounding bright viewing field. Simple light microscopes are sometimes referred to as brightfield microscopes.

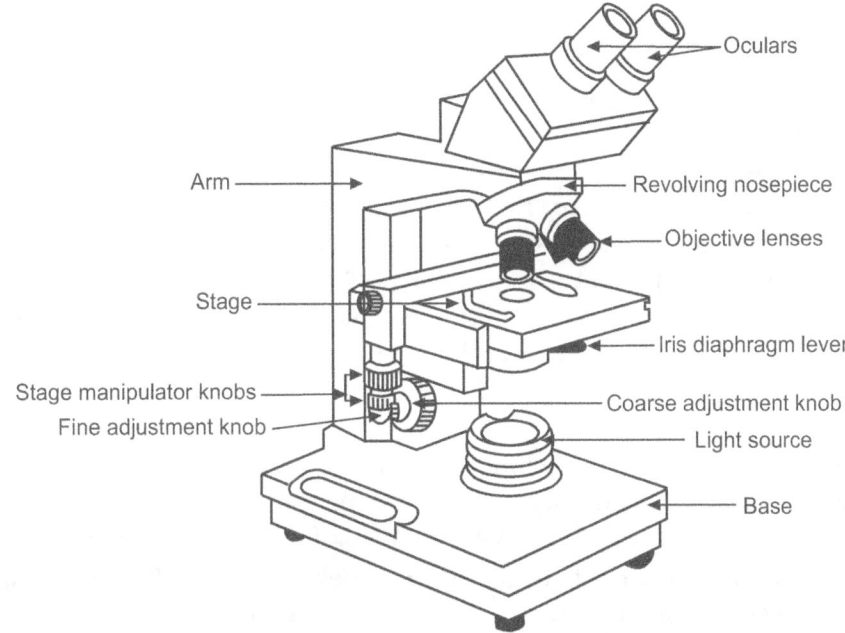

Fig. 2.2: A bright field microscopy.

In brightfield microscopy a specimen is placed on the stage of the microscope and incandescent light from the microscope's light source is aimed at a lens beneath the specimen. This lens is called a condenser.

The condenser usually contains an aperture diaphragm to control and focus light on the specimen; light passes through the specimen and then is collected by an objective lens situated in a turret above the stage.

The objective magnifies the light and transmits it to an oracular lens or eyepiece and into the user's eyes. Some of the light is absorbed by stains, pigmentation, or dense areas of the sample and this contrast allows you to see the specimen.

For good results with this microscopic technique, the microscope should have a light source that can provide intense illumination necessary at high magnifications and lower light levels for lower magnifications.

Uses and Advancements:

To some extent, brightfield microscopy is used in most disciplines requiring microscopic investigation.

Because it is a simple method, this is the first type of microscopy students learn in schools.

The life sciences, particularly microbiology and bacteriology, have always relied on the brightfield technique.

This technique can be used to view fixed specimens or live cells. Since many organic specimens are transparent or opaque, staining is required to cause the contrast that allows them to be visible under the microscope.

Different stains and staining techniques are used depending upon the type of specimen and cell structure being examined. For example :
- Fuchsin is used to stain smooth muscle cells.
- Methylene blue is used to stain cell nuclei.
- Gram stain is used on bacteria and gives rise to the name gram-negative or gram-positive bacteria based on the reaction of the bacteria to the stain. In fact, many scientific journals will not accept microbiological research for publication that is not supported by gram staining and brightfield illumination methodology. Most routine medical microscopic examination of blood and tissue is performed using this illumination technique.

Different complimentary techniques can be used to augment brightfield microscopy. By using a polarizing filter this illumination technique can be used in geological microscopic research and will reveal details not visible using white light.

Properly stained, microorganisms may be magnified to 1200x; utilizing an oil immersion objective will increase resolution at this high magnification.

Digital Imaging Options:

Although a basic method of microscopy, brightfield as a technique is well suited to mating with new technologies.

Digital imaging systems can make high resolution images of properly stained microorganisms using this technique. Three-dimensional imaging accessories can be used with the brightfield method and newer technologies will allow real time viewing in 3D. Also suited to video imaging, this enhancement will allow the user to view motile organisms interacting with their environment.

Brightfield technique has been matched with cell imaging software to better perform tasks previously delegated to fluorescence microscopy. By using multiple focal levels the cell borders and nuclei can be located in cell populations.

The benefit of using brightfield illumination for this task is that it frees fluorescent channels in microscopes and eliminates distortions caused by the overlapping of the color emissions of the stains and the excitation of the fluorescing materials.

Advantages:
- Brightfield microscopy is very simple to use with fewer adjustments needed to be made to view specimens.
- Some specimens can be viewed without staining and the optics used in the brightfield technique don't alter the color of the specimen.
- It is adaptable with new technology and optional pieces of equipment can be implemented with brightfield illumination to give versatility in the tasks it can perform.

Disadvantages:
Certain disadvantages are inherent in any optical imaging technique.
- By using an aperture diaphragm for contrast, past a certain point, greater contrast adds distortion. However, employing an iris diaphragm will help compensate for this problem.
- Brightfield microscopy can't be used to observe living specimens of bacteria, although when using fixed specimens, bacteria have an optimum viewing magnification of 1000x.
- Brightfield microscopy has very low contrast and most cells absolutely have to be stained to be seen; staining may introduce extraneous details into the specimen that should not be present. Also, the user will need to be knowledgeable in proper staining techniques. Lastly, this method requires a strong light source for high magnification applications and intense lighting can produce heat that will damage specimens or kill living microorganisms.

2. **Oblique illumination:** Microscope mirrors are occasionally knocked out of alignment at some stage during viewing, with the result that the subject is lit with an off-axis light source. This oblique illumination is in fact a useful way of improving the visibility of some low contrast subjects like protozoa and the details on diatoms.

Essentially oblique illumination works by accentuating any phase gradients within a transparent specimen. It's an easy form of lighting to achieve up to medium powers (e.g. 40x objectives) with most microscopes with or without a mirror, and is a 'cheap and cheerful' technique the amateur can use to improve visibility when studying low contrast subjects, especially if you're not fortunate enough to possess phase contrast or high power dark field illumination.

Use:
The use of this optics with axial illumination has long been the standard method for observing microscopic specimens and is widely used today. The most useful of this optics is to observe stained or naturally pigmented objects which absorb some wavelength of lights and transmit others. Such specimens are considered optically to be amplitude-modifying or absorption objects. Most of the living cell like protozoa are colorless, and although the light which passes through them is slightly retarded in phase compared with light passing with surrounding medium.

3. **Dark field:** Dark field optics are a low cost alternative to phase contrast optics. The contrast and resolution obtained with inexpensive dark field equipment may be superior to what you have with student grade phase contrast equipment. A dilute suspension of yeast cells makes a good practice specimen for dark field optics, particularly when cultured with living *Paramecium*.

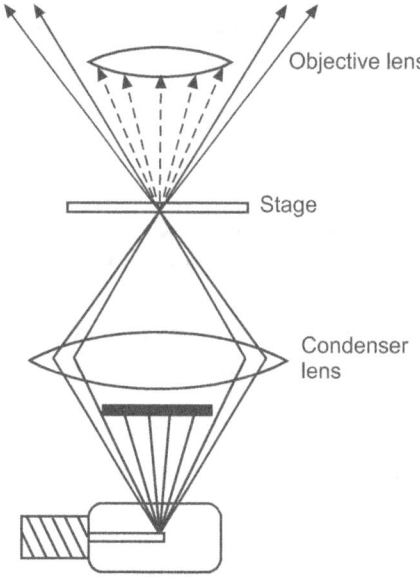

Fig. 2.3: Dark field Microscopy

Principle:

To view a specimen in dark field, an opaque disc is placed underneath the condenser lens, so that only light that is scattered by objects on the slide can reach the eye. Instead of coming up through the specimen, the light is reflected by particles on the slide. Everything is visible regardless of color, usually bright white against a dark background. Pigmented objects are often seen in "false colors," that is, the reflected light is of a color different than the color of the object. Better resolution can be obtained using dark field as opposed to bright field viewing.

Dark field illumination is most readily set up at low magnifications (up to 100x), although it can be used with any dry objective lens. Any time you wish to view everything in a liquid sample, debris and all, dark field is best. Even tiny dust particles are obvious. Dark field is especially useful for finding cells in suspension. Dark field makes it easy to obtain the correct focal plane at low magnification for small, low contrast specimens. Use dark field for

- Initial examination of suspensions of cells such as yeast, bacteria, small protists, or cell and tissue fractions including cheek epithelial cells, chloroplasts, mitochondria, even blood cells (small diameter of pigmented cells makes it tricky to find them sometimes despite the color).

- Initial survey and observation at low magnification powers of pond water samples, hay or soil infusions, purchased metazoan cultures.
- Examination of lightly stained prepared slides
- Determination of motility in cultures

4. Dispersion staining:

Dispersion staining is a group of analytical techniques based on the analytical interpretation of color effects resulting from differences in the rate of change of the refractive index with wavelength (dispersion) between a standard material and an unknown. It is an optical effect and does not involve a chemical reaction or require a chemical affinity as do chemical staining techniques. Dispersion staining has been widely used in the study of everything from dental caries to hazardous materials identification.

Significant advances in the technique of free particle analysis have occurred since the last major study of dispersion staining by G. B. Hoidale. That study, conducted in 1964, provided a description of dispersion staining as it was understood at that time and included an extensive list of references. In the intervening years dispersion staining has been much more widely applied as an analytical technique. There is now a better appreciation of the material properties underlying the dispersion of the refractive index and there have been many improvements in the detection and characterisation of these properties.

The dispersion of a material is related to the nature of the bond energies between ions in the molecules of that material and the energy of the wavelength of light used to measure those properties. The dispersion of a material is typically plotted on a graph with the abcissa being the refractive index and the ordinate being the wavelength scaled as a function of the reciprocal of the wavelength squared . Bond energies between three and five electron volts result in a very steep dispersion curve. Materials with higher bond energies have dispersion curves with a more horizontal slope, as the bond energies increase the slope of the dispersion curve decreases.

There are five basic methods of dispersion staining. These are Becke' line dispersion staining, oblique illumination dispersion staining, condenser stop dispersion staining, objective stop dispersion staining, and phase contrast dispersion staining.

Becke' line dispersion staining was first documented in 1911 by F. E. Wright. He referred to the coloured Becke' lines that could be seen around a particle when the refractive index of the particle and that of the surrounding liquid in which it was mounted matched for some visible wavelengths but not for others. The path of a parallel bundle of rays (substage condenser iris closed down) through a particle mounted in a liquid of lower and of higher refractive index respectively. The appearance of the Becke' line as the plane of focus is moved above that of the edge of the particle by defocusing the microscope. The Becke' Line is the bright band of light that moves into the particle if the particle has the higher refractive index or out into the surrounding liquid if the liquid has the higher refractive index. If the refractive index of the particle ($^{'}$obj) and the liquid (^{n}sur) match at one wavelength ($\lambda 0$) but the liquid has a steeper dispersion curve than the solid (generally the case) then two Becke' lines are created. The Becke' line moving into the particle is the combination of all of the wavelengths for which the particle has the higher refractive index. These are all the wavelengths toward the red end of the spectrum from the matching wavelength. The colour of this Becke' line will vary from pale yellow if $\lambda 0$ is in the deep blue to dark red if $\lambda 0$ is in the orange-red part of the spectrum. The Becke' line that moves into the surrounding liquid is the combination of all the wavelengths for which the liquid has the higher refractive index. These are all the wavelengths toward the blue end of the spectrum from the matching wavelength. The colour of this Becke' Line will vary from deep blue if $\lambda 0$ is in the blue part of the spectrum to pale blue if $\lambda 0$ is in the orange-red part of the spectrum.

Wright also proposed the oblique illumination method. The colors created are the same but they color significant areas of the opposite sides of the particle when the particle is in sharp focus. By using a narrow range of angles for the oblique illumination this technique can be very effective and has the advantage of keeping the particle sharply in view and of creating a larger coloured area which is easier to interpret.

Another dispersion staining method was introduced by G. C. Crossmon during the 1940's. It involved the use of a darkfield stop in the substage condenser of the microscope. A further improvement of this method was made during the 1970's by using a more limited cone of illumination (R. G. Speight). This was accomplished by using a phase annulus rather than the simpler darkfield stop. The particle appears on a black background in the complimentary color to that of the matching wavelength. The color ranges from pale yellow, to gold, to shades of magenta, and finally to blue as $\lambda 0$ moves from deep blue (400 nanometers) through dark red (700 nanometers).

In the 1950's Yu. A. Cherkasov in the Soviet Union devised another technique. He began by noting the distribution of the rays that gave rise to the coloured Becke' lines as they passed through the back focal plane of the objective. By placing opaque screens of different configurations at the back focal plane he could control which set of rays could pass to create the final image of the object. This technique was further developed by K. M. Brown and Walter McCrone and is the most common dispersion staining technique used today, though often not the most appropriate. The color sequence when a central stop is used is the same as that for the condenser stop technique above but this technique is more sensitive to smaller particles and generates brighter colors. One disadvantage is the greater loss of resolving power, the shape of object is more difficult to see. When the oblique stop is used the color sequence is the same as for oblique illumination with the same advantages and disadvantages noted for the central stop. The annular stop creates a particle image in the wavelength for which the liquid and the particle match in refractive index in theory. In fact the matching refractive index is mixed with the direct ray and a green color dominates the series of colors that is difficult to characterize as to the location of the matching wavelength. The central stop is almost exclusively used when objective stop dispersion staining is applied.

In the late 1950's and early 1960's K. G. Schmidt in Germany wrote a paper on the color effects seen when using phase contrast microscopy . These effects were due to the combination of dispersion and the phase shift in the rays of light passing through the particle compared to those passing through the mounting medium. His papers noted the effects but did not explain the origin of the colours. As a result his observations were not generally repeatable. The dependence of the phase shift as a function of particle thickness was the principle parameter missing in Schmitt's work. For particles less than ten micrometers in thickness a reliable and repeatable sequence of colors is created that can be used to determine the wavelength at which a particle and its surrounding mounting liquid match. The sequence of colors is basically the same as for the colored Becke' Lines except the blue colors become the color of the entire particle and the red colors become a halo around the particle. This system has the advantage of showing the color effect without any loss of resolving power in the image. This technique is a significant addition to dispersion staining test procedures and is vastly superior to the objective stop method for the characterization of small particles or fibers as in the analysis of asbestos.

The literature on dispersion staining methods is woefully deficient in detailed descriptions of the mechanisms involved. Cherkosov's paper on objective stop methods and a paper by Speight on condenser stop methods are two notable exceptions. Dispersion staining methods are being widely applied, not just for bulk asbestos analysis but for other types of analysis also (E. R. Crutcher).

5. Phase contrast:

The phase contrast microscope is widely used for examining such specimens as biological tissues. It is a type of light microscopy that enhances contrasts of transparent and colorless objects by influencing the optical path of light. The phase contrast microscope is able to show components in a cell or bacteria, which would be very difficult to see in an ordinary light microscope.

Altering the Light Waves

The phase contrast microscope uses the fact that the light passing trough a transparent part of the specimen travels slower and, due to this is shifted compared to the uninfluenced light. This difference in phase is not visible to the human eye. However, the change in phase can be increased to half a wavelength by a transparent phase-plate in the microscope and thereby causing a difference in brightness. This makes the transparent object shine out in contrast to its surroundings.

The invisible can be seen

The phase contrast microscope is a vital instrument in biological and medical research. When dealing with transparent and colourless components in a cell, dyeing is an alternative but at the same time stops all processes in it. The phase contrast microscope has made it possible to study living cells, and cell division is an example of a process that has been examined in detail with it. The phase contrast microscope was awarded with the Nobel Prize in Physics, 1953.

Most living bioligical specimens are translucent. When viewed under transmitted light in a high power compound light microscope, there is often little or no distinguishable contrast in the image. The solution came with the advent of the phase contrast microscope. It is well known that a change in medium will shift a ray of light out of phase, slowing it down if the medium is denser than what it was travelling in. It also bends the light, such as a flashlight beam is bent when shining into a body of water at night. This same principle of light is applied to the discovery of the phase contrast microscope.

When the light travels through a specimen, parts of the specimen are denser than other parts, so this creates the phase shift in the transmitted light. This phase shift is able to be detected and transferred to a corresponding change in light intensity in the phase contrast microscopy system. This gives the ability for a normally translucent specimen to show differing gradients of light shades, thus resulting in contrast differences.

The effect is stunning on specimens what are typically translucent under normal brightfield microscopy illumination conditions in a compound light microscope. The phase contrast microscope consists of a normal compound light microscope that has special phase contrast objectives that have a phase disc in the back aperature plane. This disc is aligned with the properly sized phase annulus ring in the light condenser. Each magnification of phase requires the corresponding magnification size of phase annulus ring in the light condenser.

A phase telescope is used to align the phase objectives with the phase annulus rings. The phase telescope allows us to view a different plan system in the microscope that is not normally in focus at the focal plane of the eyepieces. Applications for phase contrast microscopy equipment range from the study of living biological specimens, medical applications, study of live blood cells, and other biological and science applications. It is also useful for the counting of asbestos fiber concentrations since the asbestos fibers are typically translucent under normal brightfield microscopy illumination methods. Whatever your needs are for phase contrast microscopy equipment, we recommend you to contact us today to speak to a skilled microscopist professional.

6. Differential interference contrast microscopy:

Differential interference contrast microscopy takes advantage of differences in the light refraction by different parts of living cells and transparent specimens and allows them to become visible during microscopic evaluation.

How differential interference contrast microscopy works

Differential interference contrast produces contrast by visually displaying the refractive index gradients of different areas of a specimen.

This process begins with light from an incandescent illumination source passing through a polarizing filter placed between the light source and the condenser. This orients the light waves in one direction so the electromagnetic waves oscillate in only one plane. Next, this beam is directed through a two-layered modified Wollaston prism which splits the beam into two beams which are spatially separated by a distance equal to the resolution of the microscope's objective lens. The path of one beam is directed through the specimen and the other, or reference beam, merely passes through the background and the two beams are again combined by an upper Wollaston prism placed above the objective lens.

Different parts of the specimen have different refractive indices and when the beams are compiled by the second prism and a second polarizing filter, or analyzer, reconstitutes the vibrational planes of the beams, this causes amplitude variations that are visualized as differences in brightness

Advantages and Disadvantages

An advantage of Differential interference contrast microscopy is that the specimen will appear bright in contrast to the dark background.

This method can take advantage of being able to use a full width condenser aperture setting. Where originally a slit condenser had to be used to produce a thin vertical beam of light, this limited the amount of illumination that could be brought to focus on the specimen.

The lower prism allows the user to employ the full condenser aperture by compensating for the phase differences of all the emitted light and results in a brighter image. This system is relatively easy to incorporate with an existing brightfield microscope. Two of the short comings of the phase contrast method are the fact that the specimen must be very thin and a halo is produced in the viewing field. No halo effect occurs with differential interference contrast and it can be used to produce very clear images of thick specimens.

It can also be used in conjunction with digital imaging systems to add further definition to the image. Differential interference contrast imaging can be used in conjunction with fluorescence microscopy to provide a better fluorescence image and to pinpoint specific areas on a specimen before switching to the fluorescence mode to further examine the object.

A major advantage of the differential interference contrast technique is in examining living specimens when normal biological processes might be impeded by normal staining procedures. A drawback to this type of imaging is that the three-dimensional image of a specimen may not be accurate. The enhanced areas of light and shadow might add distortion to the appearance of the image.

7. Interference reflection microscopy:

Interference reflection microscopy (IRM) utilises interference of light reflected from closely apposed surfaces to provide an image containing information about the separation of those surfaces. The introduction of cell biology given by Curtis in 1964 and then interference reflection microscopy (IRM) has been used by an increasing number of researchers to study cell-substrate interactions in living cells in culture. With the use of antiflex objectives, high-contrast IRM images can now be readily obtained. From the different theories on image formation in IRM that have been put forward, it can be seen that a zero-order interference pattern is generated at high illuminating numerical aperture. This yields information on the closeness of contact between cell and substrate, with only minor perturbation by reflections from the dorsal cell surface. Therefore, the proper use of illuminating apertures is crucial. Nevertheless, IRM images have to be interpreted with caution, especially under thin cytoplasmic sheets. Quantitative IRM is possible only with a mathematical model for finite illuminating aperture interferometry and with an independent measurement of cell thickness for values up to 1 micron. IRM has been applied qualitatively to a large number of cell types, and it seems that there are two universal types of adhesion. Focal contacts are small regions of closest cell-substrate apposition, possibly of immediate contact, that are associated with the distal end of actin filament bundles. They are firm attachment structures that hold the cell in place and in its spread shape. Close contacts are broad areas of reduced cell-to-substrate distance. They are weaker but highly dynamic adhesions that sustain rapid movements of cells or cell parts over the substrate. Although a number of independent observations suggest that adhesion patterns of malignantly transformed cells differ from those of their normal counterparts, there is no simple correlation between malignancy in vivo and altered contact formation in vitro. The adhesion pattern seems to be determined by the locomotory state of the cells rather than by their tissue of origin. Finally, IRM can also be used to enhance contrast in images of fixed preparations.

Uses:

In cell biology, IRM is used to image structures at the base of adherent cells and to measure cell–substratum distances, as well as to investigate mechanisms of cell–substratum adhesion. IRM is also used to study topology and dynamics of biomimetic systems such as vesicles, supported membranes and other multilayered structures. Basic IRM optical configuration is relatively easy to set up, and image analysis can provide information about interfacial distances with nanometer precision and millisecond time resolution. IRM can be readily combined with other microscopic techniques, and with force transducing devices such as optical tweezers, micropipettes and microcantilevers. New advancements in the field include dual-wavelength IRM and fluctuation contrast IRM.

Key concepts:
- Interference reflection microscopy measures the distance between close surfaces.
- Cell adhesion areas such as focal contacts can be mapped by IRM.
- IRM provides vertical resolution in the nanometer range.
- Dual-wavelength IRM removes ambiguity in measurements of vertical distances up to 800 nm.
- IRM can determine amplitudes of local membrane fluctuations.

8. Fluorescence:

Fluorescence of a substance is seen when the molecule is exposed to a specific wavelength of light (excitation wavelength or spectrum) and the light it emits (the emission wavelength or spectrum) is always of a higher wavelength. To view this fluorescence in the microscope, several light filtering components are needed. Specific filters are needed to isolate the excitation and emission wavelengths of a fluorochrome. A bright light source with proper wavelengths for excitation is also needed. For normal fluorescence applications, this is a mercury vapor arc burner. For fluorescence confocal microscope applications where up to 95% of the emission light is filtered out, specific wavelength lasers are used as these are extremely bright. Fluorescence imaging uses high intensity illumination to excite fluorescent molecules in the sample. When a molecule absorbs photons, electrons are excited to a higher energy level. As electrons 'relax' back to the ground-state, vibrational energy is lost and, as a result, the emission spectrum is shifted to longer wavelengths.

Fluorescence emanates from the sample (and not the illuminating light). In epi-fluorescence microscopes, the objective both focuses the excitation light and collects light returning to the eyepiece or detector. Fluorescence is separated from excitation light by a dichroic mirror and appropriate filters: excitation light is reflected back into the objective while fluorescence is transmitted. Filters, excluding and / or transmitting selected wavelengths of light, optimize fluorescence and reduce unwanted 'background noise'.

Many substances auto-fluoresce and this has been exploited especially in botany, petrology, and semiconductor industry. Commercially available fluorophores, with well-defined excitation and emission spectra, can be used to 'stain' specific structures or molecules in a specimen. Judicious choice of fluorophores allows the identification of multiple targets as long as emission spectra can be cleanly separated anA fluorescence microscope is much the same as a conventional light microscope with added features to enhance its capabilities.

- The conventional microscope uses visible light (400-700 nanometers) to illuminate and produce a magnified image of a sample.
- A fluorescence microscope, on the other hand, uses a much higher intensity light source which excites a fluorescent species in a sample of interest. This fluorescent species in turn emits a lower energy light of a longer wavelength that produces the magnified image instead of the original light source.

Fluorescent microscopy is often used to image specific features of small specimens such as microbes. It is also used to visually enhance 3-D features at small scales. This can be accomplished by attaching fluorescent tags to anti-bodies that in turn attach to targeted features, or by staining in a less specific manner. When the reflected light and background fluorescence is filtered in this type of microscopy the targeted parts of a given sample can be imaged. This gives an investigator the ability to visualize desired organelles or unique surface features of a sample of interest. Confocal fluorescent microscopy is most often used to accentuate the 3-D nature of samples. This is achieved by using powerful light sources, such as lasers, that can be focused to a pinpoint. This focusing is done repeatedly throughout one level of a specimen after another. Most often an image reconstruction program pieces the multi level image data together into a 3-D reconstruction of the targeted sample.

How does fluorescent microscopy work?

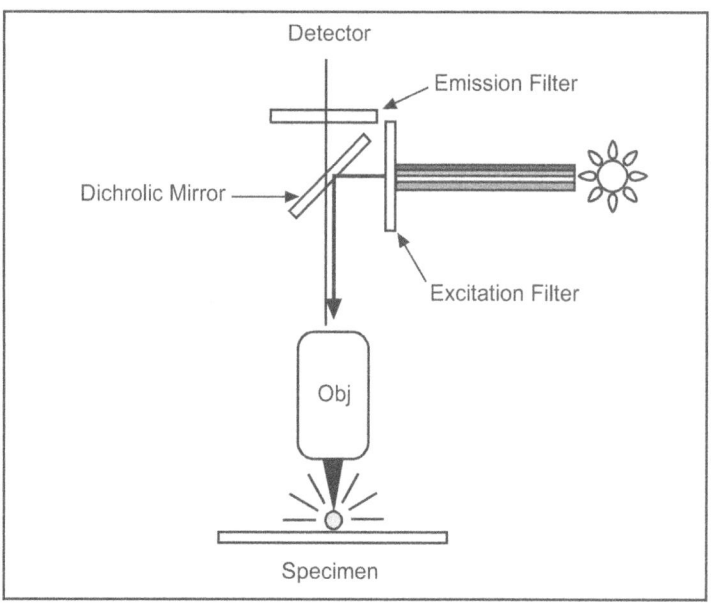

Fig. 2.4 : Showing the filters and mirror in a fluorescent microscope

In most cases the sample of interest is labeled with a fluorescent substance known as a fluorophore and then illuminated through the lens with the higher energy source. The illumination light is absorbed by the fluorophores (now attached to the sample) and causes them to emit a longer lower energy wavelength light. This fluorescent light can be separated from the surrounding radiation with filters designed for that specific wavelength allowing the viewer to see only that which is fluorescing.

The basic task of the fluorescence microscope is to let excitation light radiate the specimen and then sort out the much weaker emitted light from the image. First, the microscope has a filter that only lets through radiation with the specific wavelength that matches your fluorescing material. The radiation collides with the atoms in your specimen and electrons are excited to a higher energy level. When they relax to a lower level, they emit light. To become detectable (visible to the human eye) the fluorescence emitted from the sample is separated from the much brighter excitation light in a second filter. This works because the emitted light is of lower energy and has a longer wavelength than the light that is used for illumination.

Most of the fluorescence microscopes used in biology today are epi-fluorescence microscopes, meaning that both the excitation and the observation of the fluorescence occur above the sample. Most use a Xenon or Mercury arc-discharge lamp for the more intense light source.

Applications:

The refinement of epi-fluorescent microscopes and advent of more powerful focused light sources, such as lasers, has led to more technically advanced scopes such as the confocal laser scanning microscopes and total internal reflection fluorescence microscopes (TIRF).

CLSM's are invaluable tools for producing high resolution 3-D images of subsurfaces in specimens such as microbes. Their advantage is that they are able to produce sharp images of thick samples at various depths by taking images point by point and reconstructing them with a computer rather than viewing whole images through an eyepiece.

These microscopes are often used for -
- Imaging structural components of small specimens, such as cells.
- Conducting viability studies on cell populations (are they alive or dead?).
- Imaging the genetic material within a cell (DNA and RNA).
- Viewing specific cells within a larger population with techniques such as FISH.

3. MICROORGANISMS IN BIOTECHNOLOGY

A microorganism (from the Greek: "small" "organism"; also spelled micro-organism, micro organism or microörganism) or microbe is a microscopic organism that comprises either a single cell (unicellular), cell clusters or multicellular relatively complex organisms. The study of microorganisms is called microbiology, a subject that began with Anton van Leeuwenhoek's discovery of microorganisms in 1675, using a microscope of his own design.

Microorganisms are very diverse; they include bacteria, fungi, algae, and protozoa; microscopic plants (green algae); and animals such as rotifers and planarians. Some microbiologists also include viruses, but others consider these as nonliving. Most microorganisms are unicellular (single-celled), but this is not universal, since some multicellular organisms are microscopic, while some unicellular protists and bacteria, like *Thiomargarita namibiensis*, are macroscopic and visible to the naked eye.

Microorganisms live in all parts of the biosphere where there is liquid water, including soil, hot springs, on the ocean floor, high in the atmosphere and deep inside rocks within the Earth's crust. Microorganisms are critical to nutrient recycling in ecosystems as they act as decomposers. As some microorganisms can fix nitrogen, they are a vital part of the nitrogen cycle, and recent studies indicate that airborne microbes may play a role in precipitation and weather.

Microbes are also exploited by people in biotechnology, both in traditional food and beverage preparation, and in modern technologies based on genetic engineering. However, pathogenic microbes are harmful, since they invade and grow within other organisms, causing diseases that kill humans, other animals and plants

HISTORY OF DISCOVERY MICROORGANISMS

Antonie Van Leeuwenhoek (1632–1723) was one of the first people to observe microorganisms, using a microscope of his own design, and made one of the most important contributions to biology. Robert Hooke was the first to use a microscope to observe living things; his 1665 book *Micrographia* contained descriptions of plant cells.

Before Leeuwenhoek's discovery of microorganisms in 1675, it had been a mystery why grapes could be turned into wine, milk into cheese, or why food would spoil. Leeuwenhoek did not make the connection between these processes and microorganisms, but using a microscope, he did establish that there were forms of life that were not visible to the naked eye. Leeuwenhoek's discovery, along with subsequent observations by Spallanzani and Pasteur, ended the long-held belief that life spontaneously appeared from non-living substances during the process of spoilage.

Lazzaro Spallanzani (1729–1799) found that boiling broth would sterilise it and kill any microorganisms in it. He also found that new microorganisms could settle only in a broth if the broth was exposed to the air.

Louis Pasteur (1822–1895) expanded upon Spallanzani's findings by exposing boiled broths to the air, in vessels that contained a filter to prevent all particles from passing through to the growth medium, and also in vessels with no filter at all, with air being admitted via a curved tube that would not allow dust particles to come in contact with the broth. By boiling the broth beforehand, Pasteur ensured that no microorganisms survived within the broths at the beginning of his experiment. Nothing grew in the broths in the course of Pasteur's experiment. This meant that the living organisms that grew in such broths came from outside, as spores on dust, rather than spontaneously generated within the broth. Thus, Pasteur dealt the death blow to the theory of spontaneous generation and supported germ theory.

In 1876, Robert Koch (1843–1910) established that microbes can cause disease. He found that the blood of cattle who were infected with anthrax always had large numbers of *Bacillus anthracis*. Koch found that he could transmit anthrax from one animal to another by taking a small sample of blood from the infected animal and injecting it into a healthy one, and this caused the healthy animal to become sick. He also found that he could grow the bacteria in a nutrient broth, then inject it into a healthy animal, and cause illness. Based on these experiments, he devised criteria for establishing a causal link between a microbe and a disease and these are now known as Koch's postulates. Although these postulates cannot be applied in all cases, they do retain historical importance to the development of scientific thought and are still being used today.

1) **Antonie van Leeuwenhoek**, the first microbiologist and the first to observe microorganisms using a microscope.

2) **Lazzaro Spallanzani** showed that boiling a broth stopped it from decaying.

3) **Louis Pasteur** showed that Spallanzani's findings held even if air could enter through a filter that kept particles out.

4) **Robert Koch** showed that microorganisms caused disease

MICROORGANISMS AND TYPES

The economic importance of bacteria derives from the fact that bacteria are exploited by humans in a number of beneficial ways. Despite the fact that some bacteria play harmful roles, such as causing disease and spoiling food, the economic importance of bacteria includes both their useful and harmful aspects.

Microorganisms are unicellular, meaning they contain only a single cell. The cellular organisms are broadly classified as prokaryotes and eukaryotes, aerobic and anaerobic, and by type of metabolism.

Microorganisms play a crucial role in maintaining the delicate ecological balance of the earth. They revitalize the soil by recycling the minerals and nutrients of decaying matter, and many are essential to the healthy growth of plants. Microorganisms also affect our lives more directly in the manufacture of such items as food products, detergents, antibiotics and antitumor.

Types of cells:
1) Prokaryotes
2) Eukaryotes cell

1) Prokaryotes cell :

These are micro-organisms that are characterized by the absence of a distinct membrane-bound nucleus and by DNA that are not organized into chromosomes. They can be sub-classified into archaebacteria and eubacteria with further subclassification under those types.

(a) Archaebacteria
   (i) Methanogens– Anaerobic methane producing bacteria
   (ii) Extreme halophiles– Bacteria that require high salt concentration to survive
   (iii) Extreme thermophiles– Bacteria that require high temperatures and sulfur

(b) Eubacteria
   (i) Gram-positive bacteria– Bacteria whose cell walls retain crystal violet dye during iodine treatment, e.g. lactic acid bacteria.
   (ii) Gram-negative bacteria– Bacteria that vary in cell-wall structure and do not retain crystal violet dye during iodine treatment.

2) Eukaryotes

These are organisms that have a membrane bound nucleus in the cell containing chromosomes, and other membrane bound organelles, for example, **fungi.** These fungi can be further classified into myxomycota and eumycota.

(a) Myxomycota
These are fungi that do not contain a cell wall. They are also called slime-molds.

(b) Eumycota
These are true fungi. They are the most important class of fungi and are exploited for commercial purposes like fermentation. Examples are yeasts, mushrooms, sponge fungi, rusts, and mildews.

Micro-organisms can be classified according to their oxygen requirements, as aerobic or anaerobic.

   (i) Aerobic: These are micro-organisms that can grow and live in the presence of oxygen. In compost heaps bacteria of this type generate heat when they convert carbon and nitrogen, reducing the volume of waste. As they exhaust the oxygen in the compost pile they die leaving a germ free product.

   (ii) Anaerobic: These organisms are averse to air. They are useful in biodegradation, breaking down organic chemicals into smaller compounds, producing methane and carbon dioxide. Some anaerobic organisms can break down organic chemicals by fermentation. Such organisms are useful at hazardous waste sites.

Types of Metabolism :

Micro organisms can also be classified according to type of metabolism. Types include autotrophs, heterotrophs, chemotrophs, chemoheterotrophs, and phototrophs.

1. Autotrophs

These are microorganisms that use carbon dioxide as their carbon source.

2. Heterotrophs

These are microorganisms that use organic compounds as their carbon source.

3. Chemotrophs

These are microorganisms that use chemical bonds for production of adenosine tri-phosphate (ATP).

4. Chemoheterotrophs

These are microorganisms (such as fungi) that use organic compounds for a carbon source and the energy of chemical bonds to produce ATP.

5. Phototrophs

These are microorganisms that use light for production of ATP.

Microbial Metabolism :

Microbes used in fermentation have to grow and reproduce rapidly so that they can produce metabolites. This process is related to "metabolism". Metabolism includes two processes, namely, anabolism and catabolism.

1. Anabolism

This is the synthesis of various metabolic compounds like amino acids, proteins, nucleic acids, carbohydrates, and lipids. It is an energy-consuming process.

2. Catabolism

This is the breakdown of metabolic products to produce energy (e.g. breakdown of carbohydrates to carbon dioxide, water, and energy). It is an energy-producing process.

Carbohydrates $\leftrightarrows$ Carbon Dioxide + Water + Energy

Adenosine Tri-Phosphate (ATP) is a source of energy produced through anabolism and catabolism and is broken down into Adenosine Di-Phosphate (ADP).

Catabolic Pathways:

Catabolic pathways are means by which organic molecules are degraded to release energy for growth or degradation. They include photosynthesis, respiration, carbohydrate catabolism, pentose phosphate pathway, Entner-Doudoroff pathway, phosphoketolase pathway, tri carboxylic acid cycle (TCA), and fatty acid & hydrocarbon pathway.

1. Photosynthesis

Photosynthesis is the most important source of energy for plants. Plants have structures called *chloroplasts* that contain pigment called *chlorophyll* which plays a vital role in utilizing sunlight, carbon dioxide, and water to produce energy and organic compounds.

Carbon Dioxide + Water + Sunlight ⇌ Organic Compound + Oxygen + Energy

Some micro-organisms called phototrophic microbes contain special structures in their cells called *thylakoids* which contain *chlorophyll*. They utilize sunlight and carbon dioxide to synthesize organic compounds and energy. Bacterial photosynthesis does not require water and does not produce oxygen.

Carbon Dioxide + Hydrogen Sulfide + Sunlight ⇌ Organic Compound + Sulfur + Water

2. Respiration

The process in which organic compounds are catabolized to produce carbon dioxide is known as respiration. Aerobic micro-organisms utilize oxygen whereas anaerobic micro-organisms utilize molecules like sulfur, sulfate, nitrate, and carbonate.

3. Carbohydrate Catabolism

Carbohydrates are broken down to glucose, used as the most important carbon source. Glucose catabolism includes the metabolic pathways glycolysis and pentose phosphate. Glycolysis is the oxidation of glucose to either *lactate* or *pyruvate*.

4. Pentose phosphate pathway

Also called hexose mono phosphate (HMP) pathway, this is a biosynthetic pathway in which glucose is converted into *pentose* and carbon dioxide, the pentose sugar is then utilized for nucleic acid synthesis and as precursors for vitamins, aromatic amino acids.

5. Entner-Doudoroff pathway

This is also a biosynthetic pathway where glucose is converted to various precursors for DNA, RNA, and aromatic amino acid synthesis.

6. Phosphoketolase pathway

This is a less commonly used pathway seen only in few bacteria. Glucose is broken down to two compounds: *acetate* associated with ATP production and *pyruvate* which is in part carried out by the Glycolytic pathway.

7. Tri carboxylic acid cycle (TCA)

TCA is the most commonly used pathway for energy production and biosynthesis of important precursors. Products of glucose metabolism are further metabolized in a cyclic reaction to produce intermediates for various biosynthetic and oxidation reactions (oxidative reactions produce energy). The TCA cycle utilizes a wide variety of enzymes and co-enzymes. It is also called the citric acid cycle, or Krebs's cycle:

Pyruvate acetyl-CoA (acetyl co-enzyme A)

7. Fatty acid & hydrocarbon pathway

Microbes utilize fatty acids and hydrocarbons for their metabolism, so these are usually added to various fermentation reactions, such as the manufacture of antibiotics. Fats and hydrocarbon are converted to fatty acids which are then finally converted to acetyl-CoA after a series of reactions. This is also called *β-oxidation*.

Oxidation

1. Oxidation of methane and methanol

Micro-organisms that use methane as a carbon source are called *Methanotrophs* and those that use methanol as carbon source are called *Methylotrophs*. Methane is oxidized initially to methanol and finally to carbon dioxide in a reaction involving a series of steps. The overall reaction can be summarized as

Methane ⇋ Methanol ⇋ Formaldehyde ⇋ Formic Acid ⇋ Carbon Dioxide

2. Oxidation of amino acids

Amino acids are metabolized by microorganisms through oxidation, to be utilized as excellent source of carbon and nitrogen.

3. Oxidation of polymers

A polymer is the compound which has large number of monomeric units linked together. As an example, Polysaccharides (starch, cellulose, etc.) contain a large number of monomeric sugar (carbohydrate) molecules linked together. Proteins contain a large number of amino acids linked together to form large chains. Microorganisms metabolize polymers by breaking the chains into individual monomeric units in a process called *hydrolysis*, and it requires enzymes called *hydrolytic enzymes* or *hydrolases.* or drugs.

Biotechnology and Bacteria

The ability to form recombinant DNA molecules in vitro that can be stably replicated in a recipient host has had a major impact on biological community and on society. One aspect of this impact has been the formation of Biotechnology companies.

Biotechnology, when broadly defined as the application of biological materials to industrial processes, is not new.

Microorganisms have traditionally produced such useful compounds like alcohol and antibiotics

Biotechnology or Industrial microbiology is defined as the application of organisms such as bacteria, fungi and algae to the manufacturing and services industries.

These include:
1. Fermentation processes, much as brewing, baking, cheese and butter manufacturing, Bacteria, often *Lactobacillus* in combination with yeasts and molds, have been used for thousands of years in the preparation of fermented foods such as cheese, pickles, soya sauce, sauerkraut, vinegar, wine, and yogurt.
2. Chemical manufacturing such as ethanol, acetone, organic acid, enzymes, perfumes etc. In the chemical industry, bacteria are most important in the production of enantiomerically pure chemicals for use as pharmaceuticals or agrochemicals.
3. Pharmaceuticals, such as antibiotics, vaccines and steroids.
4. Microbial mining, which is the bacteria and other microorganisms are cultured in container and then used to bring these processes e.g., copper extraction

1. Fermentation process

Though there are different perceptions of the nature of the process, fermentation can be defined as the breakdown or catabolism of organic compounds by microorganisms under both aerobic and anaerobic conditions. This breakdown yields end products.

End-products obtained by fermentation

Types of end products of fermentation include:
- Microbial cells (e.g. bacteria, yeast, fungal spores)
- Microbial enzymes (e.g. milk clotting enzymes or rennets, recombinant fungal and bacterial rennets for cheese manufacture)
- Microbial metabolites (e.g. alcohols – ethanol, butanol, 2, 3-butanediol, isopropanol; chemicals – lactate, propionate, proteins, vitamins, antibiotics; and fuels – methane)
- Recombinant products (e.g. hormones)

Alcohol fermentation

Various bacteria and yeasts metabolize sugars into ethanol through different pathways using different enzyme systems. Alcohol fermentation is used for the industrial production of alcohols and alcoholic beverages. In the preparation of alcoholic beverages several factors have to be considered, such as flavor, taste, appearance, and safety. These require special procedures and standards. The commercial producers of alcoholic beverages each have their own protocols which give their product a distinct taste and flavor, and these are often kept confidential. The process is as follows:

Sugar (Carbohydrate) ⇌ 2Ethanol + 2Carbon Dioxide

There are four different phases in bacterial growth during fermentation. A good understanding of these phases is very important for effective management of the whole fermentation process.

a. **Lag phase:** At the start of the process microorganisms are added to the nutrient medium and allowed to grow. The number of microorganisms will not increase because they try to adapt to the environment.

b. **Log phase:** The microorganisms are adjusted to the new environment and they multiply at a very rapid pace thus increasing the cell number exponentially.

c. **Stationary phase:** As the microorganisms grow they produce metabolites which are toxic to microbial growth. Also the nutrient medium is used up, slowing down or stopping cell growth.

d. **Death phase:** Microorganisms produce toxic metabolites to the extent that they cause the death of the microorganisms.

Factors that influence microbial growth

Temperature, water, pH, and nutrients can influence microbial growth.

Temperature

Most microorganisms that are *mesophiles* require temperatures of 25-40 C for optimum growth. As temperatures increase or decrease the growth rate is adversely affected. *Thermophiles* require high temperatures over 50 C; they cannot survive at low temperatures. *Psychrophiles* require very low temperatures -15 to 20 C for survival and growth.

Water

Microorganisms require optimum amounts of water to maintain their metabolism and produce required products.

pH

Optimum pH for bacteria is 6.5-7.5, yeasts 4-5, molds 4-7. The pH of the medium should be maintained at optimum level for the micro-organism being employed to ensure better product yield.

Nutrients

Micro-organisms require optimum concentrations of nutrients like nitrogen, vitamins, and minerals for maximum growth rate. This will be different for each of the different types. The optimum concentration of nitrogen is 0.1-1mg/L.

Sources of microorganisms

Microorganisms are ubiquitous. Pond water and sand are the commonly used microbial sources since they offer greatest diversity of organisms. A sample of the microbial source is added to a sterile nutrient medium (such as agar) and incubated at suitable temperatures. This facilitates the growth of all micro-organisms that are present in the initially selected sample. The process is called microbial culture.

Identification and isolation of required micro-organisms is very critical for any microbiological process, since some micro-organisms may be toxic to the useful microbes and may use up the nutrients all by themselves, producing metabolites that are different from the desired ones. Isolation of micro-organisms also helps to screen them to determine if they can be used for any industrial process. Such microorganisms should satisfy some specified criteria. These include:
- cheap medium for growth,
- optimum growth temperature around 30 C so that the costs of cooling or heating the medium can be avoided,
- reaction of micro-organism should be suitable to the process used,
- micro-organism should be stable and should allow genetic manipulation,
- micro-organisms should convert the substrate into product rapidly,
- product formed should be easily recovered from the culture medium, and
- micro-organisms should be safe and should survive primarily in the lab only.

Isolation techniques

Several techniques could be employed for isolating micro-organisms for microbial culture growth. These include the liquid culture method, the solid culture method, and the screening of microorganisms.

1. Liquid culture method

This is carried out in shaker flasks containing nutrient liquid culture medium. The initial inoculum contains different types of microorganisms and the desired one can be isolated from others in the sub-culturing process, since each has a different maximum growth rate.

2. Solid culture method

This technique is used mainly for microorganisms that produce industrially important enzymes. The solid culture medium contains a substrate which is converted by the enzymes that are produced. Soil is first pasteurized to eliminate spores and then spread on an alkaline agar medium that contains an insoluble protein. The microorganisms which produce the desired enzyme then leave clear zones on the medium as the enzyme dissolves the protein.

Screening of microorganisms

This process is very tedious and time consuming since the microorganisms have to be tested for desired property at different concentrations and at different environmental conditions.

Preservation of microorganisms

There are different methods for microbial preservation. Suitable methods are selected based on:
- type of microorganism,

- effect of the preservation method on the viability of the microorganism,
- frequency at which the cultures are withdrawn,
- size of the microbial population to be preserved,
- availability of resources, and
- cost of the preservation method.

Desiccation

This involves removal of water from the culture. Desiccation is used to preserve actinomycetes (a form of fungi-like bacteria) for very long period of time. The microorganisms can be preserved by desiccating on sand, silica gel, or paper strips.

1. Agar slopes

Microorganisms are grown on agar slopes in test tubes and stored at 5 to -20 C for six months. If the surface area for growth is covered with mineral oil the microorganisms can be stored for one year.

2. Liquid nitrogen

This is the most commonly used technique to store micro-organisms for a long period. Storage takes place at temperatures of less than -196° C and even less in vapor phase. Micro-organisms are made stationary and suspended in a cryo-protective agent before storing in liquid nitrogen.

3. Drying

This method is especially used for sporulating microorganisms (organisms that produce spores). They are sterilized, inoculated, and incubated to allow microbial growth, then dried at room temperature. The resultant dry soil is stored at 4° to 5°C.

4. Lyophilization

This process is also known as freeze-drying. The microbial culture is first dried under vacuum, filled in ampoules (glass vessels) then frozen. This is a most convenient technique, since it is cheap to store and easy to ship. The disadvantage is that it is difficult to open the freeze dried ampoules; also, several subcultures have to be done to restore the original characteristics of the microorganisms.

Strain improvement

The yield of products will be much less when naturally available microorganisms are used for fermentation in optimum growth medium. Providing optimum growth conditions increases the yield only marginally. To increase the productivity of the microorganisms it is necessary to modify their genetic structure since it is genomes that determine the productivity of organisms. The culture medium and nutritional requirements also change slightly when the genetic structure of the microorganism is changed and hence they are also modified according to the new requirements to ensure maximum product yield.

Genetic change of the microorganism can be done by inducing mutations in the microorganisms, recombinant technology, and selecting natural variants.

Inducing mutations in the microorganisms

This is the most important microbial strain improvement technique. Large numbers of improved strains which are currently available are produced by induced mutations. This process involves subjecting the microorganisms to mutagens and then screening the mutated microbes for increased productivity and finally selecting these microbial strains. Induced mutation does not always produce useful strains so it is vital to select the strains which are of interest. UV-radiation is the most commonly used mutagen.

Recombinant technology

Recombinant DNA technology is applied to produce microbial strains that can produce desired products.

Selecting natural variants

Microorganisms undergo slight genetic change with every cell division. They undergo a very large number of cell divisions. After several divisions culture mediums include microbes with a wide range of genetic structure. From this the varieties which produce maximum product yields can be selected for industrial purposes.

Preparation of the inoculum

Microbial inoculum has to be prepared from the preservation culture so that it can be used for the fermentation process. The aim of inoculum preparation is to select microorganisms with high productivity and to minimize low productive, mutant strains. The process involves several steps.

First generation culture is prepared from the preservation culture on agar slants which is then sub-cultured to prepare "working culture". At this stage the microorganisms start growing. In small scale fermentation processes working culture is used as inoculum, but for large scale fermentation inoculum preparation involves additional steps.

Second, sterile saline water or liquid nutrient medium containing glass beads is added to the agar slants and shaken so that microbial suspension is prepared. This suspension is transferred to a flat bed bottle which contains sterile agar medium. The microorganisms are allowed to grow by incubating the bottle.

Third, the microbial cells from the flat bed bottles are transferred to a shaker flask containing sterile liquid nutrient medium and is placed on a rotary shaker bed in an incubator. Microorganisms grow at a rapid rate due to aeration.

Fourth, microbial cells from the shaker flask can be used as seed culture which are then added to a small fermenter and allowed to grow for 1-2 days. This simulates conditions that exist in the larger fermenter to be used for production of metabolites.

Finally, the microorganisms are transferred to the main fermentation vessel containing essential media and nutrients.

Culture medium

Media requirements depend on the type of microorganism being used in the fermentation process, but the basic requirements remain the same--source of energy, water, carbon source, nitrogen source, vitamins, and minerals. Designing the media for small scale laboratory purpose is relatively easy, but media for industrial purpose are difficult to prepare.

The culture medium should: allow high yield of the desired product and at fast rate,

allow low yield of undesired products, be sterilized easily, yield consistent products i.e., minimum batch variation, be cheap and readily available, be compatible with the fermentation process, and not pose environmental problems before, during, or after the fermentation process.

The culture medium will affect the design of the fermenter. For example, hydrocarbons in the media require high oxygen content so an air-lift fermenter should be used. Natural media ingredients are cheap but they have high batch variation. On the other hand pure ingredients (also called defined media or formulated media) have very little batch variation but are expensive. The media should support the metabolic process of the microorganisms and allow bio-synthesis of the desired products.

Carbon and Energy source + Nitrogen source + Nutrients $\leftrightarrows$ Product(s) + Carbon Dioxide + Water + Heat + Biomass

Media are designed based on the above equation using minimum components required to produce maximum product yield.

Important components of the medium are carbon sources, nitrogen sources, minerals, growth factors, chelating agents, buffers, antifoaming agents, air, steam, and fermentations vessels.

a. Carbon sources

Product formation is directly dependent on the rate at which the carbon source is metabolized; also the main product of fermentation determines the type of carbon source to be used. Carbon sources include carbohydrates, oils and fats, and hydrocarbons.

1. Carbohydrates

These are the most commonly used carbon sources in the fermentation process. Starch is easily available carbohydrate obtained from maize, cereals, and potatoes. It is widely used in alcohol fermentation. Grains like maize are used directly in the form of ground powder as carbohydrate. Malt and beer made from barley grains contain high concentrations of different carbohydrates like starch, sucrose, cellulose and other sugars. Sucrose is obtained from sugar cane and molasses. Molasses is one of the cheapest sources of carbohydrate. It contains high sugar concentration and other components like nitrogenous substances and vitamins and is used in alcohol, SCP (Single-cell Protein), amino acid, and organic acid fermentations.

Extraction and purification of the products is expensive. Sulfite waste liquor is the by-product of the paper industry; it contains carbohydrates and is used in yeast cultivation. Whey is the byproduct of dairy industry. It is used in alcohol, SCP, gum, vitamins, and lactic acid fermentation.

2. *Oils and Fats*

Vegetable oils are used as a carbon source. Oils provide more energy per weight compared to sugars. They also have anti-foaming properties but are generally used as additives rather than as the sole carbon source. Examples are olive oil, cotton seed oil, soya bean oil, linseed oil, and lard (animal fat).

3. *Hydrocarbons*

C12-C18 alkanes can be used as carbon sources. They are cheap, and have more carbon and energy content per weight than sugars. They can be used in organic acids, amino acids, antibiotics, enzymes, and proteins fermentation.

4. *Nitrogen sources*

Ammonia, ammonium salts, and urea are the most commonly used nitrogen sources in the fermentation process. Ammonia also serves the purpose of pH control. Other substances used as nitrogen sources are corn-steep liquor, soya meal, peanut meal, cotton seed meal, amino acids, and proteins.

5. *Minerals*

Calcium, chlorine, magnesium, phosphorous, potassium and sulfur are the essential minerals for all media. Other minerals like copper, cobalt, iron, manganese, molybdenum, and zinc are needed in trace amounts and are generally present as impurities in other components. The specific concentration on these elements depends on the micro-organism being used.

6. *Growth factors*

Vitamins, amino acids, and fatty acids are used as growth factors in the fermentation process to complement the cell components of the microorganisms.

7. *Chelating agents*

Chelating agents prevent formation of insoluble metal precipitates. They form complexes with the metal ions present in the medium and can be utilized by the microorganisms. Chelating agents are not required in large scale fermentation processes since some of the other ingredients like yeast extract will perform the function of forming complexes with the metal ions.

One example of a chelating agent is EDTA (ethylenediaminetetraacetic acid). EDTA is a versatile, being able to form six bonds with a metal ion. It is frequently used in soaps and detergents because it forms a complex with calcium and magnesium ions. These ions are in hard water and interfere with the cleaning action of soaps and detergents. Other chelating agents are citric acid and pyrophosphates

8. *Buffers*

Buffers are used to maintain the pH of the medium as microbial growth is affected by the pH changes. Optimum pH for most microorganisms is 7.0. Commonly used buffers are calcium carbonate, ammonia, and sodium hydroxide.

9. *Antifoaming agents*

Microbial process produces a large amount of foam in the fermentation vessel. This is due to microbial proteins or other components of the media. Foaming causes removal of cells from the media and their autolysis, thus, releasing more microbial foam-producing proteins, hence, aggravating the problem. Foam will reduce the working volume in the fermentation vessel, decrease rate of heat transfer, and deposit cells on the top of the fermenter. The air filter exits then become wet allowing growth of contaminating microorganisms. Antifoaming agents are also called surfactant, i.e. they reduce the surface tension in the foam and destabilize the foam producing proteins.

Commonly used antifoaming agents are stearyl alcohol, cotton seed oil, linseed oil, olive oil, castor oil, soy bean oil, cod liver oil, silicones, and sulphonates.

10. *Air*

Air is required for aeration and is supplied to the fermenter by means of pumps or compressors. It is sterilized by passing through filters before being introduced. The amount of air required and the extent of purity depends on the fermentation process being carried out.

11. *Steam*

Steam is used to sterilize fermenters and other equipment and to control temperature. Continuous dry steam supply is required for the fermentation process and care should be taken to prevent condensation.

Fermentation Vessels:

Laboratory scale fermentations are carried out in shaker flasks, and flat bed bottles. Large scale fermentations are carried out in glass or stainless steel tank fermenters. A fermentation vessel should: be cheap, not allow contamination of the contents, be non-toxic to the microorganism used for the process, be easy to sterilize, be easy to operate, be robust and reliable, allow visual monitoring of the fermentation process, allow sampling, and be leak proof.

1. *Shaker flasks*

These are conical vessels made of glass and are available in different sizes. The typical volume of these flasks is 250 ml. There are different types of shaker flasks, such as baffled, unbaffled or Erlenmeyer flask, and flying saucer. Shaker flasks are used for the screening of microorganisms and cultivation of them for inoculation.

Shaker beds or shaker tables are used to allow oxygen transfer by their continuous rotary motion. Baffled flasks are used to increase the oxygen transfer. Shaker flasks need to be plugged to prevent contamination with other microorganisms. Cotton-wool, polyurethane foam, glass, and synthetic plugs are commonly used. Fernwald shaker flasks and flat bed Thompson bottles are expensive and are not commonly used.

2. *Stirred tank fermenters*

These are the most commonly used fermenters. They are cylindrical vessels with a motor driven agitator to stir the contents in the tank. The Top-entry stirrer (agitator) model is most commonly used because it has many advantages like ease of operation, reliability, and robustness. The Bottom-entry stirrer (agitator) model is rarely used. Figure 3.3 – 3.5 shows different types of stirred tank fermenters.

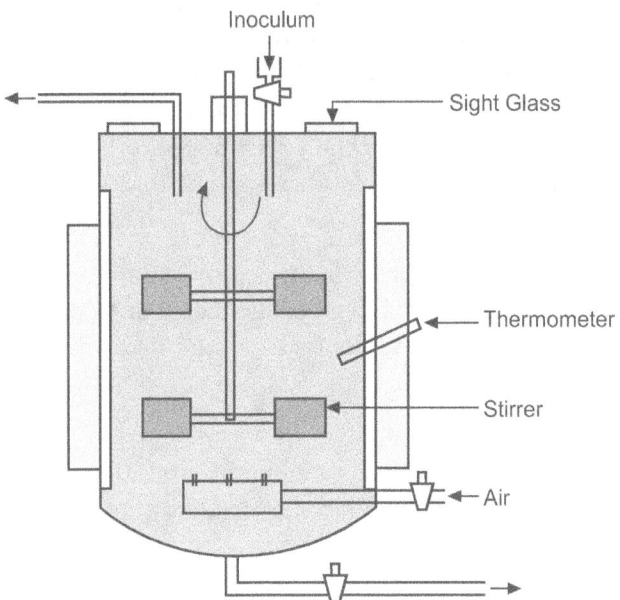

Fig. 3.1: Stirred tank fermenter.
Source: ESEL TechTra, Inc.

Fig. 3.2: Stirred tank fermenter
Source: Novaferm AB, Inc.

Laboratory scale stirred tank fermenters are made of borosilicate glass with a stainless steel lid and top-entry stirrer. Typical volume of these fermenters is 1 to 100 liters. Stirrers consist of a motor attached to the shaft. The shaft contains impellers.

Stainless steel fermenters are also used in laboratories and have special requirements. They should be made of high grade stainless steel, have an internal surface that should be polished to reduce adhesion of contents to the walls of the fermenter, and have joints that should be smooth and free from pin-holes.

Fermentation vessel additional equipment
Agitator

This consists of shaft, impellers with 4 to 6 blades and motor to drive. Shafts should have double seals to prevent leakage of the contents. The main function of the agitator is mixing of the contents, aeration, and removal of carbon dioxide produced during fermentation process by mixing action.

Different types of impellers are:
1. Rushton blade or disc turbine: This is the most commonly used impeller because of its simple design, robustness and ease of operation. It has 4 to 6 blades.
2. Open turbine impellers
3. Marine impellers

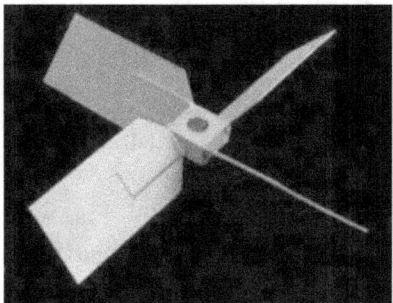

Fig. 3.3: Rushton blade/disc turbine

Fig. 3.4: Marine impeller   Fig. 3.5: Marine impeller

Source: Master Tech Marine, Inc and Henleys Propeller & Marine, Inc

Baffles

Four baffles are fixed on the walls of the fermenter which are used to prevent formation of a vortex. Impellers and baffles produce axial or radial flow patterns of the contents in the fermenter.

Compressor

Compressors are used to pump air under pressure into the fermenter from the bottom, to promote aeration and mixing. They are used mainly in the large fermenters. For laboratory scale, small fermenters air pumps are used. Compressors should be oil-free in order to provide food-grade clean air to the fermenter.

Filter

Filtration & Clarification:

Removal of suspended solids, contaminants and ions from liquid is called as Filtration, If the concentration of suspended particle is less than 1% in the slurry, process is called as clarification.

Following are the different approaches of filtration:
1) By Mechanism: Absorbance and Porosity.
2) By Fluid Flow: Dead end or Tangential.
3) By Media Structure: Depth or Surface.

1) By mechanism:

Porosity: Porosity of filter Mediums: Determines the minimum size of the solids removed.

Absorbance: by Zeta Potential charge or Brownian diffusion or affinity (Hydrophilic-Hydrophobic) attracts opposite charge particles such as polyphenols and proteins.

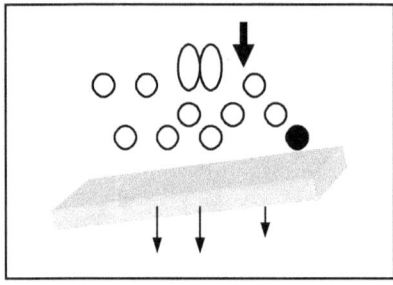
Porosity

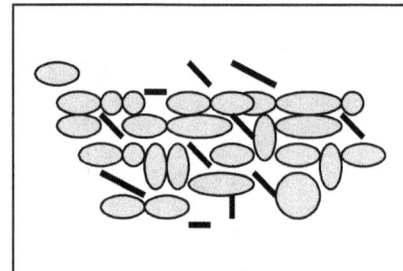
Absorbance

2) By Fluid Flow:

Dead end: In this filtration, all the fluid(that is feed) flows though the membrane and all particulates larger than the pore size of the membrane are mainly retained at its surface. In the process, the retained particulates start to build up a "Filter cake " on the surface of the membrane which has an impact on the efficiency of the process.

Cross-flow filtration: In this filtration a feed stream passes tangential to a pressure difference across the membrane, leaving the remaining feed to continue. The use of such tangential flow will prevent thicker particulates from building up a Filter cake.

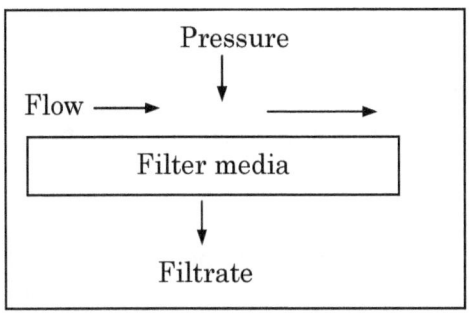 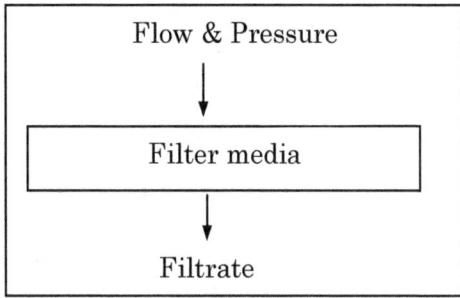

Cross Flow Filtration or Tangential filtration   Dead End Filtration

3) By Media Structure: Depth or Surface.

Filter media can be divided into two broad groups based on their pores structure:
1) Capillary - Type pores, Surface Filtration. E.g. Membrane filtration.
2) Tortuous - Type pores, Depth filtration, E.g. Quartz, Sand, filtration.

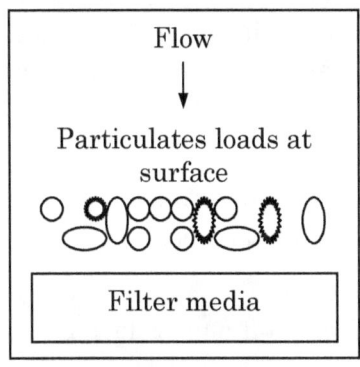 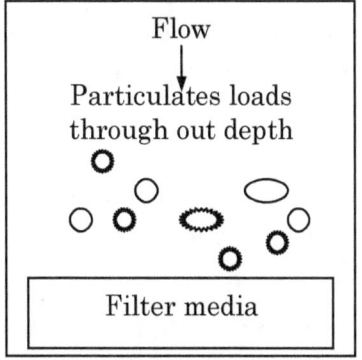

Surface filtration   Depth Filtration

FILTER RATING:

1) Absolute Filters   2) Nominal Filters

1) Absolute filters (Absolute Pore Size) : The pore size at which a challenge organism of a particular size will be retained with 99.99 to 100 % efficiency under strictly defined test conditions. These are sterilizing grade filters. (0.22 micron and lesser pore size filters.)

2) Nominal filters (Nominal Pore size): Ability of the filter media to retain the majority of particulate at 90-98 % the rated pore size.

Miscellaneous Filtration type in liquids filtration:
1) Coarse Filtration : 10 to 5 Micron meter, nominal pore size filtration.
2) Rough Filtration: 5 - to 1.5 Micron nominal Pore size, Filtration.
3) Tight or Polish: 1.5 to 0.8 micron meter, nominal pore size filtration.
4) Sterile filtration: 0.45 micron meter (earlier), 0.22 Micron meter and below Absolute pore size filtration.

Membrane filtration types on pore size:
1) Particle filtration (0.5 micron & Above).
2) Micro filtration. (0.1micron & 0.5 Micron).
3) Ultra filtration: Molecular weight based filtration(50 - 1000 Angstroms).
4) Nan filtration (10 - 50 Angstroms).
5) Reverse Osmosis(Below 10 angstroms or 0.001 micron).

This is used to filter the air supplied by the compressor before it enters the fermenter to ensure clean air. Types of filters are:

1. **Membrane filters:** They are made of cellulose acetate and nitrate with constant pore size of 0.2 mm to ensure filtering of particulate matter. They are not cheap but easy to maintain.
2. **Packed bed filters:** They contain glass wool or cotton wool packed in a container through which air is passed. Pore size is not uniform and these filters are susceptible to compaction and wetting thus causing channeling.
3. **Cartridge filters:** Filter element is present in a stainless steel or polycarbonate cartridge. They are more reliable and durable but are expensive.

Sparger

Filtered air is introduced to the fermenter from the bottom through a sparger in the form of small air bubbles to ensure proper aeration and mixing.

Sensors

These are used to monitor and control various fermentation parameters like pH, temperature and oxygen content.

Other equipment for fermenting

Autoclave

Autoclaves are used to sterilize equipment, media, and other components of fermentation. They are similar to pressure cookers. Different sizes of autoclaves are available on the market.

Ovens

Hot air ovens are used to sterilize or dry the equipment used in the fermentation process. The equipment to be dried or sterilized should withstand high temperatures, borosilicate or pyrex glass equipment being good examples. The inner chamber is made of heat resistant stainless steel and has a fan to circulate the hot air evenly throughout the chamber to ensure proper heat transfer. Microwave ovens are used to perform drying and melting agar. The main advantage of micro wave ovens is they take a very short time to do the job.

Incubators

Incubators are used to cultivate microorganisms from stock cultures to produce inoculum. Incubators provide optimum temperature for growth of microorganisms.

Fig. 3.6: Incubator

Source: Smulders Bakery and Cooking Equipment, Inc.

Pumps

Liquid/media is introduced to the fermenter by a pump. There are various types of pumps available, including:

1. **Peristaltic:** They provide constant flow rate and mild pumping. Liquids do not back-flow, so check valves are not required
2. **Mini or Delta:** They are used for adding pH control agents like acid, alkali, and adding anti foam agents. Mini pumps are fixed-speed pumps and can pump against the pressure.
3. **Larger pump:** They are used to add nutrients to the medium. Speed can be varied by altering the bore size of the tubes.

Air-lift fermenters

These fermenters do not have mechanical agitation systems (motor, shaft, impeller blades) but contents are agitated by injecting air from the bottom. Sterile atmospheric air is used if microorganisms are aerobic and "inert gas" is used if microorganisms are anaerobic. This is a gentle method of mixing the contents and is most suitable for fermentation of animal and plant cell cultures since the mechanical agitation produces high shearing stress that may damage the cells. Air-lift fermenters are most widely used for large-scale production of monoclonal antibodies.

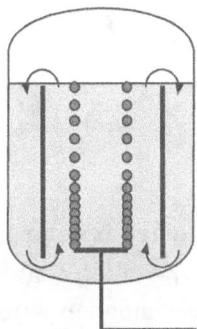

Fig. 3.7: Air-lift fermenter

Source: Kang, X. Department of Chemical and Biochemical Engineering, University of Maryland, Baltimore County.

Draft tubes are used in some cases to provide better mixing, mass transfer, and to reduce bubble coalescence by inducing circulatory motion.

Fixed bed fermenters

These are also called immobilized cell fermenters. The cells are absorbed onto or entrapped in the solid surfaces like plastic beads, glass or plastic wool and solidified gels to render them

Fixed bed fermenters are most commonly used for waste water treatment and as biological filters in small aquarium water recycling systems and production of amino acids and enzymes.

Tower fermenters

Tower fermenters are simple in design and easy to construct. They consist of a long cylindrical vessel with an inlet at the bottom, an exhaust at the top, and a jacket to control temperature. They do not require agitation hence there are no shafts, impellers or blades. Tower fermenters are used for continuous fermentation of beer, yeast and SCP.

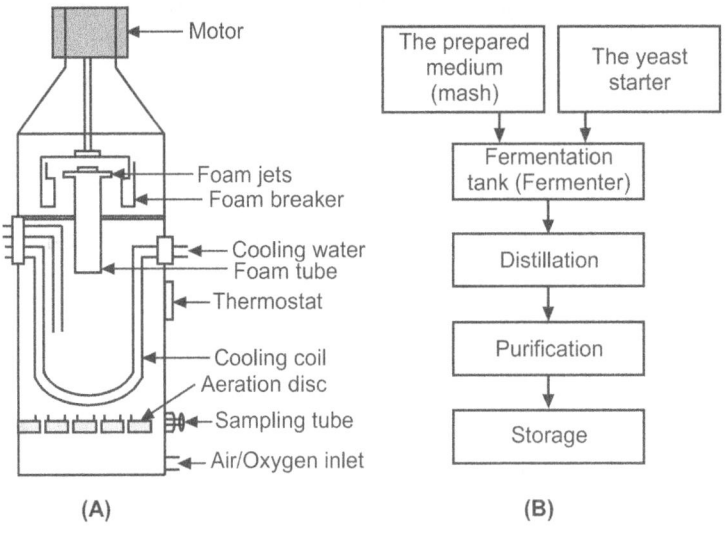

Source: PinkMonkey, Inc.

Fig. 3.8: Tower fermenter

Batch culture fermentation

This type of fermentation is also called a *closed culture* system because nutrients and other components are added in specific amounts at the start of the process and are not replenished once the fermentation has started. At the end of the process the product is recovered; then, the fermenter is cleaned, sterilized, and used for another batch process.

In the initial stages microorganisms grow at a rapid rate in the presence of excess nutrients but as they multiply in large numbers they use up the nutrients.

They also produce toxic metabolites which retard further growth of microorganisms during the later stages of the fermentation process.

Fed-batch culture

In this process the nutrients and substrates are added at the start of the process and at regular intervals after the start. This is called controlled feeding. Inoculum is added to the fermentation vessel when microorganisms are in exponential growth phase. Fed-batch culture is controlled by *feed-back control* and *control without feed-back*.

1. Feed-back control: The fermentation process is controlled by monitoring process parameters like dissolved oxygen content, carbon dioxide to oxygen ratio, pH, concentration of substrate, and concentration of the product.
2. Control without feed-back: The substrates and nutrients are added at regular intervals.

Fed-batch culture requires special equipment such as a reservoir which holds the nutrients, pH modifiers so that they can be added to the fermenter at regular intervals, and pumps to deliver culture medium aseptically to the fermenter.

Continuous culture fermentation

This method prolongs the exponential growth phase of microbial growth as nutrients are continually supplied and metabolites and other wastes are continually removed thus promoting continual growth of the microorganisms. Continuous culture fermentation is advantageous because of its high productivity.

Two control methods are used in continuous culture fermentation, namely, *chemostat* and *turbidostat*.

Chemostat

This medium contains excess of all but one of the nutrients which determine the rate of growth of the microorganism. At steady state of the chemostat the rate of input of medium into the fermenter is equal to the rate of output out of the fermenter.

Turbidostat

This medium contains excess of all nutrients so the microbial growth is at its maximum specific growth rate. The system consist of a photoelectric cell which is a turbidity sensor that detects changes in turbidity of the contents in the fermenter and then controls the amount of medium fed to the fermenter.

Sterilization

It is essential for all fermentation processes to ensure yield of desired product as this allows growth of the desired microorganisms. All the components of fermentation need to be sterilized, including the nutrient medium and other ingredients. The fermentation vessel and other accessory equipment must also be sterilized to ensure pristine conditions and virtually no contamination. Different techniques of sterilization are available based on the properties of the component being sterilized. Most commonly used techniques include: heat sterilization– moist heat sterilization, dry heat sterilization, incineration, and boiling; sterilization by chemicals; sterilization by filtration; and sterilization by radiation.

Moist heat sterilization

This is the most commonly used technique for sterilization of a wide variety of fermentation components. Steam is used at high pressure and temperature 121° C for 15 minutes causing denaturation of enzymes and degradation of the nucleic acids resulting in death of the microorganisms. This process is carried out by using an autoclave in which the components to be sterilized are placed in water and heated. Steam is produced and high pressure is developed inside the autoclave. Most of the fermentation components like culture medium, small fermenters and glassware are sterilized by this technique.

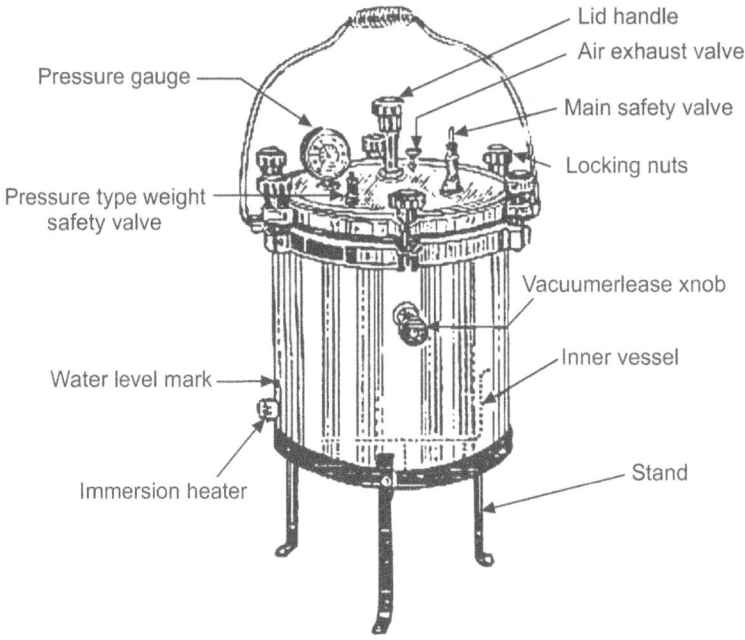

Fig. 3.9: Autoclave
Source: Narang Medical, LTD.

Dry heat sterilization

Hot air is used to sterilize by oxidizing the cellular components of the microorganisms. Dry heat is less effective than moist heat so high temperatures of 160°-180° C are used for about 1 hour to attain complete sterilization. Hot air ovens are used to sterilize equipment in the fermentation process. The equipment to be sterilized should withstand high temperatures, like borosilicate or Pyrex glass equipment. The inner chamber of the oven is made of heat resistant stainless steel and has a fan to circulate the hot air evenly throughout the chamber to ensure proper heat transfer.

Incineration

The objects to be sterilized are directly exposed to flames to kill all microorganisms. This is the most effective method of sterilization but suitable only for heat stable components like metal and some glass objects such as inoculation loops, needles and heat stable glassware.

Boiling

Liquids are sterilized by boiling at 100° C for 30 minutes which kills most of the microorganisms except the spores. Spores can be killed for boiling for a longer period of time.

Sterilization by chemicals

Gases like ethylene oxide, and formaldehyde gas, and liquids such as chlorine, ethyl alcohols, hydrogen peroxide and formaldehyde are some of the chemicals used to sterilize fermentation components which cannot withstand the high temperatures of heat sterilization.

Sterilization by filtration

Filters are used to sterilize liquids which are heat sensitive and gases used in fermentation process.

Sterilization by radiation

Ionizing radiations and UV light are used to perform sterilization. Filters, gases, and other heat sensitive components are sterilized by radiation.

Product recovery

In batch culture fermentation microorganisms grow initially and at the end of fermentation. The resultant broth contains product and dead microorganisms, thus it is essential to separate out the desired product. Microorganisms can be removed from the broth by filtration or centrifugation to separate microbial cell from the cell free solution containing the product. The product is isolated from cell free solution by precipitation, adsorption, or solvent extraction techniques.

Precipitation

This is the simplest method of isolation. Fermentation products like carbohydrates are precipitated by adding alcohol, while organic acids are salted out of the solution.

Solvent extraction

This technique provides isolation and purification of product in a single step. Organic solvent is added to the fermentation broth which dissolves the product to form a solvent layer which is separated from the aqueous layer and is evaporated to obtain the pure product.

Ion exchange

Ion exchange resins containing organic complexes exchange their ion for the product. The process involves two steps, adsorption and elution.

1. Adsorption– The fermentation broth when passed through a column containing the resin gets absorbed to the resin.

2. Elution– Product is separated from the resin by passing suitable reagent through the column. The advantage of this technique is reusability of the ion-exchange resin after the product is isolated.

Genetic Engineering and Bacteria:

Genetic engineering is the manipulation of genes. It is also called recombinant DNA technology. In genetic engineering, pieces of DNA (genes) are introduced into a host by means of a carrier (vector) system. The foreign DNA becomes a permanent feature of the host, being replicated and passed on to daughter cells along with the rest of its DNA. Bacterial cells are transformed and used in production of commercially important products. The examples are production of human insulin (used against diabetes), human growth hormone (somatotrophin used to treat pituitary dwarfism), and infections which can be used to help fight viral diseases.

So what is biotechnology **and** genetic engineering. There are three major developments that act as the signature of biotech, with many more surprises coming down the road:

- Bacterial production of substances like human interferon, human insulin and human growth hormone. That is, simple bacteria like E. coli are manipulated to produce these chemicals so that they are easily harvested in vast quantities for use in medicine. Bacteria have also been modified to produce all sorts of other chemicals and enzymes.

- Modification of plants to change their response to the environment, disease or pesticides. For example, tomatoes can gain fungal resistance by adding chitinases to their genome. A chitinase breaks down chitin, which forms the cell wall of a fungus cell. The pesticide Roundup kills all plants, but crop plants can be modified by adding genes that leave the plants immune to Roundup.

- Identification of people by their DNA. An individual's DNA is unique, and various, fairly simple tests let DNA samples found at the scene of a crime be matched with the person who left it. This process has been greatly aided by the invention of the polymerase chain reaction (PCR) technique for taking a small sample of DNA and magnifying it millions of times over in a very short period of time.

To understand some of the techniques used in biotechnology, lets look at how bacteria have been modified to produce human insulin.

Insulin is a simple protein normally produced by the pancreas. In people with diabetes, the pancreas is damaged and cannot produce insulin. Since insulin is vital to the body's processing of glucose, this is a serious problem. Many diabetics, therefore, must inject insulin into their bodies daily. Prior to the 1980s, insulin for diabetics came from pigs and was very expensive.

To create insulin inexpensively, the gene that produces human insulin was added to the genes in a normal E. coli bacteria. Once the gene was in place, the normal cellular machinery produced it just like any other enzyme. By culturing large quantities of the modified bacteria and then killing and opening them, the insulin could be extracted, purified and used very inexpensively.

The trick, then, is in getting the new gene into the bacteria. The easiest way is to splice the gene into a plasmid -- a small ring of DNA that bacteria often pass to one another in a primitive form of sex. Scientists have developed very precise tools for cutting standard plasmids and splicing new genes into them. A sample of bacteria is then "infected" with the plasmid, and some of them take up the plasmid and incorporate the new gene into their DNA. To separate the infected from the uninfected, the plasmid also contains a gene giving the bacteria immunity to a certain antibiotic. By treating the sample with the antibiotic, all of the cells that did not take up the plasmid are killed. Now a new strain of insulin-producing E. coli bacteria can be cultured in bulk to create insulin.

Using biotechnology techniques, bacteria can also be bioengineered for the production of therapeutic proteins, such as insulin, growth factors or antibodies

Once the bacteria become the host for the production of bioengineered products MCB is prepared from a single clone. MCB is extensively characterized and expanded to prepare WCB. When future cells are needed, they are taken from the working cell bank.

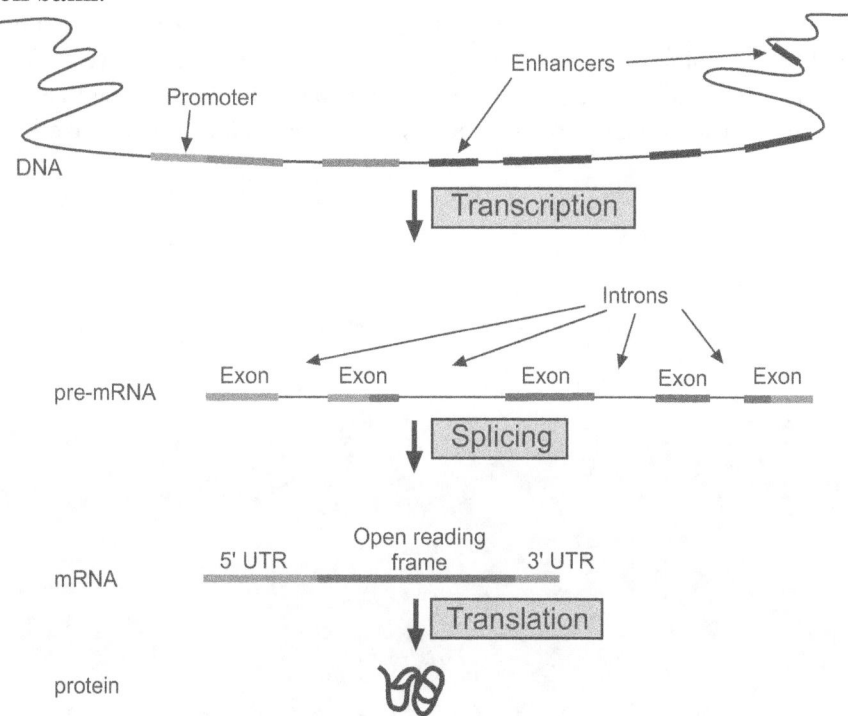

Eukaryotic protein coding gene

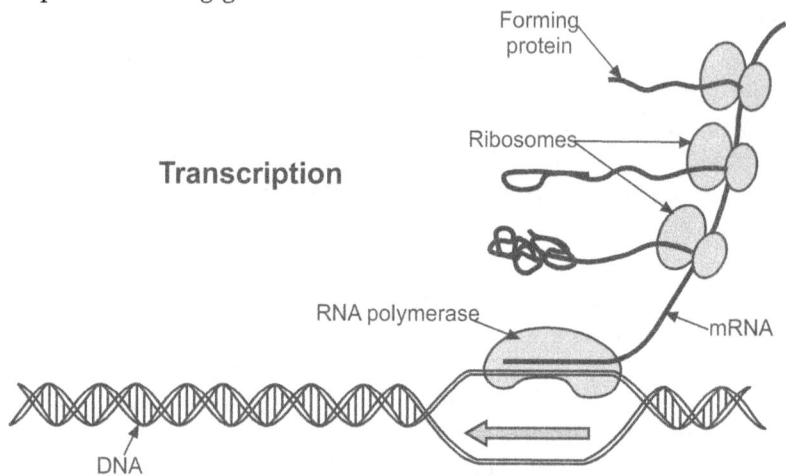

Fig. 3.10: **Transcription in bacteria**

A gene is a unit of heredity in a living organism. It is a name given to some stretches of DNA and RNA that code for a type of protein or for an RNA chain that has a function in the organism. Living things depend on genes, as they specify all proteins and functional RNA chains. Genes hold the information to build and maintain an organism's cells and pass genetic traits to offspring, although some organelles (e.g. mitochondria) are self-replicating and are not coded for by the organism's DNA. All organisms have many genes corresponding to various different biological traits, some of which are immediately visible, such as eye color or number of limbs, and some of which are not, such as blood type or increased risk for specific diseases, or the thousands of basic biochemical processes that comprise life.

❖❖❖

4. BIOTECHNOLOGY INDUSTRY SET UP

There are so many steps, which are to be followed while setting up of the biotechnology manufacturing and testing facility. The first and most important step is market survey and selection of product, then Research & Development, regulatory approvals, setting up of production and testing unit, licencing and effective marketing of these products. Biotechnology companies are places where scientific discoveries are transformed into commercial products. This transformation begins in the research and development,(R & D) unit.

A) R & D *is the organizational unit that finds ideas for products, performs research and testing to see if the ideas are feasible, and develops promising ideas into actual products.*

Responsibilities of the research and development unit:
1. Finding a potential product with commercial value - performing research relating to the potential product
2. Characterizing the properties of the product, such as: composition, physical, and chemical properties strength, potency or effect of the product purity of the product and steps required to avoid contamination stability and shelf-life of the product applications of the product safety concerns in the use of the product
3. Establishing product specifications (descriptions of properties that every batch of the final product must have to be released for sale)
4. Developing methods to test the product to ensure that it meets its specifications
5. Developing processes to make the product
6. Describing any cells or microorganisms required to make the product
7. Determining what raw materials are required to make the product and establishing specifications to characterize these materials
8. Describing equipment required to make the product
9. Developing a plan for production of the product

B) The production unit

The production unit in a company is responsible for making products. The systems used for production in biotechnology companies are diverse. Manufacturing a product may involve growing bacteria in laboratory flasks and isolating products from the cultures. In other situations, manufacturing involves growing bacteria, or other types of cells, in fermenters that are several stories tall and using industrial-scale equipment to purify products from the cultures. Production may involve growing cells in petri dishes, cultivating crops in a field, maintaining laboratory animals or even farm animals. Thus, the details of production vary greatly from company to company. However, certain functions, are generally the responsibility of the production team.

Responsibilities of the production unit
1. Making the product
2. Working with large-scale equipment and/or large-volume reactions (not applicable to all biotechnology products or companies)
3. Routine monitoring and control of the environment as required for the product (for example, maintaining the proper temperature or sterility requirements)
4. Routine cleaning, calibration and maintenance of equipment
5. Following written procedures
6. Monitoring processes associated with making the product
7. Initiating corrective actions if problems arise Completing forms, labeling, filling in logbooks, and maintaining other required documents

C) The Quality Control/Quality Assurance Unit

The quality control/assurance unit (QC/QA) in a company is responsible for ensuring the quality of the product. We define "**quality control**", QC, *as a subsection of QA chiefly responsible for monitoring processes and performing laboratory testing.* "**Quality assurance**", QA, *refers to all the activities and people who work to ensure the final quality of products.* Although the terminology varies, the goal of the quality team is to assure a quality product.

Responsibilities of the Qc/Qa Unit
1. Monitoring equipment, facilities, environment, personnel and product
2. Reviewing all production procedures used in the company
3. Ensuring that all documents are accurate, complete and available
4. Testing samples of the product and the materials that go into making the product Comparing data to established standards
5. Deciding whether or not to approve the product for release to consumers
6. Reviewing customer complaints

D) The "Life Cycle" of a Biotechnology Company

Small, start-up biotechnology companies that are in the early stages of developing marketable products may be almost entirely devoted to R & D. As products are being developed, a single individual may play multiple roles. For example, the research scientists who develop a product may also initially produce and package it for sale and may also deal with quality assurance and regulatory issues. The same facilities and the same types of equipment may be used to perform research and to make products. Thus the distinction between R & D, production, and QC/QA may be blurred in a start-up company.

A start-up company in its early stages of development must not only create new products, but must also find ways to finance its growth when it has no products to sell. As it does so, a business culture begins to evolve. Assuming the company successfully develops a product(s), more employees are hired, some of them specializing only in production or quality assurance activities. The equipment and facilities used for production typically become larger and distinct from those used for product development. As this maturation of the company occurs, government regulations and standards may play an increasingly important role and the quality assurance unit grows to keep up with these changes. As a company matures, its "feeling" also changes. It is sometimes said that there are three cultures within a mature biotechnology company – R and D, production, and QC/QA.

The R and D people work in an atmosphere of change and unpredictability. They often do not know which ideas will result in a product, which methods will work best, and how much success they will have in their endeavors. Creativity and a willingness to work with uncertainty characterize most investigators in R and D and in academic research laboratories.

In production situations, attention to detail is critical and deviations from established procedures must be carefully considered and approved. The production team therefore works in a more predictable environment. The quality team is intent on assuring product integrity. The quality team interacts closely with outside agents, such as auditors, inspectors, and customers, and also works closely with the company's R and D and production personnel. The quality assurance team must effectively manage problems and be conscious of the ramifications of particular courses of action.

E) Other Functions in a Company

There are other important areas in a biotechnology company including:

1. ***Engineering (or facilities management),*** which is responsible for ensuring that the systems that control the building environment are operating properly and that large equipment is properly installed and functioning.
2. ***Facility maintenance and housekeeping,*** which performs critical day to day functions, such as cleaning and certain building repairs.
3. ***Receiving and shipping,*** which assures that incoming raw materials are properly routed and that products go to the proper destination.
4. ***Dispensing,*** which puts products that are produced in bulk into individual containers for consumer use.
5. ***Metrology,*** which ensures that instruments (such as those used in laboratories and those used to monitor production conditions) operate properly.
6. ***Marketing and sales,*** which is responsible for interacting with customers.

The Biotechnology Workplace

A. Biotechnology Laboratory Work Places

Let's consider biotechnology laboratory workplaces in more detail.

1. **Laboratory** *is a place where people produce knowledge, data, or information.* While people in laboratories produce tangible products such as photographs, antibodies, purified proteins, and printouts, these materials are produced with the purpose of learning more about a system or a sample, answering a research question, or documenting a discovery.

   Small biotechnology companies often produce products in facilities that are also used for research or that are similar to research laboratories. However, we call any facility used for producing a commercial product a production facility, rather than a laboratory.

2. **Research laboratory** is one kind of laboratory. *It is a space set aside to study the complexities of nature in a controlled manner.* Experiments can be performed in a research laboratory in which the researcher controls the factors of interest. Universities house many of the research laboratories in which are made seminal discoveries that drive the biotechnology industry. So, the university biology research laboratory might be considered a biotechnology workplace. The methods used in research and development laboratories associated with biotechnology companies have much in common with university laboratories, but company R and D scientists are more focused on commercial applications of their work than are academic scientists.

3. **Testing laboratory** is another sort of laboratory environment. *It is a place where analysts test samples.* The product of a testing laboratory is a test result. A quality control laboratory is a type of testing laboratory where samples of products and raw materials are tested to see if they are of good quality. Once a biotechnology company begins to manufacture a product, it needs to create a QC laboratory and assign analysts to this important laboratory work.

   Testing laboratories play a key role in biotechnology by testing the effects of drugs and other products that are in development. For example, before a drug can be marketed, it is tested in a multitude of ways in cells, in animals, and finally in human volunteers.

   Sometimes a biotechnology company does this testing in its own facilities. But, very often biotechnology companies do not perform all these tests themselves but rather contract with specialized testing companies to get their product tested. Thus, a testing laboratory is the workplace for many biotechnologists.

B. Biotechnology Workplaces are Diverse

It is evident that there is not a single biotechnology workplace. For example, the work Environment of an operator in a production facility is different than that of a person who works with documents in a quality assurance department or someone who works in the laboratory doing research and development tasks. The work of a production person in a start-up biotechnology company is different from that of an operator in a large production facility. Working in a company whose products are crop plants, is different than working in a company manufacturing drug tablets.

Thus, a person entering biotechnology as a career will have many options and can find a place that suits their personality and interests.

CELL CULTURE LABORATORY AND EQUIPMENT

Design of the laboratory

Design of the tissue culture laboratory is very important for the success of tissue culture since almost all the procedures dealing with cells require an aseptic environment. Cell culture laboratories should be separated from contaminating environments like microbiological laboratories or animal houses and should have restricted access so that only authorized personnel can enter and carry out procedures. These laboratories should provide clean, dust free environments by using air filters since making the whole lab sterile is practically impossible. Aseptic environments at the work place, i.e., while carrying out cell culture procedures, can be provided by using laminar flow cabinets. The laboratory should have all the required equipment (refrigerator, freezer, oven etc.), working bench to carry out the procedures, storage area, chemicals, air purifiers, air-conditioning, sinks with constant water supply, power supply and trash cans. The laboratory should be easy to clean and should have good drainage. Procedures such as sterile handling, incubation, preparation, washing, and storage should be done in separate areas of the laboratory to avoid contamination.

Equipment

The equipment required by the cell culture laboratory depends on various factors such as size of the laboratory, scale of manufacturing, economic constraints, and availability of equipment. However, there are some basic pieces of equipment that every laboratory should have regardless of the above mentioned constraints. These are essential equipment without which cell culture procedures cannot be done.

Laminar-flow hood cabinet

An aseptic environment is required to carry out cell culture activities such as preparing reagents, preparing media, and culture transferring. This can be provided effectively and cheaply by laminar-flow hood cabinets.

Autoclave

This is required to sterilize heat sensitive equipment and the culture media.

Oven

Used for dry heat sterilization of equipment and for mild to moderate heating of media and reagents.

Incubator

Culture cells require optimum temperature for growth which can be provided by the incubator where the temperature can be controlled as per the requirements.

Incubators with constant humidity create an environment for the support and growth of bacteria, mold, and spores.

Centrifuge

Cell culture suspensions are centrifuged to increase the concentration of cells.

Cell counting counter

Cell counting is vital to determine viability and to assess growth rate of the cells in culture. This, in turn, determines the success of the procedure on the whole. Therefore, the cells are counted at regular intervals using tools like hemocytometer slide and Coulter counters for automated counting. Cell counts are enumerated using a flow cytometer, which is a machine in which the cells of interest in a sample of blood are tagged with florescent monoclonal antibodies and passed in a single-cell column in front of laser light. The light then illuminates the cells so that they may be read by a photosensor to indicate the size of the cells. In a similar way, when the laser light hits an antibody, it shines brightly and the cell is counted by the sensor attached to a microscope.

Refrigerator and Freezer

Cell culture components such as cells, chemicals, reagents, and enzymes should be stored in low temperatures, thus, refrigerator ($-4°C$) and freezer ($-20°C$) are compulsory for any cell culture laboratory. Domestic refrigerators and freezer are cheap and effective and are therefore most commonly used.

Microscope

Cells in culture can be monitored for growth and developments regularly, using a microscope with good magnification, since cells are too small to be visible to the naked eye. Recently, microscopes have been made available with built in cameras so that pictures can be taken while observing the cells. This is useful for documentation and publication purposes.

The inverted microscope is used for the examination of biological and metallurgical specimens, tissue cultures, microbes, and other living specimens in their natural form, in Petri dishes, or in the examination of culture bottles.

Glassware

The cell culture laboratory should include glass vessels because of properties such as ease of sterilization, non toxicity, and transparency. Different types of glassware are needed to handle different components of the cell culture.

Pipettes: They are used for addition of measured amounts of reagents and chemicals to the culture and for transferring fluids from one container to another. Glass pipettes can be sterilized before each use but pre-sterilized and ready to use disposable pipettes are also available commercially and are intended for single use.

Test tubes: Small volumes of cell culture suspensions, culture media, chemicals, and reagents are stored in test tubes.

Bottles: These are available in different sizes and shapes and used to store cell cultures, chemicals, and reagents.

Conical flasks: These are commonly used to prepare the culture media and to incubate the cell cultures.

CULTURES

Types of cultures

There are three types of cultures: tissue, cell, and organ cultures.

1. *Tissue culture*

The technique of in-vitro cultivation of animal cells, tissues or organs in general is called tissue culture. Tissue culture can be further divided into cell culture and organ culture.

2. *Cell culture*

These are cultures of cells obtained from some parent tissue. The cells do not have the biochemical properties of the parent tissue but they can be grown and multiplied when provided with optimum nutrition and optimum conditions.

3. *Organ culture*

In-vitro culture and growth of the whole or part of organs is called organ culture. This technique is used to maintain the organ in-vitro allowing normal differentiation of the cells or reconstituting of the whole or part of organs while retaining all components of the tissue (anatomical, physiological, and histological properties) thus resembling the organ in-vivo. Organ culture is an extremely difficult procedure due to large experimental variation involved in the process.

Sterilization

Cell culture techniques demand strict aseptic environment for the success of its procedures. All the equipment, media, and other components used in a cell culture laboratory should be sterilized to render them free of any type of microorganisms and resistant spores that can contaminate the cell culture.

Basic sterilization techniques are previously discussed in detail in Section II.

Vessels

Vessels like glassware (bottles, pipettes, and culture flasks), plastic vessels, and caps of the vessels are sterilized in steps. First, the apparatus are washed several times with tap water while brushing to remove dirt and grease from the surfaces and water is drained completely to make them absolutely dry.

Pipettes are soaked in soap water overnight before cleaning with tap water to remove tough stains or traces of chemicals. Previously used glassware should be cleaned with a disinfectant immediately after use. In the next step, these apparatus are subjected to hot air sterilization at 160°C for 50-60 minutes using a hot air oven or moist heat sterilization at 121°C 15-20 minutes using an autoclave. The apparatus are then allowed to cool down to room temperature and should be used within 2-4 days.

Media

Autoclaving is the most commonly used technique for sterilization of culture media. Other liquid components such as chemicals and reagents can also be sterilized by autoclaving. The liquids are first poured in glass containers and sealed to prevent evaporation of liquids and contamination due to contact with the steam. Then, the sealed containers are placed in the autoclave for sterilization. Heat labile chemicals and culture media are sterilized by the membrane filtration technique.

Water

Water used in a cell culture laboratory has to be pure so it should be sterilized by advanced techniques such as reverse osmosis, distillation, deionization, and carbon filtration. Ultra pure water can be obtained by using a combination of the above mentioned techniques. In the first stage, water is subjected to reverse osmosis or distillation, secondly, the organic and inorganic compounds are removed from the water by carbon filtration. Ionized inorganic materials are then removed from the water in the third stage by deionization and in the final stage, microorganisms are eliminated by micro-pore filtration.

Requirements for Cell Growth

Culture media

The cells in culture media require a suitable environment and optimum nutrition that are similar to in-vivo for their survival, growth, and multiplication. Culture media not only provide nutrients that are not synthesized by the cells but also optimum physical conditions like pH that are essential for the survival of cells. Factors such as temperature, oxygen, and light should be controlled externally.

Based on functions the culture media can be broadly classified into four groups.

Media for immediate/short time survival of cells: This media contains an instant energy source and maintains optimum osmotic pressure needed for survival of cells. The commonly used ingredients in this type of media are inorganic salts and glucose, for example, balanced salt solution.

Media for prolonged survival of cells: This media should contain nutrients and supplements that cannot be produced by the cells in culture– nutrients which are essential for their long term survival such as amino acids, vitamins, growth factor, and hormones. For short time survival Eagle's media is commonly used.

Media for long term growth of cells: This is a complex media that can provide supplements required for long term growth and multiplication of the cells. Included are enzymes, co-enzymes, and serum proteins.

Media for specialized functions: This is also a complex media that serves special nutrients to the cells in a culture, depending on the cell types used (e.g.

estrogen for the cells of female sex organs and vitamin A for ciliated epithelial cells). Since the ingredients vary for each type of cell the media is prepared accordingly.

Based on method of preparation culture media can be classified into two types.

Natural media: This was the most commonly used culture media in the past. Natural ingredients like blood and tissues are used for the preparation of the media. There are two types of natural ingredients generally used in the preparation of natural media, namely, plasma and biological fluids.

Plasma: Plasma clots were commonly used in the past for the culture of small tissues. Plasma is one of the constituents of animal blood and is prepared from the blood collected from different types of animals.

Biological fluids: Serum is the clear liquid that is left out when the blood clots. It is prepared by allowing whole blood to clot and collecting the clear fluid that is separated from the clot. Serum is the most commonly used biological fluid used in the preparation of natural culture media because it contains proteins, growth factors, hormones, trace elements, and fatty acids, which can enhance growth rate of the cells in culture. Culture media can also be prepared using other biological fluids like embryo extracts and amniotic fluid.

Synthetic media: This type of media is prepared using different chemicals that can provide optimum nutrition and physical environment for the cells in culture, thus, promoting the cell growth. Defined media is prepared using definite amounts of chemicals in the media similar to those present in the natural ingredients. Synthetic media should also include vitamins, enzymes, amino acids, trace elements, buffers, antibiotics, indicators, and antioxidants. Natural media contain all of these ingredients, so, in some cases, serum is included in the synthetic media instead of adding all the above mentioned ingredients.

STAGES IN CELL CULTURE

Cell sources

Cells for culture can be obtained directly from organs or tissues but common sources are cell banks which are either owned by private businesses or government. The advantages of obtaining cells from cell banks are that they would have been subjected to viability and quality control tests. A protocol has to be followed when new cells are obtained by the laboratory from cell banks or any other external sources. The new cells should be quarantined and quality control tests performed before they can be added to the main cell stock of the laboratory.

Primary culture

Primary culture is the process of establishing the culture by collecting cells directly from the animal source. Different types of cells can be collected from the animal source to establish the primary culture such as normal cells, cells from a tumor, from adults, or from embryos. Cells from different species can be used depending on the type of cell culture product. Primary cells can be obtained by one of the following processes.

Mechanical Disaggregation

Mechanical disaggregation of cells from the source, involving: collecting the tissue from the animal and washing to remove blood and other unwanted tissues, mincing the tissue, rinsing the tissue with sterile BSS solution, centrifuging to collect cells, seeding the cells in large flasks with nutrient media, and incubating at approximately 37° C to allow growth of primary cells.

Enzymatic Disaggregation

Enzymatic treatment of the animal source with enzymes that can disaggregate the tissue into individual cells. EDTA is used since it chelates. Mg^{++} and collagenase is often used as well. Enzymes like trypsin and pronase are used for this purpose. This process involves: collecting the tissue from the animal and washing to remove blood and other unwanted tissues, mincing the tissue, treating the tissue with 0.25%w/v trypsin for 30-40 minutes at 37 °C, adding serum to neutralize trypsin, collecting the cells, seeding the cells in flasks containing nutrient media, and incubating at 37C to allow growth of primary cells.

Growing cells

Allowing the cells to grow out of the animal tissue.

Types of Cells

There are two types of cells used in culture based on their growth characteristics. They are: adherent cells and suspension cells.

1. Adherent cells

The cells are adhesive and depend on a substrate, matrix, micro-carriers, or other supporting material for their growth and development. These cells require treatment with the enzyme trypsin before they can be sub-cultured since the cells bond with the substrate.

2. Suspension cells

These cells are non-adhesive or less adhesive and do not depend on the substrate or other supporting material for their growth and development. They can be maintained while held in suspension. The suspension cells can be sub-cultured easily by dilution and do not require trypsinization.

Stages of Growth:

The growth of cells in culture follows a similar pattern as that of microbial growth in a fermentation tank. Cell growth can be classified into three phases or stages.

1. *Lag phase*

   In this phase cells do not appear to grow but instead they prepare for the growth.

2. *Log phase*

   In this phase the cells grow at very rapid pace using the nutrients provided by the culture media and the cell number increases exponentially.

3. *Stationary phase*

   In this phase cell growth is retarded and it reaches a plateau due to accumulation of toxic wastes released by the rapidly growing cells or due to exhaustion of nutrients in the culture media. Cell senescence is also a factor because of its limited replicative capacity.

Assessing Cell Growth:

Cell growth should be assessed at regular intervals during the cell culture process so that if growth rate is low appropriate steps can be taken. Counting the number of cells in specified amount of sample is the effective way of assessing the growth rate of cells. This can be done using two types of methods.

1. *Direct method*

   The cell numbers are directly counted using a hemocytometer.

2. *Indirect method*

   The cell numbers are counted indirectly by measuring the DNA and protein in the sample to determine the number of cells present.

SECONDARY CULTURE/SUBCULTURE

This is a technique employed to maintain the cells in logarithmic phase in the culture so that they continue to grow and increase in number in a way not possible after a stage, since growth is retarded due to accumulation of wastes or to exhaustion of nutrients in the culture medium. The cells can be sub-cultured during the later stages of the lag phase. Sub-culturing is also used to obtain a culture with a homogenous population of cells from the existing primary culture. Such cultures are very useful to scale up the cell culture procedures to an industrial level and to carry out experiments on one type of cell more easily. Sub-culturing can be done either by adding fresh nutrient media to the cells in primary culture or by adding the cells from a primary culture to the fresh nutrient media.

Cell Line preservation

Homogeneous cell lines are obtained from primary cultures and subsequent secondary cultures and the entire process is not only laborious and time consuming, but also, expensive. Cell lines are also susceptible to microbial contamination, hence, it is absolutely necessary to take appropriate steps to preserve them for later use and to prevent loss due to microbial contamination.

Cryopreservation

This is a technique of preserving the cell line at very low temperatures. At such temperatures cell metabolism is reduced significantly, but cells retain their viability when they are thawed.

Cell banks

This is the collection and preservation of cell lines in liquid nitrogen such that their viability and other characteristics are not altered. Cell banks provide a continuous supply of cells for various procedures in the laboratory.

CLONING OF A CELL LINE

Cell lines are susceptible to genetic variation over the course of time. There is the possibility of growth of unwanted cells which can affect the growth and viability of the original cell lines. Cloning of cell lines is the effective way of dealing with the above mentioned situation as large number of identical cells can be produced in a short period of time. Cell lines can be cloned using three techniques

Soft agar technique

This technique is used for cloning suspension cultures.

Cloning rings technique

This is the technique used for cloning adherent cells where the cells are allowed to grow in conventional vessels. Small, hollow, sterile stainless steel rings called cloning rings are used to isolate each of the discrete colonies.

Limiting dilution technique

This is the most common technique which can be used for both suspension cells and adherent cell lines. Three dilutions of cell suspensions are prepared. Cell suspension is added to a 96 well tray followed by medium and the process is repeated for each of the three dilutions. The 96 well trays are then incubated at a suitable temperature to allow the growth of cells. The wells which show growth of colonies of single type cells are selected and further sub-cultured to produce large numbers of similar cells which can then be maintained by cryopreservation.

CLONING OF ANIMALS

Cloning creates a genetically identical copy of an animal or plant. Plants are cloned through cutting. In humans identical twins are clones.

Dolly the sheep has been the world's most famous clone because she was the first mammal to be cloned from an adult cell, rather than an embryo. Thinking of cloning in the broad senses as splitting an egg or embryo, then, it is easy to understand that a number of animals such as frogs, mice, sheep, and cows had been cloned prior to Dolly.

The production of dolly

To clone Dolly scientists used the nucleus of an udder cell from a six year old Finn Dorset white sheep. The nucleus contained almost all the cell's genes so the scientists had to find a way to reprogram the udder cells in order to keep them alive and stop them from growing. This was achieved by altering the growth medium. The cell was then injected into an unfertilized egg cell whose nucleolus had been removed. The cells were then fused with the use of electrical pulses. The unfertilized egg cell came from a Scottish Blackface ewe.

After the scientists had fused the nucleus from the cell of the adult white sheep with the cell from the black-faced sheep, they cultured it for six to seven days to make sure that the cells divided and developed normally. This was then implanted into a surrogate mother, which was another Scottish Blackface ewe. A total of 277 cells were fused, with 29 early embryos being developed and implanted into surrogate mothers. However, only one pregnancy went to full term and produced a 6.6kg Finn Dorset lamb called Dolly which was born with a white face after 148 days from the work of scientists at the Roslin Institute in Scotland.

ORGAN CULTURE

The process of maintaining the whole organs in-vitro without affecting its properties is called organ culture . Organ culture can be carried out by using the following methods.

Watch glass

A clot is prepared on a watch glass using a mixture of chicken plasma and chick embryo extract. The animal tissue is placed on the clot and the watch glass is then placed in a petri dish containing moist cotton wool. The petri dish is covered and incubated at 37° C.

Single slide

This technique is also called Maximow single slide technique where the organs are dissected and treated with HBSS. Chicken plasma and chicken embryo extract are added on a cover slip mixed and allowed to clot. The organ is added to the clot formed on the cover slip. The cover slip with the clot and the organ is mounted on a Maximow slide. The sides of the cover slip are sealed with wax and the slide is placed in the incubator at 37° C.

Agar gel

The organs, after treating with HBSS, are placed in a watch glass containing agar gel along with chick embryo extract, chicken serum, Gey solution and Tyrode solution. The watch glass is then sealed with glass lid using wax and incubated at 37° C.

CELL CULTURE ON A LARGE SCALE

Cell culture experiments in the laboratory are useful to examine morphological, physiological, and functional properties of the cells. But for bulk production of cell culture products such as vaccines, antibodies, and hormones automated techniques are required. Suspension cultures are easy to scale up. Large scale cell cultures require slight modifications of the procedures used in laboratory scale.

Media

The medium should be very rich in nutrients since the cell density in large scale cell culture is very high and the nutrients are used up quickly.

Oxygen

The cells require oxygen continuously.

pH

Optimum pH for most of the cultures is 7-7.4 and this can be maintained by carbon dioxide-bicarbonate present in the medium as well as phosphates (also present in the medium). If these natural buffers fall short, pH buffers can be used.

Temperature

In large scale cell culture procedure temperatures higher than optimum range are produced that can adversely effect the growth of cells in culture, so it is very important to control the temperature. This can be done through internal heat exchangers which circulate cold water through cylinders or coiled tubes immersed in the medium.

Culture vessels

Large volumes of cell suspensions can be handled by using large fermentation tanks and large roller bottles, depending on the type of cells being used.

Sterilization

On laboratory scales most of the equipment and vessels can be sterilized easily by autoclaving but it is difficult to autoclave large culture vessels and other equipment. In-situ sterilization is employed for this purpose, done by pumping steam at high pressure over the surface of the vessel.

Large scale culture of adherent cells

Adherent cells are difficult to scale up since they have to be trypsinized first. They require special vessels for culture and have special nutritional and physical requirements. The culture vessels used for large scale cell culture of adherent cells are considered below.

Roller Bottles

These are cylindrical plastic bottles of volumes in the range of 1000-1500 ml. Roller bottles provide large surface areas for the cells, as well as, good gas exchange compared to conventional culture vessels. Large numbers of bottles are stacked and placed horizontally on rollers, rotated at a specific rpm, and incubated. Roller bottles are also called Roux bottles.

The surface area of the roller bottles can be increased by filling with sterile spiral plastic film or with sterile small glass tubes.

Multi-plate Unit

This consists of flat chambers placed together and interconnected to allow transfer of culture medium between the units; the apertures in the chambers allow gas transfer. The multi-plate unit is also called *cell factory*.

Fermentation tanks which can support adherent dependant cells by allowing a substratum to be in suspension are generally used for adherent cell culture. Glass bead bioreactors contain small glass beads packed in the column through which the medium passes freely. The glass beads act as substratum over which the cells can grow by adhering to them.

Large Scale Culture of Suspension Cells

Suspension cultures are much easier to scale up since what's involved is increasing the culture volume in appropriate culture vessels. Bioreactors/fermentation tanks are the most commonly used culture vessels for large scale cell culture procedures.

Stirred Tank Bioreactors

These are large steel fermentation tanks which can handle culture volumes of up to 8000 liters. They are provided with either a mechanical or magnetic stirrer to ensure homogenous mixing and aeration of the contents.

Air-lift Bioreactors

These are bioreactors which do not have stirrers. The stirring action is provided by the continuous pumping of air through a sparger located at the bottom.

Membrane Bioreactors

These are generally used for treatment of waste water due to their ability to increase the rate of separation of solid wastes from the water. This property can be utilized in cell culture to improve the concentration of cells. Membrane bioreactors are also well suited to handle very large volumes of cell suspensions.

Note: For detailed explanation of bioreactors refer to fermentation vessels section in the chapter on fermentation.

SAFETY IN CELL CULTURE LABORATORY

Cell culture laboratories handle harmful materials like chemicals, reagents, blood products, other animal cell products, and viruses. Some of them are carcinogenic and even classified as Biologically Hazardous Materials by the regulating authorities. Hence, it is very important that the cell culture laboratory personnel follow strict rules and protocols to ensure their personnel safety, safety of their co-workers, and thus, ensuring safety of the laboratory on the whole. Occupational Health and Safety Administration (OHSA) a division of Department of Labor developed regulations that should be followed in all cell culture laboratories. Information about safety, guidelines, and regulations should be made available to the personnel. Good Laboratory Practice (GLP) guidelines should be followed in the cell culture laboratory.

Some of the safety measures taken in the cell culture laboratory are:

Personnel Safety Measures

The personnel working in the cell culture laboratory should: attend safety and precautions training sessions before starting the employment, wear protective clothing like lab coat and disposable gloves to protect hands when entering the lab and should remove them before leaving the lab, clean hands with soap or specified disinfectant before entering and leaving the lab, wash the body parts immediately with water if contacted with harmful materials and bio-hazardous materials, and avoid eating and storing food in the laboratory.

Safe Handling of Equipment

Equipment such as glassware, autoclave, oven, centrifuge, and sharp equipment like syringe and scalpels, should be handled with caution to ensure safety.

Handling Bio-hazardous Materials

Cell culture laboratories contain various bio-hazardous materials. Some steps taken to handle such materials safely are use of gloves while handling such materials to avoid direct contact since they are harmful, avoidance of spilling and production of aerosols, availability of disinfectants, decontaminants for cellular, chemical, and microbial contaminants at all times in the laboratory to be used in case of spillages, proper cleaning of work benches before and after handling of cell products, and transferring of cellular and microbial products for sub-culturing only in bio-safety hood.

WASTE DISPOSAL

Cell culture laboratory wastes should be disposed of appropriately since they contain harmful equipment like needles, broken glass, bio-hazardous materials and harmful chemicals. Other recommended practices include chemical wastes should be disposed in labeled containers before disposal, glassware should be treated with bleach solution immediately after their use, broken glassware, syringes, needles, other sharp objects should be treated with bleach before disposing in containers marked Sharps, bio-hazard wastes should be disposed in special containers marked bio-hazard wastes, disposable equipment and gloves, among others, should be sterilized prior to disposal, mixing of incompatible chemicals should be avoided even after disposal as this may result in dangerous reactions, and metal cans should not be used for waste disposal; explosive resistant plastic containers should be used.

5. BIOTECHNOLOGY FOR HEALTHCARE : PREVENTIVE MANAGEMENT

Modern biotechnology is rooted in hundreds of years of basic biological research into the intricacies of living systems. In the early 1970s, *Drs. Herbert Boyer and Stanley Cohen* published the results of basic scientific research demonstrating that genetic information could be intentionally transferred from one organism to another. In 1976, venture capitalist Robert A. Swanson and Dr. Boyer founded a company, Genentech Inc., to apply this genetic methodology to the production of commercial products. In 1977, Genentech Inc. reported production of the first human protein manufactured in bacteria, somatostatin, a hormone that has many effects in the body. Genentech is generally considered to be the first "modern" biotechnology company, but many others were quickly founded. There are now hundreds of biotechnology products such as: human growth hormone, used to treat dwarfism; Interferon α-2b, used to treat a variety of viral diseases and cancers; and Hepatitis B vaccine, used to immunize people against the Hepatitis B agent. **Gene therapy** is a promising application of biotechnology that *involves replacing a gene that is missing, or correcting the function of a faulty gene, in order to cure an illness.*

Following are the some of the genetically produced product and used in treating the human illness.

1. Products of human therapeutic proteins:

   Some of the important Products and indication are as follows:

Erythropoietin	Anaemia.
Epidermal Growth Factor	Ulcer.
Factor VIII	Haemophilia.
Factor IX	Christmas Disease.
Granulocyte colony stimulating factor	Cancer.
Hepatitis B surface antigen	Hepatitis B (Vaccination).
Human serum albumin	Plasma supplements.
Human Insulin	Diabetes.
Human Somatotropin.	Dwarfism.
Interleukin	Cancer.
Interferon - Alpha	Leukaemia and other cancer.
Interferon - Beta	Cancer.
Relaxin	Child Birth.
Tissue Plasminogen Activator (tPA)	Heart Attack.
Vascular Endothelial growth factor.	CVS Disorders.

2. In the treatment of diseases.
3. Production of desired characteristic organisms.
4. Production of desired plants seeds
5. Production of citric acid
6. Various drugs and pharmaceutical.

1. Biotechnology for healthcare - Preventive Management:

Biotechnology products are being used for prevention and cure of various diseases. These products are as below:

(i) Vaccine

Through genetic engineering, scientists can isolate specific genes and insert them into DNA of certain microbes or mammalian cells; the microbes or cells become living factories, mass producing the desired antigen. Then, using another product of biotechnology, a monoclonal antibody that recognizes the antigen, the scientists can separate the antigen from all the other material produced by the microbe or cell. This technique has been used to produce immunogenic but safe segments of the hepatitis B virus and the malaria parasite.

In another approach, scientists have inserted genes for desired antigens into the DNA of the vaccinia virus, the large cowpox virus familiar for its role in smallpox immunization. When the reengineered vaccinia virus is inoculated, it stimulates an immune reaction to both the vaccinia and the products of its passenger genes. These have included, in animal experiments, genes from the viruses that cause hepatitis B, influenza, rabies, and AIDS

Instead of adding a gene, some scientists have snipped a key gene out of an infectious organism. Thus crippled, the microbe can produce immunity but not disease. This technique has been tried with a bacterium that causes the severe diarrheal disease cholera; such a vaccine is commercially available against a virus disease of pigs totally different approach to vaccine development lies in chemical synthesis. Once scientists have isolated the gene that encodes an antigen, they are able to determine the precise sequence of amino acids that make up the antigen. They then pinpoint small key areas on the large protein molecule, and assemble it chemical by chemical. Wholly synthetic vaccines are being explored for malaria and for the major diarrheal diseases that are so devastating in developing countries.

Another pioneering vaccine strategy exploits antiidiotype antibodies (see A Web of Idiotypes). The original antibody (or idiotype) provokes an antiantibody (or antiidiotype) that resembles the original antigen on the disease-causing organism. The antiidiotype will not itself cause disease, but it can serve as a mock antigen, inducing the formation of antibodies that recognize and block the original antigen. To make such a vaccine, scientists inject animals with a monoclonal antibody (idiotype) against a disease-causing microorganism, then harvest the antiidiotypes produced in response.

(ii) Biotechnology for curative (theraputic) management:

Following are the some products used for cure of the various diseases.

a) Monoclonal antibodies:

Substances foreign to the body, such as disease-causing bacteria and viruses and other infectious agents, known as antigens, are recognized by the body's immune system as invaders. Our natural defenses against these infectious agents are antibodies, proteins that seek out the antigens and help destroy them.

Antibodies have two very useful characteristics. First, they are extremely specific; that is, each antibody binds to and attacks one particular antigen. Second, some antibodies, once activated by the occurrence of a disease, continue to confer resistance against that disease; classic examples are the antibodies to the childhood diseases chickenpox and measles.

The second characteristic of antibodies makes it possible to develop vaccines. A vaccine is a preparation of killed or weakened bacteria or viruses that, when introduced into the body, stimulates the production of antibodies against the antigens it contains.

It is the first trait of antibodies, their specificity, that makes monoclonal antibody technology so valuable. Not only can antibodies be used therapeutically, to protect against disease; they can also help to diagnose a wide variety of illnesses, and can detect the presence of drugs, viral and bacterial products, and other unusual or abnormal substances in the blood.

Given such a diversity of uses for these disease-fighting substances, their production in pure quantities has long been the focus of scientific investigation. The conventional method was to inject a laboratory animal with an antigen and then, after antibodies had been formed, collect those antibodies from the blood serum (antibody-containing blood serum is called antiserum). There are two problems with this method: It yields antiserum that contains undesired substances, and it provides a very small amount of usable antibody.

Monoclonal antibody technology allows us to produce large amounts of pure antibodies in the following way: We can obtain cells that produce antibodies naturally; we also have available a class of cells that can grow continually in cell culture. If we form a hybrid that combines the characteristic of "immortality" with the ability to produce the desired substance, we would have, in effect, a factory to produce antibodies that worked around the clock.

In monoclonal antibody technology, tumor cells that can replicate endlessly are fused with mammalian cells that produce an antibody. The result of this cell fusion is a "hybridoma," which will continually produce antibodies. These antibodies are called monoclonal because they come from only one type of cell, the hybridoma cell; antibodies produced by conventional methods, on the other hand, are derived from preparations containing many kinds of cells, and hence are called polyclonal. An example of how monoclonal antibodies are derived is described below.

A myeloma is a tumor of the bone marrow that can be adapted to grow permanently in cell culture. When myeloma cells were fused with antibody-producing mammalian spleen cells, it was found that the resulting hybrid cells, or hybridomas, produced large amounts of monoclonal antibody. This product of cell fusion combined the desired qualities of the two different types of cells: the ability to grow continually, and the ability to produce large amounts of pure antibody.

Because selected hybrid cells produce only one specific antibody, they are more pure than the polyclonal antibodies produced by conventional techniques. They are potentially more effective than conventional drugs in fighting disease, since drugs attack not only the foreign substance but the body's own cells as well, sometimes producing undesirable side effects such as nausea and allergic reactions. Monoclonal antibodies attack the target molecule and only the target molecule, with no or greatly diminished side effects.

2. Biotechnology in production of proteins:

Protein biotechnology and **proteomics** are exciting and fast- growing areas of research, with numerous industrial applications. The great challenge of contemporary Biotechnology is found in the characterization of properties of proteins & their development in industrial applications, in development of pharmacies, in treatment of diseases, in agriculture & the environment.

Proteins are the major components of living organisms and perform a wide range of essential functions in cells. While DNA is the information molecule, it is proteins that do the work of all cells - microbial, plant, animal. Proteins regulate metabolic activity, catalyze biochemical reactions and maintain structural integrity of cells and organisms

The unique structure and chemical composition of each protein is important for its function; it is also important for separating proteins in a protein purification strategy. Each of these differences in properties can be used as a basis for the separation methods that are used to purify proteins. Because these differences in protein properties originate from differences in the chemical structure of the amino acids that make up the protein, we need to explore the structure of amino acids and their contribution to protein properties in more detail

A protein is formed by amino acid subunits linked together in a chain. The bond between two amino acids is formed by the removal of a H_2O molecule from two different amino acids, forming a dipeptide

The bond between two amino acids is called a peptide bond and the chain of amino acids is called a peptide (20 amino acids or smaller) or a polypeptide.

Each protein consists of one or more unique polypeptide chains. Most proteins do not remain as linear sequences of amino acids; rather, the polypeptide chain undergoes a folding process. The process of protein folding is driven by thermodynamic considerations. This means that each protein folds into a configuration that is the most stable for its particular chemical structure and its particular environment. The final shape will vary but the majority of proteins assume a globular configuration. Many proteins such as myoglobin consist of a single polypeptide chain; others contain two or more chains. For example, hemoglobin is made up of two chains of one type (amino acid sequence) and two of another type.

Although the primary amino acid sequence determines how the protein folds, this process is not completely understood. Although certain amino acid sequences can be identified as more likely to form a particular conformation, it is still not possible to completely predict how a protein will fold based on its amino acid sequence alone, and this is an active area of biochemical research.

3. siRNA:

Small interfering RNA (siRNA), sometimes known as short interfering RNA or silencing RNA, is a class of double-stranded RNA molecules, 20-25 nucleotides in length, that play a variety of roles in biology. Most notably, siRNA is involved in the RNA interference (RNAi) pathway, where it interferes with the expression of a specific gene. In addition to their role in the RNAi pathway, siRNAs also act in RNAi-related pathways, e.g., as an antiviral mechanism or in shaping the chromatin structure of a genome; the complexity of these pathways is only now being elucidated.

siRNAs were first discovered by David Baulcombe's group at the Sainsbury Laboratory in Norwich, England, as part of post-transcriptional gene silencing (PTGS) in plants

The scientific community considers RNA interference the breakthrough biological discovery of the decade with the potential to change how diseases are treated. Sirna Therapeutics is at the forefront of the effort to create RNAi- based therapies and leverage the vast potential of this technology to ultimately treat patients

Using siRNA for gene silencing is a rapidly evolving tool in molecular biology. There are several methods for preparing siRNA, such as chemical synthesis, in vitro transcription, siRNA expression vectors, and PCR expression cassettes.

RNA interference is a process of gene silencing that plays an important role in development and maintenance of the genome. The RNAi pathway is complex. It is initiated by the enyzme dicer which cleaves double stranded RNA (dsRNA) into 20-25 bp fragments. An RNA-induced silencing complex (RISC) is then formed by base pairing between complementary mRNA and 1 of the 2 strands of each new fragment. This formation of the RISC complex is followed by degradation of the complementary mRNA by the endonuclease argonaute. Argonaute is the catalytic component of the complex. The short 20-25 bp fragments are known as small interfering RNA (siRNA) when they are artificially introduced and microRNA (miRNA) when they are produced endogenously. RNA interference has become a valuable research tool since it allows the prevention of translation of specific genes by introducing siRNA complementary to the mRNA one wishes to suppress.

4. Gene:

Defination: Gene therapy is an experimental technique that uses genes to treat or prevent disease. In the future, this technique may allow doctors to treat a disorder by inserting a gene into a patient's cells instead of using drugs or surgery. Researchers are testing several approaches to gene therapy, including:
- Replacing a mutated gene that causes disease with a healthy copy of the gene.
- Inactivating, or "knocking out," a mutated gene that is functioning improperly.
- Introducing a new gene into the body to help fight a disease.

Although gene therapy is a promising treatment option for a number of diseases (including inherited disorders, some types of cancer, and certain viral infections), the technique remains risky and is still under study to make sure that it will be safe and effective. Gene therapy is currently only being tested for the treatment of diseases that have no other cures.

Working principle:

Gene therapy is designed to introduce genetic material into cells to compensate for abnormal genes or to make a beneficial protein. If a mutated gene causes a necessary protein to be faulty or missing, gene therapy may be able to introduce a normal copy of the gene to restore the function of the protein.

A gene that is inserted directly into a cell usually does not function. Instead, a carrier called a vector is genetically engineered to deliver the gene. Certain viruses are often used as vectors because they can deliver the new gene by infecting the cell. The viruses are modified so they can't cause disease when used in people. Some types of virus, such as retroviruses, integrate their genetic material (including the new gene) into a chromosome in the human cell. Other viruses, such as adenoviruses, introduce their DNA into the nucleus of the cell, but the DNA is not integrated into a chromosome.

The vector can be injected or given intravenously (by IV) directly into a specific tissue in the body, where it is taken up by individual cells. Alternately, a sample of the patient's cells can be removed and exposed to the vector in a laboratory setting. The cells containing the vector are then returned to the patient. If the treatment is successful, the new gene delivered by the vector will make a functioning protein.

Researchers must overcome many technical challenges before gene therapy will be a practical approach to treating disease. For example, scientists must find better ways to deliver genes and target them to particular cells. They must also ensure that new genes are precisely controlled by the body.

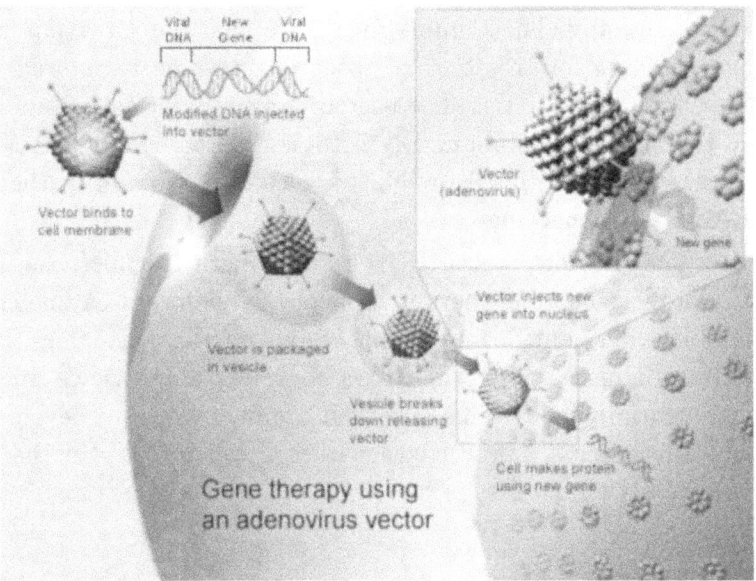

Fig. 5.1: Gene therapy using Adeno Virus vector
Source – U.S. national library of medicine,

A new gene is injected into an adenovirus vector, which is used to introduce the modified DNA into a human cell. If the treatment is successful, the new gene will make a functional protein.

Safety:

Gene therapy is under study to determine whether it could be used to treat disease. Current research is evaluating the safety of gene therapy; future studies will test whether it is an effective treatment option. Several studies have already shown that this approach can have very serious health risks, such as toxicity, inflammation, and cancer. Because the techniques are relatively new, some of the risks may be unpredictable; however, medical researchers, institutions, and regulatory agencies are working to ensure that gene therapy research is as safe as possible.

Comprehensive federal laws, regulations, and guidelines help protect people who participate in research studies (called clinical trials). The U.S. Food and Drug Administration (FDA) regulates all gene therapy products in the United States and oversees research in this area. Researchers who wish to test an approach in a clinical trial must first obtain permission from the FDA. The FDA has the authority to reject or suspend clinical trials that are suspected of being unsafe for participants.

The National Institutes of Health (NIH) also plays an important role in ensuring the safety of gene therapy research. NIH provides guidelines for investigators and institutions (such as universities and hospitals) to follow when conducting clinical trials with gene therapy. These guidelines state that clinical trials at institutions receiving NIH funding for this type of research must be registered with the NIH Office of Biotechnology Activities. The protocol, or plan, for each clinical trial is then reviewed by the NIH Recombinant DNA Advisory Committee (RAC) to determine whether it raises medical, ethical, or safety issues that warrant further discussion at one of the RAC's public meetings.

An Institutional Review Board (IRB) and an Institutional Biosafety Committee (IBC) must approve each gene therapy clinical trial before it can be carried out. An IRB is a committee of scientific and medical advisors and consumers that reviews all research within an institution. An IBC is a group that reviews and approves an institution's potentially hazardous research studies. Multiple levels of evaluation and oversight ensure that safety concerns are a top priority in the planning and carrying out of gene therapy research.

Ethical issues:

Because gene therapy involves making changes to the body's set of basic instructions, it raises many unique ethical concerns. The ethical questions surrounding gene therapy include:

- How can "good" and "bad" uses of gene therapy be distinguished?
- Who decides which traits are normal and which constitute a disability or disorder?
- Will the high costs of gene therapy make it available only to the wealthy?
- Could the widespread use of gene therapy make society less accepting of people who are different?
- Should people be allowed to use gene therapy to enhance basic human traits such as height, intelligence, or athletic ability?

Current gene therapy research has focused on treating individuals by targeting the therapy to body cells such as bone marrow or blood cells. This type of gene therapy cannot be passed on to a person's children. Gene therapy could be targeted to egg and sperm cells (germ cells), however, which would allow the inserted gene to be passed on to future generations. This approach is known as germline gene therapy.

The idea of germline gene therapy is controversial. While it could spare future generations in a family from having a particular genetic disorder, it might affect the development of a fetus in unexpected ways or have long-term side effects that are not yet known. Because people who would be affected by germline gene therapy are not yet born, they can't choose whether to have the treatment. Because of these ethical concerns, the U.S. Government does not allow federal funds to be used for research on germline gene therapy in people.

Disorder treatment:

Gene therapy is currently available only in a research setting. The U.S. Food and Drug Administration (FDA) has not yet approved any gene therapy products for sale in the United States.

Hundreds of research studies (clinical trials) are under way to test gene therapy as a treatment for genetic conditions, cancer, and HIV/AIDS. If you are interested in participating in a clinical trial, talk with your doctor or a genetics professional about how to participate.

5. Cellular Therapy:

Cell therapy is the transplantation of human or animal cells to replace or repair damaged tissue.

Cellular therapy also called live cell therapy, cellular suspensions, glandular therapy, fresh cell therapy, siccacell therapy, embryonic cell therapy, and organotherapy refers to various procedures in which processed tissue from animal embryos, fetuses or organs, is injected or taken orally

(a) Purpose

The purpose of cell therapy is to introduce cells into the body that will grow and replace damaged tissue. Cell therapy differs from conventional stem cell therapy in that the cells injected into the body in cell therapy are already differentiated (e.g., muscle cells, gland cells), whereas conventional stem cell therapy utilizes undifferentiated, usually embryonic cells. Cell therapy has long been used by alternative medicine practitioners who have claimed great benefits; these have not been replicated by conventional medical practitioners.

(b) Description

The theory behind cell therapy has been in existence for several hundred years. The first recorded discussion of the concept of cell therapy can be traced to Phillippus Aureolus Paracelsus (1493-1541), a German-Swiss physician and alchemist who wrote in his *Der grossen Wundartzney* (Great Surgery Book) in 1536 that "the heart heals the heart, lung heals the lung, spleen heals the spleen; like cures like." Paracelsus and many of his contemporaries agreed that the best way to treat an illness was to use living tissue to restore the ailing. In 1667, at a laboratory in the palace of Louis XIV, Jean-Baptiste Denis (1640-1704) attempted to transfuse blood from a calf into a mentally ill patient. Since blood transfusion is, in effect, a form of cell therapy, this could be the first documented case of this procedure. However, the first recorded attempt at non-blood cellular therapy occurred in 1912 when German physicians attempted to treat children with hypothyroidism (underactive thyroid gland), with thyroid cells.

In 1931, Dr. Paul Niehans (1882-1971), a Swiss physician, became known as "the father of cell therapy" quite by chance. After a surgical accident by a colleague, Niehans attempted to replace a patient's severely damaged parathyroid glands with those of a steer. When the patient began to rapidly deteriorate before the transplant could take place, Niehans decided to dice the steer's parathyroid gland into fine pieces, mix the pieces in a saline solution, and inject them into the dying patient. He reported that immediately the patient began to improve and, in fact, lived for another 30 years.

(c) Cell therapy as alternative medicine

Cell therapy as performed by alternative medicine practitioners is very different from the controlled research done by conventional stem cell medical researchers. Alternative practitioners refer to their form of cell therapy by several other different names including xenotransplant therapy, glandular therapy, and fresh cell therapy. The procedure involves the injection of either whole fetal xenogenic (animal) cells (e.g., from sheep, cows, pigs, and sharks) or cell extracts from human tissue. Several different types of cells may be administered simultaneously.

Just as Paracelsus's theory of "like cures like," the types of cells that are administered correspond in some way with the organ or tissue in the patient that is failing. In other words, the cells are not species specific, but only organ specific. Alternative practitioners cannot explain how this type of cell therapy works, but proponents claim that the injected cells travel to the similar organ from which they were taken to revitalize and stimulate that organ's function and regenerate its cellular structure. Supporters of cellular treatment believe that embryonic and fetal animal tissue contain active therapeutic agents distinct from vitamins, minerals, hormones, or enzymes. This theory and these claims are rejected by practitioners of conventional medicine.

Proponents of cell therapy claim that it has been used successfully to rebuild damaged cartilage in joints, repair spinal cord injuries, strengthen a weakened immune system, treat autoimmune diseases such as AIDS, and help patients with neurological disorders such as Alzheimer's disease, Parkinson's disease, and epilepsy. Further claims of positive results have been made in the treatment of a wide range of chronic conditions such as arteriosclerosis, congenital defects, and sexual dysfunction. The therapy has also been used to treat cancer patients at a number of clinics in Tijuana, Mexico. Most of these claims are anecdotal. None of these application is supported by well-designed, controlled clinical studies.

(d) Key terms

Cell therapy as conventional medicine

Cell therapy in conventional medicine is still in the research and early clinical trial stage. This research is an outgrowth of stem cell research, and is performed in government-regulated laboratories by traditionally trained scientists. Embryonic stem cells are cells taken from an embryo before they have differentiated (specialized) into such specific cell types as muscle cells, nerve cells, or skin cells. In laboratory test tube and animal experiments, stem cells often can be manipulated into differentiating into specific types cells that have the potential to replace differentiated cells in damaged organs. For example, in early 2008, researchers at the Diabetic Research Institute at the University of Miami in Florida were able to convert embryonic stem cells into insulin-producing cells and use them to treat insulin-dependent diabetes in mice.

Stem cells also have been found in bone marrow, and work is underway to see if other cells can be manipulated into transforming into differentiated cells. In January 2009, researchers at Northwestern University's Feinberg School of Medicine in Chicago announced that they had used a patient's own bone marrow stem cells to improve early symptoms of multiple sclerosis. Researchers noted improvement only in patients with early symptoms; in earlier research those with advanced symptoms had not improved. Other researchers are working on treating symptoms of muscular dystrophy with fully differentiated myoblasts (a kind of muscle cell) with mixed results. Still other are working with using cartilage cells (chondrocyte cells) to repair cartilage in joints such as the knee.

Stem cell therapy has potential to treat a wide range of diseases and disorders, but it is, for the most part, still in the test tube and animal research stage of development. Because of the ethical questions raised when the harvesting of stem cells destroys embryos, the United States has placed restrictions on some human stem cell research. These restrictions, however, do not apply to research that does not destroy embryos. However, much stem cell research is being carried out in other countries, especially Thailand, South Korea, and China, where fewer restrictions are placed on obtaining human stem cells for experimentation. A list of FDA-approved clinical trials involving stem cell therapy can be found at http://www.clinicaltrials.gov.

(e) Preparations

Alternative practitioners use several processes to prepare cells for use. One procedure involves extracting cells from the patient and then culturing them in a laboratory until they multiply to the level needed for transplantation back into the same patient. Another procedure uses freshly removed fetal animal tissue that has been processed and suspended in a saline (salt water) solution. The preparation of fresh cells then may be either injected immediately into the patient or preserved by being freeze-dried or deep-frozen in liquid nitrogen before being injected. Injected cells may or may not be tested for pathogens, such as bacteria, viruses, or parasites, before use. Conventional cell therapy researchers work in laboratories where the growing environment of the cells is highly controlled and monitored to prevent contamination.

(f) Precautions

Many forms of cell therapy in the United States are highly experimental procedures. Patients should approach any cell therapy treatments with extreme caution, inquire about their proven efficacy and legal use in the United States or their home country, and should only accept treatment only from a licensed physician who should educate the patient completely on the risks and possible side effects involved with cell therapy. These same cautions apply for patients interested in participating in FDA-approved clinical trials of cell therapy treatments.

(g) Side effects

Because cell therapy encompasses a wide range of treatments and applications and many of these treatments are unproven and highly experimental, the full range of possible side effects of the treatments is not yet known. Anaphylactic shock, immune system reactions, and encephalitis are just a few of the known reported side effects in some patients to date.

Patients undergoing cell therapy treatments which use cells transplanted from animals or other humans run the risk of cell rejection, in which the body recognizes the cells as a foreign substance and uses immune system cells to attack and destroy them. Some forms of cell therapy use special coatings on the cells in an attempt to trick the immune system into recognizing the new cells as native to the body. There is also the chance of the cell solution transmitting a bacterial, viral, fungal, or parasitic infection to the patient. Careful screening and testing of cells for pathogens can reduce this risk.

(h) Research and general acceptance

Cell therapy as alternative healers practice it is generally rejected as effective by the traditionally-trained scientific community. Most of the claims made for these therapies are based on anecdotal evidence and are not backed by controlled clinical trials. While some mainstream cell therapy procedures have shown some success in clinical studies, others are still largely unproven, including cell therapy for cancer treatment. Until large, controlled human clinical studies are performed on cell therapy procedures, they will remain fringe treatments.

6. Tissue Engineering

Tissue engineering / regenerative medicine is an emerging multidisciplinary field involving biology, medicine, and engineering that is likely to revolutionize the ways we improve the health and quality of life for millions of people worldwide by restoring, maintaining, or enhancing tissue and organ function. In addition to having a therapeutic application, where the tissue is either grown in a patient or outside the patient and transplanted, tissue engineering can have diagnostic applications where the tissue is made in vitro and used for testing drug metabolism and uptake, toxicity, and pathogenicity. The foundation of tissue engineering/regenerative medicine for either therapeutic or diagnostic applications is the ability to exploit living cells in a variety of ways.

Tissue engineering research includes the following areas:

1) **Biomaterials:** including novel biomaterials that are designed to direct the organization, growth, and differentiation of cells in the process of forming functional tissue by providing both physical and chemical cues.

2) **Cells:** including enabling methodologies for the proliferation and differentiation of cells, acquiring the appropriate source of cells such as autologous cells, allogeneic cells, xenogeneic cells, stem cells, genetically engineered cells, and immunological manipulation.

3) **Biomolecules:** including angiogenic factors, growth factors, differentiation factors and bone morphogenic proteins

4) **Engineering design aspects:** including 2-d cell expansion, 3-d tissue growth, bioreactors, vascularization, cell and tissue storage and shipping (biological packaging).

5) **Biomechanical aspects of design:** including properties of native tissues, identification of minimum properties required of engineered tissues, mechanical signals regulating engineered tissues, and efficacy and safety of engineered tissues

6) **Informatics to support tissue engineering:** gene and protein sequencing, gene expression analysis, protein expression and interaction analysis, quantitative cellular image analysis, quantitative tissue analysis, in silico tissue and cell modeling, digital tissue manufacturing, automated quality assurance systems, data mining tools, and clinical informatics interfaces.

6. REGULATORY APPROVAL

In India, Genetically Modified Organism (GMOs) and products there of are regulated as per "Rules for the manufacture, use/import/export and storage of hazardous microorganisms/genetically engineered organisms or cells, 1989" notified by the ministry of environment and forests (MoEF), government of India under the environment protection act 1986. These rules are implemented by ministry of environment and forests (MoEF), the Department of Biotechnology (DBT), Ministry of science and technology and the state governments through the six competent authorities notified under the rules which are as follows:

1. The Recombinant DNA Advisory Committee (RDAC)
2. Institutional Biosafety Committee (IBSC)
3. Review Committee on Genetic Manipulation (RCGM)
4. Genetic Engineering Approval Committee (GEAC)
5. State Biotechnology Coordination Committee (SBCC)
6. District Level Committee (DLC)

While the RDAC has advisory in function, IBSC, RCGM and GEAC are involved in regulatory functions. SBCC and DLC are responsible for monitoring the activities related to GMOs in state/district level.

Out of the above, IBSC is the nodal point for interaction within an organization for implementation of the biosafety regulatory framework. An IBSC is to be constituted by every organization engaged in research, handling and production activities related to GMOs

Flow chart to start up Biotechnology Industry:

Registration of company under companies act.
↓
Approval from Department of Biotechnology, Ministry of science and health
↓
Registration of IBSC (Institutional Biosafety Committee)
↓
Form 29 from local FDA (manufacture for examination test or analysis)
↓
Approval from IBSC committee (for development, preclinical and clinical)
↓
Approval from RCGM (For development, Preclinical and clinical)
↓
Approval from DCGI (for Clinical and manufacture and marketing)

1. **Registration process of industry**

   The start up process for any industry is to first make registration of the company in the office of registrar of companies.

   Registrars Of Companies (ROC) allocated under Section 609 of the Companies Act enveloping different States and Union Territories, is authorized to register a company in India and guarantees that such firms abide by the constitutional prerequisites under the Act.

   The detailed procedure is as under

   (a) Step 1: The methods of registering a company in India are as under: Step 1 - Attain director identification number (DIN) by filling Form DIN-1. The temporary DIN is instantly issued which must then be printed, signed and sent to the Ministry of Corporate Affairs for its consent along with the identity and address proof.

   The Identity Proof should contain any one of the following:
   - PAN card
   - Driving licence
   - Passport
   - Voter Id card

   The residence proof should contain any one of the following:
   - Driving licence
   - Passport
   - Voter Id card
   - Telephone bill
   - Ration card
   - Electricity bill
   - Bank statement

   The involved authority authenticates all the credentials and, upon agreement, drafts a permanent DIN.

   (b) Step 2: Acquire digital signature certificate to utilize the latest electronic registration system under MCA 21. This certificate can be acquired from any one of the six private bureaus sanctioned by MCA 21. Director of the company is required to submit the recommended application form along with the identity and residence proof.

   (c) Step 3: Cache the company name with the Registrar of Companies (ROC). To attain name consent for the suggested firm, Form No. 1A should be presented to the Registrar of Companies (ROC) of the state citing the address of the Registered Office of the projected firm along with the signature of one of the promoters.

   A maximum of 6 proposed names can be presented which are verified by RoC staff for any resemblance with other company names in India. This process takes two days for attaining consent of the name if the suggested name exists and matches to the naming values instituted by the Company Act.

(d) Step 4: Seal the company credentials at the State Treasury (State) or certified private bank. The appeal for stamping the inclusion certificates should be complemented by unsigned copies of the Articles of Association, Form - 1 and Memorandum and Articles of Association. The firm must make sure that no promoter has written anything nor have signed on the documents which are deposited to the Superintendent of Stamps or to the certified bank for stamping. The price of stamp duty differs from state to state.

The documents should be signed by the firm's promoters after the MOA and AOA have been stamped. Besides the promoter's signature, other information which must be filled in applicant's handwriting is the company's name, description of company's activities and motive, father's name, address, occupation and number of shares subscribed.

(e) Step 5: Attain the Certificate of Incorporation from the Registrar of Companies, Ministry of Corporate Affairs. The forms which are required to be filled online on the Ministry of Company Affairs website are: e-form 1; e-form 18; and e-form 32. Along with these papers, copies of agreement of the original directors and signed and sealed form of the Memorandum and Article of Association must be enclosed in Form 1.

(f) Step 6: Make a seal (applicable for the private limited companies). Making a company seal is not a legal obligation for the firm to be integrated, but firms require a seal to deliver share certificates and other certificates.

(g) Step 7: Attain a Permanent Account Number (PAN) from a certified franchise or agent allotted by the National Securities Depository Ltd. (NSDL) or the Unit Trust of India (UTI) Investors Services Ltd., as outsourced by the Income Tax Department (National). Each person is entitled to state his or her Permanent Account Number (PAN) for the purpose of tax payment under the Income Tax Act, 1961 and the Tax Account Number (TAN) for submitting tax reduced at source. One can get PAN application from IT PAN Service Centers or TIN Facilitation Centers using Form 49A with the acknowledged copy of the certificate of registration, released by the Registrar of Companies along with the identity and residence proof.

(h) Step 8: Acquire a Tax Account Number (TAN) for income taxes abstracted at source from the Assessing Office of the Income Tax Department. The Tax Account Number (TAN) is required by anyone accountable for deducting or gathering tax. The prerequisites of Section 203A of the Income Tax Act state that all individuals who subtract or collect tax at the source must submit an application for a TAN. The submission for allotment of a TAN must be registered using Form 49B and deposited at any TIN Facilitation Center certified to accept e-TDS returns.

(i) Step 9: Enroll with the Office of Inspector, Shops, and Establishment Act (State/Municipal). Under this procedure, a proclamation incorporating the names of employer's and manager's and the establishment's name (if any), postal address, and group must be delivered to the local shop inspector with the pertinent fees.

(j) Step 10: Enroll for Value-Added Tax (VAT) at the Commercial Tax Office (State). Registration of VAT requires filling up of Form 101. Other credentials which need to be enclosed with Form 101 are:

Attested copy of memorandum and articles of association of the company
- Residence proof
- Proof of location of company
- Applicants one current passport size photograph
- Copy of PAN card
- Challan on Form No 210

Regulatory guidelines for biologics development

The following are the steps to start product development work

Statutory Bodies:
1. The Recombinant DNA Advisory Committee (RDAC)
2. Institutional Biosafety Committee (IBSC)
2. Review Committee on Genetic Manipulation (RCGM)
3. Genetic Engineering Approval Committee (GEAC)
4. State Biotechnology Coordination Committee (SBCC)
5. District Level Committee (DLC)

At first make registration of the company to start development /manufacturing of the biologic products. The company registration can be made in registrar of companies.

There is special requirement to take approval from Department of Biotechnology, Ministry of health and science, government of India for start of biologics manufacturing activity.

The registration of IBSC (Institutional Bio-Safety Committee):

IBSC is the committee in which the at least three members of related work, one biosafety office, one outside expert on biologics and one member appointed as nominee from Department of Biotechnology(DBT). This IBSC(Institutional Biosafety committee) committee will decide strategy on development of the project activity. The main functions of IBSC committee is:

To note, examine and approve proposals involving r-DNA work; to ensure adherence of r-DNA Safety Guidelines- 1990 of Government; inspection of containment facilities at R&D and production units and to inform the RCGM about the facilities;

To prepare emergency plan according to guidelines;

To approve experiments utilizing the organisms and genetic elements from Risk Group-I and II organisms up to laboratory fermentation 20 ltrs capacity with intimation to RCGM; for using organisms falling in Risk Group III & above, recommend to RCGM for approval to conduct laboratory studies;

To recommend for import/ exchange of GMOs/LMOs/Transgenic seeds, vectors, gene constructs, plasmids, etc., for research purposes;

To inform DLC and SBCC as well as GEAC about the experiments where ever needed; to act as a nodal point for interaction with statutory bodies; to ensure experimentation at designated location taking into account of approved protocols etc.

To examine the description of the target gene and source; nucleotide sequence and amino acid sequence of target gene and the target protein; the composition of the vector used; schematic diagram of the expression cassette; restriction map of vector indicating the location of the target gene; cloning strategy; description of the host cell line including genera and species; risks involved in handling of cell line; methods of maintenance of cell line; classification of the host cell line as per the guidelines;

To approve category I & II experiments, as per the Guidelines 1998 of DBT, up to green house level with intimation to RCGM in category III & above experiments, RCGM to approve conduct lab & green house studies. To recommend all open field experiments in any of the category, for any purpose (biosafety studies, seed increase experiments, agronomic studies, etc) for the approval of RCGM.

To examine protocols for toxicity/allergenicity studies as per national and international guidelines and their recommendations to RCGM

RCGM (Review Committee on Genetic Manipulation)

RCGM(Review Committee on genetic manipulation) is a statutory body notified under the Rules, 1989 of environmental Protection Act, 1986 to ensure that the R&D activities undertaken by DBT are carried out in a safe and sound manner. It comprises of 29 experts from various multi-disciplinary fields. The development of product (including imports for research) at the laboratory stage, contained multi-location trials and protocols for the biosafety studies require prior approval of the RCGM.

To bring out manuals of guidelines specifying producers for regulatory process on GMOs in research, use and applications including in industry with a view to ensure environmental safety.

To review all on going r-DNA projects involving high risk category and controlled field experiments

To lay down producers for restriction or prohibition, production, sale, import & use of GMOs both for research and applications.

To permit experiments with category III risks and above with appropriate containment.

To authorize imports of GMOs/ transgenes/ transgenic seeds for research purposes.

To guide the applicant to generate relevant biosafety data on transgenic materials in appropriate test systems.

To examine information on preparation of MCB and WCB; QC tests conducted on the cell line; approaches adopted for expression of target gene in the host cell line; genetic analysis including copy number of inserts, stability; level of expression of target gene; description of production process; growth kinetics; fermentation parameters; in-process control measures; quality control & quality assurance data; approaches adopted for extraction and purification of the target gene product; examine data on physico-chemical, biochemical, immunological and pharmacological characterization of the bulk; characterization of the finished formulation; acceptability criteria for bulk and formulation as per IP, USP, BP or other national/international specifications etc; efficacy tests on the target product; trial batch fermentation data on the product; estimation of contaminants like DNA, RNA, lipids, carbohydrates, proteins etc, derived from the host organism and any toxic processing materials in the product;

To approve the protocols for conducting animal toxicity and allergenicity studies and examination of in-process and final QC data on the product etc; to submit its recommendation on the preclinical studies/data directly to the DCGI; for the products from Risk group III & above organisms, to examine the information on containment facilities at the R&D and production sites as well as the results of the pre-clinical studies and submit their recommendations both to the GEAC and DCGI.

To authorize field experiments in 20 acres in multi-locations in one crop season with up to one acre at one site.

To examine the data generated in the Lab & Green house on the points like: source and sequence of trans-gene; cloning strategy; characteristics of expression vector(s); characteristics of inserted genes with detailed sequences; characteristics of promoters; transformation/cloning methods of target gene; genetic analysis including copy number of inserts, stability, level of expression of trans-gene, characterization of expressed gene product; mode of action of gene product; compositional analysis; description of the host plant; rationale for the development of transgenic plants in terms of agronomic, nutritional and other benefits; centers of origin of the host plant; geographical distribution of the host plant in the country of development;

To evaluate the data on back crossing duration; seed setting characteristics; germination rates; phenotypic characteristics; target gene efficacy tests; observations on the implications of toxicity and allergenicity, if any during handling, etc. (These points are indicative only. Depending up on the nature and characteristics of the target gene & the transgenic crop additional information may require to be generated).

Also to evaluate information generated during the contained open field trials on the transgenic crops on the points like: comparison of germination rates and phenotypic characteristics; study of gene flow; possibility of transfer of gene to near relatives through out crossing; implications of out crossing; invasiveness; possibility of weed formation; susceptibility to diseases and pests; toxicity and allergenicity implications of plants/fruits/seeds and any other plant parts; food/feed safety evaluation in animals; handling procedures for allergenic substances; agronomic advantages etc.

To inform and recommend to the GEAC about the containment facilities at R&D and production sites.

Terms of Reference of RCGM
1. The RCGM shall function in the DBT to monitor the safety related aspects in respect of all ongoing r-DNA projects & activities involving Genetically Engineered Organisms/ Hazardous Micro-organisms and controlled field experiments as per the Rules-1989 of EPA-1986.
2. The RCGM shall constitute Monitoring-cum-Evaluation Committee (MEC) through DBT as per the 'Revised Guidelines for Research in Transgenic Plants and Guidelines for Toxicity and Allergenicity Evaluation of Transgenic Seeds, Plants & Plant Parts-1998'. RCGM may also appoint subgroups to undertake specific activities related Biosafety.
3. The RCGM shall bring out manuals of guidelines specifying procedure for regulatory process with respect to activities involving genetically engineered organisms in research, use and application including industry with a view to ensure environmental safety.
4. The RCGM shall lay down procedures restricting or prohibiting production, sale, importation and use of such genetically engineered organisms or products thereof for research and applications that may have biohazard potential.
5. The RCGM shall review all on-going research projects involving high-risk category and controlled field experiments.
6. The RCGM or its constituted subgroups shall visit periodically the experimental sites where projects with biohazard potential are being pursued to ensure that adequate safety measures have been taken as per the guidelines.
7. The RCGM would issue the clearance for import of genes, DNA fragments, vectors, plasmids, etiologic agents & vectors, transgenic germplasm(s) including transformed calli, seeds, plants & plant parts for research use only.
8. The RCGM can authorize applicants to conduct contained field trials limited to a total of 20 acres in multi-locations in one crop season in the country to seek answers to relevant and necessary questions on biosafety including

risks related to environment, animal and human health. In one location, where the experiment is conducted with transgenic plants, the land used should not be more than one acre. The design of the trial experiments is either provided by the RCGM or it may approve the protocol designed by the Investigator.

9. The RCGM, on case-by-case basis, can authorize applicants to use bioreactors beyond 20 ltrs capacities exclusively for research purposes only to produce sufficient material/ products of GMOs required for generating pre-clinical and other relevant data required to establish the product for commercial use.
10. The RCGM, if required, can direct the applicants to generate toxicity, allergenicity and any other relevant data on transgenic materials/ GMOs in appropriate test systems. The RCGM may design or approve a protocol for conducting experiments to seek answers to the above.
11. The RCGM, if required, can direct the applicants to generate long term environmental safety data, who are seeking release of transgenic plants into the open environment after completion of initial safety evaluation.
12. The RCGM, if required, can generate or examine the research projects, proposals for conduct of workshops, seminars, symposia, training courses etc., creation of information systems/ data banks in electronic media, websites etc. and recommend to the DBT for funding of specific projects for furthering the cause of generating specific biosafety data related to use of GMOs in the environment and strengthening infrastructure facilities & dissemination of biosafety rules, regulations & guidelines in the country.
13. The RCGM may also invite, induct or appoint experts in their individual capacities for furthering the cause of RCGM.
14. The RCGM shall maintain the classified information provided by the applicants as confidential.
15. The RCGM shall function for a period of three years from the date of notification.
16. The RCGM shall meet at least twice in a year or as and when required
17. The Members of RCGM shall be paid TA/DA and honorarium as per the Government rules and regulations.

The biosafety officer and biosafety committee

It is essential that each laboratory organization has a comprehensive safety policy, a safety manual, and supporting programmes for their implementation. The responsibility for this normally rests with the director or head of the institute or laboratory, who may delegate certain duties to a biosafety officer or other appropriate personnel.

Laboratory safety is also the responsibility of all supervisors and laboratory employees, and individual workers are responsible for their own safety and that of their colleagues. Employees are expected to perform their work safely and should report any unsafe acts, conditions or incidents to their supervisor. Periodic safety audits by internal or external personnel are desirable.

1. Biosafety officer

Wherever possible a biosafety officer should be appointed to ensure that biosafety policies and programmes are followed consistently throughout the laboratory. The biosafety officer executes these duties on behalf of the head of the institute or laboratory. In small units, the biosafety officer may be a microbiologist or a member of the technical staff, who may perform these duties on a defined part-time basis. Whatever the degree of involvement in biosafety, the person designated should possess the professional competence necessary to suggest, review and approve specific activities that follow appropriate biocontainment and biosafety procedures. The biosafety officer should apply relevant national and international rules, regulations and guidelines, as well as assist the laboratory in developing standard operating procedures. The person appointed must have a technical background in microbiology, biochemistry and basic physical and biological sciences. Knowledge of laboratory and clinical practices and safety, including containment equipment, and engineering principles relevant to the design, operation and maintenance of facilities is highly desirable. The biosafety officer should also be able to communicate effectively with administrative, technical and support personnel.

The activities of the biosafety officer should include the following:
1. Biosafety, biosecurity and technical compliance consultations.
2. Periodic internal biosafety audits on technical methods, procedures and protocols, biological agents, materials and equipment.

2. Biosafety committee

A biosafety committee should be constituted to develop institutional biosafety policies and codes of practice. The biosafety committee should also review research protocols for work involving infectious agents, animal use, recombinant DNA and genetically modified materials. Other functions of the committee may include risk assessments, formulation of new safety policies and arbitration in disputes over safety matters.

The membership of the biosafety committee should reflect the diverse occupational areas of the organization as well as its scientific expertise. The composition of a basic biosafety committee may include:
1. Biosafety officer(s)
2. Scientists
3. Medical personnel
4. Veterinarian(s) (if work with animals is conducted)
5. Representatives of technical staff
6. Representatives of laboratory management.

The biosafety committee should seek advice from different departmental and specialist safety officers (e.g. with expertise in radiation protection, industrial safety, fire prevention, etc.) and may at times require assistance from independent experts in various associated fields, local authorities and national regulatory bodies. Community members may also be helpful if there is a particularly contentious or sensitive protocol under discussion.

Ref,NO:_____

FORM 29

[See Rule 89]

License to manufacture Drugs for purposes of Examination, Test or Analysis.

1. ---------(name of company) is hereby licensed to manufacture the drugs specified below for purposes of Examination, Tests or Analysis at ---------------- (address of company)

2. This license is subject to the conditions prescribed in Part VIII of the Drugs and Cosmetics Rules 1945.

3. This license shall be in force for one year from the date specified below

FROM .... TO ....

Name of the Drug:

Date:

Joint Commissioner
(Division)
Food & Drug Administration

Proposed Time Lines:

The recommended protocol requests for the ideal time lines:

1. RCGM approval for pre-clinical animal studies	45-60 days
2. RDAC approval for Human Clinical Trials protocol	45-60 days
3. RDAC(DCGI) examination of trial data and approval	Case specific

Simultaneous DCGI and GEAC approvals: 45-60 days after submission of acceptable trial data

3. Biosafety guidelines

There are certain cardinal rules and regulations which one has to follow while working a science laboratory or else even the slightest of carelessness can lead to major accidents. It is wise to have a laboratory safety sign chart displayed in a lab. Below mentioned are few safety precautions which can come handy while working in a science laboratory:

- Avoid all kinds of eatables or eating and drinking in the lab. Things like gum, cough drops etc. should not be carried in the lab, besides, useless activities like chewing hair ends or applying chapstick etc. should also be avoided by all means.

- One needs a good microbiological practice for working safely in a science laboratory. Try and handle everything including laboratory equipments and laboratory apparatus as if it is pathogenic. The soil and water samples used for culturing etc. should be handled with a standard microbiological practice under adult supervision.

- Make sure that the flame and flammable solutions are kept far apart. This can reduce the chances of a hazardous situation manifold. Try to have an open alcohol beaker far away from the flame so that some of the containing alcohol evaporates till the time the tool is brought to the flame.

- Electrical equipments should be kept far away from water making sure that the areas around electrical equipments is dry and common laboratory apparatus must be handled with care.

- A person should be equipped with lab safety equipments like fume hood, gloves, goggles etc. while working in the lab. Avoid wearing latex gloves if you are allergic to it.

- Make sure you clean the glass wear nicely before using it. The residues should be wiped clean and some water must be added before adding any liquid or solid solutes in it.

- Returning the excess material back to the stock container must be strictly avoided hence, one should be sure of the quantity of chemicals and reagents before pouring them out.

7. FINANCIAL SUPPORT FROM GOVERNMENT OF INDIA AND OTHER COUNTRIES

DBT invites Proposals from Biotech Companies for BIPP Scheme (An Advanced Technology Scheme). BIPP Announces Online Submission of Proposals Department of Biotechnology (DBT) invites proposals from Indian Biotechnology Companies under the Biotechnology Industry Partnership Program (BIPP), a Government partnership with industry for support on a cost sharing basis for development of novel and high risk futuristic technologies mainly for viability gap funding and enhancing existing R and D capacities.

BIPP has been initiated under Biotechnology Industry Research Assistance Program (BIRAP), a unique initiative of DBT being implemented in partnership with ABLE and BCIL to nurture R and D and innovation in Biotech Industry. Biotech Consortium India Limited (BCIL) is the BIPP Management Agency and will ensure maintenance of strict confidentiality of the proposals as per DBT norms.

Who can apply?

A single or consortia of Indian "for profit" company(ies) - Small, Medium or Large having DSIR* recognized in-house R&D unit(s). An Indian Company is defined as one, which is registered under the Indian Companies Act 1956 and in which more than 51% of the ownership is held by Indian Citizens (including NRIs). The proposals can be submitted: solely by an Indian Company; or jointly by an Indian Company and National R and D Organizations and Institutions; or by a group of Indian Companies along with National Research Organizations etc. (*The companies who are in the process of obtaining Department of Science and Industrial Research (DSIR) recognition may also apply along with the proof of application to DSIR. However, the final decision on such applications would be subject to their getting DSIR recognition.)

How to apply

There is provision for online submission of proposals under BIPP. To submit a proposal online under BIPP, please follow the following steps:

Log on the website **www.birapdbt.nic.in**

Click on the New User Registration for registering your Company

A computer-generated password would be sent to your email-id provided at the time of registration (password can be changed later).

For submitting the proposal, log in by entering your user name and password and you would be navigated to the page displaying BIPP link.

Further details on How to submit a proposal would be available in the BIPP User Guide available on the website.

*User Registration and online proposal submission has started from 15th February. 2010. *No Hard Copy to be submitted.

For details contact:
Advisor Incharge BIPP, Department of Biotechnology,
Block No: 2, 7th Floor, CGO Complex, Lodi Road,
New Delhi - 110003, India.

Following are the some schemes from Government of India & other countries:

1. **Call for Proposals within the New INDIGO Partnership Programme (NPP) on Biotechnology applied to Human Health:**

    Aim of the NPP Call: The NPP's primary aim is to reinforce EU-India cooperation in thematic areas of mutual interest. Recognising the fact that Biotechnology is one of India's research strengths while health is a field of rising importance both in India and Europe, a joint call for proposals in **Biotechnology applied to Human Health is announced.**

    Participating countries: The following partners have agreed to open a call for funding multilateral research projects in the field of biotechnology applied to human health:

India	-	*Department of Biotechnology (DBT);*
Austria	-	*Austrian Science Fund (FWF), Federal Ministry of Science & Research (BMWF)*
France	-	*Agence Nationale du Financement de l'Innovation (Oséo)*
Germany	-	*Federal Ministry of Education and Research (BMBF)*
Israel	-	*Israeli Industry Center for R&D (MATIMOP)*
Norway	-	*Research Council Norway (RCN)*
Portugal	-	*Fundação para a Ciência e Tecnologia (FCT)*
Spain	-	*Ministry of Science and Innovation (MICINN)*

    Funding instruments: Funding can be applied for multilateral research projects with durations of three years. Projects will start in September 2012.

    For each project a sum in the range of € 150.000 (~ € 50.000 p.a.) of eligible costs from each funding country can be applied for.

    Within the framework of a multilateral research project funding can be applied for:
    - **Mobility:** exchange research visits by European and Indian scientists between Europe and India. Travel costs and living expenses and visa costs of scientists are eligible for funding
    - **Workshops:** organisation costs, including rents for the event location, catering, communication materials and the invitation of external experts

- **Research costs:** equipment and consumables, project related miscellaneous expenses and project related larger equipment; the extend to which equipment costs are eligible for funding depends on national regulations
- **Personnel costs:** are eligible if designated as such by the respective funding agency; to which extent they are eligible is according to national rules and regulations

It is not possible to apply for individual exchanges or single workshops.

Financial Implementation: DBT would fund the Indian Researchers: The NPP follows the "juste retour" principle, which means national funding will be assigned to participants of that respective country. Researchers participating in a multinational project therefore receive funding from their national representative, in accordance with the national regulations.

How to apply

Who can apply: Scientists from universities, research institutions and small and medium enterprises / companies from India conducting research within the health science biotechnology area can apply. The small and medium enterprises is as defined by BIRAP, DBT.

Eligibility: Only trans-national projects will be funded. Each proposal must involve eligible researchers/research institutes from a minimum of two different European New INDIGO funding members, as well as one or more eligible partners from India.

Research groups from non-funding New INDIGO partner countries may participate in projects if they secure their own funding. Their participation and their secured funding need to be confirmed through signing a Letter of Commitment uploaded as PDF with the full proposal application.

Application process: The application procedure has two stages: pre-registration and the full project proposal submission. A full project proposal may only be submitted after pre-registration. All pre-proposals will undergo an eligibility check as well as an evaluation by a scientific council. Only those consortia who have handed in the 30 best pre-proposals will be invited to submit a full proposal. Applications are submitted electronically using PT-Outline which is accessible through the New INDIGO website (www.newindigo.eu/npp).

For technical reasons and to prevent multiple versions, only one of the two project coordinators is given access to the web tool for submission. This project coordinator is called principal coordinator for this purpose.

For further information please refer Department of Biotechnology's web-site www.dbtindia.nic.in or contact Dr. Shailja Gupta, Joint Director, International Collaboration, E-mail: shailja@dbt.nic.in; Tel.: 91 11 24363748.

2. SUSTAINABLE BIOENERGY AND BIOFUELS (SuBB): CASE FOR SUPPORT TEMPLATE

A. GENERAL INFORMATION

Project Title *[up to 150 characters]*

Applicants

*Please provide the names, full affiliations and contact details of all lead and co-investigators. Please indicate lead investigator from each country in **bold** font.*

UK Applicants

Position	Name	Organisation	Department/Division	E-mail

India Applicants

Position	Name	Organisation	Department/Division	E-mail

Summary

Please provide a short summary of the project [circa 4000 characters]

Project Aims

Please describe the main objectives of the proposed research [circa 4000 characters]

Summary of resources required for the project

Summary of UK costs: *Please give the total cost of the project (in £ sterling) of UK project component*

Directly Incurred Indirect	**Directly Allocated**
Staff:	Investigators:
Travel and Subsistence:	Estates:
Equipment:	
Other:	
Total:	

Summary of India costs: *Please give the total cost of the project (in Indian Rupees) of Indian project component*

A. Non-Recurring
  1. Equipment

TOTAL A:

B. Recurring
  1. Consumables
  2. Travel
  3. Contingency
  4. Overheads

TOTAL B:

C. Manpower

TOTAL C:

Total Project Cost (£ Sterling):

B. DETAILED SCIENTIFIC INFORMATION

Previous track record

Please refer to SuBB:Call for proposals for guidance on what to consider when completing the following section [up to 4 sides of A4]

Detailed description of project

Objectives

List the overall aims and objectives of the proposed research [up to 1 side of A4]

Current Landscape

Describe the current landscape relevant to the project in India, the UK and other countries [up to 1 side of A4]

Description of proposed research

Please give a detailed project description, highlighting novelty and originality [up to 8 sides of A4]

Added value of the proposed collaboration

Please describe how the transnational project will be managed with emphasis on communication strategies, data management and data sharing across the project and management of intellectual property [up to 2 sides of A4]

Information dissemination and knowledge exchange

Describe potential routes to translate the outcomes from the project into genuine impacts that benefit the UK and India. Include interaction with private sector, policy makers and other relevant stakeholders [up to 1 side of A4]

Workplan

Please provide a Gantt chart, or diagrammatic workplan, for the project including milestones [up to 1 side of A4]

Justification for Resources

Please provide a description and justification of resources requested for the project [up to 2 sides of A4]

C. DESCRIPTION OF PROJECT TEAMS

Please include brief CVs of all investigators, including the three most significant, recent, publications [up to 1 side of A4 per investigator]

3. *SUSTAINABLE BIOENERGY AND BIOFUELS (SuBB) SCHEME:* Below is the form & information for financial support under this scheme.

DEPARTMENT OF BIOTECHNOLOGY, MINISTRY OF SCIENCE AND TECHNOLOGY, Government of India

BBSRC / DBT joint initiative on:

SUSTAINABLE BIOENERGY AND BIOFUELS (SuBB)

PROFORMA: INDIAN COSTS

Please complete the following information as completely as possible. This form should be submitted as *part* of your application to the SuBB collaboration. It should be uploaded as an 'other attachment' to the 'je-s application form' by the overall principal investigator for the proposal.

Indian lead Investigator/ organisation

Name	
Organisation	
Division or Department	

Names of any other co-investigators based in India

Name	Email address	Organisation	Division or Department

Name of UK Principal Investigator	
Organisation and Department:	
Project Title:	

Duration of project in months (including start and end date):

Summary of Resources Required for Project
(INDIAN PARTNERS ONLY)
(₹ in Lakh)

Format for Budget

Sl#	Item	Year I	Year II	Year III	TOTAL
A.	**Non-Recurring**				
1.	Equipments				
	Total A				
B.	**Recurring**				
1.	Consumables				
2.	Travel i) Domestic ii) International iii) Local Hospitality for visiting scientist				
3.	Contingency				
4.	Overheads				
	Total B				
C.	**Manpower**				
1.					
2.					
	Total C				
	TOTAL A+B+C				

Notes:
- For proposals involving multiple Indian organisations, please copy the above table and provide financial Requirements for Each Indian organisation separately.
- The 'totals' columns above reflect the totals requested *from DBT by financial year*.
- Normal DBT financial norms and regulations for manpower salaries apply. Further information can be found at: http://dst.gov.in/whats_new/whats_new07/ fellowship.pdf
- Travel costs for employees of Indian institutions should be estimated in accordance with the Government of India's normal rules. This usually means

that DBT will bear the cost of local hospitality and local transport for non-Indian visitors within India, and also that DBT will cover the international airfares of Indian scientists travelling overseas for the purposes of the project.
- International travel for non-Indian collaborators, as well as local travel and subsistence for Indian collaborators when outside India, will not usually be covered by DBT and should be entered in the main

  Je-S form rather than in this proforma.

Related Grants

Provide the DST, DBT, CSIR etc. reference numbers of any current grants held by any of the Indian applicants that are related to this proposal.

Other Information

1. List of facilities, equipment and other resources available at Indian institutions involved in the collaboration
2. Endorsement from Head of the Institution of the Indian lead organisation *(this page with signatures should be signed, scanned and sent to the investigator responsible for submitting the proposal via Je-S)*

Signature of Indian lead investigator:

Name:

Date:

Signatures of Head of lead Indian Institute

Name:

Date:

Note: Users are requested to see the current versions of forms, regulatory guidelines and time limitations on the Government websites. This is guidance only.

❖❖❖

8. LIST OF BIOTECH INDUSTRIES IN INDIA AND THEIR PRODUCTS

The Department of Biotechnology (DBT) was set up by the Government of India under the Ministry of Science and Technology in 1986, to give a boost to the Biotech industry in India. Since then there has been no looking back. The funding and initiatives of DBT have been successful in generating a rich pool of academicians and scientists. India has become a hub of Biotechnology activity in the last decade. It is an ideal ground to set up biotech companies not only by Indian ventures, but also MNCs. India provides a sound knowledge base combined with skilled manpower. It is also a great place to set up manufacturing units, not to mention research laboratories.

Success didn't come early to the biotech industry in India. Due to the prolonged period of research involved in the development of the processes and products, it was difficult for the industry to sustain itself in the face of scant funding. The high initial investment required and the uncertain nature of research made investors wary of funding activities, till a developed and tested product was available. But India could not afford to lag behind in the face of the huge benefits of Biotechnology. The science of biotechnology is a dynamic one, adopting the principles of various disciplines such as Biology, Biochemistry, Genetics, Cytology, Chemistry, Pharmacology, Bioinformatics and impacting important areas such as medicine, agriculture and environment. The applications of biotech research are many, some of which are cited below.

The field of medicine is making rapid progress and breakthroughs, thanks to new biotechnological processes and products. Traditional medicine cured the symptoms of various diseases. But biotechnological processes, in combination with pharmacology have the capability to develop proteins or molecules, which target the pathway of the disease and provide a permanent cure. Microorganisms can be manipulated to produce insulin, human growth factors, blood clotting factors, fertility drugs, antibiotics, vaccines and enzymes, which can be used to cure many human disorders. Gene therapy, a gift of biotechnology can cure genetically acquired diseases. It involves replacing defective genes, which may (somatic treatment) or may not (germline treatment) be transmitted to the next generation, as the need may be. Genetic testing can confirm paternity in the case of disputed parentage or help in solving a crime using DNA manipulative techniques available. A whole range of diseases like AIDS, cancer, sickle cell anemia, hemophilia, cystic fibrosis, diabetes, etc., can be detected and treated using biotechnological procedures which can detect mutations and address them at a genetic level.

The production of high yielding and disease resistant crops through biotechnological means is a real boon to agriculture. Plants can be engineered with new genes for a favorable trait. They can be induced to form more nutritious fruits and/or vegetables. Their color and size too can be manipulated by altering their genetic constitution, viz. replacing defective genes or incorporating new genes. Banana and tomato plants have been engineered to produce vaccines. If clinical trials are successful, we are in for a revolution in biopharmaceuticals. Disease resistance crop varieties can be produced by incorporating Bt (*Bacillus thuringiensis*) gene in the crops, which when expressed produces the Bt toxin.

When the insect feeds on the plant, the toxin acts on its metabolism and causes the death of the pest. Crops can also be engineered to tolerate biotic and abiotic stress conditions. Biotechnology has erased the divide of the seasons, allowing us to enjoy our favorite fruits, vegetables and flowers all through the year.

The environment around us is undergoing a lot of change due to increased amounts of pollutants and climatic changes around the globe. To maintain a sustainable environment, it is necessary to cleanse our habitat.

Biotechnology helps us to study the existing degradation pathways and improvise on them. For example, the oil spills in coastal regions and petroleum seepage into water bodies, can be controlled by bioengineered microorganisms, which can degrade these harmful pollutants. Biotechnology in conjunction with environmental sciences provides valuable insights into the different pathways and networks of important elements in nature, thereby helping in bioremediation.

The Government of India is going all out to embrace the biotech industry and its products. Funds are flowing through Venture Capitalists (VCs) to biotech startups. Rebate on R&D, 100% foreign direct investment, excise and customs duty waiver on certain products, etc., are some of the incentives introduced by the government. India has made great strides in all the above biotechnological applications.

The Indian biotech industry today encompasses 325 companies, some of them including Biocon, Serum Institute of India and Panacea Biotec alone, contributing to 27% of revenues. According to the 5th BioSpectrum-ABLE (Association of Biotechnology Led Enterprises) Biotech Industry Survey, of April-May 2007, the industry has grown by 30.9% in 2006-2007 alone. The contract research industry in India could reach as high as US $ 270 million by 2009 (Asia Specific Biotechnology Market 2007-2010, June 2007).

The top ten biotech companies of India listed below have broken new grounds and given new products and technologies to the world (for information only).

1. Biocon
2. Serum Institute of India

3. Panacea Biotec
4. Nicholas Piramal
5. Wockhadrt Limited
6. GlaxoSmithKline
7. Bharat Serum
8. Krebs Biochemicals and Industries Limited
9. Zydus Cadila
10. Indian Immunologicals

Close on the heels of the companies listed above, are Shantha Biotechnics, Biological E, Mahyco Monsanto, Bharat Biotech, Ranbaxy and Novozymes to name a few. Biocon is the first and presently the leading biotech company in India. Initially it brought in revenues by manufacturing enzymes. But it has gradually become more research oriented with the goal of introducing new drugs to the market. Its manufacturing capabilities include microbial and mammalian cell culture fermentation, synthetic chemistry and therapeutic drugs for the treatment of cancer, autoimmune and metabolic diseases. Serum Institute of India, Indian Immunologicals and Bharat Biotech specialize in the production of vaccines. Serum Institute of India is the world's largest producer of measles and DTP vaccines. Panacea Biotec has recently set up a plant in Himachal Pradesh, India, for production of bacterial and viral vaccines.

Wockhardt is a biopharma powerhouse with 11 world class manufacturing plants in India. Shantha Biotechnics is located in Hyderabad and its products include Hepatitis B vaccine, Streptokinase drug and Interferon alpha-2b. The big player in agro-biotech, MAHYCO Monsanto has released a number of Bt cotton hybrids, which have been approved for commercial cultivation. The significant reduction in the use of pesticides and higher and better quality yields will result in increased incomes to farmers.

Genetically modified field crops like rice, mustard, groundnut, maize, tubers like potato, vegetables like tomato, cabbage, okra, etc., are also under various stages of field trial led by Indian biotech companies. Development of products tailored to the needs of the Indian agricultural sector, will go a long way in making the country self-sufficient.

The above-mentioned achievements of Indian biotech companies have started attracting overseas partners and investors. Indian biotech firms have started scaling up their capabilities to become global players. With proactive government schemes, VC funding, new products and groundbreaking research, India is fast emerging as a biotech leader in the Pacific, alongside Singapore, Japan, Taiwan, Korea and China.

The medical/pharmaceutical industry is not the only one impacted by the methods of modern biotechnology.

For example, farmers commonly plant crops that are genetically modified to be resistant to herbicides. Genetically modified microorganisms are sometimes used to detoxify contaminated soil and/or water. Crime investigators use DNA methods to link a suspect to a crime scene. Biotechnology is thus a collection of technologies that have profoundly impacted many human enterprises.

9. CLASSIFICATION OF INSULIN PREPARATIONS BASED ON DURATION OF ACTION

Insulin preparations are available in various different injectable dosage forms. Different dosage forms are having different onset of action and duration of action. Following is the classification of insulin preparation intended for subcutaneous administration.

Sr. No.	Type	Synonym	Common classification	Approximate duration of action after subcutaneous administration
1.	Soluble insulin (also known as regular or unmodified insulin)	1. Neutral Insulin. 2. Soluble insulin. 3. Acid insulin	Short acting	6-8 hours
2.	Biphasic insulins	1. Biphasic insulin. 2. Biphasic isophane insulin.	Intermediate acting	Upto 24 hrs.
3.	Insulin suspension	1. Isophane protamine insulin injection. 2. Isophane insulin. 3. Isophane insulin (NPH). 4. Amorphous insulin Zinc suspension, semi-lente		
		1. Insulin Zinc Suspension (I.Z.S.) (mixed), Insulin lente. 2. Insulin zinc.	Intermediate or long acting.	UPto 30 Hours.
		1. Crystalline I.Z.S Insulin ultra lente. 2. Insulin protamine zinc.	Long acting	Upto 36 hours

10. OPERATIONAL EXCELLENCE AND SIX SIGMA IN PHARMA INDUSTRY

Now days various tools of Operational excellence are used to reduce the rejects rate, workplace management, increase productivity, reduce the cost of product & inventory control. Following are the few tools of operational excellence.

1. KAIZEN.
2. LEAN
3. SIX SIGMA
4. POKAYOKE
5. JIT (JUST IN TIME)
6. ISO 9000

1. KAIZEN:

This is useful for

- Workplace Management
- Change for betterment
- Changeover time Reduction (SMED-single minute exchange die)
- Autonomous maintenance

2. LEAN:

This is useful for

- Respond to pull. (car – When one car get sold, sold car invoice generate mfg order.)
- Reduce waste. (time, manpower, material, intellect etc.)
- Reduce non value added activity. (ex sorting of tablets.)
- Flow increase. (flow of river) – maximum out put in lesser time.
- Customer focus. (What customer expects different from commodity to commodity.)

3. SIX SIGMA :

This is useful for

- Perfection and Zero defect /error product.
- Data base analysis
- Works on variation. Reduce variance.
- Useful for Process capability, process performance & standard .deviation.

It is measured by two methods

1) Defect Rate (DPMO- defects per million opportunity)
2) Process capability Ratio & index.

4. POKAYOKE :

This is useful for

- Mistake proofing.

E.g. Design of process or product shall be such that there is no chance of making mistake. For example- Mobile charger pin, Mobile battery. Wrong charger pin will not fit in other mobile.

5. **JIT (JUST IN TIME):**

   This is useful for
   - Inventory management.

6. **ISO 9000:**

   This is quality management system.

SIX SIGMA

1.0 Introduction

Sigma that is Standard deviation and it is used to designate the distribution or spread of any process about the mean (average). The sigma value indicates how well that process is performing. The higher the sigma value 2,3,4, 5 and 6, the better the process performance. Sigma measures the capability of process to perform defect free work. A defect is anything that results in customers dis-satisfaction. With six sigma, the common measurement index is defect per unit, where unit can be virtually anything – a component, a piece of material, a line of code an administrative form, a time, a distance etc. The sigma value indicates how often defects are likely to occur. As sigma values increases, cost goes down, cycle time goes down and customer satisfaction goes up.

The name Six Sigma comes from the fact that it is a managerial approach designed to create processes that result in no more than 3.4 Defects Per Million. One of the aspects that distinguishes Six Sigma from other approaches is a clear focus on achieving bottom-line results in a relatively short three- to six-month period of time. After seeing the huge financial successes at Motorola, GE, and other early adopters of Six Sigma management, many companies worldwide have now instituted Six Sigma management programs.

The DMAIC Model

To guide managers in their task of improving short- and long-term results, Six Sigma uses a five-step process known as the DMAIC model, named for the five steps in the process: Define, Measure, Analyze, Improve, and Control.

Define: The problem is defined along with the costs, benefits, and impact on the customer. Clearly define the problem and relate it to the customer's needs (generally, with a cost benefit to the organization identified).

Measure: Operational definitions for each critical-to-quality (CTQ) characteristic are developed. In addition, the measurement procedure is verified so that it is consistent over repeated measurements. Measure what is key to the customer and know that the measurement is good.

Analyze: The root causes of why defects occur are determined, and variables in the process causing the defects are identified. Data are collected to determine benchmark values for each process variable. Search for and identify the most likely root causes

Improve: The importance of each process variable on the CTQ characteristic are studied using designed experiments. The objective is to determine the best level for each variable. Determine the root causes and establish methods to control them.

Control: The objective is to maintain the benefits for the long term by avoiding potential problems that can occur when a process is changed. Monitor and make sure the problem does not come back.

The sigma level numbers often associated with six Sigma represents the capability of a core business process, as measured in **defects per million opportunities**:

Sigma level	Defects per Million Opportunities	Yield
6	3.4	99.9997 %
5	233	99.977%
4	6,210	99.379%
3	66,807	93.32%
2	308,537	69.2%
1	690,000	31%

Six Sigma should not replace GMP; however, its application may be used as a first step towards GMP. In countries where appropriate regulations exist and are enforced, compliance with GMP (including validation), drug regulatory activities and inspections provide good assurance that risks are largely controlled. In countries where control is less effective, however, patients may be put at risk through the production of drugs of inadequate quality. The assessment of individual process status related to specific pro-ducts and starting materials, and the recognition of problems at specific stages of production or distribution should permit regulatory authorities to improve drug control by increasing the effectiveness of their activities within the limits of the available resources. The present guidelines are aimed at assisting industry to develop and implement effective 6-sigma plans covering activities such as research and development, sourcing of materials, manufacturing, packaging, testing and distribution.

In each stage of the manufacture and supply of pharmaceuticals, the necessary conditions should be provided and met to protect the pharmaceuticals concerned.

This has traditionally been accomplished through the application of Good Clinical Practice (GCP), Good Laboratory Practice (GLP), GMP and other guidelines, which are considered to be essential to the development and implementation of effective 6 sigma plans. 6 Sigma plans are focused on Defect free product, the overall objective being to ensure that pharmaceuticals are safe for use. The existence and effectiveness of GCP, GLP and GMP should be assessed when drawing up6 Sigma plans.

Although Six Sigma and the DMAIC toolkit focused on eliminating process variability, there still remained the need to bring products to market faster and more cheaply. As a result, the biopharmaceutical industry has turned to the principles of Lean Manufacturing to increase the efficiency of our processes. The ideas of Lean Manufacturing are based on the Toyota Production System approach of eliminating waste in every aspect of a company's operation. Lean focuses on time variability, in contrast to Six Sigma's focus on process variability.

2.0 ORGANIZATION CHART & RESPONSIBILITY IN 6 SIGMA.

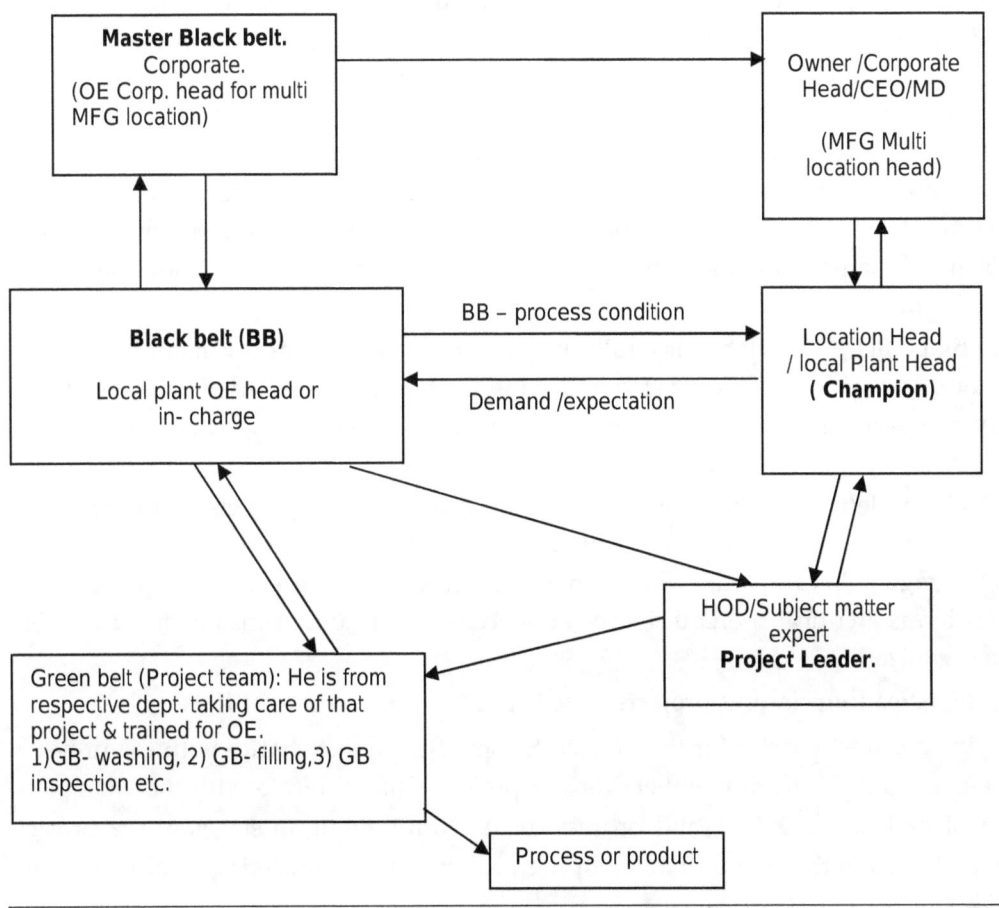

Based on some review of data BB will do the background analysis of product and process and he will present to Champion . Background analysis is which process or product is defective more as compaired to other and there is scope for improvement. How much cost will be saved. Champion will study the analysis report and give the project to BB that reduce the this much time of break down.BB in coordination with HOD will prepare a project Charter (See annex II.). BB will give training to the dept person who will take care of project and may be called as Green belt. Project leader will ask for resources to Champion. If not granted, BB will inform to MBB and MBB will get it sanctioned from Owner/CEO. Also see the defn topic.

2.0 DIFINATIONS:

The following definitions apply to the terms as used in these guidelines. They may have different meanings in other contexts.

1. Master Black Belt : A master black belt takes on a leadership role as keeper of the Six Sigma process and advisor to senior executives or business unit managers. He or she must leverage his or her skills with projects that are led by black belts and green belts. Frequently, master black belts report directly to senior executives or business unit managers. A master black belt has successfully led many teams through complex Six Sigma projects. He or she is a proven change agent, leader, facilitator, and technical expert in Six Sigma management. It is always best for an organization to develop its own master black belts. However, sometimes it is impossible for an organization to develop its own master black belts because of the lead time required to become a master black belt. Thus, circumstances sometimes require hiring master black belts from outside the organization.

2. Black Belt: A black belt is a full-time change agent and improvement leader who may not be an expert in the process under study [see Reference 4]. A black belt is a quality professional who is mentored by a master black belt, but who may report to a manager for his or her tour of duty as a black belt.

3. Green Belt: A green belt is an individual who works on projects part-time (25%), either as a team member for complex projects or as a project leader for simpler projects. Most managers in a mature Six Sigma organization are green belts. Green belt certification is a critical prerequisite for advancement into upper management in a Six Sigma organization.

Green belts leading simpler projects have the following responsibilities:

Refine a project charter for the project. Review the project charter with the project's champion. Select the team members for the project. Communicate with the champion, master black belt, black belt, and process owner throughout all stages of the project. Facilitate the team through all phases of the project. Schedule meetings and coordinate logistics. Analyze data through all phases of the project. Train team members in the basic tools and methods through all phases of the project. In complicated Six Sigma projects, green belts work closely with the team leader (black belt) to keep the team functioning and progressing through the various stages of the Six Sigma project.

4. **Central Tendency :** one of the silent characteristics of the distribution of the sample data is that most of the observations tend to concentrate in the centre of the distribution. This characteristic of the distribution is known as central tendency. Central tendency is usually expressed in three ways : Arithmetic Mean, Median, Mode.

5. **Arithmetic mean (The average Value) : (X)** The arithmetic mean is the average of all the values of the variets in the sample.

If $X_1, X_2, X_3, X_4 \ldots X_n$ are the n values of varies X in the sample, then their arthematic mean is, $X_1 + X_2 + \ldots + X_n / n$

The arithmetic mean is used to report average size, average yield, average percent defects etc.

6. **Median (The middle values) :** When all the observations are arranged in ascending or descending order, then the median is the magnitude of the middle case, it has half the observation above it & half below it. If there are "n" observations of the variate and they are arranged in ascending order then median is given by $(n + 1/2)$ if n is odd. If n is even the median is taken as the average of n/2 th and (n/2 + 1 th value.

7. **Mode (Most frequently occurring values) :** The mode is the value that occurs most frequently, in a frequency histogram or frequency polygon. It is observed value corresponding to high point of the graph. Ex- 2, 3, 5, 2, 6, 2, 4, 2, 8, 2, 9 = 2 occurs most frequently, hence Mode is = 2.

8. **Dispersion :** The extent to which the data is scattered about the zone of central tendency is known as dispersion. The Range (R), Standard Deviation (sigma) and Variance are the important measures of dispersion.

9. **Range :** Rang eis the simplest measure of dispersion in a sample. It is used particularly in the control chart. It is the difference between the largest observed value and the smallest observed value.

10. **Standard Deviation (Sigma) :** It is the root Mean square of the differences between the observations and the mean. It is used in control charts, Process capability studies, and also when the data have extremely high or low value the SD is more desirable than the range.

11. **Variance :** It is another measure of dispersion. This is the sum of the square of the deviations from the Arithmetic mean divided by the number of observations n. In another word, the variance is the square of the standard deviation.

12. Process capability Ratio (Cp) : It is Ratio of Specification range to the process capability. Process capability indicates the ability of the process to hold product tolerance. That is if the Product tolerance is 110 ml to 120 ml, Process capability is to holds all the bottles within tolerance of 110 to 120 ml. IT is calculated by Usl- Lsl/6Sigma. (6 sigma is 6 × SD). If this ratio is 2 then process is complying 6sigma.

13. Process capability Index (Cpk) : It is minimum Ratio of either (Mean-LSL/3sigma) or (USL-mean/3sigma.), Process capability index indicates the ability of the process to hold product within tolerance but closer to the mean. That is if the Product tolerance is 110 ml to 120 ml, Process capability index is to holds all the bottles within tollerance of 110 to 120 ml but closure to the mean fill volume that is 115ml . that is even though the tollerance limit if 110 to 120 ml all the bottles will be closer to 115 msl that is within 114 to 116 ml & not from 110 to 120 ml. Mean-Lsl/3sigma) or USL-mean/3sigma.). For new process Cpk shall be 1.5 for 6 sigma process, but as the process become older there should be more perfection in the process & sigma shift by 1.5 so for old process Cpk shall be 2.0. That means if the old process is complying with six sigma means Cpk 1.5, it should be considered 4.5 sigma & Cpk 1.5. this is 1.5 sigma shift. for old process Cpk shall be 2 for 6 sigma compliance.

Example for CP & CPk

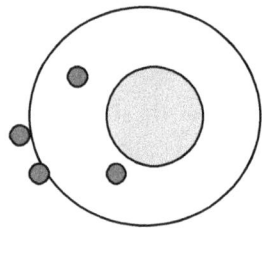
Circle 1

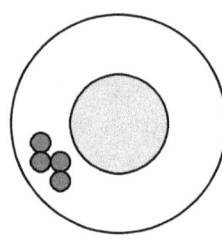
Circle 2

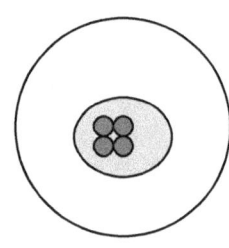
Circle 3

1) **Outer circle is Tolerance limit, inner circle is Target that is mean of tolerance. small circle is bullets.**

   Circle 1 : Bullets are hit but not in the tolerance limit so it is not considered for Cp or Cpk.

   Circle 2: All the bullets are hit preciously within the limit and in the same range but not closer to the mean so it is Cp.

   Circle 3: All the bullets are hit in the target that is within specified limit and also closer to the mean or center of the specification. That is Cpk.

Process Range: CP & Cpk

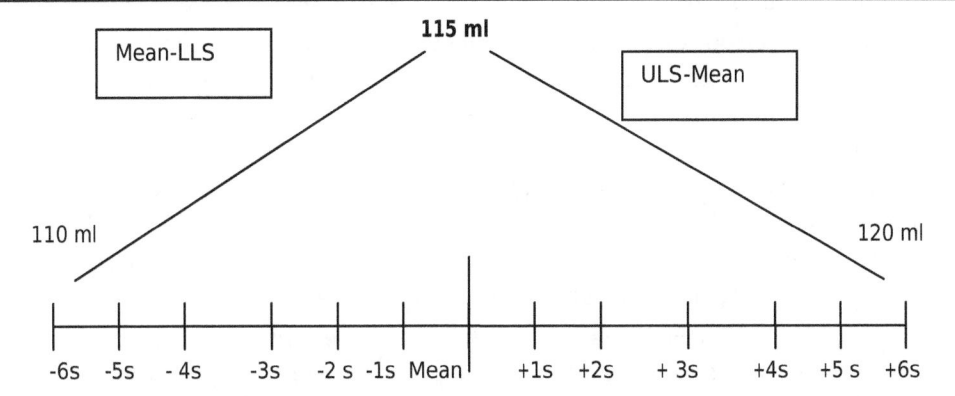

Above is the Process Range, If it is divided by 6 sigma (6 x SD) then it is CP.

And if (Usl-mean)is divided by 3s or (Mean-LSL)is divided by 3s. the minimum of one of this is call CPK. (120-115)/3s or 115-110 /3s = min value is Cpk.-
Distribution graph.

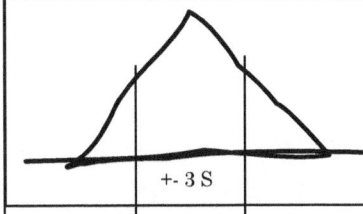

See the distribution of values of any process top of the triangle is mean. Base line is + 6s to -6 sigma. If the area under curve is 100 %, up to +,- 3 s shall be above 70 %,, from 3 s to 4s is 20%. from 4 S to 5 S is 7 %. from 5 to 6 s is 3 %

3.0 PRINCIPLES:

The 6 sigma system is based on five principles. In applying these principles, 17 steps are recommended. Some Stapes are linked to specific principles while others serve as an Introduction to the concept.

The Five DMAIC principles are:
1. Define
2. Measure
3. Analyze
4. Improve
5. Control

1. **Define:** The problem is defined along with the costs, benefits, and impact on the customer. Clearly define the problem and relate it to the customer's needs (generally, with a cost benefit to the organization identified).
2. **Measure:** Operational definitions for each critical-to-quality (CTQ) characteristic are developed. In addition, the measurement procedure is

verified so that it is consistent over repeated measurements. Measure what is key to the customer and know that the measurement is good.

3. **Analyze:** The root causes of why defects occur are determined, and variables in the process causing the defects are identified. Data are collected to determine benchmark values for each process variable. Search for and identify the most likely root causes

4. **Improve:** The importance of each process variable on the CTQ characteristic are studied using designed experiments (see Chapter 8, "Design of Experiments"). The objective is to determine the best level for each variable. Determine the root causes and establish methods to control them

5. **Control:** The objective is to maintain the benefits for the long term by avoiding potential problems that can occur when a process is changed. Monitor and make sure the problem does not come back.

The sigma level numbers of ten associated with six Sigma represents the capability of a core business process, as measured in **defects per million opportunities** :

Following are the stages of implementation of 6 sigma Tools under the five basic principals.

1. Define :
   o Establish Team Charter
   o Identify Team Sponsor & team resources.
   o Administer Pre- Work.
2. Measure
   o Confirm Team Goals
   o Define current state
   o Collect & display data
3. Analyze
   o Determine Process capability & speed.
   o Determine Sources of variance and time bottle necks.
4. Improve
   o Generate Ideas
   o Conduct experiments.
   o Creates Straw models.
   o Conducts B's & C's
   o Develop action plan.
   o Implement.
5. Control
   o Develop control plan
   o Monitor performance.
   o mistake proof process

4.0 METHODOLOGY FOR, 6-δ PROCESS EVALUATION & IMPROVEMENT

4.1 GUIDANCE FOR APPLICATION OF 6- SIGMA WITH GMP SYSTEM :

The following guidelines will be found useful in applying the 6-Sigma system:
- Before 6-sigma is applied to any sector, that sector should be operating in accordance with the principles of good practices and the relevant legislation.
- Management commitment is necessary if an effective 6-Sigma system is to be implemented.
- 6-Sigma should be applied to each specific operation separately.
- Problem analysis tools & process improvement recommendations identified in any given example in any reference document (including GMP guidelines) may not be the only ones identified for a specific application or may be of a different nature.
- The 6 Sigma application should be reviewed and necessary changes made when any modification is made in the product or process, or in any step.
- It is important, when applying 6 Sigma, to take into account the nature and size of the operation.
- There should be a 6 sigma plan. The format of such plans may vary, but they should preferably be specific to a particular product, process or operation. Generic 6-Sigma plans can serve as useful guides in the development of product and process 6 sigma plans; however, it is essential that the unique conditions within each facility are considered during the development of all components of the 6 Sigma plan.

4.2 DMAIC TOOLS METHODOLOGY :

It is used for compliance & implementation of 6 sigma in pharmaceutical industry . Procedure for 6 sigma methodology based on 17 steps of DMAIC tools is given below.

1. Define :
   o Establish Team Charter
   o Identify Team Sponsor & team resources.
   o Administer Pre- Work
2. Measure
   o Confirm Team Goals
   o Define current state
   o Collect & display data
3. Analyze
   o Determine Process capability & speed.

- o Determine Sources of variance and time bottle necks.
4. Improve
    - o Generate Ideas
    - o Conduct experiments.
    - o Creates Straw models.
    - o Conducts B's & C's
    - o Develop action plan.
    - o Implement.
5. Control
    - o Develop control plan
    - o Monitor performance.
    - o Mistake proof process

4.2.1 DEFINE:

The problem is defined along with the costs, benefits, and impact on the customer. Clearly define the problem and relate it to the customer's needs (generally, with a cost benefit to the organization identified).

Step 1: Establish Team Charter:

Team charter is the face of the project. In this stage identify the Project. If you have 10 processes in your dept or 10 products then select such process or product for 6 sigma where the rejection rate is is higher and there is scope for improvement. While selecting the project perform the Project Background analysis, and based on background analysis prepares the project Charter.

1) **Project back ground Analysis: (Annexure 1):** First decide the project analysis say, yield improvement, reduce break down timing etc. based on this collect the data, monthly meeting Review, Internal quality audits or such other reviews. This is responsibility of Location OE in charge (black belt) . Collect the data and Prepare the graphs by digging the process where there is more scope. After background analysis OE In charge black belt will inform and present the data to the location plant head (Champion), Location plant head (champion will study the data and instruct to OE in charge to start the project and prepare the Project charter. For example, in monthly review meeting it is observed that last month m breakdown time is more in production area. Then OE In charge will first collect the data Process wise like name of process and total break down time and prepare background analysis to present to Location head (Champion)

Annexure I
Project Background Analysis (Define)

Responsibility: Black belt (location OE in charge)

Step -1 -Production area Break down analysis- **process wise**

Sr. No.	Process	Down time
1.	granulation	200 min
2.	Compression	300 min
3.	coating	200 min
4.	Sorting	50 min
5.	Blister packing	**5050 min**
6.	Bottle packing	800 min
7.	Strip packing	900 min
	Total	7400 min

Plot the graph of above

> Plot here Process vs downtime graph.

Analysis: From above data it is clear that production major break down time is in packing dept on Blister machine. So further analysis shall be completed for blister packing machine.

Done by   checked by

Step -2 Blister packing Break down analysis- Packing line wise.

Sr. No.	Process	Down time
1.	Blister Line I	**3000 min**
2.	Blister Line II	300 min
3.	Blister Line III	200 min
4.	Blister Line IV	1000 min
5.	Blister Line V	200 min
6.	Blister Line VI	150 min
7.	Blister Line VII	200 min
	Total	5050 min

Plot the graph of above

> Plot here Process vs downtime graph

Analysis: From above data it is clear that Blister line major break down time is on dept on Blister machine I. So further analysis shall be completed for blister packing machine I.

Done by   checked by

Step -3 : **Blister packing I** Break down analysis- **machine wise**

Sr. No.	Process	Down time
1.	Blistering machine	**2500 min**
2.	Cartoning machine	20 min
3.	counter	20 min
4.	Shrink wrap machine	350 min
5.	BOPP taping machine	10 min
6.	Utility	100 min
	Total	3000 min

Plot the graph of above

> Plot here Process vs downtime graph

Analysis: From above data it is clear that Blister line I major break down time is on on Blister machine it self & Cartoning machine. So project shall be targeted on these two machine, because if we will solve the problem of these two machine 80 % of production time breakdown will be avoided & and there is cost saving.

Done by   checked by

2) **Project charter:** Annexure II : once the background analysis is completed, OE in charge will present this data to champion . Champion will give the demand of total process improvement or yield improvement to OE in charge (OEI). OEI will prepare a Project charter and after approval will start the project. Following Points shall be included in the Project Charter.
   1) Business Opportunity: Include the current status /figures of process or product, or in %. Mention the opportunity in terms of % or unit tha can be achieved to improve the process or product quality.
   2) Project Target: Specify the target from current stage to achieved stage ex- to reduce break down time from 4 % to 2% for xyz line.
   3) Project Scope: Specify the machine name, product name which is targeted for improvement.
   4) Project Methodology: Project will follow the DMAIC Methodology.
   5) Project saving: Specify the saving in terms of money, month, spare, product unit.
   6) Project Team: Prepare project team.

The roles of senior executive (CEO or president), executive committee, champion, process owner, master black belt, black belt, and green belt are critical to the Six Sigma management process.

The senior executive provides the impetus, direction, and alignment necessary for Six Sigma's ultimate success. The most successful, highly publicized Six Sigma efforts have all had unwavering, clear, and committed leadership from top management. Although it may be possible to initiate Six Sigma concepts and processes at lower levels, dramatic success will not be possible until the senior executive becomes engaged and takes a leadership role.

The members of the executive committee are the top management of an organization. They should operate at the same level of commitment for Six Sigma management as the senior executive.

Champions take a very active sponsorship and leadership role in conducting and implementing Six Sigma projects. They work closely with the executive committee, the black belt assigned to their project, and the master black belt overseeing their project. A champion should be a member of the executive committee or at least a trusted direct report of a member of the executive committee. He or she should have enough influence to remove obstacles or provide resources without having to go higher in the organization.

A process owner is the manager of a process. He or she has responsibility for the process and has the authority to change the process on his or her signature. The process owner should be identified and involved immediately in all Six Sigma projects relating to his or her own area.

6 SIGMA TEAM

The pharmaceutical manufacturer should assure that product-specific knowledge and expertise are available for the development of an effective 6 sigma plan. This may be best accomplished by assembling a multidisciplinary team. Team members should therefore represent all the relevant disciplines, such as research and development, production, quality control, quality assurance, microbiology, engineering and distribution or others as applicable. Team members should have specific knowledge and expertise regarding the product and process. Where such expertise is not available on site, expert advice should be obtained from other sources. Team members should be able to:

(a) Under stand the process or product;
(b) Define the goals & targets;
(c) Measure the current status of the process based on available data;
(d) Know the sources of problems & probable causes of defects in the process;
(e) Give the ideas & solutions to solve the identified problems to improve the process;
(f) Control the improved level process consistently.;
(g) Verify the 6 sigma plan.

Project team shall consists of 1) Team leader, Spencer, BB,GB,

Annexure II
PROJECT CHARTER (Define)
Responsibility: Black belt (location OE in charge)

PROJECT NAME :	
Reduction of breakdown time in packing area by 25 %.	
BUSSINESS OPPORTUNITY: Current breakdown time of the packing lines for blister line is 50 % . There is opportunity to reduce this break down time to 25 % to improve the operational efficiency.	**PROJECT TARGET :** **Reduction of Break down time :** Blister Line NO -I : 5 % to 3.5%
PROJECT SAVING : The project will save the loss of operational time in month. 1) Blister packing line – I - 600 min (1.25 Shift)	**PROJECT TEAM** 1) Group leader – HOD 2) Sponsor – HOD (Cost center) 3) Green belt. 4) Members – 5) Black Belt (Site OE leader) -

PROJECT SCOPE: Blister packing Line – I is scope .	PROJECT METHODOLOGY : Project will follow the methodology of 6Sigma DMAIC. (Define, Measure, Analyse, Improve and control)
PROJECT PLAN Project start date : Project End date :	OTHER REMARK : Remark for any delay or change in above plan.
PREPARED BY	APPOVED BY :

Step 2: Identify Team Sponsor & team resources.

After completion of team charter identify the project sponsor that is from whose account resources will be purchased. That is cost centre for that dept. and also the benefits will be credited to the same person who is sponsor of the project. There may be one or two sponsors like Engineering and productions for Purchase of purchase spare and consumables. Also enlist the resources to be required for the completion of project. See annexure III.

Annexure III
PROJECT SPONSOR & RESOURCES
Responsibility: PROJECT TEAM

PROJECT NAME : Reduction of breakdown time in packing area by 25 %.	
NAME OF THE SPONSOR	COST CENTER (IF REQUIRED):
1) 2) 3)	

Resources Required :	Remark :
PREPARED BY	APPROVED BY :

Step 3: Administer pre-work.

Explain the Project charter to each project team member. Explain them Why this project is selected, What is base line & what is target. Also explain the Background work so that they will know the rejection/ loss ration & source of it. See annexure. IV

Annexure IV
Team pre-work
Responsibility: Project leader

PROJECT NAME :

Reduction of breakdown time in packing area by 25 %.

Following points from project background & project charter are discussed to the team
1) Why project is selected?
2) Base line and target.
3) Probable reasons.
4) Background analysis.(Pre-work)

Sign. Of All team members: 1) 2) 3) 4) 5)	Any remark
PREPARED BY	APPROVED BY :

4.2.3 MEASURE
Step 4: Confirm Team Goals

Distribute the responsibility within the team and finalize the team goals. The team goal is base line to to the target. See annexure. Explain the individual responsibility. See Annexure V

Annexure V
Team Goal

PROJECT NAME : Reduction of breakdown time in packing area by 25 %.	
TEAM GOAL : Reduction of breakdown time in packing area by 25 %.	
Team Member	Responsibility
PREPARED BY	APPROVED BY :

Step 5: Define current state.

Current state is base line that is current status of the rejection or breakdown. The data can be collected from background analysis also. in this step you have to do the measuring system Analysis that is verify that all the measuring equipments are sufficient and calibrated and gives the correct.

In this step 1) Measuring equipment calibration, 2) Base line status 3) current status of sigma of the process or product is carried out.

1) **Measuring equipment Calibration:** Check the calibration of the measuring equipments on the process line. If not calibrated then calibrate the equipments before measuring the current Sigma status. Take the trial of the process using different equipment, different operator, and different time. And record the data.
2) Mention the base line status that is current status of process r project.
3) Current sigma level of the process or product: sigma status of the process or product is carried out by two methods.
    a) Product sigma : Defect rate analysis:
    b) Process sigma status: process capability ration & index.

a) Product current sigma level status :

1) Minimum 30 reading may be considered. For 30 batches. Batch size, OK units and defects units, Loss.
2) Arrange the values as below, that is sr. NO, Lot No, Specification, Output, Loss of defectives and DMPO.
3) How to calculate, rejects and defectives. If in a lot size of 100 no of bottles, out put of which OK bottle is 90 Bottles and 10 bottles are rejects then analyze the 10 bottle, for number of defects in each bottle. If out of 10 bottle 5 bottles are with single defects of volume variation & 5 bottle are with two defects that is volume and seal rejection then consider the total rejection as 15 that is 10 bottle Vol. variation and 5 bottle seal rejection.
4) Calculate the rejection for one million units (10 lacs) lot
5) At the end make the total of specification, Rejection and DMPO (defects per million opportunity.
6) Compare the DMPO with standard comparison table and know the current status of quality of product in terms of 6 sigma.
7) Also plot the graph of B.NO vs Loss.

Sr. No.	Batch No A	Batch Size(input) B	Yield OK units C	Loss D	DPMO (defect per million opportunity)
1.	ABC 001	10000 unit	9000	1000	100000xD/B
2.	ABC 002	10000 unit	9500	500	100000xD/B
3.	ABC 003	10000 unit	9800	200	100000xD/B
4.	ABC 004	10000 unit	8000	2000	100000xD/B
5.	ABC 005	10000 unit	8000	2000	100000xD/B
---	ABC 006	10000 unit	8500	8500	100000xD/B
30	ABC 007	10000 unit	9500	500	100000xD/B
	Total	Bt	Ct	Dt	100000xDt/Bt = 540

Standard Comparison table:

Defect per million (DPMO)	Sigma level with 1.5 sigma shift	Cpk (Sigma level /3) with 1.5 sigma shift
933200	0.000	0.000
915450	0.125	0.042
894400	0.250	0.083
869700	0.375	0.125
841300	0.500	0.167
809200	0.525	0.208
773400	0.750	0.250
734050	0.875	0.292
691500	1.000	0.333
645650	1.125	0.375
598700	1.250	0.417
549750	1.375	0.458
500000	1.500	0.500
450250	1.525	0.542
401300	1.750	0.583
354350	1.875	0.625
308500	2.000	0.667
265950	2.125	0.708
226600	2.250	0.750
190800	2.375	0.792

Contd...

158700	2.500	0.833
130300	2.525	0.875
105600	2.750	0.917
84550	2.875	0.958
66800	3.000	1.000
52100	3.125	1.042
40100	3.250	1.083
30400	3.375	1.125
22700	3.500	1.167
16800	3.525	1.208
12200	3.750	1.250
8800	3.875	1.292
6200	4.000	1.333
4350	4.125	1.375
3000	4.250	1.417
2050	4.375	1.458
1300	4.500	1.500
900	4.525	1.542
600	4.750	1.583
400	4.875	1.625
230	5.000	1.667
180	5.125	1.708
130	525.000	1.750
80	5.375	1.792
30	5.500	1.833
23.4	5.525	1.875
16.7	5.750	1.917
10.1	5.875	1.958
3.4	6.000	2.000

8) The DPMO is 540 that means if you produce 10 Lac. (1 million bottle) there will be 540 defect bottle.

9) 540 DPMO mean Sigma level in between 4.75 to 4.875.

10) Then How to calculate Actual sigma. In excel

= NORMSINV(1-DPMO)/1000000) + 1.5

= NORNSINV(1-540)/ 1000000) + 1.5

= **4.768 is actual sigma level.**

Annexure VI
Measuring Equipment calibration

PROJECT NAME :

Reduction of breakdown time in packing area by 25 %.

Srl	Equipment name	Code/Make	Calibration. Ok/not ok	Remark	Ckd by

PREPARED BY   CHECKED BY :

Annexure VII
CURRENT STATUS OF PRODUCT – SIGMA LEVEL

Project Name:
Product Name:
Batch Size:

DEFECT RATE ANALYSIS

Sr. No.	Batch No A	Batch Size (input) B	Yield OK units C	Loss D	DPMO (defect per million opportunity)
1.	ABC 001	10000 unit	9000	1000	100000xD/B
2.	ABC 002	10000 unit	9500	500	100000xD/B
3.	ABC 003	10000 unit	9800	200	100000xD/B

4.	ABC 004	10000 unit	8000	2000	100000xD/B
5.	ABC 005	10000 unit	8000	2000	100000xD/B
---	ABC 006	10000 unit	8500	8500	100000xD/B
30.	ABC 007	10000 unit	9500	500	100000xD/B
	Total	Bt	Ct	Dt	100000xDt/Bt = 540

- 540 DPMO mean Sigma level in between 4.75 to 4.875.
- Then How to calculate Actual sigma. In excel = NORMSINV(1-DPMO)/1000000) + 1.5 = NORNSINV(1-540)/1000000) + 1.5

  = 4.768 is actual sigma level.

Result: The current sigma level of this product as per DPMO method is 4.768 Sigma.

PREPARED BY   CHECKED BY :

b) Process sigma status: process capability ratio & index:
1. When there is variation in the process results then defect rate method cannot be used for example, temp. fill volume, assay, dissolution, pH etc
2. Process capability is variation within specification limit but not closer to mean, Process capability index is variation within the specified limit but closer to mean.

   For example: if the Bottle fill volume specification if 100 ml to 120 ml and mean is 110 ml then if the batch fill volume is from 100 ml to 120 ml but the reading are from 101 ml to 119 ml, then it is called cp process capability ratio but when these fill volume readings are in between 108 ml to 112 ml closure to the mean then it is called cpk Process capability index .
3. At least 30 readings or values shall be taken for calculation
4. **How to calculate Cp**

   a) Arrange the 30 reading in one column

   b) Calculate the arithmetic mean by Excel formula (=average(select the reading column) or by calculator sum of all reading divided by total numbers of readings

5. Calculate the Standard deviation by using Excel formula (=STDEV(column selection)) or (= STDEV(click first reading then coma...) or
6. Use calculator as below : under root √ (first reading -mean) 2+ (second reading- mean) 2+....+(last reading-mean)2 / total no of readings
7. First deduct the mean from reading, then square the reading, then do the addition of these square then divide by numbers of reading & lastly calculate the square root of this figure. Put the value on calculator and press square root sign. This will be your std.deviation
8. Calculation of square root by using excel formula- (=power(Value,0.5))
9. After calculation of SD, calculate the Cp & Cpk. For this calculate the following
10. Cp is Tolerance divide by 6 sigma. And tolerance is Upper specification level - lower specification level
11. Put the Upper specification level- USL
12. Put the Lower specification level – LSL
13. Calculate Mean – LSL
14. Calculate USL – mean
15. SD is called as Sigma
16. Calculate +3 sigma = mean+(3*SD)
17. Calculate - 3 sigma = Mean -(3*SD)
18. Calculate 3 sigma = 2 *SD
19. Calculate 6 sigma = 6 * SD
20. 6sigma is called Process capability
21. Formula for calculation of process capability ration
22. CP= Usl-Lsl/6sigma that is specification range divided by process capability.
23. Compare these values with the standard table and know the current status of your process.

> 2 CP = 6 sigma

24. ***How to Calculate Cpk*** = Process capability index = min (mean-Lsl/3sigma,(or) USL-mean/3sigma)
25. Calculate the A= mean -Lsl/3 sigms values & B=Usl-mean/3sigma values
26. Lowers values among the A or B is Cpk.
27. Compare the Cpk to the standard table and know the

> 1.5 Cpk = 6 Sigma = 3.4 PPM defect

28. The higher the value of Cpk the lower will be the amount of product which is out of specification limit.
29. If the actual average is equal to the midpoint of the specification range, then Cpk = Cp.

Example: 100ml bottle filling line with below fill volume, calculate the sigma level.
Specification - 101 ml- 120ml
Specification mean – 110 ml

	Fill volume readings
1	110
2	108
3	109
4	110
5	111
6	112
7	108
8	110
9	114
10	110
11	115
12	112
13	108
14	108
15	114
16	115
17	107
18	107
19	108
20	105
21	110
22	110
23	112
24	112

25	**110**
26	**113**
27	**111**
28	**112**
29	**108**
30	**108**

Mean	**110.2333333**
STDEV (sigma)	**2.51455533**
Usl	**120**
Lsl	**101**
Mean- Lsl	**9.233333333**
Usl-Mean	**9.766666667**
+3 Sigma	**117.7769993** for graph
-3 Sigma	**102.6896673** for graph
3 Sigma	**7.543665989**
6 Sigma	**15.08733198**
Usl-Lsl	**19**

Calculation of cP

C_p = USL-Lsl/6 sigma
 =19/15.08   2

$\boxed{C_p\ =\ 2.0}$

Calculation of Cpk

Cpk= min (mean-Lsl/3sigma,(or) USL-mean/3sigma)

1) Mean-Lsl/ 3sigma
 =110.23-101/7.54   1.22398491
 = 1.223

2) USL-mean/3sigma)

=120-110.23/7.54   1.294684399

= **1.294**

A= 1.223 & B =1.294, minimum of these is Cpk =1.223

If Cpk is 1.223 the Sigma level is = 3.75

How to plot graph (Excel sheet)
1. Prepare Bin Column, Bin is marking range on axis. First the bin in one column.

Bin
101
102
103
104
105
106
107
108
109
110
111
112
113
114
115
116
117
118
119
120

Use following commends in Excel to plot graph.
1.

Tools	Click
Data analysis	Click
Histogram	Click
Input range	Click in white block and select fill volume all column.

Bin range	Click in white block and select Bin all column.
Output range	click in white range and then on excel sheet where you want graph.
Chart Output	Click
Ok	Click

2. Stretch the Boundaries of graph to enlarge it.
3.

Bin	Frequency
101	0
102	0
103	0
104	0
105	1
106	0
107	2
108	7
109	1
110	7
111	2
112	5
113	1
114	2
115	2
116	0
117	0
118	0
119	0
120	0

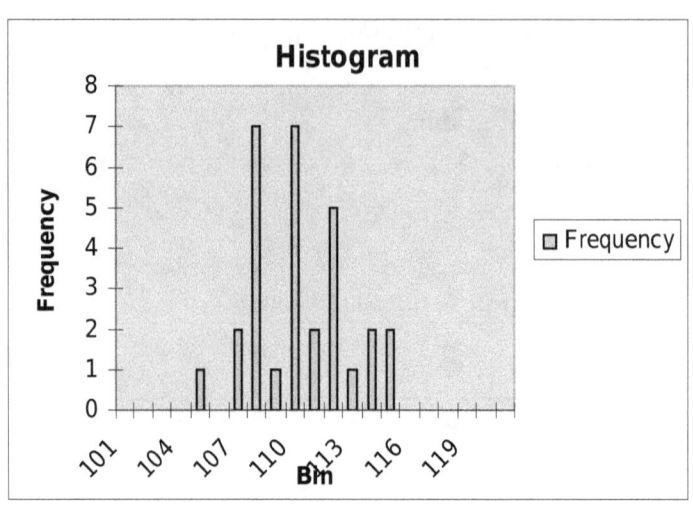

Annexure VIII
CURRENT STATUS OF PROCESS –SIGMA LEVEL
(Cp & Cpk status)

Project Name:
Product Name:
Batch Size:

Observation table of the process values. (USE excel sheet)

Specification : 101 ml- 120ml
Specification Mean: 110 ml

Sr. No.	Fill volume readings	Checked by	Sign	Remark

Calculation :

Mean	**110.2333333**
STDEV (sigma)	**2.51455533**
Usl	**120**
Lsl	**101**
Mean- Lsl	**9.233333333**
Usl-Mean	**9.766666667**
+3 Sigma	**117.7769993** for graph
-3Sigma	**102.6896673** for graph
3 Sigma	**7.543665989**
6 Sigma	**15.08733198**
Usl-Lsl	**19**

Calculation of cP

Cp = USL-Lsl/6 sigma
=19/15.08   2

$\boxed{Cp = 2.0}$

Calculation of Cpk
Cpk= min (mean-Lsl/3sigma,(or) USL-mean/3sigma)

1) Mean-Lsl/ 3sigma
=110.23-101/7.54   1.22398491
= **1.223**

2) USL-mean/3sigma)
=120-110.23/7.54   1.294684399
= **1.294**

A= 1.223 & B =1.294, minimum of these is Cpk =1.223

If Cpk is 1.223 the Sigma level is = 3.75

Result : **If Cpk is 1.223 that is the Sigma level is = 3.75.**

Done by   **Checked by**

Annexure IX
CURRENT STATUS OF PROCESS –SIGMA LEVEL
(Cp & Cpk status)
GRAPHICAL REPRESENTATION

Project Name:
Product Name:
Batch Size:

Bin	Frequency
101	0
102	0
103	0
104	0
105	1
106	0
107	2
108	7
109	1
110	7
111	2
112	5
113	1
114	2
115	2
116	0
117	0
118	0
119	0
120	0

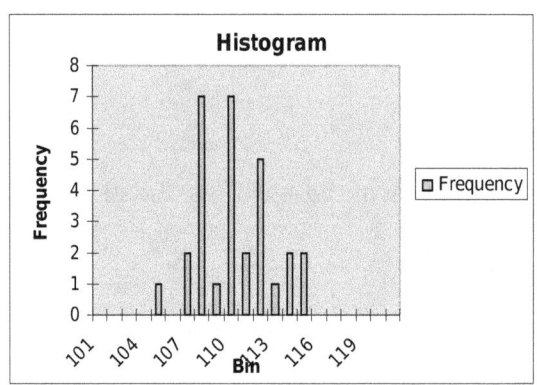

Done by **Checked by**

Industrial Biotechnology - I.154

Step VI: Collect and display data.
1) Establish the process flow sheet.
2) Collect the data of process. For example for Blister Line -1, take the machine trial or take the data from history for number of times break down for each component of blister line such as forming forming, Leaflet catcher, cartoner, pusher, pusher alarm and such other component because of which break down is happened and plot graph & measure which component is repeatedly faulty, and rectification this problem will improve the major break down.
3) From above data if it is cleared that blister line -1 has more break down time because of cartooning machine. Then enlist the different cartooning machine parts & number of times break down. Plot the graph (use excel sheet.).

Annexure X
<u>Flow sheet for projected process</u>

Name of project:
Name of Process:

Process flow diagram
Receipt of table/Packing material
↓
Loading in Blister Machine
↓
Loading of Foil
↓
Loading of cartons & literatures
Blistering of tablets
↓
Cutting
↓
Counting
↓
Cartooning
↓
Wrapping
↓
Shippering
↓
Bopp Sealing

Prepared by   **Checked by**

Annexure XI
Data colletion sheet for breakdown time

Name of project :
Name of Process :

Sr. No.	Blister line Component	Break down time/ attempt	

Measure Result : xyz component has frequently break down and repeated breakdown. So focus on that component.

Prepared by   **Checked by**

Annexure XII
Breakdown time- Graph

Name of project:
Name of Process :

> Graph component vs breakdown time or attempt.

Prepared by   **Checked by**

Annexure XIII
Data colletion sheet for Cartoning machine

Name of project:
Name of Process:

Srl	Cartoning m/s parameters	Break down time/ attempt	

Measure Result: xyz component has frequently broken down & repeated breakdown. So focus on that component.

Prepared by   **Checked by**

Annexure XIV
Breakdown time- Graph

Name of project:
Name of Process:

> Graph component vs breakdown time or attempt.

Prepared by   **Checked by**

4.2.4 ANALYZE :

Step 7: Determine process capability and speed.(cp & Cpk)

Carry out the process capability as mentioned above step 5.Analysie the impact of saving the time if you rectify the problem of above problematic machine. plot the graph of machine wise on this blister line -1, against the earlier time & improved time . Also check by taking trial whether the line speed affects the process capability & defects rates.

Annexure XV
Analysis - break down and saving

Name of project:
Name of Process:

Machine	Down Time	7 significant contributors	Target reduce half	New future state
Cartoning Machine	9845	7070	3535	6310
Blister machine	7259	4974	2487	4772
Shrink wrap machine	835			835
Utility	390			390
weigher	255			255
Other	2100			2100
Total	20684		6022	14662

Machine	Existing Break	7 significant contributors	Target	New future state
Cartoning Machine	47.6%	34.18%	17.1%	30.51%
Blister machine	35.1%	24.05%	12.0%	23.07%
Shrink wrap machine	4.0%			4.0%
Utility	1.9%			1.9%
Weigher	1.2%			1.2%
Other	10.2%			10.2%
Total	100.0%			70.9%

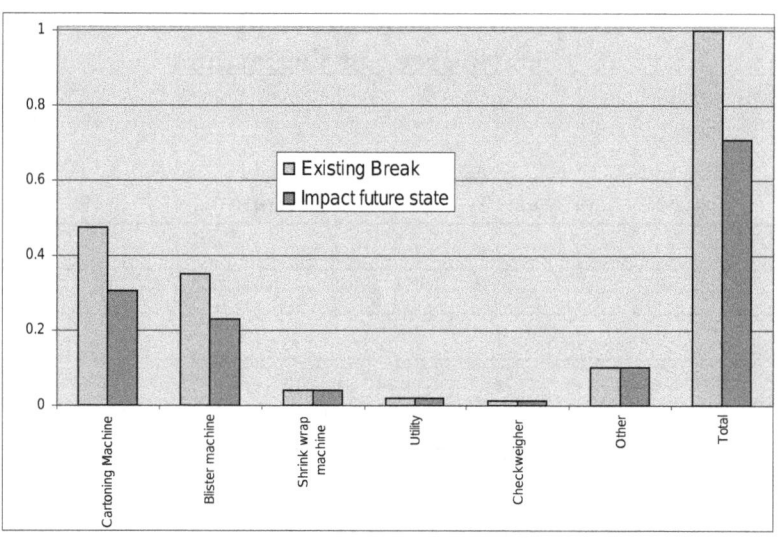

Done by : ----------------   Checked by : ----------------

Step 8: Determine the sources of variation and time bottle necks:

Determine the sources of variation in the process take the trial runs of the process, observe the process closely & note down the sources of variation.(SOV). Also use the collected data to determine the sources of variation. History data can be used for the determination of sources of variations.

Cause and effect diagram can be used know the sources of variations.

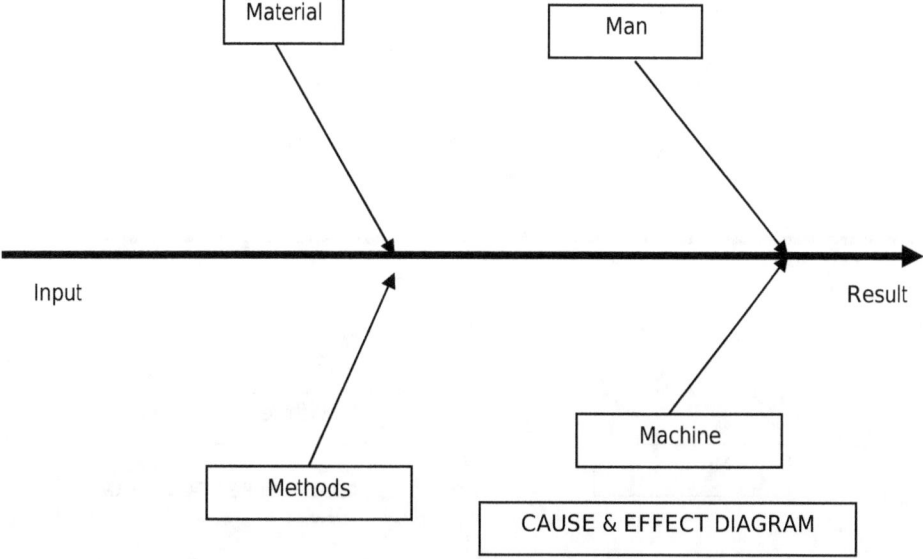

Annexure XVI
Sources of Variations

Name of project:
Name of Process:

Srl	Source of variation	% impact.	Remark

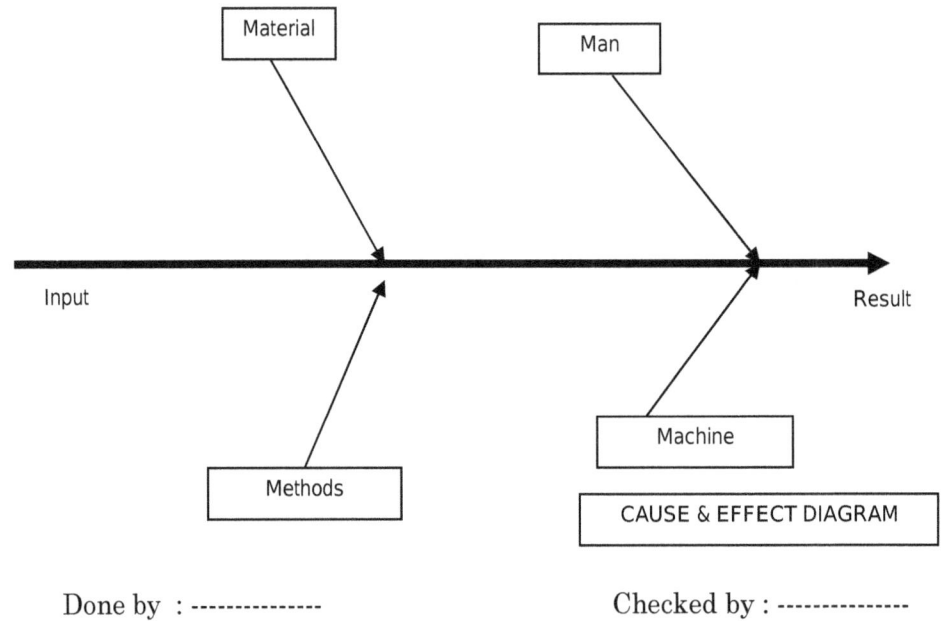

Done by : ---------------   Checked by : ---------------

Industrial Biotechnology - I.160

4.2.5 IMPROVE :

Step 9: Generate Ideas:

Carry out the brain storming of the team members & generates the ideas to improve the process. Enlist the ideas & resources required in annexure to improve the process.

Annexure XVII
Problems & Suggestions for improvement.

Name of project:

Name of Machine : blister machine :

Srl	Major Problem	Problem details	Suggested action for improvement.	Status (action plan
1	Sealing problem	- Sealing temp. problem - Sealing roller problem - Sealing heater regulation problem - SH carbon brush problem - Sealing temp fluction problem	New heater brush less coupler implementation.	Date ------
	y			
	x			
	1			

Name of Machine cartoner machine :

Srl	Major Problem	Problem details	Suggested action for improvement	Status (action plan
	z			
	y			
	x			
	1			

Done by : ---------------   Checked by : ---------------

Step 10: Conduct experiments : based on the above table of ideas conduct the experiment, not on the batch, on empty run by implementation of suggestion . For example if there is problem in filling machine volume variation, and if suggestion is replace the defective syringe with new. Then replace the new syringe and take trial on water filling. If trial is successful then take trail on some batches of bottles.

Step 11: Create straw models : that design a pilot scale model, carry out the trial on pilot scale, in this run whole batch shall be filled. This is actual run after modification.

Step 12: Control Bs and Cs: List down the do & do not during process run.

Step 13: Develop action plans : once the pilot trial is Ok, then Develop action plan that, Who will, DO what, when, where, why and resources.

Annexure XVIII
Action Plan for improvement

Name of project:

Name of Machine: blister machine:

Srl	Problem details	Suggested action for improvement	Resource	Responsibility	Status (action plan
1	- Sealing temp. problem - Sealing roller problem - Sealing heater regulation problem - SH carbon brush problem - Sealing temp fluction problem	New heater brush less coupler implementation.			Date -----
	y				
	x				
	1				

Name of Machine cartoner machine :

Srl	Problem details	Suggested action for improvement	Resource	Responsibility	Status (action plan
1	- Sealing temp. problem - Sealing roller problem - Sealing heater regulation problem - SH carbon brush problem - Sealing temp fluction problem	New heater brush less coupler implementation.			Date ------
	y				
	x				

Done by : ---------------   Checked by : ---------------

Step 14: Implement : Implement the above action plan. And mention the date of implementation.

Annexure XIX
IMPLEMENTATION RECORD.

Name of project:
Name of Machine : blister machine :

Srl	Problem details	Suggested action for improvement	Date of implementation	Checked by	Remark
1	- Sealing temp. problem - Sealing roller problem	New heater brush less coupler implementation.			

Industrial Biotechnology - I.163

	- Sealing heater regulation problem - SH carbon brush problem - Sealing temp fluctuation problem				
	y				
	x				
	1				

Name of Machine cartoner machine :

Srl	Problem details	Suggested action for improvement.	Date of implementation	Checked b y	Remark
1	- Sealing temp. problem - Sealing roller problem - Sealing heater regulation problem - SH carbon brush problem - Sealing temp fluctuation problem	New heater brush less coupler implementation.			
	y				
	x				

Done by : ---------------   Checked by : ---------------

4.2.6 Control :

Step 15: Develop Control plan: after successful implementation develop the control plan. Who, when, where, how long will the monitor the process results.

Annexure XX
Control plan

Name of project:
Name of Machine: blister machine :

Srl	Parameter to be monitored	Frequency	Duration	Responsible person	remark
1					

Done by : -------------- Checked by : --------------

Step 16: Monitor performance:

Monitor the process performance for 3 months or else & plot the histograms and also check the sigma levels.

Plot the histograms showing the earlier defect or break down against current after modification.

Annexure XXI
Check sheet for performance Monitoring
: _____ .

Name of project:
Name of Machine: blister machine:

Srl	Date /Time	Parameter to be monitored	Earlier values	Current values	Specification	Checked by	Remark
1.							
2.							
3.							
4.							

```
┌─────────────────────────────────────────┐
│ graph                                   │
│                                         │
│                                         │
│                                         │
│                                         │
└─────────────────────────────────────────┘
```

Done by : ---------------   Checked by : ---------------

Step 17: Mistake proofing: After completion of project do the mistake proofing that is the solution of design shall be such that the mistake will not happen. For example. To avoid the mix up of PP caps for two different product. Design the PP cap for one product with 13 mm and for another product 25 mm so that even there is mix up of two product 13 mm cap will not fit to 25 mm and 25 mm cap will not fit to 13 mm bottle neck. Another example is of mobile charger plug and pin.

Sr. No.	Name of part	Mistake proofing (How)	Done by	Sign.

4.3 DOCUMENTATION *AND RECORD KEEPING*

Efficient and accurate documentation and record keeping are essential to the application of a HACCP system and should be appropriate to the nature and size of the operation.

8.0 TRAINING

As 6 Sigma is a relatively new concept in the pharmaceutical industry, training of personnel in industry, government and universities in 6 sigma principles and applications is essential for its effective implementation. In developing specific training to support a 6 sigma plan, working instructions and procedures should be drawn up which define the tasks of the operating personnel to be stationed at each control point. Specific training should be provided in the tasks of employees monitoring each process parameter. Cooperation between producers, traders and responsible authorities is of vital importance. Opportunities should be provided for the joint training of industrial staff and the control authorities to encourage and maintain a continuous dialogue and create a climate of understanding in the practical application of OE six sigma. The success of a OE 6 sigma system depends on educating and training management and employees in the importance of their role in producing safe pharmaceuticals. Information should also be provided on the control of process at all stages of production and supply. Employees must understand what OE 6 sigma is, learn the skills necessary to make it function properly, and must also be given the materials and equipment necessary to control the product & process..

9.0 DEVIATIONS

Deviation from any part or the protocol or any procedure or parameter shall be addressed as per SOP NO-----. Corrective and preventive actions to the deviations shall be mentioned in the report.

10.0 CHANGE CONTROL

Any change in document, system, machine and equipment, sequence of act shall be addressed through filing and approval of change control. Refer SOP No. ---

11.0 LIST OF APPENDIX

List out the Reports, certificates as Appendix to main report.

Sr. No.	Appendix No.	Description
1.	1.	Project background analysis (define)
2.	2.	Project charter (define)
3.	3.	Project sponsor and resources
4.	4.	Team pre-work
5.	5.	Team goal
6.	6.	Measuring Equipment calibration
7.	7.	Current status of **PRODUCT** – sigma level (DPMO method)
8.	8.	Current status of **PROCESS** – sigma level (cp and cpk method)
9.	9.	Graphical representation current status of process – sigma level (Cp and Cpk method)
10.	10.	Flow sheet for projected process
11.	11.	Data collation sheet for breakdown time

12.	12.	Breakdown time - Graph
13.	13.	Data collection sheet for Cartoning machine
14.	14.	Breakdown time - Graph
15.	15.	Analysis - break down and saving
16.	16.	Sources of Variations
17.	17.	Problems and Suggestions for improvement
18.	18.	Action Plan for improvement
19.	19.	Implementation record
20.	20.	Control plan
21.	21.	Check sheet for performance Monitoring

12.0 SUMMARY OF 6-sigma PROCESS EVALUATION & IMPROVEMENT.

Write the summery of the target and achievement in view of operational excellence with 6 sigma tool.

13.0 CERTIFICATION OF REPORT.

Certify the report by the concerned personnel's and authorities after completion and final compilation.

❖❖❖

SECTION-II

DOCUMENTATION AND cGMP FOR BIOTECHNOLOGY AND PHARMACEUTICAL INDUSTRY

1. DEFINITIONS OF GMP, cGMP, QA, QC AND IPQC

Good Manufacturing Practices (GMP):

GMP is that part of quality assurance which ensures that products are consistently produced and controlled to the quality standards appropriate to their intended use and as required by the marketing authorization or product specifications. GMP is concerned with both production and Quality control.

Current Good Manufacturing Practices (cGMP):

Current Good manufacturing Practices (21 CFR 210 - 229) are promulgated by the commissioner of the Federal Food and Drug Administration (FDA) under section 701 (a) of the Food, Drug [21 USC (a) (2) (B)] in furtherance of the requirement of section 501 (a) (B) of the Act [21 USC 351 (a) (2) (B)], Which specifies that a drug is deemed to be adulterated "if the methods used in, controls used for, its manufacture, processing, packing or holding do not conform to or are not operated or not administered in conformity with Current Good Manufacturing Practices.

The manufacture of a pharmaceuticals must be by current methods with current control as a requirement that which is current or generally, accepted in the drug industry as appropriate equipment, methodology, controls and records. The standards is not only that practices be current. But that they also be "Good". Thus if a new practice is introduced anywhere in the industry which is better than what is current, then all manufacturers may seem obligated to adopt the better practices. Therefore it can be seen that being in compliance with GMP is not a static situation, but requires the manufacturer to be aware of innovations which may be good. Even if current practices were available, the FDA holds that it has special technical and scientific experience to determine which of the current practices are also good.

A current, although not necessarily predominant, practice is considered "good" if:

1. It is feasible for manufacturers to implement.
2. It considers to ensuring or added assuring the safety, quality or purity of the drug product.
3. The value of the contribution or added assurance exceeds the cost in money of implementing or continuing the practice.

Quality Assurance (QA):

QA is a wide ranging concept which covers all matters which individually or collectively influence the quality of the product. It is the sum of the total organized arrangements made with the object of ensuring that medicinal products are of the quality required for their intended use.

QA is related to all operations including manufacturing, testing and records.

Quality Control (QC):

QC is that part of GMP which is concerned with sampling, specifications and testing and with the organization, documentation and release procedures which ensures that the necessary tests are actually carried out and that materials are not released for use, nor products released for sale or supply, until their quality has been judged to be satisfactory.

In Process Quality (Production) Controls:

These are the checks performed during production in order to monitor and if necessary to adjust the process to ensure that the product conforms to its specifications. Environmental Controls and equipment controls are also considered as in process control. Temperature, Humidity, microbial count of area may be considered as IPQC/IPC.

Quality Unit (QU):

Now QC and QA is combinely called as Quality unit. So quality unit includes functions of quality control and Quality Assurance.

2. CERTIFICATIONS FOR PHARMACEUTICAL INDUSTRIES

Following are the certificates, which are applicable for pharmaceuticals for regulatory or commercial purposes.

1. Indian GMP. (Schedule M) Statutory from June 1988 in India.
2. International Organization for Standards (ISO 9001 and 14001).
3. World Health Organization (WHO GMP).
4. Therapeutic Goods Administration (TGA), Australia.
5. Medicines and Health Care Products Regulatory Agency (MHRA).
   (Formerly, Medicine Control Agency), United Kingdom.
6. Medicine Control Council (MCC), South Africa.
7. cGMP Certification from US Food and Drug Administration (US FDA).
8. International Conference on Harmonization (ICH) USA, Europe and Japan.
9. Certificate Of Suitability (COS) – Europe.

Stages and steps of US FDA guidelines:

It is very important to understood that structure of every guideline, rules and regulation. Unless we know the structure, the guidelines are difficult to understand. For understanding purpose the structure of guideline is given as below:

(1) CRF: This is the code of Federal Regulations, such as - 1, 2, 3, ...21, ... 40 etc. Those Numbers has different Heading such as 21 CFR-Food and Drug.
   ↓
(2) Chapter: I, II, III etc.
   ↓
(3) Parts: There are parts in every CFR. Like Part 211 of is Current Good Manufactures Practices for finished Pharmaceuticals" of the CFR 21.
   ↓
(4) Subpart: Again Part is divided in to the Supports. Such as A, B, C, D, E ..... Z.
   ↓
(5) Section: Subparts are divided in to the various numbers of Section, It is Part No. along with Sr. No . Such as Section 211. 1 Scope.

US FDA guideline for Finished Pharmaceutical product is given under 21 CFR and Part 210 and 211, name as below:

PART 211 - CURRENT GOOD MANUFACTURING PRACTICE FOR FINISHED PHARMACEUTICALS

Subparts and sections under the Part 211 of 21 CFR are summarized below, as below

Subpart A - General Provisions

Sec.
211.1   Scope.
211.3   Definitions.

Subpart B - Organization and Personnel

211.22   Responsibilities of quality control unit.
211.25   Personnel qualifications.
211.28   Personnel responsibilities.
211.34   Consultants.

Subpart C - Buildings and Facilities

211.42   Design and construction features.
211.44   Lighting.
211.46   Ventilation, air filtration, air heating and cooling.
211.48   Plumbing.
211.50   Sewage and refuse.
211.52   Washing and toilet facilities.
211.56   Sanitation.
211.58   Maintenance.

Subpart D - Equipment

211.63   Equipment design, size, and location.
211.65   Equipment construction.
211.67   Equipment cleaning and maintenance.
211.68   Automatic, mechanical, and electronic equipment.
211.72   Filters.

Subpart E - Control of Components and Drug Product Containers and Closures

211.80   General requirements.
211.82   Receipt and storage of untested components, drug product containers, and closures.

211.84	Testing and approval or rejection of components, drug product containers, and closures.
211.86	Use of approved components, drug product containers, and closures.
211.87	Retesting of approved components, drug product containers and closures.
211.89	Rejected components, drug product containers, and closures.
211.94	Drug product containers and closures.

Subpart F - Production and Process Controls

211.100	Written procedures; deviations.
211.101	Charge-in of components.
211.103	Calculation of yield.
211.105	Equipment identification.
211.110	Sampling and testing of in-process materials and drug products.
211.111	Time limitations on production.
211.113	Control of microbiological contamination.
211.115	Reprocessing.

Subpart G - Packaging and Labeling Control

211.122	Materials examination and usage criteria.
211.125	Labeling issuance.
211.130	Packaging and labeling operations.
211.132	Tamper-evident packaging requirements for over-the-counter (OTC) human drug products.
211.134	Drug product inspection.
211.137	Expiration dating.

Subpart H - Holding and Distribution

211.142	Warehousing procedures.
211.150	Distribution procedures.

Subpart I - Laboratory Controls

211.160	General requirements.
211.165	Testing and release for distribution.
211.166	Stability testing.
211.167	Special testing requirements.
211.170	Reserve samples.
211.173	Laboratory animals.
211.176	Penicillin contamination.

Subpart J - Records and Reports

211.180	General requirements.
211.182	Equipment cleaning and use log.
211.184	Component, drug product container, closure, and labelling records.
211.186	Master production and control records.
211.188	Batch production and control records.
211.192	Production record review.
211.194	Laboratory records.
211.196	Distribution records.
211.198	Complaint files.

Subpart K - Returned and Salvaged Drug Products

211.204	Returned drug products.
211.208	Drug product salvaging.

Subpart L - Validation

211.220	Process validation.
211.222	Method validation.

Subpart M - Contamination

211.240	Control of chemical and physical contamination

There are Five centers which are established for the purpose of control of food, Drug and health care products in USA. These are as below.

1) Center for Biologics Evaluation and Research **(CBER)**.
2) Center for Drug Evaluation and Research **(CDER)**.
3) Center for Devices and Radiological Health **(CDRH)**.
4) Center Food Safety and Applied Nutrition **(CFSAN)**.
5) Center for Veterinary Medicine **(CVM)**.

3. CLASSIFICATION AND DEFINITIONS OF VARIOUS DOSAGE FORMS

DEFINITIONS AND CLASSIFICATIONS:

Definition: Dosage form of a drug is a product designed for administration to the patient for the diagnosis or treatment of disease.

Pharmaceutical preparations are recognized by the Pharmacopoeias and other official and unofficial compendia.

Classification of Dosage Forms: Based on the physical state of formulation pharmaceutical dosage forms are classified as follows:

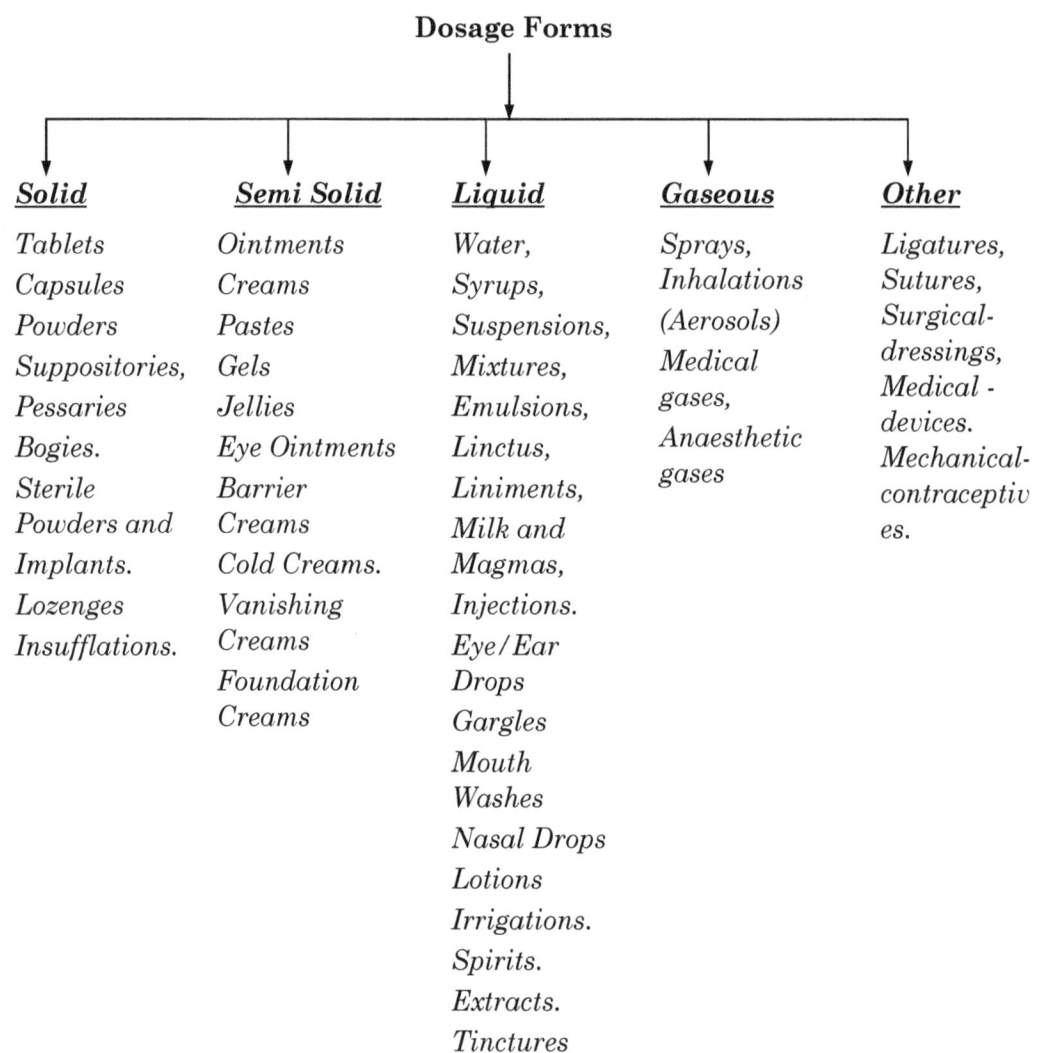

Solid	Semi Solid	Liquid	Gaseous	Other
Tablets	Ointments	Water,	Sprays,	Ligatures,
Capsules	Creams	Syrups,	Inhalations	Sutures,
Powders	Pastes	Suspensions,	(Aerosols)	Surgical-dressings,
Suppositories,	Gels	Mixtures,	Medical gases,	Medical-devices.
Pessaries	Jellies	Emulsions,	Anaesthetic gases	Mechanical-contraceptives.
Bogies.	Eye Ointments	Linctus,		
Sterile Powders and Implants.	Barrier Creams	Liniments,		
Lozenges	Cold Creams.	Milk and Magmas,		
Insufflations.	Vanishing Creams	Injections.		
	Foundation Creams	Eye/Ear Drops		
		Gargles		
		Mouth Washes		
		Nasal Drops		
		Lotions		
		Irrigations.		
		Spirits.		
		Extracts.		
		Tinctures		

1) **Applications:** These are fluids or semi-fluid preparations intended for application to the skin.
2) **Cachets:** Cachets are moulded from rice paper, a material made by pouring a mixture of rice flour and water, between two, hot, polished revolving cylinders, these are used to enclose the nauseous or disagreeable powders in tasteless powders for administration.
3) **Collodions:** These are fluid preparations for external use. These are applied with the help of a brush or rod. After application volatile solvent evaporates leaving flexible, protective film covering the site.
4) **Draughts:** Draughts are liquid oral preparations of which only one or two rather large doses of the order of 50 ml are prescribed. Each dose is issued in separate container.
5) **Dusting Powders:** These are powders which are in a fine state of subdivision, for external, applications.

   They are not to be applied to the broken skin. Dusting powders are sterile powders.
6) **Ear Drops:** These are solutions of drugs that are instilled into the ear with a dropper.
7) **Elixirs:** These are clear, liquids, oral preparations of potent or nauseous drug. They are pleasantly flavoured and usually attractively coloured.
8) **Emulsions:** These are biphasic, dispersed, liquid dosage forms, in which two immiscible liquids are mixed with the help of emulsifying agent.
9) **Enemas:** An emulsion are solutions, suspensions or Oil in water emulsion of medicaments intended for rectal use.
10) **Gargles:** It is aqueous solutions used to prevent or treat throat infections. Usually they are dispensed in concentrated forms with directions for dilution with warm water before use.
11) **Effervescent Granules:** These are the mixture of citric acid and tartaric acid with sodium bicarbonate.

    One or more Organoleptic agents are used. After addition of granules in to water, bicarbonate reacts with acid and produces carbonic acid and preparation is taken during effervescence and immediately afterward.
12) **Inhalations:** These are liquid preparations of, or containing, volatile substances. These are used to relieve congestion and inflammation of the respiratory tract infections.
13) **Insufflations:** These are medicated dusting powders that are blown by insufflators into regions such as the nose, throat, body cavities and the ear, to which it would be difficult to apply the powder directly.

14) **Irrigations:** These are solutions of medicaments used to treat infections of the bladder, vagina and less often, the nose. Thin, soft, rubber, tubes used for irrigation solutions administration are Catheter (Bladder), A vulcanite or plastic pipe (Vagina), Special Glass Irrigator (nose).

15) **Jellies (Gels):** Jellies are transparent or translucent, non-greasy, semisolid preparations mainly used externally.

16) **Linctuses:** These are viscous liquids, oral preparations that are usually prescribed for the relief of Cough. The dose is small and to ensure prolonged action, they should be sipped slowly and swallowed neat.

17) **Liniments:** These are fluid semisolid, or semi fluid preparations intended for application to the skin. These are rubbed to affected area of the skin for their counter irritant or stimulating effect but some are applied on a warm dressing or with a brush for analgesic and soothing effect. They should not be applied to broken skin.

18) **Lotions:** These are fluid preparations for external application without friction.

19) **Lozenges (Troches):** These are solid dosage forms consisting mainly of sugar and gum, the gum gives hardness and cohesiveness and ensuring slow release of the medicaments. They are used to medicate the mouth and throat and for slow administration of the indigestion and cough remedies.

20) **Mixtures:** These are the most common form of liquid orals preparations usually with aqueous vehicle and the medicaments may be in solution or suspension.

21) **Mouthwashes:** These are similar to gargles but are used for oral hygiene and to treat infections of the mouth.

22) **Nasal Drops:** These are solutions of drugs that are instilled into the nose with a dropper. They are usually aqueous because oily drops inhibit movement of cilia in the nasal mucosa and long term use may cause Lipoidal Pneumonia.

23) **Ointment:** These are semisolids, greasy preparations for external use to skin, rectum and nasal mucosa.

24) **Paediatric Drops:** Occasionally, the children's dose of a preparations is very small and stability considerations preclude dilution to 5 ml. Then the dose is prescribed as a fraction of ml and is given by a calibrated dropper.

25) **Paints:** These are liquids for application to the skin or mucosa, usually with a soft brush. Skin paints often have a volatile solvent that evaporates quickly to leave a dry or resinous film of medicament.

    Throat pains are more viscous due to high concentration of Glycerin.

26) **Pastes:** These are semi-solid preparation for external application that differ from similar products in containing high proportion of finely powdered

medicaments. The base may be anhydrous or water soluble. Their stiffness makes them useful as protective coating.

27) **Pastilles:** Pastilles are solid medicated preparations intended to dissolve slowly in the mouth. They are softer than lozenges and their basis is either glycerol or acacia and sugar.

28) **Pills:** Pills are oral dosage forms that have largely been replaced by tablets and capsules. They are spherical or less often, ovoid and usually sugar-coated.

29) **Poultices:** These are paste like preparations used externally to reduce inflammation because they retain heat well. After heating, the preparation is spread thickly on a dressing and applied, as hot as the patient can bear it, to the affected area.

30) **Powders:** Powders may be defined as the fine particles which are result of combination or granulation of the dry substance.

    A Powder can be mixture of drugs or chemicals which are uniformly mixed together and presented in dry form. Powders are intended for internal and external usages.

31) **Solutions:** These are used for many purposes. For some of these sterility is necessary, e.g. Parenteral, Peritoneal dialysis and Anticoagulant solutions, Bladder irrigations and Dermatological solutions for application to broken skin. Non-sterile solutions are used orally and externally.

32) **Solution Tablets:** These are compressed tablets that are dissolved in water to produce solution for application to the skin or mucosa. They are formed to dissolve quickly.

33) **Sprays:** Sprays are preparations of drugs in aqueous, alcoholic or glycerine containing media. They are applied to the mucosa of nose or throat with an atomiser or nebuliser.

34) **Syrups:** These are Aqueous concentrated, sucrose solutions with or without one or more medicaments.

    Organoleptic agents are added in syrups.

35) **Vitrellae:** Are thin walled glass capsules containing a volatile ingredients and protected by absorbent cotton wool and an outer silk bag. For use, in angina pectoris, these capsules are crushed and the vapours are inhaled.

36) **Extracts:** These are concentrated preparations containing the active principles of vegetable or animal drugs. The drugs are extracted with suitable solvents and the product is concentrated to Liquid or Dry or Soft Mass extracts.

37) **Glycerines:** These are solutions of medicaments in glycerol with or without addition of water.

38) **Infusions:** Fresh infusions, made by extracting drugs for a short time with cold or boiling water are no longer used because they quickly deteriorate as a result of microbial contamination and therefore must be used within 12 hours of preparation.

39) **Oxymels:** As the name suggests, these are preparations in which the vehicle is a mixture of acid (Acetic) and Honey.

40) **Spirits:** Spirits are alcoholic or Hydro-alcoholic solutions of volatile substances. Most are used as flavouring agents but a few have medicinal values.

41) **Tinctures:** These are alcoholic preparations containing the active principles of vegetable drugs. They are relatively weak compared with extracts.

42) **Aromatic Waters:** These are dilute, usually saturated, solutions of volatile oils or other volatile substances (Chloroform, Camphor and Menthol). They are mainly used as flavouring agents and carminatives.

4. DETERGENTS AND THEIR CONCENTRATION USED IN PHARMACEUTICALS AND HOSPITALS

Detergents are material used for cleaning and they help to remove the extraneous material from surfaces and, or objects.

Antiseptics are drugs that are applied to living tissues for the purpose of killing bacteria or inhibiting their growth.

Disinfectants are bactericidal (Bacteria killing) drugs that are applied to inanimate objects (Tables, Surgical dressing, instruments, bed Pans, dishes, rooms, wards, lavatories etc.) to destroy micro-organism and prevent infection.

Germicide is frequently used to cover both antiseptic and disinfectants.

Sanitizer is chemical agent used to reduce the number of bacterial contaminants to a safe level in items like the utensils and cutlery used in cafes, public eating houses and restaurants as prescribed by authorities.

Sr. No.	Brand Name	Active ingredients	Concentration	Applications
1.	Avipol	Anionic Liquid detergent of the sodium alkyl sulphate type.	1 % V/V	Tanks and Vessels in oral dosage forms.
2.	Glosol	-	5 % V/V	Floors of Toilets and Table tops in canteen.
3.	Liquid Soap	-	As is or may be diluted as per concentration required	For washing hands, Gloves and Machine parts.
4.	Teepol	Sodium benzene sulphate, alcohol ether sulphate and alcohol ethoxylate.	0.1 % V/V	It is multipurpose cleaning agent and used for cleaning of equipments, floors and glassware.
5.	Vim	Mixture of Detergents.	As is or as per requirement	Outer surface of tanks, Glass wares, Filter press, Other stainless steel equipments, Toilets, Floors, Areas behind sinks and Metal fittings.

❖❖❖

5. DISINFECTANTS & THEIR CONCENTRATIONS USED IN PHARMACEUTICALS & HOSPITALS

S.N.	Brand Name	Active ingredients	Concentration	Applications
1.	Cidex	Glutaraldehyde (2 %)	2 % V/V	Dilutions are not recommended.
2.	Dettol	Chlorxylenol and Terpineol	2.5 % V/V	Antiseptic for floor, tables, Hand wash, and as spray for air disinfection.
3.	Formalin	Formaldehyde	30 to 40 % to generate gas	Fumigation with Hot Water or with Potassium Permagnet.
4.	Sodium Hypochlorite Solution	Sodium Hypochlorite (NaOCl)	0.1 to 1 %	Disinfection of Clean surfaces and Decontamination of DM Water Plants and resins, Pipelines.
5.	Isopropyl Alcohol. (IPA)	Isopropyl Alcohol	70%	Sanitation of equipments, Work surfaces, and Hands areas behind sinks and metal fittings.
6.	Phenyle (Phenolic comp.)	Phenolic Compounds	1 – 3% or may be up to 5%.	Disinfection.

Mode of Action:

1) **Phenols:** Disruption of cells, Precipitation of cell protein, Inactivation of enzymes and Leakages of amino acids from cells.

2) **Alcohols:** Alcohols are protein denaturants. Alcohols are also solvents for lipids and hence they may damage lipid complexes in the cell membrane. They are also denaturating agents. Severe dehydration occurs under high concentration condition which would in turn result in bacteriostatic actions.

6. US FEDERAL STANDARD 209E CLASSIFICATION, TESTING AND MONITORING REPORTS

CLEAN ROOM CLASS DESIGNATION:

The proper way to designate class is to give the class in metric or English units along with the size or sizes of particles which are to be measured for quality or certify the class.

For example:

Class M 2.5 (at 0.2 μm and 0.5 μm) describes air with not more than 2650 particles per cubic meter of a size 0.2 μm and larger and not more than 353 particles per cubic meter of a size 0.5 μm and larger.

Class 10 (at 0.1 μm and 0.3 μm) describes air with not more than 350 particles per cubic foot of a size 0.1 μm and larger and not more than 30 particles per cubic foot of a size 0.3 μm and larger.

'U' DESCRIPTORS:

In addition, we may use a "U" descriptor to describe the number of ultra fine particles allowed per cubic meter or cubic foot of air. Ultra fine particles are described as particles between approximate - 0.02 μm diameter and the upper limit of the Discrete Particles Counter (DPC) being used (typically a condensation nuclei counter). The "U" descriptor is designated as follows:

U (X): means not more than x ultra fine particles per cubic meter of air.

Example:

U (100): means not more than 100 ultra fine particles per cubic meter of air.

Class M 1.5 (at 0.1 μm and 0.2 μm and 0.5 μm) U (2200):

It means that the air contains not more than 1240 particles of 0.1 μm and larger size per cubic meter, not more than 265 particles of 0.2 μm and larger size per cubic meter, not more than 35.3 particles of 0.5 μm and larger size per cubic meter, and not more than 2200 ultra fine particles per cubic meter.

But these are obsolete method, now ISO 14644 -1 Classification shall be used for your clean room classification.

PERIODIC MONITORING AND REQUIREMENTS IN TESTING REPORTS:

Unlike 209 D, 209 E (Obsolete) requires that in addition to initially verifying the clean room class requirements a plan for verification tests at periodic or other intervals shall be in place and conducted after the initial verification tests have been performed in order for the clean room to be certified.

MONITORING AND REPORTS REQUIREMENTS:

The following is to be reported along with the final results when reporting the certification or monitoring particle counts or ultra fine particles:

(a) Identification and location of the clean room (or clean zone).
(b) Identification of the DPC and it's calibration status.
(c) Background noise count for the DPC.
(d) Date and time when DPC was used.
(e) Clean Room (or Clean Zone) status: "As – built", "At rest", Operational, or as otherwise specified.
(f) Type of test, verification or monitoring.
(g) Target level of verification of the clean room or clean zone.
(h) Range(s) of the particle sizes measured.
(i) DPC inlet sample flow and sensor measured sample flow.
(j) Location of sampling points.
(k) Sampling schedule for verifications or sampling protocol for monitoring.
(l) Raw data for each sample point, as required.

7. FUMIGATION TECHNOLOGY FOR INDUSTRY AND HOSPITALS

Fumigation is a process of gaseous sterilization which is used for killing of micro-organisms and prevention of microbial growth in air, on surface of wall or floor. It is generally used in the pharmaceuticals, operation theatres, hospitals, hotels, offices and wherever required. Generally for fumigation, chemicals like formaldehyde and potassium permanganate is used. It is also helpful for removing lizards, cockroaches, cobwebs, rodents, flies and insects from the area.

PRINCIPLE

Formaldehyde (chemically H – CHO) in its pure form is a gas at room temperature, with a boiling point of –19°C but readily polymerises at temperature below 80°C to form white solid. The important polymer is Para formaldehyde, a colourless substance which rapidly yields formaldehyde on heating.

Formaldehyde is also marketed in aqueous solution as formalin which contains 37 to 40 per cent formaldehyde. The vapours can be generated from solid polymers such as Para formaldehyde or from a solution of 37 per cent formaldehyde in water (formalin). Formalin usually contains 37 per cent methanol to prevent polymerization. Its bactericidal power is superior to ethylene oxide but it has weak penetrating power and it is only a surface disinfectant.

Absorbed gas is very difficult to remove and long airing times are required. One of the disadvantage of this process is limited ability of formaldehyde vapours to penetrate covered surface.

Formalin and Para formaldehyde are two principle sources of formaldehyde. It is used for sterilization of air.

MODE OF ACTION

It's mechanism of action is thought to involve in the production of intermolecular cross link between proteins together with interaction with RNA and DNA. It acts as mutagenic and alkylating agent reacting with carbonyl, thiol and hydroxyl groups.

In order to be effective, the gas has to dissolved in the film of moisture surrounding the bacteria and for this reason relative humidity in the order of 75 % RH are required (limit humidity 60 – 80 per cent and temperature 22°C).

METHOD AND CONCENTRATION

Steam can be used to increase humidity and temperature in room up to required limit. Aerosol generator can be used to a generate fumes. Following are two different concentrations for fumigation:

1. 500 ml. formaldehyde and one liter distilled water for 28 cubic meter of area for four hours or overnight.

2. 170 g Potassium permanganate and 500 ml formaldehyde for 28 cubic meter for four hours or overnight.

These concentration may be changed after proper validation and keeping the supporting record.

PRECAUTIONS

1. Raw material, finished goods, intermediates or in process goods should be remove from the area of fumigation. If unavoidable cover it with thick polythene cover.
2. Formaldehyde fumes are irritating and toxic to human eye, nose and throat. Therefore use of nose-mask and goggles while doing fumigation is advisable.
3. Windows, doors should be closed. AC and AHU should be switched off before starting fumigation.
4. 'Area under fumigation, do not enter' status label should be displayed on either side of the entrance.
5. Intimation of fumigation and for additional rounds should be given to security.
6. Before entry into fumigated area, half an hour exhaust should be given.

Now-a-days this method is not Recommended, because of it's disadvantages. Hydrogen peroxide can be used using fogger for fumigation in pharmaceuticals.

HYDROGEN PEROXIDE FUMIGATION:

This is non-toxic, eco friendly, chlorine free, non-mutagenic fumigating agent. Various formulation of H_2O_2 are available in market having concentration of H_2O_2 10% with acidic pH and odourless. It is water miscible and it does not coat material. 10% market formulation may be used for fumigation. For 1000 ft^3 of area to be fumigated use 20% (i.e. 200 ml of solution in 800 ml of DM water) and spray it with the help of fogger for 30 min. Fogging may be done at 130 ml/minute rate. The contact time shall be at least one hour.

Mode of action: It is strong oxidizing agent. It oxidizes toxins and bacteria and make them inert.

Virosil Pharma ™ is preparation available in market in 10 % Hydrogen Peroxide concentration. The recommended concentration of the same are as below:

1) Surface disinfection – 5%.
2) Instrument disinfectant – 10 %.
3) Resin and filter disinfection – 1 to 3 % .
4) Storage tank disinfection – 5%.
5) Laundry disinfection – 10%.

8. CALIBRATIONS

Calibration can be defined as the set of operations that establish, under specified condition, the relationship between values indicated by an instrument or system for measuring (especially weighing, recording and controlling, or the values represented by a material measure, and the corresponding known values of reference equipment standard. Limit of acceptance of the results of measuring equipment should be established. Equipment shall be adequately inspected, cleaned, and maintained. Equipment used for generation measurement, or assessment of data shall be adequately tested, calibrated and or standardized. A laboratory shall establish schedules for such operations based on manufacturer's recommendations and laboratory reference.

STANDARDS FOR CALIBRATION:

GLP requires the laboratory's system of calibration and measurement be designed and operated to ensure that calibrations or tests and supporting measurements performed by the laboratory are traceable to national or international standards of measurements.

Use Certified Standards, if available for calibrations. Wherever the concept of traceability is not applicable in practice, the laboratory shall provide satisfactory evidence of correlation of calibration or test procedures.

List of equipments which requires calibration should be prepared for in-house calibration and External party calibrations equipments. List shall include minimum following information.

1. Name and Model No. of Equipment.
2. In-house Code No.
3. Location.
4. Capacity/Sensitivity.
5. Calibration Frequency.
6. Address for External Party Calibration.
7. Acceptance Limit (Tolerance Limit).
8. Reference to Master Equipment.

9. VALIDATIONS

Validation (US FDA) is establishing documented evidence which provides a high degree of assurance that a specified process will consistently produce a product meeting it's predetermined specifications and quality attributes.

Validations (WHO) is establishment and performance of activities required to obtain documented assurance that a manufacturing process or a part thereof - during routine use are correct so that specified requirements on process variables and product properties are complied with.

Validation is the process of evaluating products or analytical methods to ensure compliance with products or cleaning method requirements.

Validation is a concept that has been evolving continuously since its first formal appearance in United States in 1978. FDA and European Community for Medical Products (EC) has developed general non-mandatory guidelines.

Validation is a mandatory (Statutory requirement) in GMP. Validation master plan shall be prepared for regular validation in organization.

Validation and Testing:

Validation and testing are not same. Testing is defined as the identification of errors (difference between expected and actual results) in a system. Validation is defined as documented evidence that a system performance as expected. Validation includes testing but it is more - for instance, the checking the documentation for completeness and correctness.

Types of Validations:

Process Validations and Analytical Method Validations are two major types recognized. But Cleaning Method and utility validations are also another type to be considered for validations.

Importance of Validation:

Validation assures a great importance for - Quality Assurance and cost reduction. Validation produces product fit for intended use. Quality; Safety and Effectiveness may be designed and built into product.

Validation is key element in assuming the quality of the product.

10. URS, FAT, DQ, SAT, IQ, OQ, PQ OF MACHINE and EQUIPMENTS

Validation activities that centers on equipment, machine rather than process is referred as qualifications.

Qualifications are divided in to four parts:
* Design Qualifications.
* Installation Qualifications.
* Operational Qualifications.
* Performance Qualifications.

Now a days procurement of machine or equipment is not easy because of so much GMP documentation for any machine. But it is GMP requirement to document all events of procurement of machine. The document involved is also confusing to the most of the user. What document, at what time, what is to be incorporated in these document is still unclear to the most of people in the pharmacy and engineering. From the point of view of understanding following are the documents required to be prepared at the time of machine, equipment and software procurement. Following are the documents with sequence of their generation during the life of machine, equipment or soft ware.

1) URS,
2) DQ,
3) FAT,
4) SAT,
5) IQ,
6) OQ,
7) PQ.

All above documents shall be prepared for the one time in the life of system except PQ, PQ shall be repeated after scheduled interval through out the life of machine, equipment or software. But if the machine is to be relocated, location is changed, then based on movement, wear and tear prequalification (IQ, OQ and PQ) shall be performed. Some times only OQ and PQ can be performed based on change in site, and location. User has to decide the criteria for requalification based on criticality of occasion.

1. URS (Users Requirement Specifications): User department will raise the indent for his requirement regarding machine, equipment or software. He will give his requirement in one format called URS which includes the functional and technical specification for the machine, equipment soft ware. These specifications in the written formats is defined as URS. Suppose one software is required to production dept, then production department (or user) along with EDP department person will prepare the specification for the purchase of soft ware. URS shall be very specific, there should not be any confusion. Functional as well as technical aspects shall be clearly mentioned. Quantity of spares, change parts required shall be mentioned in URS. While preparing URS national, international rules and regulation shall be taken in to consideration, Environmental safety, Machine safety controls, health shall also be considered while preparing the URS. User should also give the other areas which are going to affect, if this machine is procured or which are the other areas, which needs to modify, such are environmental(AHU) control system. Also think whether this modification are possible and feasible, Will it impact on other existing systems. URS is supporting document for the preparation of DQ.

General format for URS is given below, but user can add much more information depending on machine, equipment or software.

NAME OF THE ORGANIZATION

USERS REQUIREMENT SPECIFICATIONS

Date: _____

Name of the User department:_____

Location   :_____

Name of the machine/equipment/software:_____

Purpose of the machine/equipment/software:_____

Other area of impact (AHU, movement, space):_____

Sr. No.	Parameters	Specification	Quantity /Remark
1.	Name		
2.	Model		
3.	Make		
4.	Capacity /sensitivity		
5.	Material of construction.		
6.	Instruments on machine		
7.	Calibrations		
8.	Spares		
9.	Change parts,		
10.	Tools		
11.	Documentation (FAT / SAT / Qualifications / Manuals)		
12.	Environmental / health safety requirements and controls		
13.	Critical control Points.		
14.	Other		

Prepared by   Reviewed by   Approved by

At the end review, revise and approve the URS, the next step is Design Qualifications.

2. DESIGN QUALIFICATION: Once the URS is finalized, the engineering department, R and D, User, QA, department will prepare the design qualification, which includes drawings, calculations, samples, and other design documents. Identify the manufacturer and These DQ will then be sent to various manufacturers of machines for their comments and Quotation. Manufacturer will study the design. If design is OK, from the construction point of view manufacturer will quote to the user. If the design is not OK from the construction, national and international standards point of view, machine manufacturer will prepare new drawing from the construction as well as legal and user point of view, Then this drawings and specifications will be send to Users for approval . User will amend / revise the DQ if possible, Approve the revised the drawing and DQ . Finalize the commercial aspects of the dealing and send the final DQ with the purchase order to the machine manufacturer.

Some times User provides the URS to the Machine manufacturer, and manufacturer prepares the design qualification, these DQ will be sent to user for review and approval. DQ can be prepared either by User or manufacturer, but it should be reviewed and approved by User as well as machine manufacturer. So DQ is commercial as well as technical agreement between machine manufacture and users .

After finalization of design qualifications construction of machine will start . During the period of construction of machine user should visit the manufacturer site in order to check whether the construction of machine is going as per design or not. Any deviation from DQ or any mistake will be identified on line and it will avoid the loss of time and money, if inspected at the end of construction . After completion of manufacturing of machine, machine manufacturer will review the as build construction of machine as per DQ and then he will prepare the next document FAT.

DQ protocol contents:

General,
Document Approval,
Version control,
Abbreviations,
Objective,
Responsibility (User and manufacturer)
URS
Equipment description.
Technical design specification of machine . equipments.
Functional design specification
Technical specifications of the components used
Cabling / power details,

- Utility required details
- Identification of components for calibrations test
- MOC and Finish of all components
- P and I Drawings / Other drawings / calculations
- Critical control Parameters.
- Safety features.
- Change control and deviation procedure.
- DQ review and Approval.
- Appendix.

Any other important information can be incorporated which is related to design of the machine.

3) FAT (Factory Acceptance Test): After completion of construction of machine, inspection of machine at the factory site as per DQ shall be carried out by user/client. This inspection before delivery to the user site is called FAT. Manufacturer of machine will prepare the factory acceptance test protocol based on DQ, as built machine specifications, calibration certificates, documents of spares and equipments mounted on machine, then this FAT protocol will be sent to client/user for review and approval. User will review and approve the FAT protocol. The user/client will visit the factory of machine manufacturer to inspect the ready for delivery machine as per FAT protocol.

FAT is generally first stage of system testing and should be witnessed by the customer prior to agreement for the machine to be delivered to the user site. The manufacturer should ensure that machine can pass the predefined test prior to the witnessed acceptance testing so as to minimize the risk of any testing.

During factory acceptance testing, users should test and verify every component of machine for operation and functioning as per predefined acceptance criteria. User will also verify as built drawing with machine, calibration of instruments, documents of calibrations, other calibration and MOC certificates. Check the safety controls, signals and critical control points as per DQ. Perform the functional test as per requirement and FAT protocol.

If the machine complies the URS, DQ and Acceptance criteria, it is recommended for the delivery to the site. The fat protocol and report shall be reviewed, approved by manufacturer and user after completion of FAT and before delivery of the machine.

If the m/c does not complies the acceptance criteria, modifications shall be approved through change control system. or can be accepted with deviation system. RE FAT shall be carried out in case of modifications. Machine will be delivered/shipped to site after completion FAT.

FAT protocol content:
  General,
  Document Approval,
  Version control,
  Abbreviations,
  Objective,
  Responsibility (User and manufacturer)
  Procedure
  Completing and correcting documents,
  Instruments and tools.
  Equipment description.
  Tests and Checks
  Equipment / machine components,
  Material of construction.
  Change Parts
  Operational Checks and Tests.
  Documentation Checks
  Utilities checks
  Dimensions of machine/equipments.
  Drawings and wiring diagrams, layout with electrical components.
  Personnel's performing FAT.
  Identification f personnel trained
  Change control and deviation procedure.
  FAT review and Approval.
  Appendix.
  Acceptance criteria
  Summery and results .
  Conclusion.

4) SAT (Site Acceptance test): Once the machine has been delivered to the user site. It will be received by the user as per SOP of receipt of machines and equipments. Manufacturer will sent engineering for installation of machine at the user site. Machine will be removed out from the packaging, then machine will be inspected for any damage during shipment and transport and handling. Check the spares, parts, tools as per packing list and record the observations. Also check the documents such as manuals and excise and transport documents. Hand over the documents to the concern department. Carry out the sanitation and cleaning of machine as per SOP before transferring it to the concerned department clean atmosphere. After sanitation wrap the machine with film or poly ethylene paper. Transfer the machine to the intended location. Install the machine properly and connect the utilities and service lines such as water, air, vacuum to the machine. Area qualifications shall be completed prior to the installation of machine in new facility. After ensuring proper installation and connections of power and service lines machine is ready for SAT. Site acceptance test is the process of inspection with documentation the machine at the user site for any change, damage, ware and tare during the transportation and shipping before installation of machine.

SAT protocol will be prepared by the machine manufacturer and it will be reviewed by both manufacturer and user before implementation. Machine manufacturer will also check and verify the site for machine installation, such as temperature, humidity, flooring, power supply, service lines, etc, if it not as per requirement to the machine, machine manufacturer can ask to rectify the things prior to FAT and IQ. SAT is performed to check that, is there any wear and tear or damage to the machine during transport/ shipping vibrations, due to handling, loading and unloading . Both the critical and non critical parameters and functions shall be challenged during SAT. It shall also include: Component unpacking, Inspection and storage, Installation and power Up, Installation of instruments, Instrument recalibration, functional testing, as built engineering drawing, Operation and maintenance manuals, and any other checks.

Record the observations and results in SAT protocols if machine complies SAT specifications and acceptance criteria. Review and Approve the SAT protocol and report after completion of documentation machine is recommended for IQ .

Now perform the IQ, OQ and PQ as per protocols, Up to IQ, OQ it is responsibility of machine manufacturer as well as User. PQ shall be carried out by user on actual production or process.

We will consider the Software system for IQ/OQ and PQ.

5) IQ (Installation Qualifications): IQ is documented verification that the system is installed satisfactorily and is compliant with appropriate engineering codes. Manufacturer recommendations and approved specifications, and that the instrument is calibrated and all services are available and of adequate.

IQ protocol for software system should cover:
1) Validation file
2) Security access,
3) Environmental
4) System diagnostics.
5) Hardware components
6) Instrument installation and calibration.
7) Electrical power and circuit protection.
8) Instrument air supply.
9) Loop wiring / tubing and cabling.
10) Hardware configuration.
11) Software backup and restoration.
12) General system inspection.

On issue of satisfactory and approved IQ summary report the computer system can proceed to OQ.

3) Operational Qualifications (OQ): (For software system)

The computer system must be powered up and checked to ensure it is functioning correctly. This may involve observing and recording system status lamp and /or rerunning diagnostic checks.

OQ protocol should cover:
1) Operator interface and screen displays.
2) Input/output signals
3) Data storage, Backup, and restore.
4) Electronic records and Electronic Signatures, archive and retrieval.
5) System report printout.
6) Trend display.
7) Alarm, events and messages.
8) Process and safety interlocks.
9) Control and monitoring loop operation.
10) Software process logic and sequence operation.
11) SOP preparation and approval.
12) Power failure and data recovery.

Qualification testing of electronic record will need to:
1) Verify GMP electronic raw data in the system.
2) Verify GMP electronic records within scope.
3) Justify electronic records not within scope.
4) Verify use of hybrid record.
5) Verify ability to generate paper copy of electronic record.
6) Verify controls for systems.
7) Verify electronic record responsible person.
8) Verify access and physical security.
9) Verify operational checks.
10) Verify secure and no modifiable audit trails.
11) Test data integrity.
12) Verify accuracy of generated hard copy.
13) Verify management, record periodic revision, renewal and misuse detection controls for password authority to electronic records.
14) Verify the use of document encryption and appropriate digital signature standard to ensure record authenticity, integrity, and confidentiality.

Qualification testing of electronic signatures will need to:
1) Verify electronic signature applied to GMP electronic records.
2) Justify electronic signature not within scope.
3) Verify within scope electronic signatures as communicated to regulatory authority.
4) Verify individual responsibility / accountability for electronic signature.
5) Test identification code / password or biometric electronic signature / devices.
6) Test immutable linking of electronic signatures to electronic records.
7) Verify management, record, periodic revision, renewal, and misuse detection controls for electronic signatures.

4) Performance Qualification (PQ): (For soft ware system)

Performance qualification is documented verification that the computerized operations consistently performs as intended in the URS through out all the anticipated operating ranges.

As relevant, OQ test procedures can therefore be used for PQ testing. In particular, consideration should be given to tests directly related to data integrity and system repeatability with focus on critical parameters such as, System access security, Diagnostic checks, Operator interface, Software installation verification, software backup and restoration. Control and monitoring loop operation, alarm, event and messages handling, safety operational interlocks, software logic functions and authentic process sequence operation, standard operating procedures verifications, data record and reports, Power loss and recovery.

On issue of satisfactory and approved PQ summary report, it is demonstrated that computer system supports computerized operations and conditional on satisfactory process validation is available for use in the GMP operating environment.

11. WHO – GMP MINIMUM DOCUMENTS CHECK LIST

Following are the minimum documents required, in addition to this more documents may be required:

1. Site Master File.
2. Air Quality Manuals.
3. Water Quality Manual.
4. All process related SOPs.
5. Standard Testing Procedures and Specifications for Raw Material, Packing Material, Intermediate, and Finished Product.
6. Market Complaints Record.
7. Calibration Record.
8. Process Validations.
9. Analytical Method Validations.
10. Cleaning Method Validations.
11. DQ/IQ/OQ/ PQ.
12. Internal Quality Audit Reports.
13. Medical Check up Record of Employee.
14. Master Formula Records.
15. Batch Manufacturing Records.
16. Batch Packing Records.
17. List of Machine and Equipments for Production and QA/QC(QU: Quality Unit).
18. List of Competent Technical Staff.
19. Latest FDA Approved Plan.
20. Short Term, Long Term and Photo stability. (Zone wise.)
21. Approved Vender List and Vender Evaluation Record.
22. Employee Training Record.
23. Pest Control, Premises Maintenance Record (Sanitation, Cleaning etc.).
24. Cloth Washing and Laundering Record.
25. Preventative and Break Down Maintenance Record.
26. All other Records as per WHO GMP Guidelines.
27. Annual product quality review (APQR)
28. Growth promotion test evaluation.
29. Preservative efficacy testing.
30. Risk analysis and critical control point documentation

12. SCHEDULES FROM DRUG AND COSMETIC ACT 1940

DRUG AND COSMETIC ACTS SCHEDULES:

The First Schedule -

Names of books of the Ayurvedic, Sidha and the Unanai Tibb systems of medicines. These are authoretive books of these three systems of medicines recognized for the purpose of this Act.

The Second Schedule -

Standard to be complied with by (Allopathic Drugs and Homoeopathic Medicines) which are imported, manufactured, sold or distributed in the country.

13. SCHEDULES FROM DRUG AND COSMETIC RULES 1945

Drug and Cosmetic Rules Schedules: 1945

Schedule A	Applications for licenses for import, manufacture, and sale of drug and cosmetics, the forms in which the licenses are granted and renewed and other forms.
Schedule B	Fees for analysis of drug and cosmetics that have to be paid to the Central Drug Laboratories or other Govt. Laboratories.
Schedule C	List of Biological and Immunological Products, Antibiotics and Opthalmic lotions and Ointments and all products for parenteral use (Injections)
Schedule C (I)	List of drugs, from biological origin, namely Alkaloids, Hormones, Vitamins and Antibiotics for oral use.
Schedule D	Exemptions that have been granted to drugs and importers of drugs from complying with the requirements of import of drugs and also the conditions for such exemptions.
Schedule E	List of poisons for which labeling and other requirements were to be complied with. This schedule has been deleted
Schedule E (I)	List of poisonous substances under the Ayurvedic, Sidha and Unani Systems of medicines.
Schedule F	Special provisions to be complied with, for the manufacture, testing and labeling of biological products for human use like Sera and Vaccines. These provisions have now been deleted. The requirements for running Blood Banks and other requirements are now included in this schedule.
Schedule F (I)	Special provisions to be complied with for the manufacture, testing and labeling of Veterinary Biological Products.
Schedule F (II)	Standards for Surgical Dressings.
Schedule F (III)	Standards for Umbilical Tapes.
Schedule FF	Additional standards for Ophthalmic preparations.
Schedule G	List of drugs which should be used by patient under medical supervision and which shall be labeled with the words "Caution - It is dangerous to take this preparation except under medical supervision".
Schedule H	List of drugs which are to be sold by retail against the prescription of Registered Medical Practitioner and which shall be labeled with words "Schedule H Drug. Warning: to be sold by retail on the prescription of a Registered Medical Practitioner only."

Schedule I	List of poisons and particulars about the proportion of poison in certain cases. Schedule I was linked with Schedule E. When schedule E was deleted in 1982, Schedule I was also deleted.
Schedule J	Names of diseases and ailments (by whatever name described) which a drug may not purport to prevent or cure by means of claims made on the label of the container of the drug.
Schedule K	Names of drugs or classes of drugs which are exempted from complying with the provisions for manufacture, sale and standards of drugs and the conditions of such exemption.
Schedule L	List of drugs which were required to be sold by retail against the prescription of Registered Medical Practitioner. Subsequently the drugs listed in Schedule L were transferred to Schedule H. Schedule L was deleted in 1982.
Schedule M	Good Manufacturing Practices (GMP) and the requirements of premises, plant and equipments for manufacture of drugs.
Schedule M (I)	Requirements for factory premises of Homeopathic Medicines.
Schedule M (II)	Requirements for factory premises of Cosmetics.
Schedule M (III)	Requirements of factory premises for manufacture of Medical Devices.
Schedule N	List of minimum equipments, requirements of premises for the effective running of a pharmacy.
Schedule O	Standards for Disinfectant fluids.
Schedule P	Life Period and Conditions of Storage of Drugs.
Schedule P(I)	Pack sizes of drugs
Schedule Q	List of Coal Tar colours permitted to be used in cosmetics.
Schedule R	Standards and labeling requirements of Condoms, Copper T and Contraceptive Tubal Rings.
Schedule R(I)	Standards to be complied with by medical devices.
Schedule S	Standards for Cosmetics.
Schedule T	Requirements of factory premises and hygienic conditions to be complied with by the manufacturer of Ayurvedic, Siddha and Unani Drugs.
Schedule U	Particulars to be shown in the manufacturing records, record of raw materials and in the analytical records of drugs.
Schedule V	Standards for patient and proprietary medicines and the maximum and minimum quantities of vitamins that are permitted to be added in such preparations for oral use.
Schedule W	Names of drugs which shall be marketed under generic names only.
Schedule X	Names of psychotropic drugs for which special control measures have been laid down.
Schedule Y	Requirements and guidelines on clinical trials for import and manufacture of new drugs.

❖ ❖ ❖

14. FOOD AND DRUG ADMINISTRATION (FDA) LICENSING FORMS

Only selected and frequently used forms are mentioned:

1) **Import licenses:**
   Form 8 to Form 12 B

2) **Sales License:**
   (Forms - 19, 19 A, 19 AA, 19 C, 20, 20A, 20 B, 20 BB, 20F, 20 G, 21, 21 A, 21 B, 21BB, 21 C, and 21CC.)

   Form 19 - is the application which has to be made for grant or renewal of sale license by retail or Wholesale to the State Licensing Authority.

   Form 20 - is the License granted to sell by retail drug, drugs other than Schedule C and C (1) drugs.

   Form 20B - is the license granted to sell by wholesale drugs other than Schedule C and C(1).

   Form 21 - is the license granted to sell by Retail drugs specified in Schedule C and C (1).

   Form 21B - is the license granted to sell by Wholesale to distribute drugs specified in Schedule C and C (1).

3) **License to Manufacture Drugs:**
   (Form 24, 24A, 24B, 24F, 25, 25A, 25B, 25F, 26, 26A, 26B, 26F, 26G, 26H, 27A, 27B, 27C, 27D, 28A, 28B. 28C, 28D, and 30.)

   Form 24 - is the application which has to be made for the grant or renewal of a license to manufacture drugs other than, Schedule C, C(1), and X drugs.

   Form 24A - is the application which has to be made for the grant or renewal of loan license to manufacture drugs other than, Schedule C, C(1), and X drugs.

   Form 25 - is the license granted to manufacture drugs other than Schedule C, C (1) and X drugs.

   Form 25A - is the Loan license granted to manufacture drugs other than Schedule C, C(1) and X drugs.

   Form 27 - is the application which has to be made for grant or renewal of a license to manufacture drugs included in Schedule C, C(1) drugs excluding Schedule X drugs.

   Form 27A - is the application which has to be made for grant or renewal of a Loan license to manufacture drugs included in Schedule C, C(1) drugs excluding Schedule X drugs.

Form 27C - is the application for grant or renewal of license for operation of blood bank, processing of Whole Blood for components.

Form 27D - is the application for grant or renewal of license to manufacture Large Volume Parenterals/Sera and Vaccines (and biotechnology products).

Form 28 - is the license granted to manufacture drug included in Schedule C and C(1) excluding Schedule X drugs.

Form 28A - is the Loan license granted to manufacture drugs included in Schedule C and C(1) excluding Schedule X.

Form 28C - is the license granted to operate Blood bank, for processing Whole Blood for Components.

Form 28D - is the License granted to, manufacture Large Volume Parentrals/Sera and Vaccine.

Form 29 - is the license granted to manufacture drugs for the purpose of examination, test or analysis.

Form 30 - is the application which has to be made for grant of a license to manufacture drugs for the purpose of examination, test or analysis.

4) License for Homeopathic medicines:

(Form 19B, 20C, 20D, 20E, 24C, 25C and 26C).

Form 19B - Application for grant of license to sell by Wholesale or by Retail Homeopathic Medicines.

Form 20C - Retail sale Homeopathic Medicines License.

Form 20D - Wholesale selling Homeopathic Medicines License.

Form 24C - is the application for grant or renewal of a license to manufacture Homeopathic Medicines or a license to mfg. Potentised preparation, from back potencies.

Form 25 C - is the license granted to manufacture Homeopathic Medicines.

Form 26C - is the certificate of renewal to manufacture Homeopathic Medicines.

5) Licence for Ayurvedic, Siddha or Unani Drugs:

(Form 24D, 24E, 25D, 25E, 26D, and 26E.)

Form 24D - is the application for grant or renewal of a license to manufacture Ayurvedic, Siddha or Unani Drugs.

Form 24E - is the application for grant or Renewal of loan License to manufacture Ayurvedic, Siddha or Unani Drugs.

Form 25E - is the Loan licence granted or Renewal of Loan License to manufacture the Ayurvedic, Siddha or Unani Drugs.

6) **Licenses for Cosmetics:**

(Form 31, 31A, 32, 32A, 33 and 33A)

Form 31 - is the application for grant or renewal of a license to manufacture cosmetics.

Form 31A - is the application for grant or renewal of loan license to manufacture cosmetics.

Form 32 - is license to manufacture cosmetics.

Form 32A - Loan license to manufacture cosmetics.

7) **Approval of Institutions (Private Testing Laboratories) for carrying out tests on Drugs and Cosmetics:**

(Form 36, 37, 38, and 39)

Form 36 - is the application for grant or renewal or approval for carrying out tests on drugs and cosmetics.

Form 37 - is the approval granted to an institution for carrying out tests on drugs and cosmetics.

Form 38 - is the certificate of renewal of approval granted to an institution for carrying out tests on drugs and cosmetics.

Form 39 - Report of test or analysis by approved institution.

15. LIST OF MACHINERIES AND EQUIPMENTS FOR PHARMACEUTICAL PLANT WITH ADVANCED TECHNOLOGY

CHANGE ROOM:
1. Stainless steel cross over bench.
2. Stainless steel shoe racks.
3. Apron cabinet with UV light.
3. Hand wash system.
4. Auto hand drier system.
5. Stainless steel foot deep trays or foot wash system.
6. Hand gloves cabinet.
7. Bowel with stand for disinfectant or IPA.
8. Stainless steel lockers.
9. Shoe polishing and cleaning cabinet.
10. Stainless steel drain traps (U traps).

CANTEEN:
1. Stainless steel baking oven.
2. Stainless steel chapatti plate and puffer.
3. Stainless steel stock pot range.
4. Stainless steel cafeteria service counter.
5. Stainless steel hot cabinet.
6. Stainless steel canteen tables.
7. Stainless steel pot racks.
8. Stainless steel linen trolley.
9. Stainless steel work table.
10. Stainless steel vessels.
11. Stainless steel bussing trolley .
12. Stainless steel can trolley.
13. Stainless steel hot food trolley.
14. Stainless steel sink unit.
15. Stainless steel kitchen cabinet.

PARENTERAL PRODUCT MANUFACTURING:
Solution, Suspension, Powders and Ointments:

Water system (Softener, EDI water treatment plant, Multicolumn automatic distillation plant with PLC control .RO system, DM water plant with auto regeneration system. Ozonization, Alum dosing, UV sterilization filtration unit. Online flow meter, pH meter, UV intensity meter, conductivity meter. Stainless Steel 316/ Stainless Steel 316 L water storage tank with Stainless Steel loop recirculation system. Heating facility to water tank, Inbuilt Steam In Place (SIP) and Clean In Place (CIP) facility to tank, sanitation facility, calibrated flow meters for water dispensing system, (Clean Room complying to ISO clean room standard.14644, Temperature and Humidity control in built in AHU, SS air risers, and grills. Manometers and UV lights (for disinfections.) Stainless Steel pendant. Air shower Class M 3.5 or ISO Class 5.

Stainless Steel Storage tanks. Stainless Steel double door interlocked pass box with UV lights. Stainless Steel garment cabinets. Pressure vessels, (Stainless Steel).Stainless Steel pallets, Inter lock air lock doors. Vial and ampoule SS Boxes. Stainless Steel drain traps. Stainless Steel trolley. Stainless Steel tables. Stainless Steel chairs and tools. Electronic balances of appropriate capacities, sensitivity and printing facility. Stainless Steel scoops, spatulas, trays of different capacities. Membrane filter assembly, cartridge filter holders. Stainless Steel jacketed tanks with SIP and CIP facility in built stirrer, homogenizer, aeration facility whatever is required. Silicon tubing's. Stainless Steel transfer pumps, peristaltic pump Stainless Steel pipelines, filter press, PLC control double door, hot air sterilize with printer and data logger. PLC control double door moist heat sterilizer with data logger and printer. ETO Sterilizer . Automatic vial washing machine GMP model and with air wash. Automatic ampoule Washing machine with air wash. (0.3 μ) Automatic vial filling machine with bunging machine. Automatic rubber stopper washing machine. Automatic GMP model rubber stoppering and cap sealing machine. Automatic ampoule filling and sealing machine.

Ointment MFG tanks with transfer pump, temperature control, printing and with CIP and SIP system. Automatic and VIDEO system for ampoule and vial optical inspection. Ampoule and vial leak test machine. Measuring cylinders of suitable capacities.

Planetary mixer for powder mixing, Pulverizer, automatic powder filling in to vial and sealing machine. Including rubber stoppering. Automatic ointment tube filling sealing and crimping machine. Automatic ampoule and vial labeling machine. Automatic label, carton, and catch cover overprinting machine. Inkjet coding machine. Bar code printer and scanner ,ampoule blister packing machine. Auto cartoner machine. Auto DFC box filling, BOPP sealing and loading machine. Auto DFC box weighing machine with printer.

Automatic shrink wrap machine. Automatic strapping machine. Ointment jar filling and sealing machine. Automatic sticker labeling machine. Automatic poly bag sealing machine.

Polyethylene granules bottle making and filling/sealing machine. Stainless Steel oilcan and tool boxes. Stainless Steel conveyor belts and Stainless Steel turn tables. Cold storage cabinet.

Ionizers for particle control in clean room. Air curtains of appropriate velocity and CFM. Automatic prefilled syringes filling sealing and labeling machine. Boiler, Non-lubricating air compressor, water chillier, cooling towers, DG sets, vacuum system.

AEROSOLS /INHALERS:

Process vessels with SIP and CIP system. lobe pump. Filler, valve fitting, crimping and gasketing machines. Toner for propellant liquification balances automatic labelling machine. Shrink wrap machine. canister leak test checking machine. canister destruction cabinet. water and air system as per Injectables. Meter dose counter machine. Balance general and packing machineries are same as injectables. Pressure vessels.

TABLETS:

Rapid mixer granulator with sifter facility. Planetary mixer. sieve sifter, Multi mill with dust collector. FBD with auto temperature control and print facility. Paste vessel. Fluid bed spiral granulator and drier.

Auto MFG and PCK line for tablet Includes following:

One tank auto sifting, dry mixing, paste making, damp mass, wet mixing, drying, dry sifting and sizing of granules, lubrication, auto transfer of granules to compression machine, auto compression and in process auto check and record and printing, auto blister packing with multistage, auto checking, counting, carton filling, DFC packing, (sealing overprinting with weighing of box and printing). Metal detector, polishing pan, deburing and dedusting machine,

PLC base, auto GMP model double, triple rotary compression machine. Dies and punches cabinet, microprocessor control auto tablet counting, bottle filling and sealing machine. Roll compactor, triple roller mill. Colloidal mill, oscillating granulator. Slugging machine.

Punch: Maintenance, Inspection kit and Storage cabinet.

Chemical dehumidifiers, hardness tester, digital vernier calliper, microprocessor control . friability tester, high accuracy balances, auto PLC control DT apparatus.

PLC Dissolution test apparatus, pH meter with temperature display. Tablet inspection and sorting table with conveyor. Blister packing machine, strip packing machine, aluminium – aluminium Blister packing machine, leak test apparatus, auto PLC pinhole inspection unit. Strip counter, auto cartoner, and Box filling machine, BOPP sealing machine, Inkjet printer, Bar code printing and scanning machine, auto carton label and catch cover batch coding machines. IR moisture balance.

CAPSULES:

Accurate and appropriate capacity balances, scoops, spatula and spoons all made up of Stainless Steel. Stainless Steel mass mixer, octagonal blender, planetary mixer, drum blender, close type sieve sifter, Stainless Steel storage vessels, communating mill, automatic hard gelatin capsule filling machine, auto capsule polishing and inspection sorting machine, soft gelatin capsule filling sealing, polishing and inspection machine. Blister packing machine, strip packing machine, Aluminium – Aluminium. Blister packing machine, leak test apparatus, Auto PLC pinhole inspection unit. Strip counter, auto cartoner, and box filling machine, BOPP sealing machine, Inkjet printer, Bar code printing and scanning machine, auto carton label and catch cover batch coding machines. chemical dehumidifiers, PLC control DT apparatus, digital vernier calliper, pH meter, balances.

Liquid Orals:

Water system refer injection part. Balances, stainless steel scoops, spatula, spoons trays, vessels, jacketed manufacturing tank with homogenizer, stirrer, measuring strip or tank on load cell, with Clean in place facility Suitable liquid (RM) transfer facility stainless steel pipelines,

Ordinary sugar addition facility to tank, filter press, transfer pump, lobe pumps, colloidal mill Jacketed, Insect killer, storage tanks, turn tables, stainless Steel conveyor belts, auto GMP bottle washing machine with hot air washes, empty bottle inspection machine, filled bottle inspection cabinet, automatic bottle filling sealing machine with volume control, No bottle-no liquid, no cap-no bottle-facility counter, no liquid-no fill facility. Automatic bottle labeling machine, cartoner, Box filler, BOPP sealing machine and on line DFC Overprinting, Weighing, Printing facility, shrink wrap machine, packing conveyor belt. pH meter, with temperature and pH display.

External Preparations:

Liquid, Powder, Ointment and Creams:

For liquid refer liquid orals. Powder sifting machine, mass mixer or planetary mixer, double cone blender, automatic powder filling sealing machine, powder bottle capping machine, plastic bottle printing machine, cartoner machine, box-BOPP sealing machine, label, carton auto overprinting machine. weighing balances (Electronic) water phase tank, oil phase tank and ointment cream final mixing tank, all with jacket, temperature control, stirrer, emulsifier, phase transfer pump with filters, pH meter, Brookfield visco meter, penitrometer, heating, cooling facility, ointment jar filling sealing and labeling machine, ointment tube filling sealing and crimping machine, auto cartoner, auto Box filling, BOPP sealing and overprinting machine, sticker labeling machine, shrink wrap machine.

QUALITY CONTROL

(a) Microbial Testing

- Laminar Air Flow
- Zone Reader
- Colony Counter
- Microscope
- Inoculating Loop.
- Autoclave Fully Auto
- Incubator
- BOD Incubator
- Weighing Balance
- Cycle Mixer
- Air Sampler
- Refrigerator.
- Sonicator

(b) Sterility, Pyrogen and Abnormal Toxicity Testing

Animal House with testing animals such as albino rabbit, albino mice, etc. Stainless Steel Animal cages, Animal feed trays, Animal holders, LAL test kits, Laminar Air Flow, sterility test membrane filtration assembly. Pyrogen testing equipment.

(c) Chemical and Instrumental Analysis:

All instruments shall have Automatic and Self calibration and Printing facility.

The instruments depends on the types of products to be tested:

Auto sampling HPC, FTIR, NIR, Gas chromatography, gel chromatography, thin layer chromatography, KBR pallet press, flame photo meter, pH meter, hot plate, hot water bath, distilled water still, heating mantles, sonicator, Lab. stirrer, magnetic stirrer, Shaker water bath, Kjeldahl distillation assembly .Stability and photo stability chamber, Karl fisher's auto titrater, hot air oven, muffle furnace, electric bunsen, vacuum oven, brook field viscometer, penetrometer, digital melting point apparatus, instrument sterilizer, desiccator's cabinet, auto pipette washer and drier, fluoculator, centrifuge, Griffin flask shaker, sieve shaker rotap, vortex mixer, digital bulk density apparatus, digital tablet/capsule DT apparatus, dissolution test apparatus auto sampler, tablet friability test apparatus, UV inspection cabinet, fuming chamber, spectrophotometer, tablet hardness tester, Keep's H_2S Gas apparatus, leak test apparatus, desiccators, IR moisture balance, polarimeter, refractometer, conductivity meter, colorimeter, colour measuring kit, colour grading kit, Ultrasonic cleaner, flame photo meter. Total dissolved solid meter, digital dissolved oxygen meter, TOC measurement equipment, UV Intensity measurement meter, turbidity meter/Nephelometer, LUX meter, aerosol leak test apparatus, DFC bursting strength machine, vernier caliper, screw gauge, Class A glass wares, Calibrated thermometers, hygrometers, pressure gauges, manometers, auto titrater etc.

16. ACCELERATED STABILITY TESTING AND SHELF LIFE CALCULATION

Simplified graphic techniques have been employed to predict the breakdown that may occur over prolonged periods of storage at normal conditions, **Free** and **Blythe** describe such a technique for liquid products where the decomposition behaves according to the general kinetic laws.

For example, if degradation of product is following First Order Kinetic Reaction the time required for loss of potency at several temperature and to reach 90 % of the potency of the theoretic potency is calculated by plotting a graph and lines. These time values are plotted at different temperature can be plotted and time for 10 % loss of potency at room temperature can be obtained from the resulting straight line by extrapolation to 25°C. If the extrapolated data shows that the time to reach 90 % potency at room temperature is too rapid to provide an adequate shelf life for the product, it is possible to determine the overages required for the product to maintain at least 90 % potency for a prescribed time.

Certain Kinetic paths have been described by Kenan, Which can be used for the purpose of certain comparison during formulation development work. Using standard kinetic equations, Kenan calculated the paths that reactions would follow, if a 10% potency loss in two years at room temperature were permitted. By choosing activation energies of 10 and 20 kcal/mol, both of which are conservatively low, and by plotting the time in months that a formulation would take to drop to 90 % potency versus 1/T, you can get the figures as shown in table below:

Maximum and minimum time at which potency must be at least 90 % of label claim at the temperature indicated in order to predict a shelf life of Two Years at Room Temperature.

Temperature	Maximum time for study	Minimum time for study
37°	12 months	6.4 months
45°C	8.3 months	2.9 months
60°C	4.1 months	3 weeks
85°C	06 weeks	2.5 days

If the potency of the formulation is found to remain above 90% of it's original concentration after storage at the various temperature for certain periods of time given in the table, there is good assurance that the formulation will meet the requirement of two year shelf life. Thus. If the assay are over 90 % of original potency at the minimum times at representative temperature, in all probability, the assay will be over 90 % after two years at room temperature.

❖❖❖

17. INTERNATIONAL CONFERENCE ON HARMONIZATION (ICH, CTD AND ECTD)

Harmonization of regulatory requirements was pioneered by the European Community, in the 1980s, as the EC (now the European Union) moved towards the development of a single market for pharmaceuticals. The success achieved in Europe demonstrated that harmonization was feasible. At the same time there were bilateral discussions between Europe, Japan and the US on possibilities for harmonization. It was, however, at the WHO Conference of Drug Regulatory Authorities (ICDRA), in Paris, in 1989, that specific plans for action began to materialize. Soon afterwards, the authorities approached IFPMA to discuss a joint regulatory-industry initiative on international harmonization, and ICH was conceived.

Commitment and Process:

Key factors in the success of ICH have been the commitment of the parties to the objectives and outcome of ICH and the development of the "ICH Process" for developing harmonized guidance on technical issues. The commitment to ICH was set out in a Steering Committee Statement from the meeting in Tokyo, October 1990.

The ICH "Process" was first drawn up at the Steering Committee meeting in Washington, March 1992 and amended in Tokyo, September 1992. The defined process with "decision points" at *Step 2* and *Step 4* has enabled the Steering Committee to monitor the progress of the topics selected for harmonization.

The birth of ICH took place at a meeting in April 1990, hosted by the EFPIA in Brussels. Representatives of the regulatory agencies and industry associations of Europe, Japan and the USA met, primarily, to plan an International Conference but the meeting also discussed the wider implications and terms of reference of ICH. The ICH Steering Committee which was established at that meeting has since met at least twice a year, with the location rotating between the three regions.

Format of Applications:

The Steering Committee has given priority to harmonizing the technical content of the sections of the reporting data where significant differences have been identified between regulatory requirements across the three regions: Europe, Japan and the USA. The first ICH Guideline to deal with harmonizing the format of reporting data was E3, *Content and Format of Clinical Study Reports*. This Guideline describes a single format for reporting the core clinical studies that make up the clinical section of a registration dossier.

A target for the first phase of ICH activities was to remove redundancy and duplication in the development and review process, such that a single set of data could be generated to demonstrate the quality, safety and efficacy of a new medicinal product. The long-term goal of developing a harmonized format has led to the creation of the ICH Guideline M4, *The Common Technical Document (CTD)*. The CTD provides a harmonized format and content for new product applications. ICH achieved *Step 4* status of the CTD at the ICH5 Conference in San Diego, California, in November 2000. The agreed upon implementation date for the CTD, in the three regions, was July 2003.

The *Electronic Common Technical Document (eCTD)* was developed subsequently by the M2 Expert Working Group. This specification document allows for the electronic submission of the CTD from applicant to regulator and provides a harmonized technical solution to implementing the CTD electronically. The eCTD has begun to be implemented across the ICH partner and observer regions.

The compiled text of the draft Common Technical Document reached Step 2 of the ICH Process at the Steering Committee Meeting in July 2000.

The full draft Common Technical Document was released for public consultation, with the deadline for comments for the end of September 2000.

A final Common Technical Document was completed in November 2000. Numbering and Section Headers have been edited for consistency and use in e-CTD as agreed at the Washington DC Meeting, September 11-12, 2002

Organization of The Common Technical Document for the registration of pharmaceuticals for human use including the Granularity document that provides guidance on document location and paginations.

In November 2005, the ICH Steering Committee adopted a new codification system for ICH Guidelines. The purpose of this new codification is to ensure that the numbering / coding of ICH Guidelines is more logical, consistent and clearer. Because the new system applies to existing as well as new ICH Guidelines a history box has been added to the beginning of all Guidelines to explain how the Guideline was developed and what is the latest version.

With the new codification revisions to an ICH Guideline are shown as (R1), (R2), (R3) depending on the number of revisions. Annexes or Addenda to Guidelines have now been incorporated into the core Guidelines and are indicated as revisions to the core Guideline (e.g., R1).

For implementation reasons, the Regulatory Authorities working within the ICH Regions (European Commission, Food and Drug Administration and Ministry of Health, Labor and Welfare) may not change the codification retrospectively.

The tables below are intended to clarify the old/new ICH Guidelines codification, with effect November 2005.

M4: The Common Technical Document

The compiled text of the draft Common Technical Document reached *Step 2* of the ICH process at the Steering Committee Meeting in July 2000. The full draft

Common Technical Document was released for public consultation, with the deadline for comments for the end of September 2000.

A final Common Technical Document was completed in November 2000.

Numbering and Section Headers have been edited for consistency and use in e-CTD as agreed at the Washington DC Meeting, September 11-12, 2002.

The Common Technical Document is divided into 5 Sections:
1) Organization / General
2) Quality
3) Safety
4) Efficacy
5) Electronic

1) M4 (R3): Organization:

Including the Granularity document that provides guidance on document location and paginations.

Re-edited with Numbering and Section Headers changes, September 2002

The Common Technical Document provides for a harmonized structure and format for new product applications. The Common Technical Document was agreed upon in November 2000, in San Diego, USA. This Common Technical Document is divided into four separate sections. The four sections address the application organization (M4: Organization), the Quality section (M4Q), the Safety section (M4S) and the Efficacy section (M4E) of the harmonized application. The agreed upon implementation date for the Common Technical Document in the three regions was July 2003.

2) M4Q (R1): Quality

Module 2: Quality Overall Summary (QOS)

Module 3: Quality

The section of the application covering chemical and pharmaceutical data including data for biological/ biotechnological products.

Re-edited with Numbering and Section Headers changes, September 2002

The Quality section of the Common Technical Document (M4Q) provides a harmonized structure and format for presenting CMC (Chemistry, Manufacturing and Controls) information in a registration dossier. The table of contents includes sections on Drug Substance and Drug Product. There are also sections for regional specific information as well as some appendices. Due to the fact that many CMC topics have not yet been the subject of ICH guidelines (e.g. drug substance synthesis, drug product manufacture, container closure), the content of M4Q is not totally harmonized. A new section on Pharmaceutical Development has been included to replace the Development Pharmaceutics Report (currently a part of the EU submission requirements). Also, a new CMC summary document, the Quality Overall Summary, has been developed.

3) **M4S (R2) SAFETY**

Nonclinical Summaries and Organization of Module 4

The non-clinical section of the application.

Re-edited with Numbering and Section Headers changes, September 2002

The CTD Safety (M4S) Guideline delineates the structure and format of the nonclinical summaries in Module 2 of the Common Technical Document, and provides the organization of Module 4, the Nonclinical Study Reports. The Nonclinical Overview should present an integrated and critical assessment of the pharmacologic, pharmacokinetic, and toxicological evaluation of the pharmaceutical, and generally should not exceed 30 pages.

The Nonclinical Written Summaries (100 - 150 pages) are recommended to provide more extensive summaries and discussion of the nonclinical information on pharmacology, pharmacokinetics and toxicology. Thirty-four templates are provided for the preparation of the Nonclincal Tabulated Summaries, and 31 example tables are provided. Finally, the organization of the Nonclinical Study Reports in Module 4 is described. Preparation of the nonclinical sections of the Common Technical Document according to the M4S Guideline results in a single harmonized dossier of the nonclinical information that is acceptable in all three ICH regions.

4) **M4E (R1): EFFICACY**

Module 2: Clinical Overview and Clinical Summary

Module 5: Clinical Study Reports

The clinical section of the Application.

Re-edited with Numbering and Section Headers changes, September 2002

CTD-Efficacy (M4E) describes the structure and format of the clinical data in an application, including summaries and detailed study reports. There are two high level clinical summaries in Module 2 of the CTD: the Clinical Overview, a short document that provides a critical assessment of the clinical data; and the Clinical Summary, a longer document that focuses on data summarization and integration. Clinical Study Reports and raw data (where applicable) are included in Module 5 of the CTD.

5) **eCTD:**

The electronic CTD

This specification has been developed by the ICH M2 Expert Working Group and maintained by the eCTD Implementation Working Group in accordance with the ICH Process as pertains to the M2 EWG and eCTD change control as it pertains to the eCTD IWG.

Steering Committee structure and participation

The existing Steering Committee structure continues to be appropriate. In the interests of greater transparency, the Steering Committee, however, welcomes the appropriate participation of other interested parties in a flexible and ad hoc manner on topics which affect them.

The Steering Committee continues to believe that regular large conferences help to communicate the results of the harmonization activities to the widest possible audience.

Global co-operation

The recent emphasis on global co-operation actions by ICH acknowledges the important role of WHO in disseminating information and providing input beyond the ICH regions. The Steering Committee recognizes the need to expand its communication and dissemination of information with non-ICH parties. A more active involvement of WHO through its regional centers is welcomed.

Structure of ICH

ICH is a joint initiative involving both regulators and industry as equal partners in the scientific and technical discussions of the testing procedures which are required to ensure and assess the safety, quality and efficacy of medicines.

The focus of ICH has been on the technical requirements for medicinal products containing new drugs. The vast majority of those new drugs and medicines are developed in Western Europe, Japan and the United States of America and therefore, when ICH was established, it was agreed that its scope would be confined to registration in those three regions.

ICH is comprised of Six Parties that are directly involved, as well as three Observers and IFPMA. The Six Parties are the founder members of ICH which represent the regulatory bodies and the research-based industry in the European Union, Japan and the USA. These parties include the EU, EFPIA, MHLW, JPMA, FDA and PhRMA.

The Observers are WHO, EFTA, and Canada (represented by Health Canada). This important group of non-voting members acts as a link between the ICH and non-ICH countries and regions.

ICH is operated via the ICH Steering Committee, which is supported by ICH Coordinators and the ICH Secretariat.

ICH Parties

1) European Commission - European Union (EU)

The European Commission represents the 25 members of the EU. The Commission is working, through harmonization of technical requirements and procedures, to achieve a single market in pharmaceuticals which would allow free movement of products throughout the EU.

The European Medicines Agency (EMEA) has been established by the Commission and is situated in London. Technical and scientific support for ICH activities is provided by the Committee for Medicinal Products for Human Use (CHMP) of the EMEA.

2) European Federation of Pharmaceutical Industries and Associations (EFPIA)

EFPIA, is situated in Brussels and has, as its members, 29 national pharmaceutical industry associations and 45 leading pharmaceutical companies involved in the research, development and manufacturing of medicinal products in Europe for human use. Much of the Federation's work is concerned with the activities of the European Commission and the EMEA.

A wide network of experts and country coordinators has been established, through Member Associations, to ensure that EFPIA's views within ICH are representative of the European industry.

3) Ministry of Health, Labour and Welfare, Japan (MHLW)

The Ministry of Health, Labour and Welfare has responsibilities for approval and administration of drugs, medical devices and cosmetics in Japan.

Technical and scientific support for ICH activities are provided by the Pharmaceuticals and Medical Devices Agency (PMDA) (which was established in April 2004 as a new administrative agency for scientific review for drug approval), and by the National Institute of Health Sciences (NIHS) and other experts from academia.

4) Japan Pharmaceutical Manufacturers Association (JPMA)

JPMA represents 75 members (including 20 foreign affiliates) and 14 committees. Membership includes all the major research-based pharmaceutical manufacturers in Japan.

ICH work is coordinated through specialised committees of industry experts who also participate in the Expert Working Groups.

Among the objectives of JPMA is the development of a competitive pharmaceutical industry with a greater awareness and understanding of international issues. JPMA promotes and encourages the adoption of international standards by its member companies.

5) US Food and Drug Administration (FDA)

The US Food and Drug Administration has a wide range of responsibilities for drugs, biologicals, medical devices, cosmetics and radiological products. The largest of the world's drug regulatory agencies FDA is responsible for the approval of all drug products used in the USA.

The FDA consists of administrative, scientific and regulatory staff organized under the Office of the Commissioner and has several Centers with responsibility for the various products which are regulated. Technical advice and experts for ICH work are drawn from the Center for Drug Evaluation and Research (CDER) and the Center for Biologics Evaluation and Research (CBER).

6) *Pharmaceutical Research and Manufacturers of America (PhRMA)*

The Pharmaceutical Research and Manufacturers of America - PhRMA - represents the research-based industry in the USA. The Association has 67 companies in membership which are involved in the discovery, development and manufacture of prescription medicines. There are also 24 research affiliates which conduct biological research related to the development of drugs and vaccines.

PhRMA, which was previously known as the US Pharmaceutical Manufacturers Association (PMA), coordinates its technical input to ICH through its Scientific and Regulatory Section. Special committees have been set up, of experts from PhRMA companies, to deal with ICH topics.

ICH Observers

Since ICH was initiated, in 1990, there have been observers to act as a link with non-ICH countries and regions. The ICH Observers are:

1) The World Health Organization (WHO).
2) The European Free Trade Association (EFTA), currently represented at ICH by Swiss medic Switzerland.
3) Canada, represented at ICH by Health Canada.
4) IFPMA.

The International Federation of Pharmaceutical Manufacturers and Associations is a non-profit, non-governmental Organization (NGO) representing national industry associations and companies from both developed and developing countries. Member companies of the IFPMA are research-based pharmaceutical, biotech and vaccine companies. IFPMA has been closely associated with ICH, since its inception to ensure contact with the research-based industry, outside the ICH Regions. IFPMA provides the ICH Secretariat.

ICH Steering Committee

ICH is administered by the ICH Steering Committee which is supported by the ICH Secretariat. The ICH Steering Committee (SC) was established in April 1990, when ICH was initiated. The Steering Committee, working with the ICH Terms of Reference, determines the policies and procedures for ICH, selects topics for harmonization and monitors the progress of harmonization initiatives. The Steering Committee meets at least twice a year with the location rotating between the three regions.

Since the beginning, each of the six co-sponsors has had two seats on the ICH Steering Committee (SC) which oversees the harmonization activities. IFPMA provides the Secretariat and participates as a non-voting member of the Steering Committee.

The ICH Observers, WHO, Health Canada, and the European Free Trade Association (EFTA) nominate non-voting participants to attend the ICH Steering Committee Meetings.

ICH Coordinators

Fundamental to the smooth running of ICH has been the designation, by each of the six co-sponsors, of an ICH Coordinator to act as the main contact point with the ICH Secretariat and ensure that ICH documents are distributed to the appropriate persons within the area of their responsibility.

Each party has also established a Contact Network of experts within their own organization or region in order to ensure that, in the discussions, they reflect the views and policies of the co-sponsor they represent. The way in which this network operates differs according to the administrative structure of the party concerned.

Due to the structural differences within the EU and MHLW, ICH Technical Coordinators are also designated from the EMEA and PMDA respectively. They support the ICH Coordinator and facilitate every action of the Steering Committee members in the region, mainly by applying their scientific knowledge. Their roles include acting as a contact point between the experts within EMEA and PMDA and the ICH Coordinator at the main regulatory body, and as a contact point with the ICH Secretariat.

The ICH Secretariat

The Secretariat operates from the IFPMA offices, in Geneva, and is primarily concerned with preparations for, and documentation of, meetings of the Steering Committee as well as coordination of preparations for Working Group (EWG, IWG, Informal WG) and Discussion Group meetings. The ICH Secretariat also provides administrative support for the GCG and MedDRA.

At the time of ICH Conferences, the Secretariat is responsible for the technical documentation and for liaison with the speakers for the Conference. Organizational aspects of the Conferences are handled by the industry and regulatory parties in the country where the Conference takes place.

Categories of ICH Harmonization Activities

The ICH harmonization activities fall into 4 categories (see Table below). The original Formal ICH Procedures involved a step-wise progression of guidelines. This process has evolved to include maintenance activities (Maintenance Procedure), as an essential part of the ICH procedure.

In addition to the maintenance activity, it is also important to have procedures in place to enable the modification of existing guidelines (Revision Procedure), as well as to assist in their implementation (Q and A Procedure).

Category	Type of procedure	Technical Discussion Group	Explanation	Example
1.	Formal ICH procedure	EWG	Development of a new guideline	M5 (Data Elements and Standards for Drug Dictionaries
2.	Q and A procedure	IWG	Creation of Q and as to assist the implementation of existing guidelines	CTD-IWG
3.	Revision procedure	EWG	Revision/Modification of existing guidelines	E2B(R3)
4.	Maintenance procedure	EWG	Adding Standards to existing guidelines and/or recommendations	Q3C(R3) M2 Recommendations

Formal ICH Procedure (Category 1)

This procedure corresponds to the original ICH process and was used for more than a decade, and it now includes some additional explanation on each activity. The Steering Committee may decide to follow an accelerated procedure for new topics, when necessary. To this end, the Steering Committee adopted the Streamlined Procedure (final version dated October 21, 2002) in Washington in September 2002.

Step 1: Consensus building

When the Steering Committee adopts a Concept Paper as a new topic, then the process of consensus building begins.

As requested in the Concept Paper, an extended EWG or original EWG shall be established. The Reporter prepares an initial draft of the guideline, based on the objectives set out in the Concept Paper, and in consultation with experts designated to the EWG. The initial draft and successive revisions are circulated for comments within the EWG, giving fixed deadlines for receipt of those comments.

To the extent possible, the consultation will be carried out by correspondence, using fax and e-mail. Face-to-face meetings of the EWG will normally only take place at the time and venue of the biannual SC meetings. Additional formal meetings of the ICH EWG need to be agreed, in advance, by the Steering Committee.

Interim reports are made at each meeting of the ICH Steering Committee.

When consensus is reached among all six party EWG members, the EWG will sign the *Step 2* Experts Signoff sheet.

If consensus is reached within the agreed timetable the *Step 2* Experts Document with EWG signatures is submitted to the Steering Committee to request adoption under *Step 2* of the ICH process.

Where complete consensus within the six ICH parties has not been reached within the agreed time frame, a report will be made to the Steering Committee indicating the extent of agreement reached and highlighting the points on which there are differences among the parties. Experts from all parties represented on the EWG will have the opportunity to explain their position to the Steering Committee. The Steering Committee may then:

- Allow an extension of the timetable, on the basis that the EWG can give assurances that consensus could be reached within a short, specified period;
- Decide to suspend or abandon the harmonization project.

Step 2: Confirmation of six-party consensus

Step 2 is reached when the Steering Committee agrees, based on the report of the EWG, that there is sufficient scientific consensus on the technical issues for the draft guideline or recommendation to proceed to the next stage of regulatory consultation. This agreement is confirmed by at least one of the SC members for each of the six ICH parties signing their assent.

The consensus text approved by the Steering Committee is signed off by the Steering Committee as *Step 2* Final Document.

Step 3: Regulatory Consultation and Discussion

a) Regional regulatory consultation

At this stage, the guideline embodying the scientific consensus leaves the ICH process and becomes the subject of normal wide-ranging regulatory consultation in the three regions. In the EU it is published as a draft CPMP Guideline, in Japan it is translated and issued by MHLW for internal and external consultation and in the USA it is published as draft guidance in the Federal Register.

The difference from normal, national/regional procedures for consultation on guidelines are that the regulatory parties exchange information on the comments they have received in order to arrive at a single, harmonized guideline. Also, there is an opportunity for industry associations and regulatory authorities in non-ICH regions to comment on the draft consultation documents, which are distributed using IFPMA and WHO contact lists.

b) Discussion of regional consultation comments

After obtaining all regulatory consultation results, the EWG who organized the discussion for consensus building will be resumed. This EWG consists of regulatory and industry parties, and Observers. If the Reporter was designated from an industry party until *Step 2*, then a new Reporter will be appointed from the regulatory party, preferably from the same region as the previous Reporter. The same procedure described in *Step 1* is used to address the consultation results into the *Step 2* Final Document. The draft document to be generated as a result of the *Step 3* phase is called *Step 4* Experts Document.

If both regulatory and industry parties of the EWG are satisfied that the consensus achieved at *Step 2* is not substantially altered as a result of the consultation, or consensus is reached on any alterations, the *Step 4* Experts Document is signed by the EWG regulatory experts. The *Step 4* Document with regulatory EWG signatures is submitted to the Steering Committee to request adoption as *Step 4* of the ICH process.

This *Step 4* Document with regulatory EWG signatures is named *Step 4* Experts Document, and this signoff is to be called *Step 4* Experts Signoff.

Where complete consensus has not been achieved within the agreed time frame, a report will be made to the Steering Committee indicating the extent of agreement reached and highlighting the points on which differences between the parties remain. Experts from all parties represented on the EWG will have the opportunity to explain their position to the Steering Committee. The Steering Committee may then:
- Allow an extension of the time frame, if the EWG can give assurances that consensus could be reached within a short, specified period;
- Decide to abandon the current draft and resume the discussion from *Step 1*;
- Decide to suspend or abandon the harmonization project.

Step 4: Adoption of an ICH Harmonized Tripartite Guideline

Step 4 is reached when the Steering Committee agrees, on the basis of the report from the regulatory Reporter of the EWG, that there is sufficient scientific consensus on the technical issues.

This endorsement is based on the signatures from the three regulatory parties to ICH affirming that the Guideline is recommended for adoption by the regulatory bodies of the three regions.

In the event that one or more parties representing industry have strong objections to the adoption of the guideline, on the grounds that the revised draft departs substantially from the original consensus, or introduces new issues, the regulatory parties may agree that a revised document should be submitted for further consultation. In this case, the EWG discussion may be resumed.

The *Step 4* Final Document is signed off by the SC signatories for the regulatory parties of ICH as an ICH Harmonized Tripartite Guideline at *Step 4* of the ICH process.

Step 5: Implementation

Having reached *Step 4* the harmonized tripartite guideline moves immediately to the final step of the process that is the regulatory implementation. This step is carried out according to the same national/regional procedures that apply to other regional regulatory guidelines and requirements, in the European Union, Japan and the USA.

Q and A Procedure (Category 2)

Additional implementation guidance/advice is usually developed in the form of Questions and Answers ("Q and As"). The development and adoption of these Q and As follows an established process described below:

The Q and A process is intended to be a mechanism by which questions received from stakeholders are collected, analyzed, reformulated and ultimately used as model questions for which standard answers are developed and posted on the ICH website.

The incoming questions will not be answered individually. They will rather serve to highlight areas that need additional clarification and will be used to develop a model question that will be answered in the Q and A document.

- Any question sent to the mailbox of the ICH website, or raised by any of the six official ICH parties, and/or by any of the official ICH Observers, will be brought to the attention of the appropriate Implementation Working Group (IWG).
- The regional questions and issues should first be handled by the regulatory party of the concerned region then shared and evaluated within the IWG, finally the proposed answer is presented to the Steering Committee for approval/endorsement before publication on the ICH website.
- The IWG Reporter will send the questions to the members of her / his IWG. Based on this information, the IWG will prepare model questions and their responses for presentation at the SC meeting. Based on the level of guidance given by the answers, the IWG will assess whether the Q and A document should be a *Step 2* Document and published for comments or should be a *Step 4* Document and published as final. The document should be *Step 2* if, by the answers provided, it sets forth substantial new interpretations of the guideline(s). The document should be a *Step 4* if, by the answers provided, it sets forth existing practices or minor changes in the interpretation or policy of the guideline(s).
- Each IWG presents its draft Q and A document to the SC meeting (including regional regulatory legal review process) and makes recommendations to the Steering Committee on the status of the document (*Step 2* or *4*).
- The Steering Committee concurs with the QandA document and its (*Step*) status.
- The document will then follow the normal path of a *Step 2/ Step 4* Document:
  - *Step 2*: the experts and the SC members will sign the QandA document. The document will then be published for comments in the three ICH regions.

- o *Step 4:* the regulatory experts and the regulatory SC members will sign the Q and A document.
- Each region should develop internal procedures to deal with the case of absence of the experts at the time of signoff, which could include the possibility for the Steering Committee to signoff the *Step 2/ Step 4* on behalf of the IWG experts.
- The Experts/Final Q and A document will be posted on the ICH website five working days after the SC meeting.

ICH Guidelines

The ICH Topics are divided into four major categories and ICH Topic Codes are assigned according to these categories.

Q

"Quality" Topics, i.e., those relating to chemical and pharmaceutical Quality Assurance.
Examples: Q1 Stability Testing, Q3 Impurity Testing

S

"Safety" Topics, i.e., those relating to in vitro and in vivo pre-clinical studies.
Examples: S1 Carcinogenicity Testing, S2 Genotoxicity Testing

E

"Efficacy" Topics, i.e., those relating to clinical studies in human subject. Examples: E4 Dose Response Studies, Carcinogenicity Testing, E6 Good Clinical Practices. (Note Clinical Safety Data Management is also classified as an "Efficacy" topic - E2)

M

"Multidisciplinary" Topics, i.e., cross-cutting Topics which do not fit uniquely into one of the above categories.
- o M1: Medical Terminology (MedDRA)
- o M2: Electronic Standards for Transmission of Regulatory Information (ESTRI)
- o M3: Timing of Pre-clinical Studies in Relation to Clinical Trials
- o M4: The Common Technical Document (CTD)
- o M5: Data Elements and Standards for Drug Dictionaries

Notes on implementation in the three ICH Regions

EU

The ICH guidelines are submitted to the Committee for Proprietary Medicinal Products (CPMP) for endorsement once they have reached *Step 2* or *Step 4* of the ICH Process. The CPMP decides on the duration for consultation with interested parties (usually 6 months).

The European Agency for the Evaluation of Medicinal Products (EMEA) publishes and distributes the *Step 2* guidelines for comments. At *Step 4* the guidelines are endorsed by the CPMP and a timeframe for implementation is established (usually 6 months).

The guidelines are subsequently published by the European Commission in Volume III of the Rules Governing Medicinal Products in the European Union. *Step 2* and *Step 4* guidelines are available from the EMEA site on the Internet: http://www.emea.eu.int

Volume III is available from the Office for Official Publications of the European Communities and on the DG III website: http://pharmacos.eudra.org/

MHLW

When *Step 2* or *Step 4* has been reached, the ICH texts are translated into Japanese. Subsequently Pharmaceutical and Medical Safety Bureau (PMSB) Notification for the promulgation or consultation of guidelines written in Japanese is issued with a deadline for comments in the case of consultation drafts, or an implementation date for finalized guidelines. The notifications on guidelines in Japanese and also English attachments (ICH Texts) are available from PMSB or on the Internet by the National Institute of Health and Science. http://www.nihs.go.jp/dig/ich/ichindexe.htm

FDA

When Step 2 or Step 4 has been reached, FDA publishes a notice with the full text of the guidance in the Federal Register. Notices for Step 2 guidance include a date for receipt of written comment; Step 4 guidance are available for use on the date they are published in the Federal Register. FDA guidance and guidelines are available on the Internet:

CDER:http://www.fda.gov/cder/guidance/index.htm
CBER: http://www.fda.gov/cber/guidelines.htmlity Guidelines

In November 2005, the ICH Steering Committee adopted a new codification system for ICH Guidelines. The purpose of this new codification is to ensure that the numbering / coding of ICH Guidelines is more logical, consistent and clearer. Because the new system applies to existing as well as new ICH Guidelines a history box has been added to the beginning of all Guidelines to explain how the Guideline was developed and what is the latest version.

With the new codification revisions to an ICH Guideline are shown as (R1), (R2), (R3) depending on the number of revisions. Annexes or Addenda to Guidelines have now been incorporated into the core Guidelines and are indicated as revisions to the core Guideline (e.g., R1).

For implementation reasons, the Regulatory Authorities working within the ICH Regions (European Commission, Food and Drug Administration and Ministry of Health, Labor and Welfare) may not change the codification retrospectively.

The tables below are intended to clarify the old/new ICH Guidelines codification, with effect November 2005.

New Codification as per November 2005   *Previously coded:*

Stability

Q1A(R2)	Stability Testing of New Drug Substances and Products	Q1A(R2)
Q1B	Stability Testing: Photostability Testing of New Drug Substances and Products	Q1B
Q1C	Stability Testing for New Dosage Forms	Q1C
Q1D	Bracketing and Matrixing Designs for Stability Testing of New Drug Substances and Products	Q1D
Q1E	Evaluation of Stability Data	Q1E
Q1F	Stability Data Package for Registration Applications in Climatic Zones III and IV	Q1F

Analytical Validation

Q2(R1)	New title: Validation of Analytical Procedures: Text and Methodology Previously: Text on Validation of Analytical Procedures	Q2A
	Validation of Analytical Procedures: Methodology (in Q2(R1))	Q2B

Impurities

Q3A(R2)	Impurities in New Drug Substances	Q3A(R)
Q3B(R2)	Impurities in New Drug Products	Q3B(R)
Q3C(R3)	Impurities: Guideline for Residual Solvents	Q3C
	Impurities: Guideline for Residual Solvents (Maintenance) PDE for Tetrahydrofuran (in Q3C(R3))	Q3C(M)
	PDE for N-Methylpyrrolidone (in Q3C(R3))	Q3C(M)

Pharmacopoeias

Q4	Pharmacopoeias	*Q4*
Q4A	Pharmacopoeial Harmonisation	*Q4A*
Q4B	Regulatory Acceptance of Analytical Procedures and/or Acceptance Criteria (RAAPAC)	*Q4B*

Quality of Biotechnological Products

Q5A(R1)	Viral Safety Evaluation of Biotechnology Products Derived from Cell Lines of Human or Animal Origin	*Q5A*
Q5B	Quality of Biotechnological Products: Analysis of the Expression Construct in Cells Used for Production of r-DNA Derived Protein Products	*Q5B*
Q5C	Quality of Biotechnological Products: Stability Testing of Biotechnological/Biological Products	*Q5C*
Q5D	Derivation and Characterisation of Cell Substrates Used for Production of Biotechnological/Biological Products	*Q5D*
Q5E	Comparability of Biotechnological/Biological Products Subject to Changes in their Manufacturing Process	*Q5E*

Specifications

Q6A	Specifications: Test Procedures and Acceptance Criteria for New Drug Substances and New Drug Products: Chemical Substances (including Decision Trees)	*Q6A*
Q6B	Specifications: Test Procedures and Acceptance Criteria for Biotechnological/Biological Products	*Q6B*

Good Manufacturing Practice

Q7	Good Manufacturing Practice Guide for Active Pharmaceutical Ingredients	*Q7A*

Pharmaceutical Development

Q8	Pharmaceutical Development	*Q8*

Quality Risk Management

Q9	Quality Risk Management	*Q9*

Safety Guidelines:

In November 2005, the ICH Steering Committee adopted a new codification system for ICH Guidelines. The purpose of this new codification is to ensure that the numbering / coding of ICH Guidelines is more logical, consistent and clearer. Because the new system applies to existing as well as new ICH Guidelines a history box has been added to the beginning of all Guidelines to explain how the Guideline was developed and what is the latest version.

With the new codification revisions to an ICH Guideline are shown as (R1), (R2), (R3) depending on the number of revisions. Annexes or Addenda to Guidelines have now been incorporated into the core Guidelines and are indicated as revisions to the core Guideline (e.g., R1).

For implementation reasons, the Regulatory Authorities working within the ICH Regions (European Commission, Food and Drug Administration and Ministry of Health, Labor and Welfare) may not change the codification retrospectively. The tables below are intended to clarify the old/new ICH Guidelines codification, with effect November 2005.

New Codification as per November 2005   *Previously coded:*

Carcinogenicity Studies

S1A	Need for Carcinogenicity Studies of Pharmaceuticals	S1A
S1B	Testing for Carcinogenicity of Pharmaceuticals	S1B
S1C(R1)	New title: Dose Selection for Carcinogenicity Studies of Pharmaceuticals and Limit Dose Previously: Dose Selection for Carcinogenicity Studies of Pharmaceuticals	S1C
	Addendum to S1C: Addition of a Limit Dose and Related Notes (in S1C(R1)	S1C(R)

18. WHO-GMP AND ICH STABILITY TESTING GUIDELINE FOR DRUG PRODUCTS

STABILITY STUDY AS PER ICH
(AS PER Q1A R2 and Q1B STEP 5)

ICH (International Conference on Harmonization) has published a guideline for the New Drug Substances and New drug product. Formal Stability studies programs for the drug product should be designed depending up on the Active ingredient, Behaviour and Properties and also upon the stability study results of active ingredients and based upon the experience of clinical formulation studies.

In general following types of stability study of drug product shall be carried out,

1) Physio - Chemical Stability Including Photo stability. These ICH guidelines were first recommended for adoption at step 4 of the ICH process on 27 Oct. 1993, by the ICH steering committee. These are then revised under step 2 of the ICH process on. 7th Oct. 1999 and recommended for adoption under step 4 of the ICH process on 8 Nov. 2000 by the ICH steering committee.

Again this guideline is revised IInd time as Q1AR2 and recommend for adoption on 6 Feb. 2003. by ICH steering committee.

2) Toxicological Stability.

3) Therapeutic Stability.

4) Microbial Stability.

But in ICH and WHO guidelines Toxicological, Therapeutic and Microbial stability are not described.

1. TERMINOLOGIES USED IN STABILITY:

1) Accelerated Testing: Studies designed to increase the rate of chemical degradation or physical change of the drug product by using exaggerated storage condition as a part of the formal stability study.

2) Bracketing: The design of a stability schedule such that only samples on the extremes of

certain design factors such as strength, pack size are tested at all time points as in a full design.

3) Climatic Zones: The four zones in the world that are distinguished by their characteristic, prevalent annual climatic conditions.

4) Expiration Date: The date placed on the container label of the product designating the time prior to which a batch of the product is expected to remain within the approved shelf life specifications, if stored under defined conditions and after the shelf life of a product.

5) Intermediate Testing: Studies conducted at **30°C/60% RH** and designed to moderately increase the rate of chemical degradation or physical changes for a product intended to be stored
long term at **25°C**.

6) Long Term Testing: Stability studies under the recommended storage conditions for the retest period or shelf life proposed for labeling.

7) Matrixing: The design of a stability schedule such that a selected subset of the total number of possible samples for all factors combination is tested at specified time point.

8) Shelf Life: The time period during which a drug product is expected to remain within the approved shelf life specifications. Provided that it is stored under the storage condition given on label.

9) Stress Testing: Studies undertaken to assess the effect of the severe conditions on the drug product. Such studies include Photo stability testing.

2. PHOTO STABILITY TESTING:

Photo stability studies should be carried out to demonstrate that, as appropriate, light exposure does not result in unacceptable change. Normally Photo stability testing is carried out on a single batch. If Changes are made in Formulation and Packaging material then Photo stability study shall be repeated.

Two additional batches should be conducted if the results of the confirmatory study are equivocal.

The Systemic approach to Photo stability testing is recommended covering, as appropriate studies such as:

1) Tests on the drug substance;
2) Tests on the exposed drug outside of the immediate pack; and if necessary.
3) Tests on the drug product in the marketing packs.

Light Sources:

a) Drug product should be exposed to any light source designated to produce an output similar to the D65/ID65 emission standard such as an artificial day light fluorescent lamp combining visible and ultraviolet outputs, xenon, or metal halide lamp.

D65 is the internationally recognized standard for outdoor day lights defined in ISO 10977 (1993). ID65 is the equivalent indoor indirect daylight standard. An appropriate filters may be fitted to light source to avoid the radiations below the wavelength of 320 nm. or

b) Sample can be exposed to both cool white fluorescent and near UV lamp. Cool white fluorescent lamp shall be as per specifications of ISO 10977(1993) A near UV fluorescent lamp having a radiation from 320 to 360 nm. Wavelength with maximum energy emission between 360 to 400 nm.

For confirmatory studies, sample should be exposed to light providing an overall illumination of not less than 1.2 million Lux hours and an integrated near UV energy of not less than 200 Watt Hours per sq. meter to allow direct comparisons to be made between the drug product. For easily identification of change in Drug product, Control sample protected by Aluminium foil Wrapping as dark control is kept with the test sample.

At the end of the exposure period, the samples should be examined for any changes in physical properties such as appearance, Clarity, Colour of solution, DT and Dissolution and for Assay.

3. SELECTION OF BATCHES:

At least three primary batches shall be studied for stability out of which two batches shall be at least pilot scale batches and third one can be small if justified.

Stability study can be performed on each individual strength and containers size of the drug product.

4. TESTING FREQUENCY:

a) For Long Term Stability:

Testing frequencies for the product with proposed shelf life of at least 12 months, should normally be every three months over first year; every 6 months over the second year, and Annually thereafter throughout the proposed shelf life.

b) For Accelerated Stability:

At the accelerated storage condition, a minimum of three time points, including initial and final points (e.g. 0, 3, 6 months), for 6 months study is recommended.

c) Intermediate Stability Studies:

A minimum of four points, including the initial and final points (e.g. 0, 6, 9, 12 months), from a 12 months study is recommended.

5. STORAGE CONDITIONS:

Drug product shall be evaluated under storage conditions with appropriate tolerance limit that test its thermal stability and if applicable, its sensitive to moisture or potential for solvent loss.

The long term testing should cover a minimum of 12 months duration on at least three primary batches at the time of submission and should be continued for a period of time up to shelf life.

Long term, Accelerated, and where appropriate, Intermediate storage conditions for drug product are detailed in the section below. The general case should be apply if the storage conditions can be used, if justified.

A. General Case:

Study	Storage condition		Minimum time period covered by data at the time of submission
	Temperature	Relative Humidity	
Long term*	25°C ± 2°C OR 30°C ± 2°C	60% ± 5% or 65% ± 5%	12 months
Intermediate**	30°C ± 2°C	65% ± 5%	6 months
Accelerated	40°C ± 2°C	75% ± 5%	6 months

If long term studies are conducted at 25°C ± 2°C/60° ± 5% RH, or 65%±5% and significant change occurs, at any time during 6 months.

* Manufacture can decided whether long term studies are performed at 25°C or 30°C.
** If 30°C ± 2°C/65% RH ± 5% RH is long term condition. Then there is no intermediate conditions.

Testing at the accelerated storage condition, additional testing at the intermediate storage condition should be conducted and evaluated against significant change criteria. The initial application should include a minimum of 6 months data from a 12 month study at the intermediate storage condition.

In general Significant Change for drug product is defined as one or more of the following:

1) A 5 % change in assay from its initial value, or failure to meet the acceptance criteria for potency when using biological and Immunological procedures.

2) Any degradation product's exceeding its acceptance criteria.

3) Failure to meet the acceptance criteria for Appearance, Physical Attributes and Functionality test, such as Colour phase separation, Resuspendibility, Caking, Hardness, Dose delivery as per actuation). However, some changes in physical attributes (e.g. Softening of suppositories, Melting of creams) may be expected under accelerated conditions.

4) Failure to meet the Acceptance Criterion for pH.

5) Failure to meet the acceptance criteria for dissolution for 12 dosage units.

B. Drug products packed in semi-permeable containers.

Study	Storage condition		Minimum time period covered by data at the time of submission
	Temperature	Relative Humidity	
Long term*	25°C ± 2°C OR 30°C ± 2°C	40% ± 5% OR 65% ± 5%	12 months
Intermediate**	30°C ± 2°C	65% ± 5%	6 months
Accelerated	40°C ± 2°C	not more than 25% RH	6 months

* Manufacturer can decide whether long term stability studies are performed at 25 ± 2°C / 40% ± 5% RH or 30°C ± 2°C/65% RH ± 5% RH.

** If 30°C ± 2°C / 65% RH ± 5%. RH is the long term condition, then there is no intermediate condition.

C. Drug products intended for storage in a refrigerator.

Study	Storage condition		Minimum time period covered by data at the time of submission
	Temperature	Relative Humidity	
Long term	5°C ± 3°C	NA	12 months
Accelerated	25°C ± 2°C	60% ± 5 %	6 months

D. Drug products intended for storage in a freezer.

Study Storage condition Minimum time period covered by Temperature/Relative Humidity data at the time of submission.

Study	Storage condition		Minimum time period covered by data at the time of submission
	Temperature	Relative Humidity	
Long term	-20°C ± 5°C	NA	12 months

E. Drug products intended for storage below - 20°C in a deep freezer.

These should be treated on a case by case basis.

Where the submission includes long term stability data from three production batches covering the proposed shelf life, a post approval commitments is considered necessary.

A systemic Approach should be adopted in the presentation and evaluation of the stability information, Which should include, as appropriate, results from the Physical, Chemical,

and Microbiological tests, Including particular attributes of the dosage form.

A storage statement should be established for labeling in accordance with relevant national/regional requirements. Terms such as Ambient conditions or room temperature should be avoided. An Expiration date should be displayed on the container label.

STABILITY STUDY AS PER WHO GMP

The stability of finished product depends, on the one hand, on environmental factors such as ambient temperature, humidity, light and on the other, product related factors such as the chemical and physical properties of the active substance, and excipients, the dosage forms and its composition, the manufacturing process. The nature of the containers and closures and the properties of the packing material.

The shelf life should be established with due regard to the climatic zones in which the product is to be marketed. For certain preparations. The shelf life can be guaranteed only if specific storage conditions are followed:

For Safety and Efficacy purpose storage conditions should be indicated on the label of the container. Stability testing is carried out in development phase. For the registration dossier, and in the post registration period.

1) Intended Market (Climatic Zones):

Four Climatic Zones can be distinguished for the purpose of worldwide stability testing, as follows:

Zone I   :   Temperate.
Zone II   :   Subtropical with Possible High Humidity.
Zone III   :   Hot and Dry.
Zone IV   :   Hot and Humid.

The mean Climatic Zones and Storage conditions for Real time stability studies is given as below:

Climatic Zone	Storage Conditions	
	Temperature °C	Relative Humidity %
Zone I	21	45
Zone II	25	60
Zone III	30	35
Zone IV	30	70

Since, there are only few countries in Zone I, the manufacturer would be well advised to base stability testing on the condition in climatic Zone II When it is intended to market the product in temperate climates. For countries where certain regions are situated in Zone III or IV, and also with view to the global market. It is recommended that stability testing programs should be based on the conditions corresponding to Climatic Zone IV.

Design of Stability Studies:

Stability study should be designed based on the properties and stability characteristic of the drug substances and climatic conditions of the intended market zone.

1. Test Samples:

For registration purposes, test samples of the product containing fairly stable active ingredients are taken from two different batches; in contrast, samples should be taken from three batches of products containing easily degradable active ingredients or substances on which limited stability data are available.

In On - Going Studies, Current production batches should be sampled, according to following schedule:

1) One batch every other year for formulations for which considered to be stable otherwise 1 batch per year.

2) One batch every 3 - 5 year for formulations for which the stability profile has been established, unless a major change has been made, e.g. in the formulation or the method of manufacturing.

2. Test conditions:

A. Accelerated Studies:

An example of conditions for the accelerated stability testing of products containing relatively stable active ingredients is shown as below:

Storage conditions for accelerated study for product containing relatively stable active ingredients.

Climatic Zone	Storage Conditions		Duration of studies in Months
	Temperature in °C	Relative Humidity in %	
ZONE II	40°C ± 2°C	75% ± 5%	6 months.
ZONE IV	40°C ± 2°C	75% ± 5%	3 months.

For products containing less stable drug substances and those for which limited stability data are available. It is recommended that the duration of the accelerated studies for zone II should be increased for 6 months.

Storage at higher temperature may be recommended, e.g. 3 months at 45 to 50°C and 75% relative Humidity for Zone IV.

When Significant changes occurs in the course of accelerated studies, Additional tests at intermediate conditions should be conducted, e.g. 30°C ± 2°C and 60% RH ± 5%.

The initial registration application should then include a minimum 6 months data from a 1 year study.

Significant Changes:

1) The assay values shows a 5% decrease as compared with the initial assay value of a batch;
2) Any specified degradation product is present in amount greater than its specification limit;
3) The pH limits for the products are no longer met;
4) The specifications limits for the dissolution of 12 capsules or tablets are no longer met;
5) The specifications for appearance and physical properties, e.g. Colour, Phase separation, Caking, Hardness, are no longer met.

B. Real Time Studies:

For registration purpose, the results of studies of at least 6 months duration should be available at the time of registration. However it should be possible to submit the registration dossier before the end of this 6 month period. Real time stability should be continued until the end of the shelf life.

Storage conditions as per climatic zones are given below.:

Climatic Zone	Storage Conditions	
	Temperature °C	Relative Humidity %
Zone I	21	45
Zone II	25	60
Zone III	30	35
Zone IV	30	70

3. Frequency of Testing:

In the development phase and for studies in support of an application for registration, a reasonable frequency of testing of products containing relatively stable active ingredients is considered to be:

1) For Accelerated studies at 0, 1, 2, 3 and when appropriate, 6 months.
2) For Real time studies: at 0, 6 and 12 months and then once a year.

For On-going studies, samples may be tested at 6 months intervals for the confirmation of the provisional shelf life, or every 12 months for well established products. Products containing less stable drug substances and those for which stability data are available should be tested every 3 months in the first year, every 6 months in the second year and then annually.

Analytical methods used for Stability study should be validated. At the end stability report should prepared.

4. Shelf Life and Recommended Storage Conditions:

Shelf Life is calculated on the basis of storage conditions. Statistical methods are often used for the interpretation of these results. Some extrapolation of real time data beyond the observed range, when accelerated studies support this, is acceptable.

A tentative shelf life of 24 months may be established provided the following conditions are satisfied:

1) The active ingredient is known to be stable (not easily degradable)
2) Stability studies as outlines in section 2.0 (Stability condition) have been performed and no significant change have been observed.
3) Supporting data indicate that similar formulations have been assigned a shelf life of 24 months or more.

4) The manufacturer will continue to conduct real time studies until the proposed shelf life has been covered, and the results obtained will be submitted to the registration authority.

After completion of stability study following recommendations as to storage conditions can be prominently indicated on the label.:

"Store under Normal storage condition"

"Store between 2 and 8°C (Under refrigeration, no freezing)"

"Store below 8°C (Under refrigeration)"

"Store Between - 5 to - 0°C (in freezer)"

"Store below - 18°C) (In a deep Freezer)"

Normal Storage conditions have been defined by WHO (3) as:"Storage in dry, well ventilated premises at temperature of 15 to 25°C or depending on climatic conditions, up to 30°C. Extraneous Odour, Contamination and intense light have to be excluded".

General Precautionary statements, such as "Protect from Light" and or "Store in a dry place", may be included, but should not be used to conceal stability problems.

Mid-stream switch of the intermediate storage condition from 30°C ± 2°C/60% RH ± 5% RH to 30°C ± 2°C/65% RH ± 5% RH can be appropriate provided that the respective storage conditions and the date of the switch are clearly documented and stated in the registration application.

It is recommended that registrations contain data from complete studies at the intermediate storage condition 30°C ± 2°C/65% RH ± 5% RH, if applicable, by three years after the date of publication of this revised guideline in the respective ICH tripartite region.

19. GOOD LABORATORY PRACTICES

GOOD LABORATORY PRACTICES are not less important than GOOD MANUFACTURING PRACTICES. In manufacturing of drugs, overall control is essential to ensure that the customer receives drugs of high quality. So there should be a comprehensive system, so designed, documented, implemented and controlled, and so furnished with information on man, machine and other sources. As to provide assurance that product will be consistent of quality, appropriate to their use.

Three type of laboratory facilities are necessary for assuring the quality of pharmaceutical products like parenteral preparations, liquid orals, capsules, tablets, ointments, creams, gels, dry syrups, etc.

These three facilities are:
1) CHEMICAL AND INSTRUMENTAL ANALYSIS.
2) MICROBIOLOGICAL CONTROL.
3) BIOLOGICAL TESTING - ANIMAL HOUSE.

GUIDLINE FOR GOOD LABORATORY PRACTICES:

Good Laboratory Practices is concerned with the Organizational processes and conditions under which laboratory tests are planned, performed, monitored, recorded, archived and reported. Adherence by test facilities to the principles of GLP ensures proper planning of tests and the provision of adequate means to carry them out. It facilitates the proper conduct of tests, promotes their full and accurate reporting and provides means whereby the validity and integrity of the tests and analytical data can be verified .

1. Objective
2. Scope
3. Personnel
4. Facilities
5. Documentation
6. Calibration
7. Out of Specification
8. Validation to Analytical Methods
9. Change Control
10. Laboratory Reagents and Reference Standards
11. Safety
12. Training
13. Quality Audit
14. Management Review

1. OBJECTIVE

Compliance with GLP is a regulatory/ legal requirement for the acceptance of certain studies, undertaken by facilities, to be submitted to Regulatory/Health Authorities, for risk assessment in Health and Environmental Safety. For example in UK the Good Laboratory Practice Monitoring Authority (GLPMA) enforces compliance. The GLP Regulations require that any test facility that conducts, intends to conduct a "regulatory study" must be a member, or prospective member, of the UK GLP Compliance program. However there are test facilities, typically as part of a manufacturing organization, that conduct studies (Tests) which are not "regulatory studies" .This document is intended for such facilities. Besides this, in the arena of Life Sciences, whether in Research or Development or Manufacture, a good testing is a must for building confidence that the basis of GMP AND PRODUCT ASSESSMENT IS LOGICALLY AND scientifically correct. However the various branches of Life Sciences need such specific testing facilities from recombinant DNA testing to Pharmacovigilence that it will not be possible to cover all such esoteric testing facilities. This document therefore provides the basic requirement in the running of a general testing Laboratory in terms of good practices. The objective is to facilitate the proper application and interpretation of GLP principles in a generic manner.

2. SCOPE

This document is designed to facilitate the proper application and interpretation of the GLP principles for the Organization and for the Management of a Quality Control Laboratory and to provide guidance for the appropriate application of GLP principles to testing. This guidance document is organized in such a way as to provide easy reference to the GLP principles.

3. PERSONNEL

The Test Facility must have adequate personnel with the required qualification, experience and training (and Approval from regulatory authorities wherever needed) to carry out the assigned functions in a timely manner According to the principles of GLP.

A Job Description of every category/level of personnel in the Test Facility must be maintained. This must cover every individual engaged in testing/analyzing or supervising the analysis. The Job Description must also specify the limits of authority at each level/category. The training record for every individual cross referenced with the Job description and Departmental training. Material Safety Data Sheet must be available.

The Test Facility Manager must have sufficient educational background, experience, training and authority to ensure that the Principles of GLP re complied with, in the test facility.

The Test Manager will ensure that the personnel clearly understand the functions they are to perform and, where necessary, provide training for these functions. The Indian Drugs and Cosmetics Act and Rules there under requires that each area of operations in the Laboratory has an "approved" person (competent technical Staff) to conduct the tests and/or sign off the documentation.

4. FACILITIES ACCESS TO PRODUCTION:

The test facility should ideally be situated with direct access to personnel working in them, without the need to enter through the manufacturing area, and should be separated form manufacturing areas. This is Particularly important for laboratories involved in the control of biological, microbiological and radioisotopes, which should also be separated from each other. Steps should be taken in order to prevent the entry of unauthorized personnel. The area must not be used as a right of way by personnel who do not work in them. Laboratory personal, however, must have access to production areas for sampling and investigation as appropriate.

Facilities should be designed to suit the operations to be carried out in them. Lighting, temperature, humidity and ventilation should be appropriate and such that they do not adversely affect the products being tested or the accurate functioning of equipment. If sterility testing is conducted then the area should mimic the aseptic production conditions and gowning and entry procedures, with the final stage of the changing room being, in the at rest state, of the some air quality/ air classification as that into which it finally opens, viz. the aseptic testing area. Sterility test must be conducted under Grade A conditions, typically in a Laminar Flow Module, placed in class 100 conditions. Sufficient space should be available to avoid mix ups and cross contamination. There should be adequate storage space for samples and records.

All laboratory instrument and equipment should be qualified and calibrated in accordance with the manufacturers recommendations and pharmacopoeial requirement. All the test instruments and equipment must have unique identification numbers, (for their use, cleaning, calibration, service and maintenance) can be linked to analytical raw data, calibration reports and logbooks.

Separate rooms which are climate controlled may be necessary to protect sensitive instruments from that electrical interference, humidity, vibrations etc.

Control samples or reference samples also will need a separate room which is equipped with temperature and humidity control capable of achieving the same storage conditions as stated on the labels of the materials being tested. Proper consideration should be given to ventilation requirements of the areas depending on the activities carried out therein e. g. extraction, handling of fuming chemicals, organic solvents, distillation involving heating etc.

Personal protective equipment should be worn by personnel in the laboratory (see chapter on Safety). Ideally a distinctive overall or lab coat is advisable for laboratory personnel.

If part or all of the testing is contracted out and a contract testing laboratory is used, this should be audited and approved based on compliance with GLP. A technical agreement must be in place between the contract giver and the contract acceptor with a system in place to provide updated authorized analytical methods and specifications for the analysis involved. A change control system must also be in place with the contract testing laboratory.

5. DOCUMENTATION

The availability of a complete set of SOPs necessary to govern all the pertinent activities and procedures in the test facility is an absolute prerequisite. They define how to carry out protocol specificities. They should be written in a chronological order listing different steps in the accomplishment of an activity. There must be a Clear mention of responsibilities. SOPs must remain user friendly. Major consideration should be given to the degree of details incorporated in them. Some of the key SOPs which need to be addressed include:

a. Samples handling and accountability.
b. Receipt, identification, storage, method of sampling of test and control articles.
c. Record keeping, reporting, storage and retrieval of data.
d. Operating of technical audit personnel in conducting and reporting audits, inspections, reports, reviews.
e. Routine inspection of cleaning, maintenance, testing, calibration of equipment.
f. Handling of Out of Specification (OOS) results.
g. Calibration management.
h. Validation of analytical methods.
i. Change control procedure.
j. Health and safety protection.
k. Animal room preparation and animal care.
l. Storage, maintenance and traceability of microbial cultures.
m. Storage, use of reference standards and Reagents.
n. Laboratory waste handling.

There must be a SOP in the laboratory for glassware cleaning and it should be based on glassware washing efficiency both related to chemical labs and micro labs. Sensitive items like cells for photometry readings must have cleaning procedures that demonstrate adequate cleaning.

All documents used should be reviewed, authored prior to use. In case of exclusive use of the electronic media, the software and processes used should be validated and suitable measures put in place to ensure password controls.

Documents should be periodically reviewed and where necessary, revised to ensure continuing suitability. Invalid or supersedes documents must be promptly removed or otherwise assured against unintended use. Changes to documents should be reviewed and approved by the same function that performed the original Review.

Procedures should be established to describe how changes in documents in computerized systems can be made and controlled. Additionally, clear cut procedures must be evolved for storage, distribution, retrieval and destruction of documents.

Provision must be made to retain raw data, SOPs, documents, final reports for a predetermined period. There should be archives for orderly storage and expeditious retrieval. Conditions of storage should minimize deterioration. Persons responsible for archiving must be identified and only authorized persons must enter the archives.

Raw data should be recorded on duly controlled raw data sheets or prepaginated authorized logbooks. It should be verified independently by another competent person. The raw data including the automated instrument printouts should be immediately signed and dated by the analyst performing the test. The data stored on temporary storage media (e.g. thermal paper) should be transferred to robust storage media (e.g. Photocopy or scan of the print out) and duly authorized establishing traceability to the original raw data . Data should be recorded, wherever possible, so as to facilitate trending.

Tests performed must be recorded and the records should include at least following data:

1. Name of the material and where applicable dosage from.
2. Batch no. and where appropriate the manufacturer and/ or the supplier.
3. Reference to the relevant specifications and test procedures.
4. Test results, including observations and calculations, and reference to any Certificates of Analysis.
5. Date of testing.
6. Initials of the person/s that performed the test.
7. Initials of the person/s who verified the testing and the calculations where appropriate.
8. A clear statement of the status decision (release or reject etc.) and the dated signature of the designated Facility Manager or Responsible Person.

6. CALIBRATION

All test and measuring equipment are likely to influence the test results directly or indirectly and be subject to calibration.

The frequency of calibration depends on the instrument, the recommendation from manufacturer, laboratory experience and extent of use Procedures employed for calibration must be clearly Written down and test report must conclude with a statement of "status". In case of nonconformilt, the report must indicate corrective and preventive action.

All the test instruments and equipment must have a unique identification number that should be linked to analytical raw data, calibration reports and logbooks for their use.

Calibration certificate/ calibration record/ calibration report should carry a unique identification number, the name and address of the agency, if outside expert is involved, in addition to the identification and description of test procedure including traceability to primary standards if used. The certificate should also indicate the calibration results and the due date for next calibration. The equipment should have a tag displaying the status of calibration.

When an instrument for calibration has been adjusted or replaced, the calibration results before and after repair, if available, should be reported. Reference materials used must be characterized, certified, purchased.

From reputable sources and traceable to national and international measures. When an instrument is found "Out of Calibration" it should be conspicuously labeled as such so that its use for testing is prevented. The test results between non-compliant calibration results and last successful calibration should be reviewed to confirm the correctness of the test result reported and appropriate action should be taken based on the outcome of the investigation. In case of frequent failures, the frequency of calibration and preventive maintenance should be reviewed and if necessary

7. OUT OF SPECIFICATION (OOS)

Out of Specification (OOS) results are those results, generated during testing that do not comply with the relevant specification or standards or with the defined acceptance criteria. If at any time during the process of study or testing, a result is obtained that is out of specification or is considered "atypical"(for example during stability testing), a defined procedure must be followed to investigate the result and

Determine the course of action.

The objective of the procedure is to ascertain if the OOS or atypical result is valid (.i. e. that the result is an accurate representation of the measured attribute of the sample taking into consideration the precision of the analytical method) and, if the results valid, to determine its probable cause and impact. OOS or atypical results can arise from causes that can be divided into 3 main categories.

. Laboratory Error
. Operator error –Non-Process Related
. Process related- Manufacturing Process Error

The first stage of the procedure is a laboratory investigation to determine if the OOS is clearly assignable to laboratory error. If so than the result may be discarded and the test repeated. If the OOS is not clearly due to Laboratory error then the investigation is expanded outside the laboratory testing and can include re-sampling. The aims of the expanded investigation are to identify the probable cause of the OOS or atypical result and to determine the significance of the result when making decisions about the material or product under test.

Under certain circumstances there may be justification for not following the above procedure when OOS or Atypical result is obtained. Examples of such situations include, but are not limited to:

* Pharmacopoeial specifications which give specific guidance in tests like Content Uniformity, Dissolution, Sterility Testing etc.
* Stability Testing, where prediction from trend analysis indicate that the result is valid.
* OOS supported by results for other tests like low assay with high result for impurity content.
* Investigation of OOS for a starting material, raw material or intermediate may, where justified, be restricted to a consideration of the suitability of the material for onward processing.

In circumstances where the procedure is not followed, the justification for this approach must be documented and approved by the Facility Manager.

8. VALIDATION OF ANALYTICAL METHODS

All analytical methods, particularly non-standard and in-house test methods must be validated by a laid down procedure. All analytical equipment must be appropriately qualified before method validation. The degree of validation should reflect the purpose of analysis and the type of product being tested. For example there should be an increasing degree between tests for packaging materials, raw materials, intermediates and finished products or clinical trial materials. The validation methodology must clearly documented and should include.

* Selectivity and specificity
* Range
* Linearity and range
* Robustness
* Bias
* Precision
* Limit of detection
* Limit of quantification

A record must be maintained of any modification of the validated method and should include reason for modification and appropriate data to verify that results are as accurate and reliable as the established method. Suitability of all methods should be verified under actual conditions of use documented. In addition, it would also be useful to perform inter-laboratory comparison of results periodically.

9. CHANGE CONTROL:

All changes in equipment, test environment, test method, services, systems or location that may affect reproducibility, accuracy or standards must be formally requested, documented and accepted. The likely impact of the change should be evaluated and the change control procedure should ensure that sufficient supporting data are generated to demonstrate that change does not affect the and result or the in-house or registered specifications.

10. LABORATORY REAGENTS and REFERNCE STANDARDS:

There must by written procedures in place for the handling of reagents and preparation of standard solutions.

A primary standard is one that has been shown by an extensive set of analytical tests to be authentic material of established quality. This standard may be obtained from a recognized source (like USP, BP etc) or may be prepared by independent synthesis or by further purification of existing production material. An "in-house primary standard" is an appropriately characterized material prepared by the manufacturer from a representative lot the purposes of physicochemical testing of subsequent lots and against which in-house reference material is calibrated. A "secondary standard" is a substance of established quality, as shown by comparison to a primary reference standard, used as reference standard for routine laboratory analysis.

Reagents should be dated as soon as received and a "use by" date assigned based on experience or alternatively a short date (1 year) first assigned which can than be extended based on retesting. Laboratory reagents intended for prolonged use should be marked with the preparation date and the signature of the person who prepared them. The expiry date of unstable reagents and culture media should be indicated on the label, together with specific storage conditions. In addition, for volumetric solutions, the last date of standardization and the last current factor should be indicated.

Reagents and chemicals should be stored be stored by their hazard class and not by alphabetical order. For example storage should be by segregating into groups of oxidizers, reactive, corrosives etc. Within the particular group alphabetical storage may than be done.

11. SAFETY

People who work in scientific laboratories are exposed to many kinds of hazards. This can be said of most workplaces; in some, the hazards are well recognized (those of ordinary fire, for example) and the precautions to be taken are obvious.

Laboratories, however, involve a greater variety of possible hazards than do most workplaces, and some of those hazards call for precautions not ordinarily encountered elsewhere. It is however not possible to enumerate each and every safety precaution that should be followed; this chapter consequently sets forth some of the major rules for safety and recommends the reader to the Bibliography at the end for wider reading and understanding of specific hazards and safety practices to deal with these.

The design and construction is the first instance of building safety features in the laboratory. Laboratory must be equipped with adequate fire extinguishers, personnel protective equipment (PPE), SAFETY SHOWERS, EYE WASH FOUNTAINS AND FIRST AID KITS. The design should facilitate the change of street clothes and footwear to specific PPE needed by the laboratory personnel.

No employee should work alone in a laboratory or chemical storage area when performing a task that is considered usually hazardous by the laboratory supervisor or safety officer. Clothing worn in the laboratory should offer protection from splashes and spills, should be easily removable in case of accident, and ideally should be fire resistant. No food, beverage or cosmetic products should be allowed in the laboratory or chemical storage area at any time.

Laboratories using compressed gas cylinders should ensure that they are secured at all times either to a wall or Placed in a holding cage to prevent tipping. Since the gases are contained in heavy, highly pressurized metal containers, the large amount of potential energy resulting from compression of the gas makes the cylinder a potential rocket or fragmentation bomb. In summary, careful procedures are necessary for handling the various compressed gases, the cylinders containing the compressed gases, regulators or valves used to control Gas glow, and the piping used to confine gases during flow. Ideally the cylinders should be located outside the lab, with clearly labeled piping identifying the gas, piped into instruments or parts of the lab.

Storage of flammable solvents should be minimized as far as possible and cabinets used for storage of flammable liquids must be properly used and maintained and only materials that are compatible must be stored together.(refer to OSHA in).Reagents, solutions, glassware or other apparatus should not be stored in fume/extraction hoods as this not only reduces the available space but more importantly may interfere with the proper airflow pattern and reduce the effectiveness of the hood as a safety device.

11. TRAINING

Test Facility management must provide training for all personnel whose duties involve the conducting of tests and analysis. Training should also be provided to other personnel whose activities could affect the quality of testing. Besides the basic training on the theory and practice of GLP, newly recruited personnel should receive

Training appropriate to the duties assigned to them. This should provide personnel with good motivation to perform the relevant tasks in a manner aiming towards full compliance of GLP.

Following the identification of training needs, general training sessions or small workshops for personnel should be laid down for successful implementation of GLP. These should be followed by "hands on" exercises leading to practical application of GLP principles. Training programs must lead to change in "cherished habits" of personnel. The importance of documentation used for legible, indelible recording of all events, data and other occurrences together with their dating and initialing, correctly introducing change into records must be highlighted. Training program should be designed so as to maintain continuity. A constant coaching may be needed to enable the immediate detection, admonition and correction of slips, errors, omission and neglect.

A formal training program, in the form of an SOP, must be in place which includes a procedure for assessing the competence/skills of the personnel undergoing training. Records must be maintained of persons who are adjudged competent and authorized, including dates of authorization to perform specific tasks such as sampling, testing, calibration, operating typical equipment, issuing of test reports, etc.

In addition, the records of their educational and professional qualification, training undergone, skills and experience shall also be maintained (See section on Personnel).

12. QUALITY AUDIT

The test Facility should have a documented Quality Assurance (QA) Program to assure that tests/studies performed are in compliance with these principles of good Laboratory Practice. The QA program or Self Audit should be carried out by an individual or by individuals who are designated by and directly responsible to the Facility Manager and who are thoroughly familiar with the test procedures. These individuals must not be involved in the conduct of the study/test being assured.

The responsibilities of these QA/Audit personnel include, but are not limited to, the following functions;

a. Maintain a copy of all approved test methods/study plans and SOPs in use in the test facility.
b. Verify that the test methods/study plans contain the information required for compliance with these principles of Good Laboratory Practice.
c. Conduct audits/inspections to assure that tests are conducted in accordance with these principles of Good Laboratory Practice. Inspections can be of three types as specified by the QA SOP:

   I. Study/Test-based inspection
   II. Facility-based inspection

III. Process-based inspection
d. Document and retain records of all inspections.
e. Inspect the final reports to confirm that the methods, procedures and observations are accurately and completely described and that the reported results accurately and completely reflect the raw data of the studies/tests.
f. Promptly report inspection results in writing to the Facility Manager and ensure that corrective action is put in place if necessary.

13. MANAGEMENT REVIEV

Management of a test facility has the ultimate responsibility for ensuring that the facility as a whole operates in compliance with the GLP principles. This will involve the implementation of Quality Assurance or Quality Audit program which is independent of the actual conduct of test/study and is designed to assure the test facility management of compliance with these principles of GLP.

The individuals responsible for conducting the program must not be involved in the test or in any study program being assured. The implementation of such an audit program is discussed under the chapter "Quality Audit". Records of these inspections along with corrective actions taken should be archived. Archival facilities should enable secure storage and retrieval of all documents like Test methods, raw data, final reports etc.

Normally an inspector from a Regulatory Agency will not request to see an actual report of an audit as such requests could inhibit auditors when preparing inspection reports. It is sufficient to show that a program of self audit exists through documented evidence and to show that a procedure for corrective action is also in place.

20. US-FDA DRUG MASTER FILES (DMF)

TYPES AND CONTENTS:

A DRUG MASTER FILE (DMF) is a submission to the Food and Drug Administration (FDA) that may be used to provide confidential detailed information about facilities, processes, or articles used in the manufacturing, processing, packaging and storing of one or more human drugs. A DMF is submitted solely at the discretion of the holder. Drug Master Files are provided for in 21 CFR 314.420.

Types and Contents of the DMF:

There are five types of Drug Master Files and they include:

1) Type I: *Manufacturing Site, Facilities, Operating Procedures, And Personnel*

A type I DMF is recommended for a person outside the United States to assist FDA in conducting on site inspections of their manufacturing facilities.

The DMF should describe the manufacturing site, equipment capabilities, and operational layout. The description of the site should include acreage, actual site address, and a map showing it's location with respect to the nearest city. An aerial photograph and a diagram of the site may be helpful.

A diagram of major production and processing areas is helpful for understanding the operational layout. Major equipments should be described in terms capabilities, application, and location. Make and model would not normally be needed unless the equipment is new or unique.

A diagram of major corporate organizational elements, with key manufacturing, quality control, and quality assurance positions highlighted, at both the manufacturing site and corporate headquarters, is also helpful.

2) Type II: *Drug Substance, Drug Substance Intermediate, and Material Used in their Preparation, or Drug Product:*

A Type II DMF should, in general, be limited to a single drug intermediate, drug substance, drug product, or type of material used in their preparation. For drug intermediate, drug substance summaries all significant steps in the manufacturing and controls of the drug intermediate or substance. For drug product manufacturing procedure and controls for finished dosage forms should ordinarily be submitted in an IND, NDA, ANDA or Exports Application. If all this information cannot be submitted in an IND, NDA, ANDA, or Export Application, It should be submitted in a DMF. When Type II DMF is submitted for a drug product and intermediate product special guide should be followed.

3) **Type III:** *Packaging Material.*

Each packaging material should be identified by the intended use, components, compositions and controls for its release. The names of the suppliers or fabricators of the components used in preparing the packaging material and acceptance specifications should also be given. Data supporting the acceptability of the packaging material for its intended use should also be submitted as outlined in the guideline.

4) **Type IV:** *Excipient, Colourant, Flavour, Essence or Material used in their Preparation:*

Each additives should be identified and characterized by its method of manufacture, release specifications, and testing methods. Toxicological data on these materials would be included under this type of DMF, if not otherwise available by cross reference to another document. Usually, the official compendia and FDA regulations for Colour additives (21 CFR Parts 70 through 82), Direct food additives (21 CFR parts 170 through 173), Indirect food additives (21 CFR parts 174 through 178) and Food substances (21 CFR Parts 181 through 186) may be used as source for release, tests, specifications, and safety.

5) **Type V:** *FDA Accepted Reference Information:*

FDA discourages the use of type V DMF's for miscellaneous information, duplicate information, or information that should be included in one of the other type of the DMF's. If any holder wishes to submit information that supporting data in a DMF that is not covered by Type I through IV, a holder must first submit a letter of intent to the DMF Staff. FDA will then contact the holder to discuss the proposed submission.

Type I, Type II and Type IV DMF's should contain a commitment by the firm that its facilities will be operated in compliance with applicable environmental laws.

21. CLEANROOM STANDARDS FOR DIFFERENT COUNTRIES AND NAMES

USA 209 E 1992		ISO 14644-1 1997	Japan B9920 1989	France X44101 1981	Germany VDI 2083 1990	UK BS 5295 1989	Australia AS 1386 1989
		ISO Class 1	1				
		ISO Class 2	2		0		
1	M1	ISO Class 3	3		1	C	0.035
10	M2	ISO Class 4	4		2	D	0.35
100	M3	ISO Class 5	5	4000	3	E, F	3.5
1000	M4	ISO Class 6	6		4	G, H	35
10000	M5	ISO Class 7	7	400000	5	J	350
100000	M6	ISO Class 8	8	4000000	6	K	3500
	M7	ISO Class 9			7	L	

22. GUIDANCE FOR PREPARATION OF SITE MASTER FILE (SMF) (MHRA)

GENERAL

The Site Master File is prepared by the manufacturer and contains specific information about the quality assurance, the production and/or quality control of pharmaceutical manufacturing operations carried out at the named site and any closely integrated operations at adjacent and nearby buildings. If only part of a pharmaceutical operation is carried out on the site, a Site Master File need only describe those operations, e.g. analysis, packaging, etc.

When submitted to a regulatory authority, the Site Master File provides information on the manufacturer's operations and procedures that can be useful in the efficient planning and undertaking of a GMP inspection.

These guidance notes have been set out in such a manner that each chapter and the paragraphs noted under "REQUIREMENT" is followed by "GUIDANCE" to provide details of how the requirements should be interpreted.

A Site Master File should be succinct and, as far as possible, not exceed approximately twenty-five to thirty A4 pages.

The Site Master File should have an edition number and an effective date.

REQUIREMENT

C.1 GENERAL INFORMATION

C.1.1 Brief information on the firm (including name and address), relation to other sites and, particularly, any information relevant to understand the manufacturing operations.

GUIDANCE

In not more than 250 words (one A4 page) outline the firm's activities, other sites, in addition to the site which is the subject of this report.

REQUIREMENT

C.1.2 Pharmaceutical manufacturing activities as licensed by the Competent Authorities.

GUIDANCE

C.1.2 Quote the relevant document as issued by the Competent Authority. State period of validity of license document (if the validity of the document is given in country concerned). Any conditions and/or restrictions should be stated.

REQUIREMET
C.1.3 Any other manufacturing activities carried out on the site.

GUIDANCE

C.1.3 This covers both pharmaceutical and non-pharmaceutical activities.
NB: See para C.1.6

REQUIREMENT
C.1.4 Name and exact address of the site, including telephone, fax and 24 hrs. telephone numbers.

GUIDANCE

C.1.4 Name and Address of Site
- a) Name of Company (and trading style if different). Postal Address including Code (street address if different).
- b) Telephone number of contact person.
- c) Fax number of contact person.
- d) 24 hour contact Telephone number

REQUIREMENT
C.1.5 Type of actual products manufactured on the site and information about specifically toxic or hazardous substances handled, mentioning the way they are manufactured (in dedicated facilities or on a campaign basis).

GUIDANCE

1) Type of Actual Products Manufactured
- a) Quote the type of actual products.
- b) Note any toxic or hazardous substances handled e.g. antibiotics, hormones, cytostatics. Note whether the products are manufactured in a dedicated facility or on a campaign basis.
- c) Mention if human and veterinary products are both prepared on the site.

REQUIREMENT
C.1.6 Short description of the site (size, location and immediate environment and other manufacturing activities on the site).

GUIDANCE

1) A Short Description of the Site
(not more than 250 words/one A4 page)
- a) The location and immediate environment.
- b) The size of the site, types of buildings and their ages.
- c) Other manufacturing activities on the site.

REQUIREMENT

C.1.7. Number of employees engaged in the quality assurance, production, quality control, storage and distribution.

GUIDANCE

(Note: Include employees working only part-time on full-time equivalent basis.

Give the rate of the academic and non-academic persons.)

a) Quality Assurance
b) Production
c) Quality Control
d) Storage and distribution
e) Technical and Engineering Support Services
f) Total of the above

REQUIREMENT

C.1.8 Use of outside scientific, analytical or other technical assistance in relation to manufacture and analysis.

GUIDANCE

1) For each outside contractor give:
   a) Name and address of the company.
   b) Telephone number
   c) Fax number
   d) Brief outline of the activity being undertaken in not more than 100 words (half an A4 page).

REQUIREMENT

C.1.9 Short description of the quality management system of the firm responsible for manufacture.

GUIDANCE

1) (Not more than 750 words or three A4 pages)
   a) State the firm's Quality Policy.
   b) Define the responsibility of the Quality Assurance function.
   c) Describe the elements of the QA system e.g. organizational structure, responsibilities, procedures, processes.
   d) Describe the audit programmers (self inspection or audits by external organisations undertaken).
   e) Describe how the results are reviewed to demonstrate the adequacy of the quality system in relation to the objective i.e. quality efficacy and safety of the product.

f) Record if standards such as ISO 9001-9004 are used by the company to assess its suppliers.

g) When suppliers of critical starting materials and packing materials actives,
excipients, containers and closures and printed materials are assessed, give details of how this is done.

i) Describe the release for sale procedure for finished products.

REQUIREMENT
C.2 PERSONNEL

C.2.1 Organisation chart showing the arrangements for quality assurance, including production and quality control.

C.2.2 Qualifications, experience and responsibilities of key personnel.

C.2.3 Outline of arrangements for basic and in-service training and how records are maintained.

C.2.4 Health requirements for personnel engaged in production.

C.2.5 Personnel hygiene requirements, including clothing.

GUIDANCE

1) PERSONNEL (500 words/two A4 pages)
   a) Organization chart
      i) Organogram for quality assurance including production and quality control. Record   senior managers and supervisors only.
   b) Qualifications, Experience and Responsibilities of Key Personnel.
      i) Brief details of academic qualifications and work related qualifications and years relevant experience since qualifying.
   c) Outline of Arrangements for Basic and In-service Training and how Records are maintained.

   Give brief details of the training program and include induction and continuous training, as follows:
      i) Describe how training needs are identified and by whom.
      ii) Give details of training relative to GMP requirements.
      iii) State the form of training e.g. in-house, external, and how practical experience is gained and which staff are involved.
      iv) Explain how the efficacy of the training is assessed e.g. by questionnaires.
      v) Explain how retraining needs are identified.
      vi) Give brief details of records kept.
   d) Health Requirements for Personnel Engaged in Production
      i) Who is responsible for checking health of employees ?
      ii) Is there a pre-employment medical examination ?

iii) Are employees routinely checked from time to time depending on nature of their work ?

iv) Is there a system for reporting sickness or contact with sick people before working in a critical area ?

v) Is there a system of reporting back after illness ?

iv) Are those who work in clean areas (grade A-D) subject to additional monitoring ?

e) Personnel Hygiene Requirements Including Clothing.

i) Are there suitable washing, changing and rest areas ?

ii) Is the-clothing suitable for the activity undertaken ? Briefly describe the clothing.

iii) Are there clear instructions on how protective clothing should be used and when it should be changed ? Detailed procedures are not needed. Is in house or external laundry used ?

REQUIREMENT

C.3 PREMISES AND EQUIPMENT

Premises

C.3.1 Simple plan or description of manufacturing areas with indication of scale (architectural or engineering drawings are not required).

C.3.2 Nature of construction and finishes.

C.3.3 Brief description of ventilation systems. More details should be given for critical areas with potential risks of airborne contamination (schematic drawings of the systems are desirable). Classification of the rooms used for the manufacture of sterile products should be mentioned.

C.3.4 Special areas for the handling of highly toxic, hazardous and sensitising materials.

C.3.5 Brief description of water systems (schematic drawings of the systems are desirable) including sanitation.

C.3.6 Maintenance (description of planned preventive maintenance programmes and recording system).

Equipment

C.3.7 Brief description of major production and control laboratories equipment (a list of equipment is not required).

C.3.8 Maintenance (description of planned preventative maintenance programmes and recording system).

C.3.9 Qualification and calibration, including recording system. Arrangements for computerized systems validation.

Sanitation

C.3.10 Availability of written specifications and procedures for cleaning manufacturing areas and equipment.

GUIDANCE
1) PREMISES AND EQUIPMENT
  a) Premises
   i) Provide a site plan highlighting production areas.
   ii) Provide a simple plan of each production area with indication of scale. Label areas and annotate plan with names.
   iii) Plans should be legible and on A4 sheets of paper. Plans could be on A3 sheets of paper if considered necessary.
   iv) For sterile product areas indicate room and area classification and pressure differentials between adjoining areas of different classifications.
  b) Nature of Construction and Finishes
  (500 words/two A4 pages)
   i) To reduce narrative for a large complex plant, the details should be limited to critical areas.
   ii) These areas must include all processing and packaging and/critical storage areas.
   iii) A narrative format is preferred.
  c) Brief Description of Ventilation Systems etc.
  (500 words/two A4 pages)

  Note 1: More details should be given for critical areas with potential risks of airborne contamination. This will include sterile product areas as well as areas for processing powders, granulation and tabletting. For sterile product areas a summary of the results of the most recent qualification/ requalification should be given.

  Note 2: To reduce the narrative, schematic drawings should be used. The following data should be given:
  i) Design criteria e.g.
  Specification of the air supply
  Temperature
  Humidity
  Pressure differentials and air change rate
  Simple pass or recirculation (%)
  ii) Filter design and efficiency e.g.
  Bag 99% efficiency.
  HEPA 99.997% efficiency .
  Details of any alarms on the ventilation system should be given.
  iii) The limits for changing the filters should be given.
  iv) If DOP (dioctyl-phthalate) is introduced, the point must be shown.
  v) Give the frequency of revalidation of the system.

d) Special Areas for the Handling of Highly Toxic Hazardous and Sensitising Materials
   i) Follow the same layout as 3.1 above.
   ii) Brief Description of Water Systems, including sanitation (500 words / two A4 pages)

   Note: Schematic drawings of the systems are preferred. The following information must appear:
   i) The schematic must go back to the city supply system.
   ii) The capacity of the system (maximum quantity produced per hour).
   iii) Construction materials of the vessels and pipework
   iv) Specification of any filters in the system must be given.
   v) If water is stored and circulated, what is the temperature at the point of retune
   vi) The specification of the water produced
       a) Chemical
       b) Conductivity

e) Microbiological
   vi) The sampling points and frequency of testing.
   vii) The procedure and frequency for sanitation.

f) Maintenance (250 words/one A4 page)
   Note: For the purpose of this guide "Maintenance" is carried out by the manufacturer and "servicing" by an outside contractor.
   i) Describe the planned preventative maintenance program.
   ii) Are there written procedures and suitable reporting forms for maintenance and servicing ? Do the documents record type frequency of services/checks, details of service, repairs and modifications ?
   iii) Are the maintenance routines that could affect product quality clearly identified ?
   iv) Are the reports made known to the users ?
   Equipment (250 words/one A4 page)

g) Brief Description of Major Production and Control Laboratory Equipment
   Note: Makes and model numbers of equipment are not required. However the following points should be addressed:
   i) Is the machinery constructed of appropriate material (e.g. AISI grade 316 stainless steel for product contact equipment ?)

ii) Have other materials been suitably validated e.g. polypropylene, chrome-plated brass, PVC (poly vinyl chloride), non-reactive plastic materials ?

iii) Is the equipment designed with ease of cleaning in mind ?

iv) Only a general description is required e.g. a rotary tablet press etc. If the equipment has additional devices, these should be recorded e.g. automatic weighing machines with printer; a labeler incorporating a bar code reader for the label; a lot number and expiry date over printer; a freeze drier equipped with a steam sterilization facility.

v) In the quality control laboratory only general descriptions such as pH meters, chromatographic equipment GLC (gas-liquid chromatography), HPLC (high performance liquid chromatography) with computer systems, particle size analyzers.

vi) In microbiology use general descriptions such as incubators (temperature ranges) facilities for LAL (limulus amebocyte lysate) testing, membrane filtration sterility testing, antibiotic assay, etc.

vii) In particular give brief information on the use of computers, microprocessors etc. in the factory.

b) Maintenance (250 words/one A4 page)

i) Who is responsible for maintenance and servicing ?

ii) Are there written procedures and contractual details for outside work ?

iii) Are maintenance routines which could affect product quality clearly identified ?

iv) Are records kept of:
   1. type and frequency of service/check;
   2. details of service repairs and modifications ?

v) Are reports made known to the users ?

h) Qualification, validation and Calibration
(750 words/three A4 pages)

i) Briefly describe the Company's general policy and protocols for qualification and validation (prospective and retrospective).

ii) Is there regular revalidation of critical equipment ?

iii) An outline of process validation may be given here or cross-referenced to production.

vi) Describe the system for the release for sale or supply of development and validation batches.

v) What are the arrangements for computer validation, including software validation ?

vi) Describe equipment calibration policy and records kept.

i) Sanitation

Cleaning procedures for manufacturing areas and equipment

(250 words/one A4 page)

i) Are there written specifications and procedures for cleaning. Cleaning agents and their concentration for the method of cleaning and the frequency?

ii) Are cleaning agents changes from time to time?

iii) Have the cleaning procedures been validated and what was the method of evaluating the effectiveness of cleaning?

iv) Are cleaning methods monitored routinely by chemical and/or microbiological methods?

v) What are the cleaning methods (and their frequency) for the water supply system, air handling system and dust extraction system?

REQUIREMENT
C.4 DOCUMENTATION

C.4.1 Arrangements for the preparation, revision and distribution of necessary documentation for manufacture.

C.4.2 Any other documentation related to product quality which is not mentioned elsewhere (e.g. microbiological controls on air and water).

GUIDANCE

1) DOCUMENTATION (500 words/two A-4 pages)

Note: This section refers to all documentation used in manufacture. Manufacture involves all activities relating to the production and control of pharmaceutical products.

2) Arrangements for the Preparation, Revision and Distribution of Documentation

   a) Is there a description of the documentation system?
   b) Who is responsible for the preparation, revision and distribution of documents?
   c) Where are the master documents stored?
   d) Is there a standard format and instruction of how documents are to be prepared?

   Are there documents for:
   1. Product Process Specifications
   2. Raw material specifications
   3. Packaging component specifications
   4. Standard process instructions including packaging
   5. Batch records including packaging
   6. Analytical methods
   7. QA release procedures.

e) How is the documentation controlled?
   f) For how long are documents kept after release of the batch ?
   g) Detail any arrangements for electronic or microfilmed records.
3) Other Documentation related to Product Quality
   Are the following documents available and in use ?
   a) Equipment specifications.
   b) Specifications for disposables i.e. cleaning materials.
   c) Standard operating procedures.
   d) Quality Control Procedures.
   e) Training procedures.
   f) Computer program specifications.
   g) Documentation control of process deviations.
   h) Calibration and test documents (see para 3. 9)
   i) Validation documents (see paras 3.9 and 5.4)
   j) Reconciliation of batches of raw materials, major packing components i.e. product-contact and printed materials.
   k) List and briefly explain the use of any additional standard documentation used routinely.

REQUIREMENT
C.5 PRODUCTION
C.5.1 Brief description of production operations using, wherever possible, flow sheets and charts specifying important parameters.
C.5.2 Arrangements for the handling of starting materials. packaging materials, bulk and finished products, including sampling, quarantine, release and storage.
C.5.3 Arrangements for reprocessing or rework.
C.5.4 Arrangements for the handling of rejected materials and products.
C.5.5 Brief description of general policy for process validation.

GUIDANCE
C.5   PRODUCTION
       This narrative should be kept to a minimum and generalized schematic layouts used where possible. The following points should be addressed.
C.5.1 Describe the operations capable of being carried out at the site with the existing facilities and specify the types of pharmaceutical products.
       When packaging only is undertaken, give a brief, description only, e.g. labeling, filling etc. and the nature of containers used e.g. sachets, tamper evident glass containers.
       If cytotoxic or radio-active substances are handled give details of the products.

Describe the production operations using flow charts if possible. Technical details are not required.

Describe how products are identified during production and how in-process storage is organized.

C.5.2 Arrangements for handling Starting Materials. Packing Materials, Bulk and Finished Products including Sampling Quarantine Release and Storage.

Identification of suppliers lot number with the company's lot number.

Sampling plans.

Status labeling e.g. by using labels or by computer.

Issue of materials to manufacture and package.

The control of weighing.

Checking methods.

How are materials being used for manufacture identified and released ?

    C.5.2.1 Control of Bulk Manufacture

        Checks on key parameters during manufacture e.g. blend times, filter integrity tests.

        Records of key parameters.

        In-process checks.

        Records of in-process checks.

        Compliance with the Marketing Authorization.

    C.5.2.2 Packing

        Release of bulk, semi-finished products, packing materials,

        Confirmation of identity and line clearance checks;

        In-process checks.

    C.5.2.3 Quarantine and release of finished products; compliance with the Marketing Authorization.

    C.5.2.4 Explain the role of the Authorized Person(s).

C.5.3 Arrangements for Reprocessing or Rework

    C.5.3.1 What arrangements are in place for reprocessing or reworking batches of products ?

C.5.4 Arrangements for Handling Reject Materials and Products

    C.5.4.1 Are reject materials and products clearly labeled ? Are they stored separately in restricted areas ?

    C.5.4.2 Describe arrangements for sentencing the materials and their disposal. Is destruction recorded ?

C.5.5 Brief Description of the General Policy for Process Validation

An outline of process validation protocol only is required.

REQUIREMENT

C.6 QUALITY CONTROL

C.6.1 Description of the Quality Control system and of the activities of the Quality Control. Department Procedures for the release of finished products.

GUIDANCE

C.6 QUALITY CONTROL

C.6.1 Activities of the Quality Control Department

    C.6.1.1 (a) Describe the elements of the QC system e.g. specifications, test methods, and other quality related data collection.

    (b) Briefly describe the activities of analytical testing, packaging component testing, biological and microbiological testing.

    C.6.1.2 If the review of batch documentation and release of final documentation takes place in this department, give details.

    C.6.1.3 Outline the involvement in the arrangements for the preparation, revision and distribution of documents in particular those for specification test methods and release criteria if not mentioned elsewhere.

REQUIREMENT

C.7 CONTRACT MANUFACTURE AND ANALYSIS

C.7.1 Description of the way in which the GMP compliance of the contract acceptor is assessed.

GUIDANCE

C.7 CONTRACT MANUFACTURE AND ANALYSIS

C.7.1 Describe briefly the details of the technical contract between the contract giver and acceptor and the way in which the GMP compliance is assessed to ensure product compliance with the Marketing Authorization.

REQUIREMENT

C.8 DISTRIBUTION, COMPLAINTS AND PRODUCT RECALL

C.8.1 Arrangements and recording system for distribution.

C.8.2 Arrangements for the handling of complaints and product recalls.

GUIDANCE

C.8 DISTRIBUTION

C.8.1 A Description of Storage and Distribution Practices

    C.8.1.1 Is the warehouse secure ?

    C.8.1.2 Is it environmentally controlled ?

C.8.1.3 Is there refrigerated storage ?
C.8.1.4 How are the materials stored e.g. pallet racking ?
C.8.1.5 How is the status of products controlled e.g. by computer, by label ?
C.8.1.6 What are the methods of distribution to customers ?
C.8.1.7 Does the dispatch order ensure first in/first out and identify the lot number ?

C.8.2 Records of Distribution

Do the retained records permit full batch traceability from the factory to the customer, in terms of the date of sale, customer details and quantity dispatched ?

C.8.2.1 Complaints
    C.8.2.1.1 Is there a written complaints procedure ?
    C.8.2.1.2 Who is responsible for:
        1. Logging;
        2. Classifying;
        3. Investigating complaints.
    C.8.2.1.3 Are written reports prepared ?
    C.8.2.1.4 Who reviews these reports ?
    C.8.2.1.5 For how long are complaints records kept ?

C.8.2.2 Product Recalls
    C.8.2.2.1 Is there a written procedure which describes the sequence of actions to be followed including:
        1. Retrieval of distribution data;
        2. Notification of customers;
        3. Receipt/segregation/inspection of returned product;
        4. Investigation/reporting of cause;
        5. Reporting corrective action.
    C.8.2.2.2 Who is responsible for co-coordinating product recalls ?
    C.8.2.2.3 Who notifies the Competent Authority of complaints and recalls.
    C.8.2.2.4 Is the Competent Authority involved in complaints and the decision to recall ?
    C.8.2.2.5 Can recalls be effected below wholesale level ?

REQUIREMENT
C.9 **SELF INSPECTION**
C.9.1 Short description of the self inspection system.

GUIDANCE

C.9.1.1 Describe how the self inspection system verifies that those activities that have a bearing on quality comply with the planned arrangement.

C.9.1.2 Are the quality systems effective ?

C.9.1.3 Are there documented procedures for the self inspection system and for the follow-up actions ?

C.9.1.4 Are the results of the self inspection system documented, brought to the attention of the personnel having responsibility for the area and activities inspected ?

C.9.1.5 Does the system ensure that those responsible for the area or activity take timely corrective actions on the deficiencies found ?

❖❖❖

23. STERILIZATION METHODS

Sterilization is killing or removal of Micro-organisms and their Spores from the substance, material, or preparation required to be used in sterile form.

METHODS OF STERILIZATION:
1) **Physical Methods:**
   a) Dry Heat Sterilization
   b) Moist Heat Sterilization.
   c) Radiation Sterilization. (UV and Gamma radiations.)
2) **Chemical Methods:**
   a) Ethylene Oxide Gaseous Sterilization
   b) Use of Antimicrobial Agents.
3) **Mechanical Method:**
   a) Filtration through Bacteria Proof Filter.

1) **Physical Methods:**

a) Dry Heat Sterilization (DHS):

It is suitable for heat stable, non-aqueous product and powders. Ampoules and Vials and Glassware's Sterilization and Depyrogenation. Time and Temperature cycle is as follows:

180 °C temp for --------------- 30 min.
170 °C temp for --------------- 1 hours.
160°C temp. for --------------- 2 hours.

Glass Depyrogenation can be done at 250 °C temp. for 2 to 3 hours.

IP 2007 sterilization methods recommends reference condition a minimum of 160°C at least for 2 hours; other combinations of time and temperature may be used provided that it has been satisfactorily demonstrated that the process chosen delivers an adequate level of lethality when operated routinely within the established tolerance. The procedures and precautions employed should be such as to give an SAL of 10^{-6} or better. An acceptable range in temperature in the empty chamber is ± 15° C when the unit is operating at not less than 250° C. An SAL (Sterility Assurance Level) of 10^{-12} is considered achievable for heat stable articles or components.

Mode of action: Bacterial Cell Protein Oxidation.

b) Moist or Steam Sterilization(autoclave):

This involves heating in autoclave with saturated steam under pressure and it is applicable for Aqueous preparations and Surgical Material. Time and Temperature cycle:

Holding Temp. °C	Minimum Holding Time minutes.
115 to 118°C	30 Minutes
121 to 124°C	15 Minutes
126 to 129°C	10 Minutes
134 to 138°C	3 Minutes

As per IP 2007 The reference condition for steam sterilization for aqueous preparations are heating at a minimum of 121°C for 15 minutes. Other combinations of time and temperature may be used provided that it has been satisfactorily demonstrated that the process chosen delivers an adequate level of lethality when operated routinely within the established tolerance. The procedures and precautions employed should be such as to give an SAL of 10^{-6} or better. F_0 concept may be used for establishing the sterilization cycles. When surgical materials are sterilized the steam used should neither be superheated nor contain 5 % of entrained moisture. Appropriate steps should be taken to ensure adequate removal of air. Most dressing are conveniently sterilized by maintaining at a temperature of 134 ° C to 138° C for 3 minutes.

Mode of action: Precipitation of Cell Proteins of Bacterial Cell Wall.

c) Radiation Sterilization:

i) UV Radiations:

The UV light of Wavelength 2537 Angstrom units is commonly employed for sterilization.

The principle effect may be on cellular nucleic acids which has been shown to exhibit strong absorption bands within the UV wavelength range. Applicable for sterilization of Room, Air, Air ducts, Water and Linens etc.

ii) Ionizing Radiation:

Sterilization of drug substances, dosage forms and medical devices may be achieved by exposure in the final containers or packs to ionizing radiations in the form of gamma radiations from suitable radio isotopic source such as Cobalt - 60 or Cesium 137. For Gamma radiation sterilization, an effective sterilizing dose which is tolerated without damaging effect is about 25 kGY (2.5 Megarads) Ionizing Radiation destroys micro-organism by stopping reproduction as a result of lethal mutation.

2) Chemical Method:

Ethylene Oxide Sterilization (ETO):

This process involves exposure to a sterilizing gas. It is used for sterilization of plastic tubing's, dressing, card boards and rubber gloves. The material to be sterilized is placed in chamber and exposed to Relative Humidity of up to 98 % for a period of 60 minutes or longer. It is then placed in chamber previously heated to about 55 °C and an initial Vacuum of approximate 27 inch of Hg is drawn. Ethylene

Oxide is then introduced, along with moisture to achieve 50 to 60 % RH. To the pressure required to give desired concentration of ETO, which is maintained throughout the exposure period.

Mode of Action: Kills micro-organism by alkylating essential metabolites, affecting particularly the reproductive system. The altered metabolites are not available to the micro-organism, and so it dies without reproduction.

3) **Mechanical Method:**

Filtration Methods:

This method may be used for certain active ingredients and preparations that are not sufficiently stable to heat to allow sterilization by steam. The process depends on the physical removal of micro-organisms by adsorption on a filter medium of nominal pore size of 0.22 micron meter or less.

❖❖❖

24. STERILIZATION INDICATORS: INCLUDING ISO AND EN

Following are the Biological Indicators recommended for use as per IP 2007:

1) For Autoclave or Steam Sterilizations:

   Spores of *Geobacillus stearothermophilus* (*Bacillus stearothermophilus*) (NCTC 10007, ATCC 7953 and 12980)

   The Number of viable spores should be not less than 10,000 (10^4) and not more than 10,00,00,000 (10^8) per carrier. D value at 121°C shall not be less than 1.5 minutes.

2) For Dry Heat Sterilisation:

   Spores of Bacillus atrophaeus (Bacillus subtilis) ATCC 9372.

   The Number of viable spores should be not less than 10,000 (10^4) and not more than 10,00,00 ,000 (10^8) per carrier. D value at 160°C shall not be less than 2.5 minutes.

3) Radiation Sterilization:

   Spores of Bacillus pumilus NCTC 10327, ATCC 27142.

   The Number of viable spores shall not be less than 10,00,0000 (10^7) viable spores per carrier. D value shall be in the range of 0.15 to 0.20 Mrad (1.5 to 2.0kGy).

4) Ethylene Oxide Sterilization:

   Spores of Bacillus atrophaeus (Bacillus subtilis) ATCC 9372.

   The Number of viable spores should be not less than 10,000 (10^4) and not more than 10,00,00,000 (10^8) per carrier. D value at 54 °C, ± 1 °C; 60%, ± 10% RH and 600mg ± 30 mg /l of Ethylene Oxide shall not be less than 2.5 minutes.

BIOLOGICAL AND CHEMICAL INDICATORS
(ISO AND EN)

At international level three primary standards organizations have developed the sterilization standards, These three organizations are as:

1) ISO: International Organization for standardization.
2) CEN: European Committee for standardization.
3) AAMI (US): Association for Advancement of medical Instrumentation USA.

ISO develops it's sterilization standards through ISO/TC 198, - *Sterilization of Healthcare product.*

CEN develops its sterilization standards through CEN/TC-204, - *Sterilization of Medical devices.*

AAMI Authors consensus standards; recommended procedures and technical information reports (TIRs) for the US medical industry. The American National Standards Institute (ANSI) approves AAMI standards. AAMI has support from FDA.

The sterilization standards produced by ISO, CEN and AAMI organizations are very similar in nature.

But to avoid the confusion in these standards, In Sep.1999, at the 12th meeting of ISO/TC198 in London, ISO/TC, 198 and CEN/TC, 204 agreed to a joint revision of sterilization standards under provision of the Vienna, agreement with ISO leading this effort, as per revision:

a) Sterilization using moist heat: ISO 11134, ISO 13683 and CEN -554.
b) Sterilization using Ethylene Oxide (ETO): ISO 11135 and CEN -550.
c) Sterilization using Radiation: ISO 11137 and CEN -552.
d) Biological Indicators (BIs): ISO 11138 and CEN -866
e) Chemical Indicators (CIs): ISO 11140 and CEN -867.

Here information regarding BIs and CIs is given for the primary knowledge of the users.

BIOLOGICAL INDICATORS (BIs)
(ISO 11138 AND EN 866)

Biological indicators are used to test the effectiveness of given sterilization processes and equipment by assessing microbial lethality. Calibrated bacterial spores preparations are used to monitor the efficacy of sterilization process. Calibration of spores is performed in Specialized test equipment called BIER (Biological Indicator Evaluator Resistometer). Spores species used are as:

a) Moist Heat Sterilization: *Geobacillus Sterothermophilus*
b) Dry heat sterilization: *Bacillus Atrophaeus*
c) Ethylene Oxide Sterilization: *Bacillus Atrophaeus*.
d) Radiation Sterilization – *Bacillus pumils* .
e) Hydrogen peroxide Sterilization - *Geobacillus Sterothermophilus*

Currently there are three parts in the ISO 11138 series of Biological Indicators.

I) Part 1- General Requirements
II) Part 2 – BI for Ethylene Oxide Sterilization process.
III) Part 3 – BI for Moist heat sterilization Process.

The EN series consists of 8 parts,
- I)   Part 1: General Requirements.
- II) Part 2: BI for ETO sterilization Process,
- III) Part 3: BI for Moist heat sterilization process
- IV) Part 4: BI for Irradiation sterilization process.
- V)   Part 5: Low temperature, Steam and formaldehyde sterilization process (LTSP)
- VI) Part 6: BI for dry heat sterilization process.
- VII) Part 7: Self contained BI system for Moist heat sterilization process.
- VIII) Part 8: Self contained BI for ETO sterilization process.

Additionally there are three AAMI/ANSI BI standards adopted from ISO 11138 Part 1 to 3, with minor deviations for US. This standards are ST59, ST 21 and ST 19.

The primary function of these standard is to specify general production, labeling and performance requirement of BIs and spores suspension used in sterilization process.

In combined revision of the ISO 11138 and EN 866 standard series there are 5 parts:

1) ISO 11138-1: Sterilization of healthcare product – BI system – Part 1 – General requirement.
2) ISO 11138-2: Sterilization of health care products – BI system – Part 2 – Use in EtO sterilization process.
3) ISO 11138-3: Sterilization of health care products – BI system – Part 3 – Moist heat sterilization process.
4) ISO 11138-4: sterilization of health care products – BI system – Part 4 – Dry heat sterilization process.
5) ISO 11138-5: sterilization of health care products – BI system – Part 5 – Low temperature, steam and formaldehyde sterilization process.

Following are the some important changes reflected in the new combined revision of the following:

1) EN 866, Part 4 and EN 866 Parts 7 are eliminated.

2) Elimination of the "10" requirement in ISO-11138-3 and EN 866-3, that is the requirement that the product of the log 10 of the population and D= D121.1°C values must be Z 10 for BI used for Moist heat sterilization process. The new value will be Z-7.5 which is the product of the log 10 of the minimum requirement [1.0 ¥. 105 CFU] and the minimum requirement for D121.1C value (1.5 minutes).

3) Calculation of D value by the Holcomb – Spearman-Karber, The limited spearman-Karber ; or the Stumbo, Murphy-Cochran procedure; current ISO 1118-1, specifies Fraction Negative D value calculation by only the Limited spearman –Karber method.

CHEMICAL INDICATORS (CIs)
(ISO 11140 AND EN 867)

Like the biological indicators, the chemical indicators have multiple parts. The harmonization process for CIs includes the combined revision of the ISO 11140 CI standards series and the EN867 CI standards. Currently there are five parts of these standards series. The ISO 11140 series consists of following parts:

1) General Requirement,
2) Test Equipment,
3) Class 2 indicators for steam penetration sheets,
4) Class 2 indicators for steam penetration test packs and
5) Class 2 indicators for air removal test sheet and packs.

The EN 867 CI series is consistent with most of ISO 11140 pats,1, 3, and 4, but differs in that part 2 is specific for process indicators, and part specifies indicators for systems and PCDs for testing small sterilizers.

ANSI /AAMI ST60 is a modified version of ISO 11140, Part 1, the general requirements and ANSI /AAMI ST66 is similar to the ISO 11140 section that deals with class 2 indicators for air-removal test sheets and packs. The primary purpose of the three general requirements documents is to define the requirements for various classes of CIs. However, there are differences in classification schemes within the three sets of CIs standards. While classes 1-4 (ISO and AAMI) and Classes A-D (EN) are basically equivalent, only the ISO and AAMI standards include a class 5 integrating indicators and only ISO 11140-1 includes a class 6 emulating indicators (or cycle verification indicators). The new combined revision of ISO 11140, general requirements, will include all six of these CI classes.

Currently ISO 1140, Parts 3-5; EN 867, Parts 3-4; and ANSI /AAMI ST66 all specify various applications of the Bowie Dick or steam-penetration tests. These standards are being developed in the combined revision process but may not be finalized at the same time as the ISO 11140-1 general requirements standard. ISO 11140, Parts 2 on test equipment will be eliminated and replaced by the BI and CI test equipment standard, ISO 18472.

Following are the some changes made in the revised general requirement section of ISO standards:

1) Testing requirement for Class 5 integrating indicators that will be aligned more closely with BI performance.
2) A statement that the class number, that is 1-6 is not hierarchal in terms of the information provided, e.g Class 2 Bowie Dick indicators are generally more sophisticated than class 3 or 4 indicators.
3) Inclusion of Class 1 process indicators for the vapour phase hydrogen peroxide sterilization process with testing requirement.

❖❖❖

25. DEFINITIONS OF PHARMACEUTICAL STANDARD AND NORMAL VALUES

1. **pH:** pH is defined as the negative logarithm of the hydrogen ion concentration.
   pH = - log [H$^+$]
2. **Buffers:** These are solutions which resist change in their pH when a small amount of acid or alkalis are added to them. Buffers act as shock absorbers, against the sudden change in pH.
3. **pK:** pK is that at which acid is half neutralized.
4. **Osmosis:** The flow of the solvent through a semi permeable membrane from pure solvent to solution, or from a dilute solution to concentrated solution is called as Osmosis. (Greek Osmo- To push)
5. **Reverse Osmosis:** It is membrane selective process in which Osmosis process is reversed with the help of pressure in which higher solute concentration solutions passed through semi permeable membrane to lower concentration solutions.
6. **Diffusion:** Solvent molecule passes from the dilute to the concentrated solution and solute molecules passes from the concentrated to the dilute solution until equality of concentration is achieved.
7. **Isotonic Solutions:** They have the same osmotic pressure as within cells.
8. **Hypertonic Solutions:** They have the higher osmotic pressure than within the cells.
9. **Hypotonic Solutions:** They have the lower osmotic pressure than within cells.
10. **Surface Tension:** The force within which the surface molecules are held together and forms a membrane over the surface of the liquid is called surface tension.
11. **Adsorption:** The Process of holding up of substances from the solution on surface is called adsorption.
12. **Hydrotrophy:** The process where by water insoluble substances are made soluble without under going any chemical change.
13. **Crystalloid:** Crystalloid are those substances which diffuse readily through membrane.
14. **Colloids:** Those are substances which do not diffuse through membrane.
15. **Dialysis:** The process of separating crystalloids by diffusion through a membrane by osmotic force.

16. **Miliequivalent:** It is 1000th of a gram equivalent weight.
17. **Rf Value:** Rf is defined as the ratio of the distance travelled by the component to the distance travelled by the solvent. It is also called Retention factor.
18. **Optical Density:** It is the logarithmic ratio of the intensity of the incident light to that of the emergent light.
19. **Mutarotation:** It is change in specific rotation of an optically active solutions without any change in other properties.
20. **Saponification:** Hydrolysis of fat by an alkali is called saponification.
21. **Electrophoresis:** Migration of charged molecules under the influence of electricity is called electrophoresis.
22. **Viscosity:** The property of a liquid owing to which it resist the relative motion of it's parts is called Viscosity.
23. **Solubility:** The number of grams of the substance which will dissolve in 100 grams of the solvent at a stated temperature.
24. **Hydrolysis:** The decomposition of a salt by water in to free acid and free base is called hydrolysis of salts.
25. **Refractive index:** Refractive index of liquid is defined as the ratio of the *Sine* of the angles of Incidence and Refraction.
26. **Boiling Point:** Boiling point of liquid is that temperature at which its vapour pressure becomes equal to the atmospheric pressure.
27. **Molecular Weight:** The Molecular weight of substance is defined as the weight of a molecule of that substance as compared to the weight of an atom of oxygen as 16.
28. **Conductivity:** Reciprocal of the resistance is called Conductivity.
29. **Partition Coefficient:** It is defined as the ratio of unionized drug distributed between the organic and aqueous phases at equilibrium.
30. **Photolysis:** It is light generated breakdown of substances.
31. **Melting Point:** Those point of substance within which or the point at which, substance begins to coalesce and is completely melted.
32. **Weight per ml:** It is the weight, in gram, of 1 ml of liquid when weighed in air at 25°C.
33. **Potency:** It is the absolute amount of a drug required to produce a given pharmacological effect.
34. **Efficacy:** It refers to the peak or maximal effect, of the drug seen on the log dose curve. Hence the maximum effect of efficacy is greatest response produced by a drug regardless of dose employed.

35. **Half Life:** It is the time in which a concentration or effect declines by one half.

36. **Percentage solutions:** Weight in grams of solute per 100 gram of solution is % by weight and that same amount dissolved in 100 ml is % by volume solutions.

37. **Molar Solutions:** Molecular weight in gram of solute dissolved in 1000 ml is molar solution.

    Example: Molecular weight of H_2SO_4 is 98.016, so a molar solution is 98.016 g per 1000 ml.

38. **Molal Solutions:** Molecular weight in gram of a solute dissolved in 1000 g of solvent.

39. **Normal Solutions:** A normal solutions is one which contains per litre, the amount equal to gram molecular weight of substance divided by equivalent weight or number of replaceable hydrogen ions.

    Example: Molecular weight of H_2SO_4 is 98.016 where $H^+ + H^+$ and SO_4^- ions are present. As number of replaceable hydrogen atoms is 2, that is 49.008 grams in a litre.

40. **Acetyl Value:** It is the number which expresses in milligrams the amount of potassium hydroxide required to neutralize the acetic acid liberated by the hydrolysis of 1 g of the acetylated substance.

41. **Acid Value:** It is the number which expresses in milligrams the amount of potassium hydroxide required to neutralize the free acid present in 1 gram of substance.

42. **Ester value:** It is the number of milligrams of potassium hydroxide required to saponify the esters present in 1 gram of the substance.

43. **Hydroxyl Values:** It is the number of milligrams of potassium hydroxide required to neutralize the acid combined by acylation in 1 gram of substance.

44. **Iodine Value:** It is the number which expresses in grams the quantity of halogen, calculated as Iodine, which is absorbed by 100 g of the substance under the described condition.

45. **Peroxide Value:** It is the number of milliequivalent of active oxygen that expresses the amount of peroxide contained in 1000 gram of substance.

46. **Saponification Value:** It is the number of milligrams of potassium hydroxide necessary to neutralize the free acids and to saponify the esters presents in 1 gram of the substances.

26. COMMONLY USED PHARMACEUTICAL WORDS

1. **Marc:** The inert insoluble material after exhausting the drug in extraction process is known as Marc.

2. **Menstrum:** The solvent capable of penetrating, the plant or animal tissues and dissolving the active medicaments present in them are known as Menstrum.

3. **Decoction:** It is process of extraction of the hard and woody crude drugs where the water is used as menstrum and the crude drugs are boiled along with menstrum. Decoction differs from infusion in the respect that the crude drugs in infusion are not boiled with the mensrtum but only boiling menstrum is poured over the crude drug.

4. **Maceration:** It is the process of extraction in which solid crude drug is placed with whole menstrum in the closed vessel and allow to stand for seven days shaking occasionally. Strain press the marc and mix the liquid obtained. Clarify by filtration or other suitable method.

5. **Percolation:** This is the process wherein the maceration is followed by downward displacement of saturated menstrum and the drug is exhausted by the slow passage of the menstrum through the column of the drug.

6. **Sterilization:** It is the process of killing or removing of micro-organisms and their spores from the substance, material or preparation required to be used in sterile form.

7. **Eutectic Mixture:** Many substances, when combined with other powders turns in to liquid or gives rise to a pasty mass. Such combinations that is which liquefy are known as Eutectic Mixtures.
Example: Phenol, Menthol and Camphor.

8. **Racemic Mixture:** Mixture of Dextrorotatory and Levorotatory compound is called Racemic Mixture.

9. **CFU:** is colony forming unit is unit used for counting the colonies of the microbial growth.

10. **BOPP:** BOPP is Biaxialy Oriented Polypropylene Tapes used for the sealing of Boxes.

11. **ROPP Caps:** These are Roll - On Pilfer Proof Caps of suitable metal like aluminum which avoids pilferage (leakage) of liquid from container.

12. **Adulteration:** It is a practice of substituting original crude drug partially or wholly with other similar looking substances but the later is either free from or inferior in chemical and therapeutic properties.

13. **Misbranded Drugs:** Drug shall be deemed to be misbranded;
    a) If it is so coloured, coated, powdered or polished that damage is concealed or if it is made to appear of better or greater therapeutic value than really it is; or
    b) If it is not labelled in the prescribed manner; or
    c) If its label or container or anything accompanying the drug bears the any statement, design or device which makes false claim for the drug or which is false or misleading in any particular.

14. **Adulterated Drugs:** The Drug is deemed to be adulterated:
    a) If it consists whole or in part, of any filthy, putrid or decomposed substance; or
    b) If it has been prepared, packed or stored under insanitary condition whereby it may have been contaminated with filthy or whereby it may have been rendered injurious to health; or
    c) If its container is composed, in whole or in part, of any poisonous or deleterious substance which may render the contents injurious to health; or
    d) If it bears or contains, for purpose of colouring only, a colour other than one which is prescribed; or
    e) If it contains any harmful or toxic substance which may render it injurious to health or;
    f) If any substance has been mixed therewith so as to reduce its quality or strength.

15. **Spurious Drug:** Drug is deemed to be Spurious -
    a) If it is manufactured under the name which belongs to another drug; or
    b) If it is an imitation of, or is a substitute for, another drug or resembles another drug in a manner likely to device or bear upon it or upon its label or container the name of another drug unless it is plainly and conspicuously marked so as to reveal its true character and its lack of identity with such other drugs, or
    c) If the label or container bears the same name of an individual or company purporting to be the manufacturer of the drug, which individual or company is fictitious or does not exit or;
    d) If it has been substituted wholly or in part by another drug or substance; or
    e) If it purports to be the product of a manufacturer of whom it is not truly product.

16. **Cosmetic:** Any article intended to be rubbed, poured, sprinkled or sprayed on, or introduced in to, or otherwise applied to, the human body or any part there of for cleansing, beautifying, promoting attractiveness, or altering the appearance and includes any article intended for use as a component of cosmetics.

17. **Incompatibility:** The undesired change, taking place in the physical, chemical or therapeutic properties of the medicaments, when two or more ingredients of a prescription are mixed together is termed as incompatibility.

18. **Fumigation:** Fumigation is process of killing or removal of Micro-organism, Insects, Lizards, Cobwebs and other crawling from the air and Premises by using suitable fumigating agent.

❖❖❖

27. LIST OF IMPORTANT SOP IN PHARMACEUTICALS

Following are the SOP generally required in every department. Process sop are not included, but depending upon the process SOP should be prepared. Also Machine and Equipments SOPs are not included, but SOP for Cleaning, Operation, Maintenance and Calibration of every M/C and equipment should be prepared authorized and implemented.

List of SOP for Stores:
SOP for department opening and closing
SOP for stores department cleaning.
SOP for stores department fumigation and environmental control
SOP for RM receipt and storage .
SOP for PM receipt and storage.
SOP for RM/PM dispensing for production.
SOP for material inward.
SOP for material out ward.
SOP for storage conditions for RM /PM.
SOP for storage of inflammable solvent.
SOP for storage of finished product.
SOP for storage of stationary, disinfectant, detergent, dusters, chemical reagents, ion exchange resins regeneration acid/alkali.
SOP for physical stock verification and stock statement.
SOP for disposal of spillage powders/liquids.
SOP for status labeling.
SOP for issue and acceptance of excess RM/PM from production.
SOP for receipt and sending of goods other than RM/PM and FG.
SOP for storage/receipt and fate of market returned goods.
SOP for storage of rejected RM/PM.
SOP for giving shortages requirement for production plan. (RM/PM and other Material.)
SOP for storage of quarantine, approved and rejected material. (RM/PM)
SOP for dedusting of material.

SOP Production:
SOP for department opening and closing.
SOP for product department cleaning.
SOP for product department fumigation.
SOP for environmental control.

SOP for bulk product hand over to packing.
SOP for finished goods BSR transfer.
SOP for manufacturing line clearance.
SOP for packing line clearance.
SOP for receiving packing material from store.
SOP for receiving raw material from stores.
SOP for in process control in manufacturing.
SOP for in process control in packing.
SOP for stereo order, receipt and issue to printing.
SOP for batch change over in MFG.
SOP for product change over in packing.
SOP for completion of batch manufacturing record.
SOP for completion of batch packing record.
SOP for GRN checking and it's approval.
SOP for disposal of departmental scrap.
SOP for destruction of rejected printed/unprinted PM like labels, cartons and leaflets.
SOP for destruction of used/rejected rubber stereos
SOP for destruction of rejected DFC, partition, inner boxes, plates and other corrugation.
SOP for destruction of glass bottles, ampoules, vials and aluminum pp caps and seals.
SOP for destruction of rejected measuring cup, plastic jars, vial closures etc.
SOP for destruction of rejected bulk product.
SOP for material receipt to and sending from department
SOP for on-line rejection of RM/PM.
SOP for in-house identification numbers/codes.
SOP for return of recovery to MFG.
SOP for leak test.
SOP for swab/residual test.
SOP for clean room entry.

LIST of SOP for P and A

SOP for change room entry procedure for male workers.
SOP for Change room entry procedure for female workers.

SOP for Change room entry procedure for staff.
SOP for personnel hygiene and clothing.
SOP for laundering of uniforms.
SOP for fire fighting.
SOP for medical checkup.
SOP for escape routes.
SOP for handling of compressed gas cylinders.
SOP for employee training .
SOP for pest controls .
SOP for First Aid.
SOP for disposal of toxic waste from department and premises disposal of non-toxic waste from department and premises .
SOP for accident emergency plan and industrial safety.
SOP for drainage disinfection and cleaning.
SOP for fumigation.
SOP for cleaning and sanitation of walls .
SOP for cleaning and sanitation of floors .
SOP for cleaning and sanitation of ceilings.
SOP for visitor's entry and employee out pass.
SOP for recruitment and selection of employee.
SOP for time keeping and shift schedule.
SOP for periodical assessment for trainee.
SOP for induction program.
SOP for departmental behavior.
SOP for cleaning, sanitation and maintenance of premises and surrounding of factory premises cleaning of tube light, A/C, fan, furniture, fire extinguisher, telephone etc.

SOP for Engineering and Maintenance:
SOP for department opening and closing .
SOP for department cleaning .
SOP for sanitation of engineering and maintenance department .
SOP for segregation of defective equipment.
SOP for maintenance intimation.
SOP for preventive maintenance.
SOP for breakdown maintenance.
SOP for defect book.

SOP for QA and QC

SOP for preparation of SOP.

SOP for in-house code and numbers.

SOP for document control, revision and authorization.

Sop for laboratory cleaning.

Sop for laboratory opening and closing.

SOP for sanitation and fumigation of laboratory.

SOP for cleaning of glass wares.

SOP for sampling of raw material.

SOP for Sampling of Packing material.

SOP for sampling of finished goods/intermediates.

SOP for testing of RM.

SOP for testing of PM.

SOP for testing of finished goods and intermediates.

SOP for approval and rejection of RM.

SOP for approval and rejection of PM.

SOP for approval and rejection of intermediates.

SOP for all AR/CR numbering system.

SOP for market complaints.

SOP for market recall

SOP for salvaged, market return and expired goods.

SOP for recovery from rejection.

SOP for recovery from market returned/recalled FG.

SOP for status labeling, and color coding in premises.

SOP for reagent preparation.

SOP for standardization of volumetric solutions.

SOP for preparation of volumetric solution.

SOP for stability testing of RM and finished product.

SOP for internal quality audit.

SOP for house keeping audit.

SOP for checking, storage and destruction of BMR/BPR and other production record.

SOP for entry in to microbiology laboratory.

SOP for control sample, sampling, storage, testing, record, and destruction of out dated samples.

SOP for laboratory environmental control.

SOP for disposal of non-toxic waste.

SOP for disposal of toxic waste
SOP for reference standard/working Standard.
SOP for raw material control sample, sampling, storage, record, and destruction of outdated samples.
SOP for storage conditions of finished goods.
SOP for disposal of left over RM test samples.
SOP for disposal of PM test samples.
SOP for disposal of left over finished product test sample.
SOP for destruction of microbial nutrient media.
SOP for preparation of media.
DOP for swab/residual testing.
SOP for handling of dangerous chemicals.
SOP for sampling of water for analysis.
SOP for line clearance
SOP for total IPQA.
SOP for process validations.
SOP for cleaning method validations.
SOP for testing method validations.
SOP for validation and periodical microbial monitoring of areas.
SOP for purified water loop validation.
SOP for equipment/machine qualification (Validation).
SOP for batch control record.
SOP for approval of batch coding and overprinting on packing material.
SOP for leak test.
SOP for cleaning and storage of quality record.
SOP for QA documentation.
SOP for stereo order /receipt /checking and issue.
SOP for disposal of out dated printed packing material.
SOP for specifications and testing method for RM.
SOP for specification and testing of PM.
SOP for specification and testing of finished product.
SOP for specifications and testing of intermediates.
SOP for disposal of spillage of chemical/cyanide.
SOP for deviation report.
SOP for validation of analyst.
SOP for vender approval and evaluation.
SOP for preservative efficacy test

SOP for growth promotion test.
SOP for preparation of inoculums.
SOP for LAL testing.
SOP for pyrogen testing
SOP for abnormal toxicity testing.
SOP related to the general test, individual material test methods.
SOP for testing of effluent water.
SOP for operation, cleaning, calibration and maintenance of all machine and equipments.
SOP for investigation of Out Of Specification (OOS)
SOP for validation of disinfectant in premises.
SOP for laboratories safety.
SOP for Change control.
SOP for Risk analysis, measurement and control.

Misc. SOP

Management review.
Ensuring the effectiveness of corrective action.
Preventive action related systems.
Control of quality records.
Quality planning.
Cause and effect diagram.
Control of non-conforming product.
Corrective action related to product.
Production planning.
For review of contracts.

28. BOWIE DICK TEST FOR AUTOCLAVE VALIDATION

Rapid and even penetration of steam into all parts of the sterilization load is important factor for achieving and holding the sterilization time. Provision of steam which contains minimum volume of non condensable gases and removal of air from the chamber ensures the even and rapid penetration of steam. Residual air and non condensable gas if any will concentrated as a bubble in the load and inhibit steam penetration. This test helps the user to know whether or not steam penetration of the test pack is even and rapid. That is presence of air pockets and non condensable gases in the load can be ensured by Bowie Dick Test. It does not confirm that the sterilization conditions in the load have been achieved.

PRINCIPLE OF THE TEST:

This test is based on the use of a chemical indicator in the form of an adhesive tape stuck to a piece of suitable paper to form a St. Andrew's cross. This indicator paper is placed at the centre of the test pack of folded huckaback towels and then subjected to an operating cycle. The indicator tape shows a change of colour in response to a combination of time, temperature and moisture. If there is no air present in the chamber, steam will penetrate rapidly and completely and the indicator will show a uniform colour change in response to the paper, because of a lower temperature, lower moisture level or both. The modern Bowie Dick Test uses a Class B chemical indicator conforming to EN 867: Part 3 contained within a standard test pack.

When used in conjunction with a standard test pack, Class B indicators are designed to show a failure either if, at the start of the holding time, the temperature at the centre of the test pack is 2°C or more below the temperature in the active chamber discharge; or if the indicator is exposed to insufficient moisture. Both conditions are usually caused by the presence of air or other non condensable gases. Because of the tolerance necessary in the manufacture of chemical indicator, users should be aware that in order to detect a temperature difference of 2°C the indicator may show signs of failure with a smaller temperature difference.

PROCEDURE:

The Bowie Dick test is normally preceded by a warm up cycle. This cycle is necessary because the effectiveness of air removal may depend on all parts of the sterilizer being at working temperature. A satisfactory sterilizer may give a fail result if this is not done. Remove the wrapping from a standard test pack and place the indicator paper in the sheet located nearest to the centre of the pack. Reassemble and secure the pack and replace the wrapping.

Place the test pack in the chamber with the bottom of the pack supported 100-200 mm above the centre of the chamber base. Select the Bowie Dick Test cycle. Ensure that the holding time will not be longer than that specified below. If this time is exceeded, the indicator may change in such a way as to make it difficult to detect the variations that would indicate a fail condition.

HOLDING TIME FOR BOWIE DICK TEST CYCLE:

Sterilization temp. °C	Minimum holding time (Min.)	Maximum Holding time (Min)
134	3.3	3.5
126	10.8	11
121	16.8	17

Start the operating cycle. During the holding time, note the reading on indicator, the chamber temperature indicator and the chamber pressure indicator. When the cycle is complete, remove the indicator paper from the test pack. The test should be considered satisfactory if the following requirements are met:

1) There is a uniform change throughout the indicator;
2) The automatic controller indicates that a Bowie Dick Test cycle has just been completed.

It is important to compare the indicator at the corners of the paper with that at the centre so that any difference can be clearly seen. If there is any discernible difference the test should be recorded as failed, and the paper marked accordingly. A large area of unchanged points to a gross failure. The indicator paper should be marked with the results and kept for reference for at least three months. The chemical reaction continues during this time and the paper may be discarded when the indicator becomes unreadable. The associated batch process record should be kept at least 11 years. An unsatisfactory test results indicates that the machine should not be used until the fault has been rectified.

Some common causes of failure include:

i) An insufficient air removal from chamber.
ii) An air leak during the air removal stage.
iii) The presence of non-condensable gases in the steam supply.

Guideline for composition of test pack:

Following test procedure is recommended by the manufacturer of Bowie Dick Test Sheet – M/s Raven LF Bowie Dick test sheet.

The Bowie Dick test pack consists of folded 100 % Cotton surgical towels, which are freshly laundered but not Ironed. The towels must be folded to a size not smaller that 9 inch (23 cm) in the other direction and then placed one above other. The height of the test pack must 10 to 11 inch (25 to 28 cm) and weight must be 7 kg

.The total number of towels may vary from test to test depending on towels thickness and wear. A commercially available Bowie Dick test sheet must be placed in the centre of the pack. A single wrap made of 100 % cotton 140 thread count , two ply fabric and freshly laundered is then loosely applied .

Test packs or devices other than those described may be use only when if the manufacturer of the test pack provides statistically valid experimental evidence demonstrating equivalence.

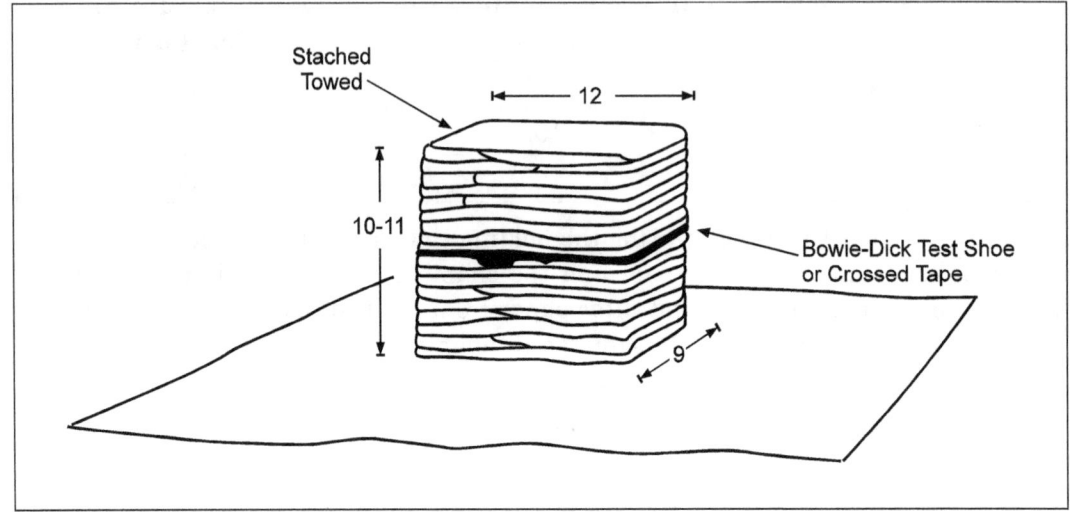

❖❖❖

29. STERILIZATION VALUES: F_0, F_H, D AND Z VALUES

Temperature, Time and Microbial resistance plays most important role in the sterilization process. Use of F, D, and Z values allows sterilization Pharmacist to compare the effectiveness of various sterilization cycles using mathematical model. These three values are used for constructing the mathematical rationale for the adequacy of sterilization.

F Value(F_0 and F_H): It is expressed in minute . It is equivalent time at specific temperature delivered to a container or unit of product. F Value centered at Autoclave is called F_0 value and for Dry heat sterilizer (De pyrogenation) it is called F_H Value.

F value is used for measurement of sterilization effectiveness. The F_0 value is the number of equivalent minutes of steam sterilization at temperature 121.1°C delivered to container of unit of product, calculated using a Z value 10°C. For example if it is states that F0 value is 8 minutes , means the process is conducted equivalent to exactly 8 minutes at 121.1°C, regardless of the process temperature and time use in the cycle. Another way if $F_{115.0}$ Value of 8 is stated then it says that the process being described is equivalent to exactly 9 minute at 115.0°C regardless of the process time and temperature used in the cycle.

The F_H is similar to F_0 and is used to describe the number of equivalent minutes of dry heat sterilization at temperature 170°C delivered to a container or units of product calculated using a Z value of 20 °C.

Following formulae is used for calculation of F_0 and F_H Value:

$$F_0 = \Delta t \times 10^{T-121.1/Z}$$

Where,

    Δt is cycle hold time,

    T - Cycle actual temperature.

    Z - Z value for steam sterilization it is assumed 10 minutes.

    121.1 is reference standard temperature for steam sterilization.

$$F_H = \Delta t \times 10^{T-170/Z}$$

Where,

    Δt is cycle hold time ,

    T - Cycle actual temperature.

    Z - Z value for dry heat sterilization it is assumed 20 minutes.

    170 is reference standard temperature for dry heat sterilization.

If suppose one sterilization cycle is run at 122.5 °C for 30 minutes, the F0 value will be.

$$F_0 = \Delta t \times 10^{T-121.1/Z}$$

$F_0 = 30 \times 10^{122.5-121.1/10}$

$F_0 = 30 \times 10^{1.4/10}$

$F_0 = 30 \times 10^{0.14}$

$F_0 = 30 \times 1.38$

$F_0 = 41.41$.

> **41.41 minute will be F_0 value for this cycle**

It means this cycle is run for 41.41 minutes at temperature exactly equivalent to 121.1°C

DETERMINATION OF MINIMUN F0 VALUE:

For new sterilization to meet desired sterility assurance level, We need to know how much F_0 to provide for sterilization. This minimum F_0 value for new sterilization value can be calculate by knowing the Bacterial resistance (D value), Bioburden on product to be sterilized and sterility assurance level in product to be sterilized.

Formula:

$$F_0 = D_{121.1} (\log_{10} A - \log_{10} B)$$

Where,

$D_{121.1}$ – D value at 121.1 of bioburden.

A – Bioburden per container.

B – Maximum acceptable sterility assurance level

For example:

The product has a bioburden of 1000 spores per container, D value of the spore is 4 minute at 121.1°C and the desired sterility assurance level is 10^{-6} that is assurance that no more than 1 unit of product in 1 million units will be nonsterile.

$F_0 = D_{121.1} (\log_{10} A - \log_{10} B)$

$F_0 = 4 [3-(-6)]$

$F_0 = 4 [3+6]$

$F_0 = 4 [9]$

$F_0 = 36$ Minutes if F_0 value for sterilization by steam sterilization.

D VALUES: It is time in minute required to inactivate 1 log of challenge microorganism.

D value is always mentioned with temperature and time, For example $D_{121.1} = 4$ Minutes, it means 4 minutes are required at 121.1°C to reduce the bacterial load by the log of 1, that is from 100 CFU to 10 CFU or 1000 CFU to 100 CFU, (90% reduction of Bioburden).

D value is calculated by Survivor Curve Method and Spearman- Karber Method.

Z VALUES: It is expressed in °C, and it is number of degree of temperature change necessary to change the D value by the factor of 10. Means it is temperature due to which D value is changed by a factor of 10 . For example, if D value at 120 °C is 60 minutes and at temperature 130°C D value of same spore is 6 Minute, This difference between 120 and 130°C is 10°C and termed as Z value, because due to change in 10°C (from 120°C to 130°C) temperature ,D value is changed by factor of a 10 (from 60 minute to 6 minute). The Z value for Same spores may be different in different medium like dextrose, Saline solution etc.

The Generally accepted Z values assumptions are:

Steam sterilization   Z = 10°C (18 °F)

Dry heat sterilization   Z = 20°C (36°F)

❖❖❖

30. CALCULATION OF IDEAL STERILIZATION CYCLE TIME AND OVERKILL APPROACH

Calculation of ideal sterilization cycle time is very important and critical technique. By using this method any one can calculate the Ideal sterilization cycle time. Exponential function can be used for the description of level of microbial inactivation. Degree of sterilization is expressed in terms of "SAL" (Sterility Assurance Level). The sterility assurance level required for parenteral preparation is 10^{-6}. SAL of 10^{-3} is required for medical device products not intended to come in contact with breached skin or compromised tissue. SAL 10^{-6} means the probability of single viable micro organism being present on a sterilized product is one vial in one million vials after completion of sterilization cycle.

1 Log reduction is decrease in the microbial population by factor by a 10. The meaning of Sterilization cycle that provides a SAL of 10^{-6} for log reduction is the micro organisms that could be present (Bioburden) are killed and additional 6 log reduction safety factor has been provided. Biobureden is total numbers of viable micro organisms present in the sample as contaminant.

EXAMPLE:

Suppose bioburden is 150 CFU, and SAL required if 10^{-6}, D value is 0.5 Minute/log at 121.1°C. Calculate the Ideal sterilization cycle time.

SOLUTION:

Bioburden is 150 CFU. SAL required is 10^{-6}

Convert bioburden from CFU in to Log reduction to 1 log. That is from 150 to 1 CFU.

Log(150) = 2.17, Means 2.17 log reduction is required to bring down the microbial population from 150 to 1.

But for SAL 10^{-6}, we have to consider safety factor of 6 Log reduction that is, from 1 microbial count to 0.000001 CFU. This will provide SAL of 10^{-6}.

So we should go for Log reduction as = 2.17 + 6 = 8.17. Total log reduction of 8.17 will provide SAL of 10^{-6} with bioburden of 150 CFU.

> Ideal Cycle time at 121.1 °C = Total log reduction required x D Value per log reduction

$$= 8.17 \times 0.5 \text{ min/log at } 121.1°C$$

$$= 8.17 \times 0.5 = 4.085$$

$$= 4.085 \text{ minutes}$$

4.085 minute is the ideal sterilization cycle time for SAL 10^{-6} and Bioburden of 150 CFU.

But this is time consuming and costly process, so Overkill approach is generally employed for non heat sensitive product. For over kill approach a bioburden of 10^6 of highly heat resistant spore forming Geobacillus Sterothermophilus bacteria is utilized. D-Value for these bacteria is slightly above 2 minutes at 121.1 °C, so use 2.5 minutes D-Value as Worst case value. Then for calculation the overkill approach log reduction we should consider bioburden of 10^6 and SAL of 10^{-6} , which is 12 log (6 + 6) reduction. So overkill approach cycle time is required log reduction multiplied by D Value .

Over kill approach cycle time = Required log reduction × D – Value.

$$= 12 \log \times 2.5 \text{ min/log}$$

$$= 30 \text{ minutes.}$$

So 30 minutes is overkill approach cycle.

31. FILTRATION BASIC CONCEPT

Filtration and Clarification:

Removal of suspended solids, contaminants and ions from liquid is called as Filtration, If the concentration of suspended particle is less than 1% in the slurry, process is called as clarification.

Following are the different approaches of filtration:
1) By Mechanism: Absorbance and Porosity.
2) By Fluid Flow: Dead end or Tangential.
3) By Media Structure: Depth or Surface.

1) By Mechanism:

Porosity: Porosity of filter Mediums: Determines the minimum size of the solids removed.

Absorbance: by Zeta Potential charge or Brownian diffusion or affinity (Hydrophilic-Hydrophobic) attracts opposite charge particles such as polyphenols and proteins.

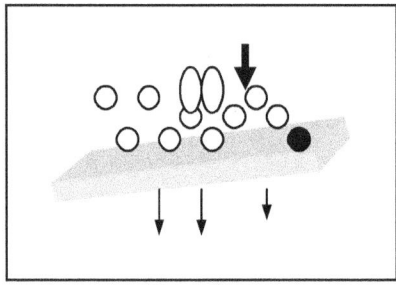
Porosity

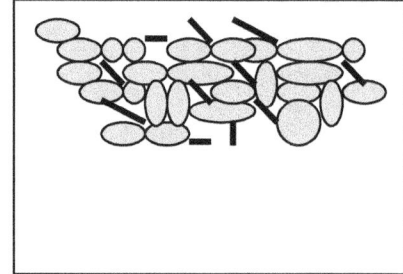
Absorbance

2) By Fluid Flow:

Dead end: In this filtration, all the fluid(that is feed) flows though the membrane and all particulates larger than the pore size of the membrane are mainly retained at its surface. In the process, the retained particulates start to build up a "Filter cake " on the surface of the membrane which has an impact on the efficiency of the process.

Cross-flow filtration: In this filtration a feed stream passes tangential to a pressure difference across the membrane, leaving the remaining feed to continue. The use of such tangential flow will prevent thicker particulates from building up a Filter cake.

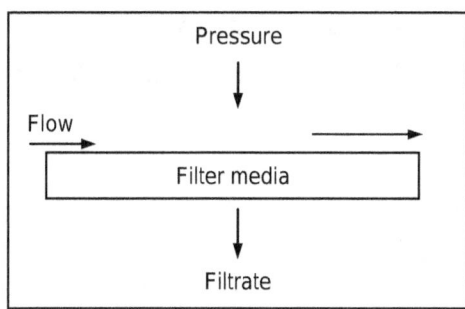
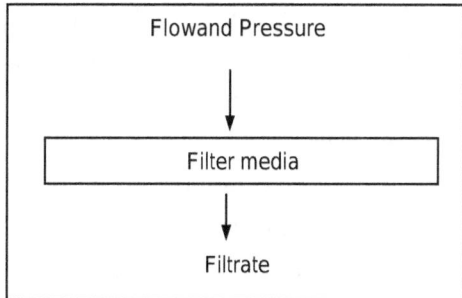

Cross Flow Filtration or Tangential filtration   Dead End Filtration

3) **By Media Structure:** Depth or Surface.

Filter media can be divided into two broad groups based on their pores structure:
1) Capillary - Type pores: Surface Filtration. E.g. Membrane filtration.
2) Tortuous - Type pores, Depth filtration, E.g. Quartz, Sand, filtration.

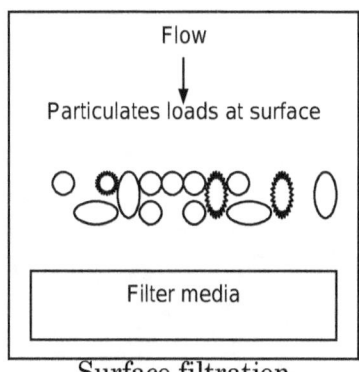
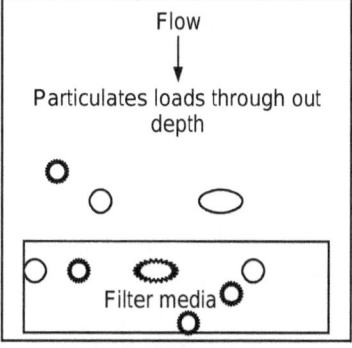

Surface filtration   Depth Filtration

FILTER RATING:
1) Absolute Filters
2) Nominal Filters

1) **Absolute Filters** (Absolute Pore Size): The pore size at which a challenge organism of a particular size will be retained with 99.99 to 100 % efficiency under strictly defined test conditions. These are sterilizing grade filters.(0.22 micron and lesser pore size filters.)

2) **Nominal Filters** (Nominal Pore size): Ability of the filter media to retain the majority of particulate at 90-98 % the rated pore size.

Miscellaneous Filtration type in liquids filtration:
1) Coarse Filtration: 10 to 5 Micron meter, nominal pore size filtration.
2) Rough Filtration: 5 - to 1.5 Micron nominal Pore size, Filtration.

3) Tight or Polish: 1.5 to 0.8 micron meter, nominal pore size filtration .
4) Sterile filtration: 0.45 micron meter (earlier), 0.22 Micron meter and below Absolute pore size filtration.

Membrane Filtration Types on Pore Size:
1) Particle filtration (0.5 micron and Above).
2) Micro filtration. (0.1micron and 0.5 Micron).
3) Ultra filtration: Molecular weight based filtration(50 - 1000 Angstroms).
4) Nan filtration (10 - 50 Angstroms).
5) Reverse Osmosis (Below 10 angstroms or 0.001 micron).

32. INTELLECTUAL PROPERTY RIGHT: PATENTS, COPYRIGHT AND TRADEMARKS

Intellectual property refers to the exclusive rights granted by the State over creations of the human mind, in particular, inventions, literary and artistic works, distinctive signs and designs used in commerce. Intellectual property is divided into two main categories: Industrial property rights, which includes patents, utility models, trademarks, industrial designs, trade secrets, new varieties of plants and geographical indications; and copyright and related rights, which relate to literary and artistic works.

Industrial Property (IP) rights are extremely important for the pharmaceutical industry. The use of the IP system in the pharmaceutical industry depends largely on the business strategy of a company, its size, resources, innovative capacity, competitive context and field of expertise. Research-teased, innovation-led companies that seek to develop new drugs, improve or adapt existing drugs or develop new pharmaceutical/medical equipment or processes, tend to rely heavily on the patent system to ensure they recover the investments incurred in research and development. Companies that rely on licensing in or licensing out of pharmaceutical products will need to be knowledgeable about the patent system to so that they are able to negotiate fair and balanced licensing contracts. Pharmaceutical industry may use the wealth of information contained in patent documents as a crucial input to their RandD work, to get ideas for further innovation, to ensure their "freedom to operate" or to find out when a patent is due to expire opening the door for the introduction of generics.

Confidential information, protected as trade secrets, is also important for many companies, as is the valuable know-how or undisclosed test data relating to new or improved drugs. Understanding the trademark system is important for companies selling branded products. Industrial designs, plant variety protection and copyright and related rights are generally less relevant to most in the pharmaceutical sector but this could vary depending on the product line and strategy of each company. Follows a brief summary of key points on each intellectual property right.

Patents

A patent is an exclusive right granted by the State for an invention that is new, involves an inventive step (or is non-obvious) and is capable of industrial application (or useful). It provides its owner the exclusive right to prevent others from making, using, offering for sale, selling or importing the patented invention without the owner's permission. A patent is a powerful business tool for companies to gain exclusivity in the market over a new product or process and develop a strong market position and/or earn additional profits through licensing.

A patent is granted by the national or regional patent office. It is valid for a limited period of time, generally for 20 years from the filing date (or priority date) of the patent application, provided the renewal (or maintenance) fees are paid to keep the patent in force. In some countries, a longer period of protection may be obtained for pharmaceutical products to compensate for the loss of effective period of protection due to delays in obtaining marketing approval from the relevant public health regulatory bodies. In return for the exclusive rights granted by a patent, the inventor is required to disclose his invention to the public in the patent application with sufficient detail to enable a person skilled in the relevant technology to practice the claimed invention. Patents, and in many countries patent applications, are disclosed to the public through publication in an official journal or gazette.

Trademarks

A trademark is a sign capable of distinguishing the goods or services produced or provided by one enterprise from those of other enterprises. Any distinctive words, letters, numerals, drawings, pictures, shapes, colors, logotypes, labels or combinations that distinguish the origin of goods or services may be considered a trademark. In some countries, advertising slogans are also considered trademarks and may be registered as such at national trademark offices. An increasing number of countries also allow for the registration of less traditional forms of trademarks such as single colors, three-dimensional signs (shapes of products or packaging), audible signs (sounds) or olfactory signs (smells). Aside from the protection of logos and brand names, in some countries, companies in the pharmaceutical industry rely on trademark protection for the distinctive shape or color of pharmaceutical products (such as capsules or tablets) and product packaging.

Trademark protection can be obtained through registration or, in some countries, also through use. Even where trademark rights can be acquired through use, companies are well advised to register a trademark by filing the appropriate application form with the national or regional trademark office. While the term of protection may vary, in a large number of countries registered trademarks are protected for 10 years. Registration may be renewed indefinitely (usually, for consecutive periods of 10 years) provided renewal fees are paid in time.

Trade Secrets

Broadly speaking, confidential business information which provides an enterprise a competitive edge may be considered a trade secret. The misappropriation, disclosure or unauthorized use of such information is regarded as an unfair practice and a violation of the trade secret. Depending on the legal system, the protection of trade secrets forms part of the general concept of protection against unfair competition or is based on specific provisions or case law on the protection of confidential information.

Confidential business information may benefit from protection as a trade secret as long as:
- It is not generally known, or readily accessible, to circles dealing with that type of information;
- It has commercial value because it is secret; and
- It has been subject to reasonable steps by the rightful holder of the information to keep it secret (e.g. through physical and electronic control mechanisms or by entering into non-disclosure or confidentiality agreements)

In the field of Pharmaceuticals, great importance is attached to the protection of undisclosed test data, which is required to be submitted for obtaining marketing approval of new drugs. Authorities in charge of marketing approval for new drugs are thus required to protect such data against unfair commercial use by competitors. Further, authorities should protect such data against disclosure, except where necessary to protect the public or unless steps are taken to ensure the protection of such data against unfair commercial use. The duration of data exclusivity varies from country to country but is often of 10 years.

Plant Variety Protection

Plant variety protection, also called a "plant breeder's right" (PBR), is a form of intellectual property right granted to the breeder of a new plant variety. According to such rights, certain acts concerning the exploitation of the protected variety require the prior authorization of the breeder. Plant variety protection is an independent sui generis form of protection, tailored to protect new plant varieties and has certain features in common with other intellectual property rights. To be granted a PBR, it is necessary to file an application for examination by the designated authority. For a variety to be protected, it must be new, distinct, uniform and stable, and must have a suitable denomination. In some countries, novel plants may be protected by patents, provided the requirements of patentability are met. In the pharmaceutical industry, plant variety protection is relevant in relation to new plant varieties used for medicinal purposes.

Industrial Designs

An industrial design is the ornamental or aesthetic aspect of a product. The design may consist of three-dimensional features, such as the shape or surface of a product, or of two-dimensional features, such as patterns, lines or color. In most countries, an industrial design must be registered in order to be protected under industrial design law. As a general rule, to be registrable, the design must be "new" or "original", and sometimes both. Once a design is registered, a registration certificate is issued. The duration of protection varies significantly from country to country, but is generally of at least 10 years, as requested by the TRIPS Agreement (though renewals may be required to benefit from the full length of protection). In the pharmaceutical industry, industrial design protection may be used, for example, to obtain exclusivity over the design of medical equipment.

Copyright and Related Rights

Copyright grants authors, artists and other creators (e.g. software companies, multimedia producers, website designers) legal protection for their literary and artistic creations. "Related rights" are the rights granted to people who often play a creative role in communicating some types of works to the public, such as performers, producers of sound recordings and broadcasting organizations. Copyright protection in the pharmaceutical industry may arise, for example, in relation to advertising campaigns or other creative output.

The remaining questions in this chapter will deal primarily with industrial property rights and, in particular, patents and trademarks.

Industrial property protection and related procedures in different countries:

Industrial property (IP) rights, such as patents, trademarks and industrial designs, are "territorial rights" that are protected through a registration or grant procedure. This means that they can only be enforced in countries (e.g. France) or regions (e.g. Member States of the African Intellectual Property Organization [OAPI]) where protection has been established and is in force. Thus, a company in the pharmaceutical industry that has duly filed an application to protect its inventions, trademarks or designs in its domestic market, and was granted patents, trademarks or industrial design protection, has no protection in export markets, unless the same rights were applied for and granted by the national (or regional) IP office of the export market in question. This is why it is important for companies operating in export markets to have a good knowledge of the IP laws, regulations, fees and procedures in those markets and ensure that their rights are adequately protected there as well. For patents, trademarks and industrial designs, the systems for international filing and registration administered by the World Intellectual Property Organization (WIPO) offer mechanisms for applying for protection in various countries through a single application for each type of IP.

Almost every country in the world has legislation protecting industrial property. Over the years, there has been significant harmonization of IP laws. Nevertheless, there still remain significant differences in terms of how the IP system operates in different countries or regions. Differences relate not only to procedure but in some cases also to what can be protected by means of which IP rights.

The best place to start looking for information on the laws, regulations and procedures for the protection of IP rights in your country or in another country is at the national and/or regional office(s) in charge of IP protection in that country (or region). IP offices are public sector bodies that generally come under the supervision of one of the government ministries (e.g. the Ministry for Trade and Industry). The primary function of these offices is the grant or registration of IP rights based on duly filled applications. While in many countries there is a single IP office covering all industrial property rights (copyright is often administered by a different office), in some countries the granting of patents and the registration of trademarks is the responsibility of different offices. The contact details of all IP offices may be found at the following web site: http://www.wipo.inl/directory/en/urls.jsp.

IP agents and IP lawyers may also be a useful source of information and advice on intellectual property issues. IP agents and lawyers are private sector service providers who are qualified to either represent clients during the application and prosecution of IP rights and/or to defend clients in the courts in case of an intellectual property dispute. Many countries require companies from overseas to hire a national IP agent domiciled in the country in question in order to file a patent or trademark application. Finally, you may consult the national legislation of a given country to obtain details on IP protection in that country. The WIPO web site includes a collection of national IP laws that may be consulted free of charge online at: http://clea.wipo.int/

What can be patented ?

In most countries, patents may be obtained for product and process in any field of technology, including Pharmaceuticals, provided that they comply with certain requirements. In patent law, an invention is generally defined as a solution to a technical problem. An invention may relate to the creation of an entirely new product or process, or may simply be a functional improvement to a product or process that provides a unique solution to a technical problem To be eligible for patent protection, an invention must meet several criteria, which may differ slightly from country to country. On the whole, however, most countries worldwide use the same (or similar) criteria for patentability, namely that:

- The invention consists of patentable subject matter;
- It is new (novelty requirement);
- It involves an inventive step or be non-obvious (inventive step or non-obviousness requirement);
- It is capable of industrial application or useful (industrial applicability or utility requirement); and
- It is disclosed in the patent application in a clear and complete manner (disclosure requirement).

Patentable subject matter

Under many national laws, patentable subject matter is defined negatively, i.e. by providing a list of what cannot be patented. However, there are important differences between countries in terms of what may represent unpatentable subject matter For example, patent legislation in some countries includes some of the following as unpatentable subject matter:

- Discoveries and scientific theories;
- Aesthetic creations (which may be protected by industrial designs);
- Schemes, rules and methods for performing mental acts;

- Newly discovered substances as they naturally occur in the world;
- Inventions the exploitation of which is contrary to "public order" or morality;
- Diagnostic, therapeutic and surgical methods of treatment for humans or animals (but not products for use in such methods);

Plants and animals other than microorganisms, and essentially biological processes for the production of plants or animals other than non-biological and microbiological processes.

In the pharmaceutical industry, types of inventions that are patentable in many countries (as long as the other criteria are met) include new pharmaceutical compounds, new or improved products for diagnostics, new dosage forms of known therapeutics, microorganisms, novel combinations of known compounds, processes and methods used for manufacturing a particular product, new and/or improved manufacturing equipment and new and/or improved drug delivery mechanisms or technologies. The list is by no means exhaustive and not all of the above are patentable in all countries.

The novelty requirement

An invention is new (or novel) if it does not form part of the prior art. The prior art is, in general, all the knowledge that has been made available to the public prior to the filing date (or priority date) of the relevant patent application or (in the United States) prior to when the invention was "made". The definition of "prior art" differs from country to country. In many countries, any invention made available to the public anywhere in the world in written form, by oral communication, by display or through use constitutes the prior art. Thus, in principle, the publication of the invention in a scientific journal, its presentation in a conference, its use in commerce or its display in a company's catalogue before the filing date (or priority date) of the application claiming that invention would constitute acts that could destroy the novelty of such invention and render it not patentable.

It is important to note, however, that in some countries, there is a grace period (usually of 6 or 12 months from the public disclosure of the claimed invention by the inventor) during which an applicant may file an application without the novelty being destroyed by such disclosure.

The inventive step/non-obviousness requirement

An invention is considered to involve an inventive step (or to be non-obvious) when, having regard to the prior art, the invention would not have been obvious to a person skilled in the particular field of technology. The non-obviousness requirement is meant to ensure that patents are not granted on developments that a person skilled in the relevant art could easily deduce from what already exists.

Industrial applicability/utility requirement

To be patentable, an invention must be capable of being used in industry (or meet the utility requirement). This means that the invention cannot be a mere theoretical phenomenon, but it must be useful and provide some practical benefit. The term "industry" is used in the broad sense, meaning anything distinct from purely intellectual or aesthetic activity, and includes, for example, agriculture. In biotechnology, the utility requirement has become particularly important in the context of the patenting of genetic sequences over which possible industrial applications are unclear. Some countries require that the utility be well established and asserted for the claimed invention in a specific, substantial and credible manner.

The disclosure requirement

According to the applicable national or regional legislation of most countries a patent application must disclose the invention in a manner sufficiently clear and complete for the invention to be carried out by a person skilled in the specific technical field (enabling disclosure requirement). For example, a patent application for a new pharmaceutical product, must include enough practical information so that anyone familiar with the relevant technical field is able to follow the indicated steps and replicate and produce an effective copy of it. In some countries, patent legislation requires the applicant to disclose the "best mode" for practicing the invention. For inventions involving microorganisms, many countries require that, if the microorganism is not accessible to the public and the claimed invention cannot be described in such a way to comply with the enabling disclosure requirement without having access to that microorganism, such microorganism be deposited at a recognized depositary institution, which is capable of maintaining the microorganism in a live culture for a prescribed period of time.

Patents in the life sciences

To comply with requirements under the TRIPS Agreement of the World Trade Organization, most countries allow for the patenting of microorganisms and, as explained above, often require the deposit of a sample of the microorganism at a recognized depositary institution when necessary to comply with the enabling disclosure requirement. Some countries exclude plants and animals (other than microorganisms) from patentability. Biological materials that have been purified and isolated from their natural environment or produced by means of a technical process are patentable in many jurisdictions. National patent law in many countries may also list some specific types of inventions that are excluded from patentable subject matter, such as processes for cloning human beings or processes for modifying the germ line genetic identity of human beings.

Depending on the country, plant varieties are protected either by the patent system, by a sui generis protection system for new varieties of plants or by a combination of the two.

Patents on improved variations and new uses

In many countries, improvements made to existing products are patentable, as are also new uses of a patented product, provided all the patentability requirements are met. In the pharmaceutical industry, it is not uncommon for companies to file patent applications for new therapeutic indications of a known drug. But such protection is not available in all jurisdictions. In addition, companies often file applications on new formulations or delivery methods of a drug, new and improved manufacturing processes, reduced dosage regimens, new versions of the active compound or other variations that meet the patentability requirements.

Rights granted by patent protection:

A patent grants its owner the right to exclude others not having his consent from commercially exploiting the invention. This includes the right to prevent or stop others from making, using, selling, offering for sale or importing the patented invention without the owner's prior permission. It is important to note that a patent does not grant the "freedom to use" the technology covered by the patent, but the right to exclude others from the use of the technology. While this may seem a subtle distinction, it is essential in understanding the patent system, its relationship to product regulatory regimes and how multiple patents can interact. In fact, there may be patents that build on previous patents or the commercialization of which require regulatory approvals or the use of other patented inventions. In some cases, a company may need to obtain a license over other people's patents in order to commercialize its own patented invention.

In the pharmaceutical industry, the right to exclude others from use of the invention does not provide the right to market a given new drug, as the drug will still have to undergo certain tests (e.g. clinical trials) and obtain marketing approval prior to commercialization, regardless of whether it has been patented or not. In short, getting a patent on a pharmaceutical product does not grant the right to put it on the market. The rights granted under a patent may be licensed, through a contract in which the patent owner agrees with a third party to allow certain specified uses of the patented invention generally in exchange for a payment of lump-sum payments and/or recurring royalties. A license may be limited according to purpose, field of use, territorial coverage and other conditions for which the authorization to use the patented invention is provided. Companies in the pharmaceutical industry may cross-license their technologies with other companies to permit both to use and benefit from their respective patented technologies. There are also situations in which a "patent pool" (or clearing house) could be created by a number of companies, in order to facilitate extensive licensing of a number of patents relating to a given technological field.

Limitations and exceptions to patent rights

Some of the basic limitations of a patent include:

- **territorial limitation** (as described above, a patent is a territorial right that only has effect in the jurisdiction for which it has been granted);

- **time limitation** (up to 20 years from the date of filing of the application, with possible extension in some countries for products that undergo regulatory approval such as certain types of pharmaceutical products);

- **limitation in scope** (a patent only provides exclusive rights over the claimed invention as described in the patent claims).

In addition, in many countries, there are exceptions to patent rights that allow third parties to use the invention without the consent of the patent owner, for example, **to conduct research for non commercial purposes** using the patented invention (often referred to as "experimental use" exception) or **to prepare and apply for regulatory approval of a pharmaceutical product before the date of expiry of the relevant patent(s)** (also referred to as "safe harbor" provisions"), so as to speed up the commercialization of a generic products after that date. Given vast differences between countries in these matters, it is generally advisable for companies to be well informed on the specific practice in each country prior to engaging in any such activities.

Compulsory licenses

Compulsory licenses are licenses granted without the consent of the patent holder. Typically, they are granted either to remedy anti-competitive practices or in situations of national emergency. They limit the exercise of the patent rights, but they do not work in the same way as exceptions. A compulsory license limits the enforcement of a patent vis-a-vis the person(s) being granted such a compulsory license. It does not revoke or invalidate the patent concerned. Compulsory licenses are granted by a national authority provided that all the necessary conditions specified in the national patent law are met. Compulsory licenses are generally subject to time and geographical restrictions. In addition, the patent holder is also entitled to compensation taking into account the economic value of the compulsory license.

Parallel imports

Parallel imports occur when goods produced in one country by an owner of IP rights, or with his consent, are imported by a third party into another country, in which the same IP rights exist, without the consent of the owner of the IP rights. Parallel imports are also often referred to as "gray market goods" as they are legitimately produced items, which are offered for sale outside the approved territory or channels of distribution established by the IP owner. Different countries or regions have different policies on parallel importation and international agreements provide national governments flexibility. Each country's law needs to be consulted.

Anti-trust or Competition law

As a general rule, governments may also invoke competition law to mitigate anticompetitive use of the exclusive rights conferred by patents, wherever it considers that a patent holder is abusing the market power provided by the patent. This sometimes occurs when a patent holder seeks to impose what are considered to be anti-competitive obligations on a licensee (such as price-fixing). There are situations in which compulsory licensing may be used as a remedy for redressing the abuse resulting from anti-competitive practices.

Obtaining patent protection in India:

In order to get a patent application for your invention, it is absolutely critical to keep it confidential prior to filing the patent application. In most circumstances, public disclosure or use of your invention, including clinical testing of a drug, prior to filing a patent application destroys the novelty of the invention, rendering it unpatentable in many countries, unless the applicable patent law provides for a "grace period" (generally of 6 months or one year) that allows the applicant to disclose the invention and file the application later within the grace period.

Prior art search

Generally the first step for any company considering patent protection for an invention is to perform a prior art search. With over 40 million patents granted worldwide, and millions of printed publications, which are all potential prior art against your application, there is a good chance that some reference, or combination of references, may render an invention, or part of it, non-novel or obvious, and therefore unpatentable. A prior art search can prevent a company from wasting money on filing and prosecuting a patent application if the search reveals prior references that are likely to preclude the patenting of a given invention.

Filing a patent application

Once a company has performed a prior art search and decided to seek patent protection for its invention, it will need to prepare a patent application and submit it in the prescribed manner to the national or regional patent office Some patent offices make it possible for applicants to submit their application on-line and may even provide discounts to those who do so. The patent application has a range of functions: - It defines the scope of the invention claimed, and thus determines the legal scope of the patent right;

It describes the nature of the invention, including detailed instructions on how to carry out the invention; and

It gives details of the inventor, the patent owner and other business and legal information.

Patent applications are similarly structured worldwide and consist of a **request,** a **description, claims, drawings** (if necessary) and an **abstract.** A patent application may be anywhere between a few pages to hundreds of pages long depending on the nature of the specific invention and the technical field.

The **claims** are generally considered the most important part of a patent application as they define the scope of the patent. They are crucial to the effective protection of an invention, for if they are badly drafted, the patent may be worthless regardless of how valuable the invention is. In enforcement actions, interpreting the claims is the first step in determining whether the patent is valid and in determining whether the patent has been infringed. It is strongly advisable to seek advice of an expert to draft patent applications, particularly the claims.

The steps taken by the patent office to grant a patent vary from country to country but, broadly speaking, follow a similar pattern:

Formal examination:

The patent office examines the application to ensure that it complies with the administrative requirements or formalities (i.e. that all relevant documentation is included, the patent application is complete and the application fee has been paid).

Search: In many countries, the patent office conducts a search to determine the prior art in the specific field to which the invention relates. The search report is used during the substantive examination to compare the claimed invention with the prior art.

Substantive examination: The aim of the substantive examination is to ensure that the application satisfies the conditions of patentability. Not all patent offices check applications against all the conditions of patentability. The applicant is given the opportunity to remove any objections that may be raised during the examination and if the applicant fails to do so in the specified time, the patent office will refuse the grant of the patent.

Publication: In many countries, the patent application is published 18 months after the filing date (or priority date) irrespective of whether it has been granted or not. In general, all patent offices also publish the patent once it is granted.

Grant: If the examination process has reached a conclusion favorable to the applicant, the patent office will grant a patent on the application and issue a certificate of grant. The time taken for a patent to be granted may vary significantly depending, among other things, on whether the patent office makes a full substantive examination on the application and/or on whether there are any pre-grant oppositions to the application and on the field of technology. In general, patent offices take between 2 and 6 years to grant a patent.

Opposition: Many countries provide a period during which third parties may oppose to the grant of a patent for example, on the basis that it is not new. Opposition proceedings may be pre-grant or post-grant procedures.

First to file vs. first to invent

In most countries, if more than one person independently made the same invention, a patent is granted to the first person to file a patent application claiming that invention. An exception is the United States of America where a first-to-invent system applies, by which, where more than one application with respect to the same claimed invention are filed, the patent will be granted to the first inventor who conceived and reduced the invention to practice. In order to prove inventorship within a first-to-invent system, it is crucial to have well-kept, duly signed and dated laboratory notebooks that may be used as evidence in case of a dispute with another company or inventor.

Protect Own IP rights in export markets:

As mentioned under Qu 2, IP rights are territorial rights, and in order to obtain protection in foreign markets, it is necessary to apply for protection with effect in those countries.

An applicant who has applied for IP protection in one country and applies for protection for the same IP right in other countries within a set period of time (referred to as the priority period under the Paris Convention) will benefit from the date of filing of the first application (priority date). This means that the subsequent applications will be regarded as if they had been filed on the priority date and your application will have priority over other applications for the same invention, trademark or industrial design filed after the priority date. The priority period is 12 months for patents and six months for trademarks and industrial designs. In the case of patents, after the expiration of 12 months from your first filing date and until the patent is first published by the patent office (generally 18 months after the priority date) you may still have the possibility to apply for protection for the same invention in other countries (assuming it has not been disclosed), but you can no longer claim priority of your earlier application. Once the invention has been disclosed or published, you may be unable to obtain patent protection in foreign countries altogether, due to loss of novelty. Therefore, as a general rule, it is highly advisable, and often indispensable, to file your foreign patent applications within the priority period.

Filing applications abroad

For IP rights that require registration (such as patents, trademarks and industrial designs) there are essentially three alternative procedures for applying for IP protection in other countries.

The national route

One option is to seek protection in individual countries separately by applying directly to national industrial property offices. Each application may have to be translated into a prescribed language. You will be required to pay the national application fees and some countries will also require that you hire a national IP agent to submit the application. If you are still in the phase of assessing the commercial viability of an invention or are still exploring potential export markets or licensing partners, the national route may be particularly expensive and cumbersome, especially where protection is being sought in a large number of countries. In such cases, the facilities offered by the WIPO-administered international filing and registration systems for inventions, marks and industrial designs (see "The international route" below) offer a simpler and generally less expensive alternative.

The regional route

Some countries have established regional agreements for obtaining IP protection for an entire region with a single application. The regional IP offices include:

African Intellectual Property Organization: http://www.oapi.wipo.net
African Regional Intellectual Property Organization: http://www.aripo.orq/
Benelux Trademark Office and Benelux Designs Office: http://www.bmb-bbm.org/ and http://www.bbtm-bbdm.org/
Eurasian Patent Office: http://www.eapo.org/
European Patent Office: http://www.epo.org
Office for Harmonization in the Internal Market (European Union Community Trademark and Community Design): http://oami.eu.int/
Patent Office of the Cooperation Council for the Arab States of the Gulf: http://www.gulf-patent-office.orq.sa/

The international route

The WIPO-administered systems of international filing and registration simplify greatly the process for simultaneously seeking IP protection in a large number of countries. WIPO-administered systems of international protection include three different mechanisms of protection for specific industrial property rights. - **A system for filing international patent applications** is provided under the **Patent Cooperation Treaty** (or **PCT**) system. An important advantage of the PCT is that it provides up to **18 additional months** on top of the 12-month priority period, during which applicants can explore the commercial potential of their product in various countries and decide where to seek patent protection. Payment of the fees and translation costs associated with national applications are thus delayed. The PCT is widely used by applicants to keep their options open for as long as possible. PCT applicants also receive **valuable information** about the potential patentability of their invention in the form of the PCT **International Search Report** and the **Written Opinion of the International Searching Authority.** This enables the applicant to make an informed decision on whether and where to pursue patent protection.

In addition, filing an applications using the PCT route significantly **reduces the initial transaction costs** of submitting separate applications to each patent office. The PCT may also be used to file applications in some of the regional systems. Guidance on how to submit an international application under the PCT can be obtained from your national patent office and/or from WIPO at www.wipo.int/pct

International protection of trademarks is facilitated by the **Madrid system for the international registration of marks.** The principal advantages of using the Madrid system are that the trademark owner can register its trademark in all the countries party to the system (over 70) by filing a single international application, in one language, subject to one set of fees and deadlines. Thereafter, the international registration can be maintained and renewed through a single procedure. More information on the international registration of marks can be obtained either from national trademark offices or on the WIPO website: www.wipo.int/madrid/.

International protection of industrial designs is provided by the **Hague Agreement Concerning the International Deposit of Industrial Designs.** An applicant from a Member country to the Hague Agreement can file a single international application with WIPO; the design will then be protected in as many Member countries of the treaty (currently 38) as the applicant wishes. The agreement provides applicants with a simpler and cheaper mechanism for applying for industrial design registration in various countries. Full ·information on the Hague Agreement, including the application form, can be obtained from the WIPO website at: www.wipo.int/hague/

Resources

1. **Secrets of Intellectual Property: A Guide for Small and Medium-sized Enterprises.** ITC/WIP0 publication on with questions and answers on intellectual property of relevance to SME exporters.

2. **Basic Facts about the PCT.** http://www.wipo.int/pct/en/basic facts/basic facts.pdf The publication provides basic information on the Patent Cooperation Treaty . For more in-depth information, see website of the PCT.

3. **Tool box for applicants of the European Patent Office.**
http://www.european-patent- office.org/ new tb applic/index.en.php

Patent information and Benefit:

"Patent information" is the technical and legal information contained in patent documents published periodically by patent offices. A patent document contains the full description of how a patented invention works and the claims that determine the scope of protection. It also contains details of who patented the invention and when it was applied for and granted, and provides references to relevant literature. It is estimated that approximately two-thirds of the technical information revealed in patent documents is never published elsewhere and the entire set of patent documents worldwide contains over 40 million items. This makes patent information the single most comprehensive collection of classified technological data. Patent information (as contained in patent databases) can be useful to pharmaceutical companies for a number of reasons. One of the most important is as a source of technical information, which companies may find of great value in their research and development and strategic business planning. Most inventions are disclosed to the public for the first time when the patent (or, depending on the national law, when the patent application) is published by the patent office. Thus, patents are a valuable source of information about current research and innovations, often long before the innovative products appear on the market. Patent databases may also be used to find out about the legal status of a patent and in particular to find out whether a specific patent has expired. This may be particularly relevant for companies considering the introduction of a generic drug once the relevant patent has expired.

Some of the most important reasons for using patent databases include:
- To avoid unnecessary expenses in researching what is already known
- To identify and evaluate technology for licensing and technology transfer
- To keep abreast of the latest technologies in a specific field of expertise
- To find solutions to technical problems
- To locate potential business partners
- To monitor activities of real and potential competitors
- To identify niche markets
- To find out about the legal status of a patent
- To avoid possible infringement problems
- To assess the patentability of an invention
- To oppose the granting of patents where they conflict with a company's own patent(s)

Freedom to operate

Using patent information is particularly important in the pharmaceutical industry when a company wishes to launch a new product or introduce an existing product into a new market. Prior to launching a new product, and often even prior to initiating a new line of research that may lead to the development of a new product, it is important that companies in the pharmaceutical industry seek to minimize the risk of infringement by securing their **"freedom to operate"** (FTO), i.e. ensuring that the commercial production, marketing and/or exporting of their new product, process or service does not infringe the intellectual property rights of others An FTO analysis invariably begins by a search of patent literature for issued or pending patents and in order to obtain a legal opinion on whether a product, process or service may infringe existing patent(s) (or patent applications) owned by others.

An FTO analysis based on the search of patent literature is in many ways just the first step. If the patent search reveals that there are one or more patents that limit your freedom to operate, your company will have to decide how to proceed. Assuming that the blocking patent(s) is/are valid, some of the most common strategies are the following:

Licensing in (i.e. obtaining authorization from the patent owner to use the technology through a licensing contract in exchange for a lump-sum payment and/or royalties).

Cross-licensing (i.e. obtaining authorization from the patent owner to use the invention in exchange for your granting to the other party the right to use one or more of your own patented inventions).

Inventing around (i.e. steering research or making changes to the product or process in order to avoid infringing the patent(s) owned by others).

Not entering a given market where the invention is protected.

Where to search for patent information

Most intellectual property offices worldwide offer facilities for the general public to consult patent databases. Some national and regional patent offices have also made their patent databases available online, generally free-of-charge. In addition, a number of private service providers offer sophisticated databases for a commercial fee. Some of the latter may be particularly important for searching chemical compounds and genetic sequences, which cannot easily be searched using the free on-line databases.

While the Internet has significantly simplified access to patent information, it is not always easy to perform a high-quality patent search, as patent jargon may sometimes appear complex and obscure and professional searching requires training. While preliminary searches may be performed through the free on-line databases, most companies requiring patent information for taking key business decisions (e.g. whether to apply for a patent or not) will generally rely on the services of skilled patent professionals who have access to some of the more sophisticated databases.

A list of on-line patent databases of national and regional IP offices is available from the following website: http://www.wipo.int/ipdl/en/resources/links.jsp In addition, there are a number of patent databases offered by commercial providers.

The International Patent Classification

The international patent classification (IPC) is a hierarchical classification system used to classify and search patent documents. The seventh edition of the IPC consists of eight sections, 120 classes, 628 subclasses and approximately 69,000 groups. The eight sections are:

A. Human Necessities;
B. Performing Operations; Transporting;
C. Chemistry; Metallurgy;
D. Textiles; Paper;
E. Fixed Constructions;
F. Mechanical Engineering; Lighting; Heating; Weapons; Blasting;
G. Physics;
H. Electricity.

Currently, over 100 countries use the IPC to classify their patents: www.wipo.int/classifications/en/ipc/index.html

Trademarks important and Trademark Registration:

While most businesses realize the importance of using trademarks to differentiate their products from those of their competitors, not all realize the importance of protecting them by registration. Given the importance that a trademark may have in determining the success of a product in the marketplace and enhancing product recognition and the development of a loyal clientele, it is essential to ensure that the company using a given trademark has obtained exclusive rights over it.

Registering a trademark gives a company the **exclusive right** to prevent others from marketing identical or similar products under the same mark or under a confusingly similar mark. Protected trademarks may also be licensed to other companies, thus providing an additional source of revenue for the company.

In some countries (particularly countries that follow a "common law" system, such as the US, Canada, the UK, Australia or India) trademark rights may also be acquired through use. The main advantages of registration in such cases are:

Registration provides proof of rights, which Is particularly important in case of disputes with third parties;

An application can be filed prior to using the mark;

Registration makes it easier and cheaper to enforce;

The trademark is included on the official trademark register; and

The ® sign can be used next to the trademark.

When choosing a trademark it is important to bear in mind the categories of signs that are usually not accepted for registration. Applications for trademark registration are usually rejected on what are commonly referred to as "absolute grounds" when the trademark is not considered sufficiently **distinctive** (e.g. it is the generic name of the product or chemical compound, it is too descriptive of the product in question or is considered deceptive).

Applications may also be rejected on "relative grounds" **when the trademark is in conflict with prior trademark rights.** Having two identical (or very similar) trademarks for the same type of product could cause confusion among consumers. Some trademark offices check for conflict with existing marks (including unregistered well-known marks) as a regular part of the registration process, while others only do so when the trademark is challenged by a third party after publication of the trademark. In either case, if the office considers a trademark to be identical or confusingly similar to one that already exists for identical or similar products, it will be rejected or cancelled as the case may be.

Trademark Registration

Before submitting an application for trademark registration, companies should ensure that a proper **trademark search** has been carried out. This is to make sure that the trademark you intend to use, or a confusingly similar one, is not already registered by another company for identical or similar products. It is advisable to conduct a trademark search not only in your own country but also, as far as possible, in potential export markets, in order to avoid problems of infringement at a later stage. A trademark search may be conducted directly by your company or you may hire the services of a trademark agent. Whatever the manner that is chosen, it is important to bear in mind that any such trademark search is only preliminary. While it is relatively simple to ensure that a trademark is not identical to an existing validly registered trademark, it may be difficult to ensure that the trademark of choice is not "confusingly similar to another trademark. This is why the guidance of an experienced trademark agent, who is familiar with the practice of the trademark office and court decisions, may be extremely helpful. A list of trademark databases is available from the following WebPages:

http://arbiter.wipo.int/trademark/output.html.

In order to register a trademark, applicants are required to send or hand in a duly completed trademark application form, which will include:

The contact details of the company,

2. FAQs on Trademarks of the International Trademark Association (INTA).

http://www.inta.org/info/faqs.html

3. Guidelines for Trademark Examination. International Trademark Association: http://www.inta.org/downloads/tap tmexam1998.pdf provides guidelines for Trademark registration offices on the criteria for evaluation of trademarks

Managing the IP assets of a company in the pharmaceutical industry:

Managing the IP assets of a company in the pharmaceutical industry is more than just acquiring the formal IP rights through the national or regional IP office. Patent or trademark rights are not worth much unless they are adequately exploited. Moreover, some types of valuable IP (such as trade secrets) do not require formal registration but call for other practical measures for their protection (e.g. confidentiality agreements). Finally, the enforcement of IP rights might be crucial to ensure that the IP rights are respected in the marketplace. Enterprises in the pharmaceutical industry willing to extract full value from their know-how, innovation and creativity should, therefore, take adequate steps to develop an IP strategy for their business and seek to integrate it within their overall business strategy. This implies, for example, including IP considerations when drafting business plans and marketing strategies. Understanding the relationship between the IP system and the system for obtaining marketing approval for new drugs by the relevant public health regulatory body is also important. A basic IP strategy would generally include at least the following:

A Strategy on the protection of IP rights

A single product or service may be protected by various forms of IP rights covering different aspects of that product or service. In the pharmaceutical industry, various aspects of a new drug may be patented (e.g. the chemical compound, processes, new uses for the same compound, improved variations, dosage regimens, etc.). Companies must consider the best protection package (including the reliance on trade secret protection, if considered appropriate) and make sure that all the formal rights are acquired in the relevant markets. Making an IP audit of the company may be an important first step for identifying protectable assets that may not have been adequately exploited by a company in the past.

Small and medium-sized exporters should also bear in mind that creating a comprehensive IP portfolio with protection in various markets may be a considerable investment. This is particularly the case for patents. Pharma industry must therefore carefully assess the costs and benefits of patenting on a case by case basis and develop a strategy/policy on the filing of patent applications that is commensurate to its budget and market opportunities.

A Strategy on IP Exploitation

IP rights may be exploited in a variety of ways. These may include the commercialization of IP-protected pharmaceutical products benefiting from the exclusive rights provided by the IP system; the entering into exclusive and/or non-exclusive licensing agreements with one or more other companies; the sale or assignment of IP assets to other firms; the creation of joint ventures or strategic alliances in order to exploit complementary IP assets of other companies; the use of IP rights to obtain access to other companies' technology through cross-licensing agreements; and/or the use of IP rights to support an application for obtaining funds to take a patented product to market.

Enterprises should decide in each case how they may best exploit their IP assets both domestically and internationally while ensuring that they have freedom to operate and do not unnecessarily run into trouble by infringing the IP rights of others.

A Strategy on IP Monitoring

Consulting patent databases regularly is important in order to find out about recent technical developments and new technologies, identify new licensing partners, suppliers or new market opportunities, ensure your freedom to operate, monitor the activities of competitors, find out about the legal status of a patent and a graphic illustration of the mark (a specific format may be required) a description of the goods and services and/or class(es) for which the company wishes to obtain trademark protection, and payment of the required fees.

Use requirement

A company may apply for trademark registration prior to using it in the market to commercialize its products or services, but some countries will not officially register the trademark until the applicant has shown proof of use (e.g. the United States). Additionally, in most cases, the registration of a trademark that has not been used for a given period of time (usually 3 to 5 years following registration) may be cancelled. This is to try to guarantee that the registration is done with the intention of actually using the trademark in the marketplace, rather than simply for the purpose of obstructing its use by others.

Trademark symbols

Many companies use signs such as ®, TM, SM, MD (French for marque deposee) or MR (Spanish for marca registrada) or equivalent symbols next to their trademark in order to inform consumers and competitors that the word, logo or other sign is a trademark. While such symbols are not a requirement and generally provide no further legal protection for the trademark, it may be a convenient way of informing others that a given sign is a trademark, thus warning possible infringers and counterfeiters and inhibits marks from losing their distinctiveness. The ® symbol, MD and MR are used once the trademark has been registered. TM denotes that a given sign is a trademark and SM is sometimes used for service marks.

Use in advertising

If your mark is registered as a logo with a specific design or font, make sure that, wherever it appears, it is represented in exactly the form in which it is registered. Monitor and supervise its use closely, as it is critical to the image of your company's products. It is also important to avoid using the trademark as a verb or noun so that it does not come to be perceived by consumers as a generic term.

Generics and brand name drugs

Dictionaries tend to define a "generic" as a product - particularly a drug - that does not have a trademark. For example, "paracetamol" is a chemical ingredient that is found in many brand name painkillers and is often sold as a (generic) medicine in its own right, without a brand name. This is "generic from a trademark point of view".

Sometimes "generic" is also used to mean copies of a patented drug, a drug whose patents have expired or a drug that is made and marketed by a company in another country in which the drug is not patented - "generic from a patent point of view". Patented drugs are almost always sold under a brand name or trademark. When a drug, protected by patent in one country, is made by another manufacturer in a country where the drug is not protected by a patent, then in such other country it may be sold under the name of the chemical ingredient (making it clearly generic), or under another trademark (which means they are still generic from a patent point of view but not from a trademark point of view).3

A Strategy on IP Enforcement

A clear strategy on IP enforcement is crucial to avoid the losses that may be incurred by the existence of infringing goods in the market and the high costs involved in some IP disputes. The main responsibility for identifying and taking action against imitators or infringers of IP rights. lies with their owner (unless such responsibility has been transferred to a licensee). A patent owner, therefore, is responsible for monitoring the use of its patented invention(s) or registered trademark(s) in the marketplace, identifying any infringers and deciding whether, how and when to take action against them:

It is advisable to contact an IP lawyer to assist in taking any steps for enforcing IP rights, both domestically and/or in any export markets, which may include the sending of a **"cease and desist letter"** informing the alleged infringer of a possible conflict between your rights and the company's business activity, approaching a court to obtain an **"interim injunction"** in order to surprise the infringer at his business premises and/or initiating **civil proceedings** against the infringing company.

In many cases, IP disputes are settled out of court and often result in a licensing agreement thus providing the authorization to the alleged infringer to continue selling the product in question in exchange for a lump-sum payment or royalties. Arbitration and mediation are often used to avoid long and expensive litigation. It is generally advisable to include a special provision in licensing contracts for any dispute that may arise to be referred first to arbitration or mediation. More information on arbitration and mediation can be found at: http://arbiter.wipo.int/cente/index.html.

33. QUALITY RISK MANAGEMENT WITH PROTOCOL AND REPORT

Risk is defined as combination of probability of occurrence of harm and the severity of that harm. Achieving a shared understanding of the application of risk management among diverse stakeholders is very difficult because each stakeholder may identify different potential harm, place different probability on each harm occurring, and characterize different severity.

An effective risk management approach can ensure the high quality of drug products to the patients in providing a proactive means to identify and mitigate potential quality issues at the early stage of product development. Additionally, use of risk management techniques can improve the decision making if a quality problem arises. It will also provide the regulators with greater assurance of a company's ability to deal with potential risks.

This guideline provides principles and examples of tools of quality risk management that may be applied to all aspects of pharmaceutical quality including development, manufacturing, distribution, inspection and submission/review processes throughout the lifecycle of drug substances and drug products, biological and biotechnological products, and the use of raw materials, solvents, excipients, packaging and labeling materials.

Two primary principles are considered for the use of quality risk management viz., (1) evaluation of the quality risk should ultimately link back to the potential harm to the patient and (2) the level of effort, formality and documentation of the quality risk management process should be commensurate with the level of risk.

Quality risk management is a systematic process for the assessment, control, communication and review of risks to the quality of drug product.

A model for quality risk management is outlined in the flowchart (Fig. 1). The emphasis on each component of the framework may differ from case to case but a robust process will incorporate all the elements at an appropriate level of detail.

Quality risk management is a joint responsibility among decision makers from various functions and departments with regulatory authorities and industry. They should ensure that a quality risk management process is defined, adequate resources are available and the quality risk management process is reviewed.

Quality risk management includes systematic processes designed to coordinate, facilitate and improve science-based decision making with respect to risk. Steps used to initiate and plan.

Initiate Risk Management Process quality risk management includes the following:
1. Define the problem and/or risk question, including pertinent assumptions identifying the potential risk.
2. Assemble background information and data on the potential hazard, harm or human health impact relevant to the risk assessment.
3. Define how decision makers will use the information, assessment and conclusions.
4. Identify a leader and necessary resources.
5. Specify a timeline and deliverables for the risk management process.

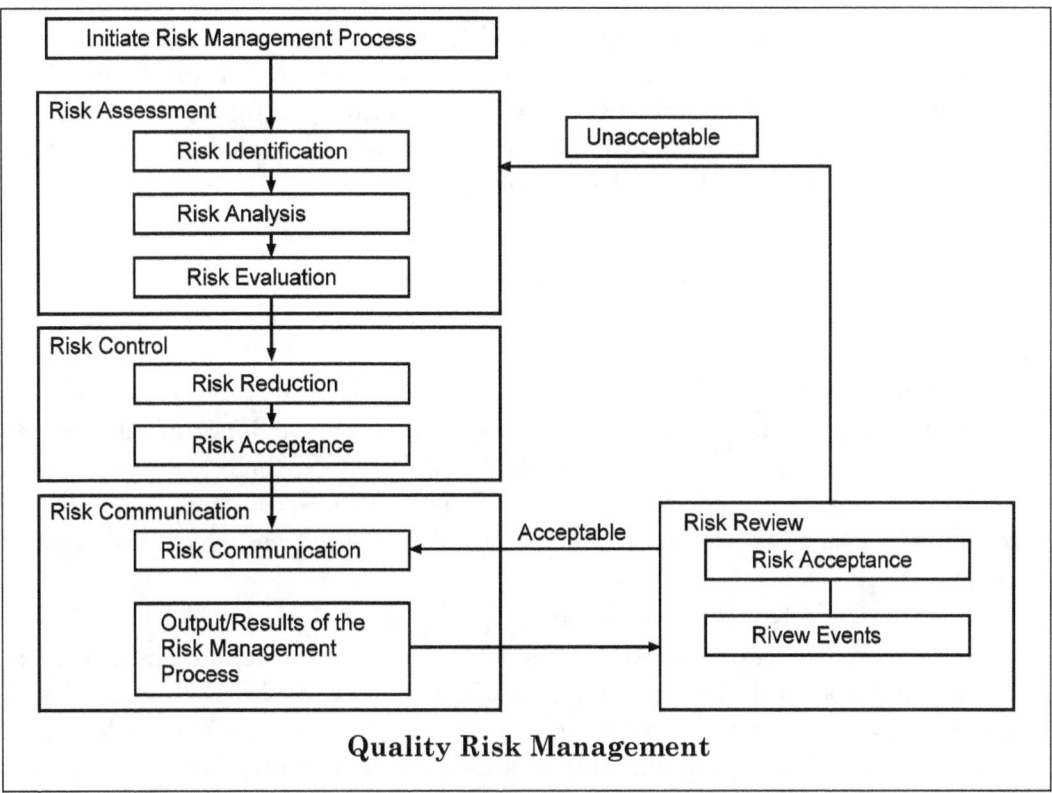

Quality Risk Management

RISK ASSESSMENT:

Risk assessment consists of risk identification, risk analysis and risk evaluation, Quality risk assessments begin with a well-defined problem description or risk question. If this is well defined, an appropriate risk management tool and the types of information needed to address the risk question will be more readily identifiable.

Risk identification is a systematic use of information to identify hazards referring to the risk question or problem description. Information can include historical data, theoretical analysis, informed opinions, and the concerns of stakeholders. Risk identification addresses the "what can go wrong" question, including identifying possible consequences.

Risk analysis is the estimation of the risk of the identified hazards. It is the process that focuses on seeking the likelihood that risks identified in risk identification might "go wrong".

Risk evaluation compares the identified and analysed risk against given risk criteria. A qualitative or quantitative process might be used to assign the probability and severity of a risk.

In doing an effective risk assessment, the robustness of the data set is important because it determines the quality of the output.

The output of a risk assessment is either a quantitative estimate of risk or a qualitative description of a range of risk. When risk is expressed quantitatively, a probability scale from 0 and 100% is used. Alternatively, ranges of risk can be expressed using qualitative descriptions, such as high, medium or low and they should be defined in as much detail as possible.

RISK CONTROL:

Risk control includes decision making to reduce and / or accept risks. The purpose of risk control is to reduce the risk to an acceptable level according to industry and regulatory standards. The efforts used for risk control should be related to the significance of the risk.

Risk reduction focuses on processes for mitigation or avoidance of quality risk when it exceeds an acceptable level. Risk reduction can include actions taken to mitigate the severity and probability of harm. Processes that improve the detectability of hazards and quality risks can also be used as part of risk control strategy.

Risk acceptance is a decision to accept risk. Risk acceptance can be a formal decision to accept the residual risk or it may be a passive decision in which residual risks are not specified. For some types of harms, even the best quality risk management practices might not entirely eliminate risk. In these circumstances, it may be agreed that the optimal quality risk management strategy has been applied and that quality risk is reduced to an acceptable level.

Risk communication is the exchange or sharing of information about risk and its management between the decision makers and others. Communication is an expected activity among appropriate parties at any stage of the risk management process. Sometimes, a formal risk communication process is developed as a part of risk management. This can include communication among many interested parties; e.g., regulators and industry, industry and the patient, within a company, industry or regulatory authority etc.

RISK REVIEW:

The results of the risk management process should be reviewed to take account of new knowledge and experience. Once a quality risk management process has been initiated, that process should continue to be utilised for events that may impact the original quality risk management decision whether these are planned or unplanned. Risk management should be an ongoing quality management process and a mechanism to perform periodic review of events should be implemented.

Risk acceptance provides for a review of the prior risk acceptance decision, considering any additional information that has become available and determination whether or not the risk is still acceptable.

RISK MANAGEMENT TOOLS:

Quality risk management tools support a scientific approach to decision making by providing documented, transparent and reproducible methods to accomplish steps of the quality risk management process.

Some of the tools are described below:

Process Mapping:

Process mapping is a prerequisite for the use of some of the tools described. The purpose of process map is to provide a clear and simple visual representation of the steps involved in the process and to show how they are interrelated. Process mapping can be used to facilitate understanding, systematically analysing complex processes and associated risks.

Hazard analysis of critical control points (HACCP):

It is a systematic, proactive, and preventive method for assuring product quality, reliability and safety. It is a structured approach that applies technical and scientific principles to analyse, evaluate, prevent and control the risk or adverse consequences of hazard due to the design, development and production and use of products.

HACCP consists of the following seven steps:

Conduct hazard analysis and identify preventive measures for each step of the process

- Determine critical control points
- Establish critical limits
- Monitor each critical control point
- Establish corrective action to be taken when deviation occurs
- Establish verification procedures and
- Establish record keeping system

It can be used to identify and manage risks associated with physical, chemical and biological hazards (including microbiological contamination). It is most useful when process understanding is sufficiently comprehensive to support identification of critical control points.

Hazard operability analysis (HAZOP):

HAZOP is based on a theory that assumes that risk events are caused by deviations from the design or operating intentions. It is a systematic brainstorming technique for identifying hazards using so-called "guide words" (e.g. no, more, other than, non part of etc.,) are applied to relevant parameters (e.g. contamination, temperature) to help identify potential deviations from normal use or design intentions. It uses a team of people with expertise covering the design or process or product and its applications.

HAZOP can be applied to manufacturing processes, equipment and facilities for drug substances and drug products. It has also been used primarily in the pharmaceutical industry for evaluating process safety hazards.

Failure mode effects analysis (FMEA):

FMEA provides for an evaluation of potential failure modes for processes and the likely effect on outcomes and / or product performance. Once failure modes are established, risk reduction can be used to eliminate, reduce or control the potential failures. It relies on process understanding. FMEA methodology breaks down the analysis of complex processes into manageable steps. It is powerful tool for summarising the important modes of failure, factors causing the failures and the likely effects of these failures.

FMEA may be used to prioritise risks and monitor the effectiveness of risk control activities. FMEA may be applied to equipment and facilities and can be used to analyse a manufacturing process to identify height risk steps or critical parameters.

Failure mode, effects and criticality analysis (FMECA):

FMECA can be extended to incorporate an investigation of the degree of severity of the consequences, their respective probabilities of occurrence and their detect ability, and can become a failure mode effect and criticality analysis. In order to perform such an analysis, the product or process specifications should be established. FMECA can identify places where additional preventive action may be necessary to minimise risks. FMECA application in pharmaceutical industry will mostly be utilised on failures and risks associated with manufacturing processes.

Fault tree analysis (FTA):

The FTA method is an approach that assumes failure of the functionality of a product or process. FTA is a method of analysis to identify all root causes of an assumed failure or problem. This method evaluates system failures one at a time but can combine multiple causes of failure by identifying casual chains. The results are represented pictorially in the form of a tree of fault modes. At each level in the tree, combinations of fault modes are described with logical operators (and or etc.). FTA relies on process understanding of the experts to identify casual factors.

The method may be used to establish the pathway to the root cause of the failure. The use of FTA may be applied while investigating complaints or deviations to fully understand their root cause and to ensure that intended improvements will fully resolve the issue and not lead to other issues. Fault tree analysis is a good method for evaluating how multiple factors affect a given issue. The output of FTA includes both a visual representation of failure modes and quantitative estimate of the likelihood of each failure mode. It is useful for both risk assessment and in developing monitoring program.

Preliminary hazard analysis (PHA):

PHA is a method of analysis based on applying prior experience or knowledge of a hazard or failure to identify future hazards, hazardous situations and events that can cause harm, as well as in estimating their probability of occurrence for a given activity, facility product or system.

PHA can be useful when analysing existing systems or prioritising hazards where circumstances prevent a more extensive technique from being used. It can be used for product, process and facility design as well as to evaluate the types of hazards for the general product type, then the product class and finally the specific product.

PHA is most commonly used in the early stages of development of a project when there is little information on design details or operating procedures; thus it will often be a precursor to further studies.

RISK RANKING AND FILTERING (RRF):

Risk ranking and filtering is a tool to compare and rank risks. Risk ranking of complex systems typically requires evaluation of multiple diverse quantitative and qualitative factors for each risk. The tool involves breaking down a basic risk question into as many components as needed to capture factors involved in the risk. These factors are combined into a single relative risk score that can then be used for ranking risks. 'Filters' in the form of weighting factors or cut-offs for risk scores, may be used to scale or fit the risk ranking to management or policy objectives.

Risk ranking and filtering can be used to prioritise manufacturing sites for inspection/audit by regulators or industry. Risk ranking methods are particularly helpful in situations in which the portfolio of risks and the underlying consequences to be managed are diverse and difficult to compare using a single tool.

Basic statistical tools can support and facilitate quality risk management. They may be helpful to enable effective data assessment and also aid in determining the significance of the data sets. Some of the principle tools used include acceptance control charts (control charts with arithmetic average and warning limits, cumulative sum charts, shewhart control charts, and weighted moving average), design of experiments (DOE), Pareto charts, probabilistic risk assessment and process capability analysis.

Quality risk management should be integrated into existing operations of the industry and regulatory authorities. When quality risk management is used, it should be included in the existing documentation for operations. Annexure 1 of the guideline proves examples of where the use of the quality risk management may provide information that can be used in a variety of pharmaceutical operations. Some of these are given in the Table1. These examples are purely illustrative and should not be taken as exhaustive list.

Source: ICH draft no. 4, Quality Risk Management Dec. 1st 2004.

TABLE 1: POTENTIAL OPPORTUNITIES FOR CONDUCTING QUALITY RISK MANAGEMENT

Sr. No.	Topic	Examples for risk assessment
1	Documentation	To determine the need and/or develop the content for SOPs, guidelines etc.
2	Training and education	To identify the training, experience, qualifications and physical abilities of personnel to perform an operation reliably and with no adverse impact on the quality of the product.
3	Quality defects	To facilitate risk communications and determine appropriate action to address significant product defects, in conjunction with regulatory authorities (e.g. recall).
4	Auditing/Inspection	Results of previous audits/inspections. Experience with manufacturing of a product (e.g. frequency, volume number of batches).
5	Periodic review	To interpret monitoring data (e.g. to support an assessment of the need for revalidation, changes in sampling).
6	Change management/ change control	To evaluate the impact of the changes on the availability of the final product. To evaluate the impact on product quality of changes to facility, equipment, material manufacturing process or conducting technical transfers.
7	Quality risk mgt. as part of regulatory	To facilitate continuous improvements of regulatory processes
8	Assessment activities	To evaluate impact of proposed variations or changes.

		To systematically evaluate information submitted by industry including pharmaceutical development information.
9	Quality risk management as part of development	To assess the critical attributes of raw materials, solvents, API starting materials, API's, use of excipients of packaging materials. To establish appropriate specifications and manufacturing controls (e.g. using information from pharmaceutical development studies) regarding the clinical significance of quality attributes and ability to control them during processing. To assess the need for additional studies (e.g. bioequivalence. stability) relating to scale up and technology transfer.
10	Quality risk management for facilities, equipment and utilities	To determine appropriate product contact material for equipment and containers (e.g. for equipment and containers (e.g. selection of stainless steel grade, gaskets, lubricants) To determine appropriate utilities (e.g. steam, gases, power source, compressed air, heating, ventilation and air conditioning (HVAC).water). To determine appropriate preventive maintenance for associated equipment (e.g. need for inventory of necessary spare parts)
11	Hygiene aspect in facilities	To protect the environment (e.g. personnel, potential for cross-contamination) from hazards related to the product being manufactured.
12	Qualification of facility / equipment /utilities	To determine the scope and extent of qualification of facilities, buildings, production equipment and/or laboratory instruments, including proper calibration methods.
13	Cleaning of equipment and environment control	To determine acceptable cleaning validation limits.
14	Calibration/preventive maintenance	To set appropriate calibration and maintenance schedules.

15	Computer systems and computer controlled equipment.	To select the design of computer hardware and software (e.g. modular, structured, fault tolerance)
16	Assessment and evaluation of suppliers and contract manufacturers	To provide a comprehensive evaluation of suppliers and contract manufacturers (e.g. auditing, supplier quality agreements).
17	Starting material	To assess differences and possible quality risks associated with variability in starting materials (e.g. age, route of synthesis).
18	Use of materials	To determine if it is appropriate to use material under quarantine (e.g. for further internal processing)
19	Storage, logistics and distribution conditions	To maintain infrastructure (e.g. capacity to ensure proper shipping conditions, interim storage, handling of hazardous materials and controlled substances, customs clearance).
20	Quality risk management as part of production validation	To determine the extent for follow up activities (e.g. sampling, monitoring and revalidation).
21	In-process sampling and testing	To evaluate and justify the use of process analytical technologies (PAT) in conjunction with parametric and real time release.
22	Stability	To evaluate adequacy of stability studies (e.g. the need for additional studies, shelf life extension, assessing frequency of extended testing, effect of variation in humidity and temperature).
23	Out of specification results	To identify potential root causes and corrective actions during the investigation of out of specification results.

Protocol No.:	LORDS PHARMACEUTICALS LIMITED	Page 157 of 222
Effective Date:	RISK ANALYSIS and RISK MANAGEMENT STUDY	Reference:
Supersede:	FOR **PURIFIED WATER PLANT**	HACCP Guideline ICH Q9

RISK ANALYSIS and RISK MANAGEMENT STUDY

FOR

PURIFIED WATER PLANT

At

LORDS PHARMACEUTICALS LIMITED.

Protocol No.:	LORDS PHARMACEUTICALS LIMITED	Page 158 of 222
Effective Date:	RISK ANALYSIS and RISK MANAGEMENT STUDY FOR **PURIFIED WATER PLANT**	Reference: HACCP Guideline ICH Q9
Supersede:		

THE PROTOCOL FOR RISK ANALYSIS and RISK MANAGEMENT FOR PURIFIED WATER PLANT PREPARED, REVIEWED AND APPROVED FOR EXECUTION BY AUTHORISED PERSONNEL FROM THE FOLLOWING HACCP TEAM. THE TEAM MEMBER REPRESENTS ALL THE RELEVANT DICIPLINES.

Prepared By:

HACCP Team	Name	Signature and Date
Engineering		

Reviewed By:

HACCP Team	Name	Signature and Date
Production		
Engineering		
Quality Assurance		

Approved By:

HACCP Team	Name	Signature and Date
Team Leader		
Quality Assurance		

Protocol No.:	LORDS PHARMACEUTICALS LIMITED	Page 159 of 222
Effective Date:	RISK ANALYSIS and RISK MANAGEMENT STUDY FOR **PURIFIED WATER PLANT**	Reference: HACCP Guideline ICH Q9
Supersede:		

INDEX

Sr. No.	Contents	Page No.
1	OBJECTIVE	
2	SCOPE	
3	RESPONSIBILITIES	
4	INTRODUCTION	
5	DEFINITIONS	
6	PRINCIPLES	
7	RISK ANALYSIS and RISK MANAGEMENT	
7.1	GUIDANCE FOR APPLICATION OF HACCP	
7.2	HACCP TEAM	
7.3	PRODUCT and PROCESS DESCRIPTION.	
7.4	IDENTIFICATION OF USE OR APPICATION OF PRODUCT	
7.5	OPEARTION / PROCESS FLOW DIAGRAM.	
7.6	ON-SITE CONFORMATION OF FLOW DIAGRAM	
7.7	LIST OF ALL POTENTIAL HAZARDS ASSOCIATED WITH EACH STEP: HAZARDS ANALYSIS	
7.8	CRITICAL CONTROL POINTS	
7.9	CRITICAL LIMITS FOR CRITICAL CONTROL POINTS (CCP)	
7.10	MONITORING SYSTEM FOR EACH CCP	
7.11	CORRECTIVE ACTIONS	
7.12	VERIFICATION PROCEDURES.	
7.13	DOCUMENTATION AND RECORD KEEPING	
8	TRAINING	
9	DEVIATIONS	
10	CHANGE CONTROL	
11	LIST OF APPENDIX	
12	SUMMARY OF RISK ANALYSIS and RISK MANAGEMENT STUDY.	
13	CERTIFICATION OF REPORT.	

Protocol No.:	LORDS PHARMACEUTICALS LIMITED	Page 160 of 222
Effective Date:	RISK ANALYSIS and RISK MANAGEMENT STUDY FOR	Reference: HACCP
Supersede:	**PURIFIED WATER PLANT**	Guideline ICH Q9

1.0 OBJECTIVE

The objective of this protocol is as follows, for Purified water plant located at _____.:

- To conduct hazards analysis as per HACCP guide.
- To identify the potential hazard.
- To identify hazard which should be controlled?
- Recommend controls and critical limits;
- To establish corrective actions.
- Verify effectiveness of procedures.
- Data reporting and conclusion on risk assessment and risk management system.

2.0 SCOPE

The scope of this protocol is limited to study risk analysis and risk management for purified water plant as per the guidelines outlined in this protocol.

3.0 RESPONSIBILITIES

The HACCP team comprising of a representative of the following departments shall be responsible for overall compliance with this protocol.

- Production Department
- Quality Control / Quality Assurance Department
- Engineering Department
- Safety dept.

4.0 INTRODUCTION

Traditionally, the Hazard Analysis and Critical Control Point (HACCP) methodology has been considered to be a food safety management system. It aims to prevent known hazards and to reduce the risks that they will occur at specific points in the food chain. The same principles are also increasingly being applied, in other industries, such as the car industry, aviation and the chemical industry. This protocol provides general guidance on the use of the HACCP system to ensure the quality of pharmaceuticals, while recognizing that the details of its application may vary depending on the circumstances. It does not provide detailed information on major hazards.

Protocol No.:	LORDS PHARMACEUTICALS LIMITED	Page 161 of 222
Effective Date:	RISK ANALYSIS and RISK MANAGEMENT STUDY FOR	Reference: HACCP
Supersede:	**PURIFIED WATER PLANT**	Guideline ICH Q9

Hazards affecting quality are controlled to a certain extent through the validation of critical operations and processes in the manufacture of finished pharmaceutical products in accordance with Good Manufacturing Practices (GMP). However, GMP does not cover the safety of the personnel engaged in manufacture, while both aspects are covered by HACCP. Procedures, including GMP, address operational conditions and provide the basis for HACCP. HACCP is a systematic method for the identification, assessment and control of safety hazards. Such hazards are defined as biological, chemical, or physical agents or operations that are reasonably likely to cause illness or injury if not controlled. In the manufacture of pharmaceuticals, these may include the manufacture of certain antibiotics, hormones, cytotoxic substances or other highly active pharmaceuticals; together with operations such as fluid bed drying, granulation is an example of hazard unit operations. The use of inflammable solvents (solutions) and certain laboratory operations may also constitute hazards. Safety hazards are common in the manufacture of active pharmaceutical ingredients; e.g., dangerous chemical conversions such as catalytic hydrogenation or nitration, or handling reactions with extremely hazardous chemicals such as phosgene or methyl-isocyanate require special precaution and control measures.

The following elements of the HACCP methodology are integral
parts of the validation master file:
— development of a flow diagram of the process;
— verification of the flow diagram on site.

In addition, HACCP will extend this concept to include an analysis of the critical quality variables as well as the assessment of hazards affecting the safety of workers and environmental pollution hazards directly related to the process (in particular in open systems) concerned. GMP for pharmaceutical products requires the validation of critical processes as well as of changes in the manufacturing process which may affect the quality of the final product. Experience shows that most manufacturing processes contain steps that are "critical" from the point of view of variations in final product quality. HACCP should not be confused with validation since its approach is broader; it thereby helps to identify matters on which validation should concentrate. It is science-

Protocol No.:	LORDS PHARMACEUTICALS LIMITED	Page 162 of 222
Effective Date:	RISK ANALYSIS and RISK MANAGEMENT STUDY FOR	Reference: HACCP
Supersede:	**PURIFIED WATER PLANT**	Guideline ICH Q9

based and systematic, and identifies specific hazards and measures for their control, as well as providing information on environmental protection and labour safety. HACCP is a tool to assess hazards and establish, control systems that focus on prevention rather than relying on corrective action based on end product testing. All HACCP systems are capable of accommodating changes, such as advances in equipment design and processing procedures or technological developments.

HACCP should not replace GMP; however, its application may be used as a first step towards GMP. In countries where appropriate regulations exist and are enforced, compliance with GMP (including validation), drug regulatory activities and inspections provide good assurance that risks are largely controlled. In countries where control is less effective, however, patients may be put at risk through the production of drugs of inadequate quality. The assessment of individual risks related to specific products and starting materials, and the recognition of hazards at specific stages of production or distribution should permit regulatory authorities to improve drug control by increasing the effectiveness of their activities within the limits of the available resources. The present guidelines are aimed at assisting industry to develop and implement effective HACCP plans covering activities such as research and development, sourcing of materials, manufacturing, packaging, testing and distribution.

Links with other programmes

In each stage of the manufacture and supply of pharmaceuticals, the necessary conditions should be provided and met with to protect the pharmaceuticals concerned. This has traditionally been accomplished through the application of Good Clinical Practice (GCP), Good Laboratory Practice (GLP), GMP and other guidelines, which are considered to be essential to the development and implementation of effective HACCP plans. HACCP plans are focussed on hazards, the overall objective being to ensure that pharmaceuticals are safe for use. The existence and effectiveness of GCP, GLP and GMP should be assessed when drawing up HACCP plans.

Protocol No.:	LORDS PHARMACEUTICALS LIMITED	Page 163 of 222
Effective Date:	RISK ANALYSIS and RISK MANAGEMENT STUDY FOR	Reference:
Supersede:	**PURIFIED WATER PLANT**	HACCP Guideline ICH Q9

5.0 DEFINATIONS:

The following definitions apply to the terms as used in these guidelines. They may have different meanings in other contexts.

1. **Control (verb):**
   The taking of all necessary actions to ensure and maintain compliance with the criteria established in the HACCP plan.

2. **Control (noun)**
   The state wherein correct procedures are being followed and criteria are being met.

3. **Control measure**
   Any action and activity that can be used to prevent or eliminate a pharmaceutical quality hazard or reduce it to an acceptable level.

4. **Corrective action**
   Any action to be taken when the results of monitoring at the CCP (see below) indicate a loss of control.

5. **Critical control point (CCP)**
   A step at which control can be applied and is essential to prevent or eliminate a pharmaceutical quality hazard or reduce it to an acceptable level.

6. **Critical limit**
   A criterion which separates acceptability from unacceptability.

7. **Deviation**
   Failure to meet a critical limit.

8. **Flow diagram**
   A systematic representation of the sequence of steps or operations used in the production, control and distribution of a particular pharmaceutical.

9. **HACCP plan**
   A document prepared in accordance with the principles of HACCP to ensure the control of hazards which are significant for pharmaceutical quality in the production and supply chain.

10. **Hazard**
    Any circumstance in the production, control and distribution of a pharmaceutical which can cause an adverse health effect.

Protocol No.:	LORDS PHARMACEUTICALS LIMITED	Page 164 of 222
Effective Date:	RISK ANALYSIS and RISK MANAGEMENT STUDY FOR	Reference:
Supersede:	**PURIFIED WATER PLANT**	HACCP Guideline ICH Q9

11. **Hazard analysis**
    The process of collecting and evaluating information on hazards which should be addressed in the HACCP plan.
12. **Monitor**
    The act of conducting a planned sequence of observations or measurements of control parameters to assess whether a CCP is under control.
13. **Verification**
    The application of methods, procedures, tests and other evaluations, in addition to monitoring, to determine compliance with the HACCP plan.

6.0 PRINCIPLES:

The HACCP system is based on seven principles. In applying these principles, 12 stages are recommended. Some stages are linked to specific principles while others serve as an introduction to the concept.

The seven principles are:
1. Conduct a hazard analysis.
2. Determine the critical control points (CCPs).
3. Establish target levels and critical limit(s).
4. Establish a system to monitor the CCPs.
5. Establish the corrective action to be taken when monitoring indicates that a particular CCP is not under control.
6. Establish procedures to verify that the HACCP system is working effectively.
7. Establish documentation concerning all procedures and keep records appropriate to these principles and their application.

12 Stages for applying HACCP:
1. Assemble a HACCP team
2. Describe the product and process
3. Identify the intended use
4. Construct a flow diagram
5. On-site confirmation of flow diagram
6. List all potential hazards associated with each step, conduct a hazard analysis, and consider any measures to control identified hazards (Principle 1)

Protocol No.:	LORDS PHARMACEUTICALS LIMITED	Page 165 of 222
Effective Date:	RISK ANALYSIS and RISK MANAGEMENT STUDY FOR	Reference: HACCP
Supersede:	**PURIFIED WATER PLANT**	Guideline ICH Q9

7. Determine critical control points (Principle 2)
8. Establish critical limits for each CCP (Principle 3)
9. Establish a monitoring system for each CCP (Principle 4)
10. Establish corrective actions (Principle 5)
11. Establish verification procedures (Principle 6)
12. Establish documentation and record keeping (Principle 7)

7.0 RISK ANALYSIS and RISK MANAGEMENT
7.1 GUIDANCE FOR APPLICATION OF HACCP
The following guidelines will be found useful in applying the HACCP system:
- Before HACCP is applied to any sector, that sector should be operating in accordance with the principles of good practices and the relevant legislation.
- Management commitment is necessary if an effective HACCP system is to be implemented.
- HACCP should be applied to each specific operation separately.
- CCPs identified in any given example in any reference document (including GMP guidelines) may not be the only ones identified for a specific application or may be of a different nature.
- The HACCP application should be reviewed and necessary changes made when any modification is made in the product or process, or in any step.
- It is important, when applying HACCP, to take into account the nature and size of the operation.
- There should be a HACCP plan. The format of such plans may vary, but they should preferably be specific to a particular product, process or operation. Generic HACCP plans can serve as useful guides in the development of product and process HACCP plans; however, it is essential that the unique conditions within each facility are considered during the development of all components of the HACCP plan.

7.2 HACCP TEAM
The pharmaceutical manufacturer should assure that product-specific knowledge and expertise are available for the development of an effective HACCP plan. This may be best accomplished by assembling a multidisciplinary team. Team members should therefore represent all the relevant disciplines, such as research and development, production, quality control, quality

Protocol No.:	LORDS PHARMACEUTICALS LIMITED	Page 166 of 222
Effective Date:	RISK ANALYSIS and RISK MANAGEMENT STUDY FOR	Reference: HACCP
Supersede:	**PURIFIED WATER PLANT**	Guideline ICH Q9

assurance, microbiology, engineering and distribution or others as applicable. Team members should have specific knowledge and expertise regarding the product and process. Where such expertise is not available on site, expert advice should be obtained from other sources. Team members should be able to:
(a) Conduct a hazard analysis;
(b) Identify potential hazards;
(c) Identify hazards which should be controlled;
(d) Recommend controls and critical limits;
(e) Devise procedures for monitoring and verification;
(f) Recommend appropriate corrective action where deviations occur;
(g) Verify the HACCP plan.

The scope of the HACCP plan should be defined. The scope should describe the segment of the process involved and the classes of hazards to be addressed should be identified.

7.3 PRODUCT and PROCESS DESCRIPTION
A full description of the product and the process should be drawn up including relevant quality information such as the composition, physical/ chemical properties, structure, pH, temperatures, method of cleaning, bactericidal/bacteriostatic treatments (e.g. heat-treatment), drying, screening, mixing, blending, packaging, and the storage conditions. The method of distribution and transport should also be described, especially where products are thermo labile.

7.4 IDENTIFICATION OF USE OR APPICATION OF PRODUCT
The intended use should be based on the expected uses of the product by the end user or consumer. In specific cases, vulnerable population groups, e.g. geriatric patients, infants and immunocompromised patients, may have to be considered.

7.5 OPEARTION / PROCESS FLOW DIAGRAM
The flow diagram should be constructed by the HACCP team, and should cover all operations and decisions in a process.When applying HACCP to a given operation, the steps preceding and following that operation should also be considered. A block-type diagram may be sufficiently descriptive.

Protocol No.:	LORDS PHARMACEUTICALS LIMITED	Page 167 of 222
Effective Date:	RISK ANALYSIS and RISK MANAGEMENT STUDY FOR	Reference:
Supersede:	**PURIFIED WATER PLANT**	HACCP Guideline ICH Q9

7.6 ON-SITE CONFORMATION OF FLOW DIAGRAM

The HACCP team should confirm the processing operation against the flow diagram during all stages and hours of operation. Amendments to the flow diagram may be made where appropriate, and should be documented.

7.7 LIST OF ALL POTENTIAL HAZARDS ASSOCIATED WITH EACH STEP: HAZARDS ANALYSIS

When hazard analysis is conducted, safety concerns must be distinguished from quality concerns.

The HACCP team should list all the hazards that may be reasonably expected to occur at each step from production, testing and distribution up to the point of use. It should then conduct a hazard analysis to identify for the HACCP plan which hazards are of such a nature that their elimination or reduction to acceptable levels is essential. A thorough hazard analysis is required to ensure an effective control point. A two-stage hazard analysis is recommended. During the first stage, the team should review the materials, activities, equipment, storage, distribution and intended use of the product. A list of the potential hazards (biological, chemical and physical) which may be introduced, increased or controlled in each step should be drawn up. In the hazard analysis, the following should be included wherever possible:
— the probable occurrence of hazards and the severity of their adverse health effects;
— the qualitative and/or quantitative evaluation of the presence of hazards;
— the survival or multiplication of microorganisms of concern;
— the production or persistence in drugs of toxins, chemicals or physical agents;
— the conditions leading to the above.

During the second stage, a hazard evaluation should be conducted, i.e. the severity of the potential hazards and the probability of their occurrence should be estimated. The team should then decide which potential hazards should be addressed in the HACCP plan, and what control measures, if any, exist that can be applied for each hazard. More than one control measure may be required to control a specific hazard(s) and more than one hazard may be controlled by a specified control measure.

Protocol No.:	LORDS PHARMACEUTICALS LIMITED	Page 168 of 222
Effective Date:	RISK ANALYSIS and RISK MANAGEMENT STUDY FOR	Reference:
Supersede:	**PURIFIED WATER PLANT**	HACCP Guideline ICH Q9

Potential hazards in relation to at least the following should be considered:
— materials and ingredients;
— physical characteristics and composition of the product;
— processing procedures;
— microbial limits, where applicable;
— premises;
— equipment;
— packaging;
— sanitation and hygiene;
— personnel;
— risk of explosions;
— mix-ups.

7.8 CRITICAL CONTROL POINTS

A CCP in the HACCP system can be more easily determined by the use of a decision-tree, which facilitates a logical approach. The way that a decision-tree is used will depend on the operation concerned, e.g. production, packing, reprocessing, storage, distribution. Training in the use of decision-trees should be given. If a hazard has been identified at a step where control is necessary for safety, and no control measure exists at that step, or any other, the product or process should be modified at that step, or at an earlier or later stage, to include such a control measure.

7.9 CRITICAL LIMITS FOR CRITICAL CONTROL POINTS (CCP)

Critical limits must be specified and verified, if possible, for each critical control point. More than one critical limit may sometimes be elaborated at a particular step. The criteria used often include measurements of temperature, time, moisture level, pH, and sensory parameters, such as visual appearance and texture. Critical limits should be scientifically based.

7.10 MONITORING SYSTEM FOR EACH CCP

Monitoring is the scheduled measurement or observation of a CCP relative to its critical limits. Monitoring should be recorded. The monitoring procedures used must be able to detect loss of control at the CCP, and this information should ideally be available in time to make adjustments to ensure control of the process and prevent violations of the critical limits. Where possible, process

Protocol No.:	LORDS PHARMACEUTICALS LIMITED	Page 169 of 222
Effective Date:	RISK ANALYSIS and RISK MANAGEMENT STUDY FOR	Reference: HACCP
Supersede:	**PURIFIED WATER PLANT**	Guideline ICH Q9

adjustments should be made when monitoring results indicate a trend towards loss of control at a CCP. These adjustments should be made before a deviation occurs. Data derived from monitoring must be evaluated by a designated person with the knowledge and authority to carry out corrective actions when indicated. If monitoring is not continuous, the amount or frequency of monitoring must be sufficient to guarantee that the CCP is under control. Most monitoring procedures for CCPs will need to be done rapidly because they relate to on-line processes and there will not be time for lengthy analytical testing. For this reason, physical and chemical measurements are often preferred to microbiological tests because they can be done rapidly and can often indicate the microbiological control of the product. The personnel conducting the monitoring of CCPs and control measures should be engaged in production (e.g. line supervisors, maintenance staff) and, where appropriate, staff from quality control. They should be trained in monitoring procedures.

Where continuous monitoring is possible, a reliable monitoring procedure and frequency should be identified. Statistically designed data collection or sampling systems should then be used.

All records and documents associated with monitoring CCPs must be signed and dated by the person(s) carrying out the monitoring and by a responsible reviewing official(s) of the company.

7.11 CORRECTIVE ACTIONS

Specific corrective actions should be developed for each CCP in the HACCP system in order to deal with deviations when they occur. These actions should ensure that the CCP is brought under control.

Corrective actions should include at least the following:
(a) Determination and correction of the cause of non-compliance;
(b) Determination of the disposition of the non-compliant product;
(c) Recording of the corrective actions that have been taken.

Specific corrective actions should be developed in advance for each CCP and included in the HACCP plan. As a minimum, this plan should specify what is to be done when a deviation occurs, who is responsible for implementing the corrective actions, and that a record will be kept and maintained of the actions taken. Individuals who have a thorough understanding of the process, product and HACCP plan should be assigned the responsibility for the oversight of corrective actions.

Protocol No.:	LORDS PHARMACEUTICALS LIMITED	Page 170 of 222
Effective Date:	RISK ANALYSIS and RISK MANAGEMENT STUDY FOR **PURIFIED WATER PLANT**	Reference: HACCP Guideline ICH Q9
Supersede:		

As appropriate, experts may be consulted to review the information available and to assist in determining the disposition of noncompliant product. Actions taken must also include the proper disposition of the affected product. Deviation and product disposition procedures must be documented in the HACCP records.

7.12 VERIFIATION PROCEDURES.

Procedures should be established for verification.

Verification and auditing methods, procedures and tests, including random sampling and analysis, can be used to determine whether the HACCP system is working correctly. The frequency of verification should be sufficient to confirm the proper functioning of the HACCP system.

Examples of verification activities includes:
— review of the HACCP system and its records;
— review of deviations and product dispositions;
— Confirmation that CCPs are kept under control.

Initial verification of the HACCP plan is necessary to determine whether it is scientifically and technically sound, that all hazards have been identified, and that, if the HACCP plan is properly implemented, these hazards will be effectively controlled.

Information reviewed to verify the HACCP plan should include:
(a) Expert advice and scientific studies;
(b) in-plant observations, measurements and evaluations. For example, verification of the moist heat sterilization process for sterile injectables should include the scientific justification of the heating times, pressure and temperatures needed to obtain an appropriate destruction of pathogenic microorganisms (i.e. enteric pathogens) and studies to confirm that the sterilization conditions ensure that the whole load is kept at the required temperature for the time required. Subsequent verifications should be performed and documented by a HACCP team or an independent expert, as needed. For example, Verifications may be conducted when there is an unexplained system failure, a significant change in product, process or packaging occurs, or new hazards are recognized. In addition, a periodic comprehensive evaluation of the HACCP system by an unbiased, independent

Protocol No.:	LORDS PHARMACEUTICALS LIMITED	Page 171 of 222
Effective Date:	RISK ANALYSIS and RISK MANAGEMENT STUDY FOR	Reference:
Supersede:	**PURIFIED WATER PLANT**	HACCP Guideline ICH Q9

third party is useful. This should include a technical evaluation of the hazard analysis and each element of the HACCP plan as well as an on-site review of all flow diagrams and appropriate records of the operation of the plan. Such a comprehensive verification is independent of other verification procedures and must be performed in order to ensure that the HACCP plan is resulting in the control of the hazards. If the results of the comprehensive verification identify deficiencies, the HACCP team should modify the HACCP plan as necessary. Individuals doing verification should have appropriate technical expertise to perform this function. Where possible, verification should include actions to confirm the efficacy of all elements of the HACCP plan.

7.13 DOCUMENTATION AND RECORD KEEPING

Efficient and accurate documentation and record keeping are essential to the application of a HACCP system and should be appropriate to the nature and size of the operation.

Examples of activities for which documentation is required include:
— hazard analysis;
— CCP determination;
— HACCP plan;
— Critical limit determination.

Examples of activities for which records are required include:
— CCP monitoring activities;
— process steps;
— associated hazards;
— Critical limits;
— Verification procedures and schedule;
— Deviations;
— associated corrective actions;
— Modifications to the HACCP system.

8.0 TRAINING

As HACCP is a relatively new concept in the pharmaceutical industry, training of personnel in industry, government and universities in HACCP principles and applications is essential for its effective implementation. In developing specific training to support a HACCP plan, working instructions and procedures should be drawn up which define the tasks of the operating

Report No.:	LORDS PHARMACEUTICALS LIMITED	Page 172 of 222
	REPORT ON	
	RISK ANALYSIS and RISK MANAGEMENT	Protocol Refn No:
Report Date:	STUDY	
	FOR	
	PURIFIED WATER PLANT	

personnel to be stationed at each critical control point. Specific training should be provided in the tasks of employees monitoring each CCP. Cooperation between producers, traders and responsible authorities is of vital importance. Opportunities should be provided for the joint training of industrial staff and the control authorities to encourage and maintain a continuous dialogue and create a climate of understanding in the practical application of HACCP. The success of a HACCP system depends on educating and training management and employees in the importance of their role in producing safe pharmaceuticals. Information should also be provided on the control of hazards at all stages of production and supply. Employees must understand what HACCP is, learn the skills necessary to make it function properly, and must also be given the materials and equipment necessary to control the CCPs.

9.0 DEVIATIONS

Deviation from any part or the protocol or any procedure or parameter shall be addressed as per SOP NO-----. Corrective and preventive actions to the deviations shall be mentioned in the report.

10.0 CHANGE CONTROL

Any change in document, system, machine and equipment, sequence of act shall be addressed through filing and approval of change control. Refer SOP No. ---

11.0 LIST OF APPENDIX

List out the Reports, certificates as Appendix to main report.

Sr. No.	Appendix No.	Description

12.0 SUMMARY OF RISK ANALYSIS and RISK MANAGEMENT STUDY.

Write the summery of the Risk analysis and Risk Management in the report.

13.0 CERTIFICATION OF REPORT.

Certify the report by the concerned personnel's and authorities after completion and final compilation.

Report No.:	LORDS PHARMACEUTICALS LIMITED	Page 173 of 222
Report Date:	REPORT ON RISK ANALYSIS and RISK MANAGEMENT STUDY FOR **PURIFIED WATER PLANT**	Protocol Refn No:

RISK ANALYSIS and RISK MANAGEMENT STUDY REPORT

FOR

PURIFIED WATER PLANT

At

ORGANIZATION ADDRESS,
(LORDS PHARMACEUTICALS LIMITED)

Report No.:	LORDS PHARMACEUTICALS LIMITED	Page 174 of 222
	REPORT ON RISK ANALYSIS and RISK MANAGEMENT STUDY FOR **PURIFIED WATER PLANT**	Protocol Refn No:
Report Date:		

PRE-APPROVAL:

THE PROTOCOL FOR REPORT ON RISK ANALYSIS and RISK MANAGEMENT FOR *PURIFIED WATER PLANT* PREPARED, REVIEWED AND APPROVED BY AUTHORISED PERSONNEL FROM THE FOLLOWING HACCP TEAM. THE TEAM MEMBER REPRESENTS ALL THE RELEVANT DICIPLINES.

Prepared By:

HACCP Team	Name	Signature and Date
Engineering		

Reviewed By:

HACCP Team	Name and Date	Signature and Date
Production		
Engineering		
Quality Assurance		

Approved By:

HACCP Team	Name	Signature and Date
Team Leader		
Quality Assurance		

Report No.:	LORDS PHARMACEUTICALS LIMITED	Page 175 of 222
	REPORT ON RISK ANALYSIS and RISK MANAGEMENT STUDY	Protocol Refn No:
Report Date:	FOR **PURIFIED WATER PLANT**	

INDEX

Sr. No.	Contents	Page No.
1	OBJECTIVE	
2	SCOPE	
3	RESPONSIBILITIES	
4	RISK ANALYSIS AND RISK MANAGEMENT	
4.1	GUIDANCE FOR APPLICATION OF HACCP	
4.2	HACCP TEAM	
4.3	PRODUCT AND PROCESS DESCRIPTION.	
4.4	IDENTIFICATION OF USE OR APPICATION OF PRODUCT	
4.5	OPEARTION / PROCESS FLOW DIAGRAM.	
4.6	ON-SITE CONFORMATION OF FLOW DIAGRAM	
4.7	LIST OF ALL POTENTIAL HAZARDS ASSOCIATED WITH EACH STEP: **HAZARDS ANALYSIS**	
4.8	CRITICAL CONTROL POINTS.	
4.9	CRITICAL LIMITS FOR CRITICAL CONTROL POINTS (CCP).	
4.10	MONITORING SYSTEM FOR EACH CCP.	
4.11	CORRECTIVE ACTIONS.	
4.12	VERIFIATION PROCEDURES.	
4.13	DOCUMENTATION AND RECORD KEEPING.	
5	TRAINING.	
6	DEVIATIONS	
7	CHANGE CONTROL.	
8	LIST OF APPENDIX.	
9	SUMMARY OF RISK ANALYSIS AND RISK MANAGEMENT STUDY.	
10	CERTIFICATION OF REPORT.	

Report No.:	LORDS PHARMACEUTICALS LIMITED	Page 176 of 222
	REPORT ON	
	RISK ANALYSIS and RISK MANAGEMENT	Protocol Refn No:
Report Date	STUDY	
	FOR	
	PURIFIED WATER PLANT	

1.0 OBJECTIVE

The objective of this report is as follows, for Purified water plant located at _____.:

- To conduct hazards analysis as per HACCP guide.
- To identify the potential hazard.
- To identify hazard which should be controlled?
- Recommend controls and critical limits;
- To establish corrective actions.
- Verify effectiveness of procedures.
- Data reporting and conclusion on risk assessment and Risk management system.

2.0 SCOPE

The scope of this report is limited to report the Study of risk analysis and Risk management for Purified water plant as per the guidelines outlined in the protocol.

3.0 RESPONSIBILITIES

The HACCP team comprising of a representative of the following departments shall be responsible for overall compliance with the protocol.

- Production Department
- Quality Control / Quality Assurance Department
- Engineering Department
- Safety dept.

4.0 RISK ANALYSIS and RISK MANAGEMENT

4.1 GUIDANCE FOR APPLICATION OF HACCP:

HACCP Plan:

HACCP plans can serve as useful guides in the development of product and process. HACCP plan for Risk management is as follow:

Sr. No	HACCP Plan Process/product	Responsibility	Date	Remark

Report No.:	LORDS PHARMACEUTICALS LIMITED	Page 177 of 222
	REPORT ON	
	RISK ANALYSIS and RISK MANAGEMENT	Protocol Refn No:
Report Date:	STUDY	
	FOR	
	PURIFIED WATER PLANT	

4.2 HACCP TEAM

Following are the team for HACCP:

Sr. No.	Name	Responsibility	Department
1		Team Leader (TL)	QA
2		Associate Team Leader (ATL)	Production
3		Team member (TM)	Safety
4		Team member (TM)	Rand D
5		Team member (TM)	Eng and maint.
6		Team member (TM)	Stores and distribution
7		Team member (TM)	QA/QC
8		Team member (TM)	
9		Team member (TM)	
10		Team member (TM)	
11		Team member (TM)	

4.3 PRODUCT and PROCESS DESCRIPTION

Product Description:

Purified water IP: Give description.

Process description:

(Give the water pretreatment and treatment, storage and distribution)

4.4 IDENTIFICATION OF USE OR APPICATION OF PRODUCT

The purified water is the product of the process, the intended use of the purified water generated by this process is for the manufacturing of medicinal products. This is also used for the rinsing of the equipment used for the manufacturing of the medicinal product used for treating and diagnosing the ailments in animal and human beings of all the age groups.

This water is also used for the testing of the medicinal product manufactured in this organization.

Report No.:	LORDS PHARMACEUTICALS LIMITED	Page 178 of 222
	REPORT ON RISK ANALYSIS and RISK MANAGEMENT STUDY FOR **PURIFIED WATER PLANT**	Protocol Refn No:
Report Date:		

4.5 OPEARTION / PROCESS FLOW DIAGRAM

MIDC water collection- under ground storage tank – lifting to over head tank – filtration 5 micron - NaOcl dosing – Flocculants dosing – Multigrade filter- NaOCl dosing – SMBS dosing – RO treatment (SDI) – De ionization with Resins –UV treatment for TOC- DM water storage- Filtration 5 and 1 micron – UF treatment- Purified water storage – UV treatment for disinfection- Sampling testing – for use – return to storage tank.

4.6 ON-SITE CONFORMATION OF FLOW DIAGRAM

MIDC water collection- under ground storage tank – lifting to over head tank – filtration 5 micron - NaOcl dosing – Flocculants dosing – Multigrade filter- NaOCl dosing – SMBS dosing – RO treatment (SDI) – De ionization with Resins –UV treatment for TOC- DM water storage- Filtration 5 and 1 micron – UF treatment- Purified water storage – UV treatment for disinfection- Sampling testing – for use – return to storage tank.

Above is the onsite diagram, which is identical to the process flow diagram and there is no variation in actual and on paper flow diagram.
This time required for process steps is also equal to flow diagram.

4.7 LIST OF ALL POTENTIAL HAZARDS ASSOCIATED WITH EACH STEP: HAZARDS ANALYSIS

List all the hazards that may be reasonably expected to occur at each step from production, testing and distribution up to the point of use.

Expected hazards are studied during process run and these are as follows.
Stage 1: Review of the materials, activities, equipment, storage, distribution and intended use of the product

Sr. No.	Process step	Expected Hazards		Adverse health effect
		Hazard	Potential hazard (biological, chemical and physical	

Report No.:	LORDS PHARMACEUTICALS LIMITED	Page 179 of 222
Report Date:	REPORT ON RISK ANALYSIS and RISK MANAGEMENT STUDY FOR **PURIFIED WATER PLANT**	Protocol Refn No:

Stage 2: A hazard evaluation is conducted in this stage, i.e. the severity of the potential hazards and the probability of their occurrence should be estimated. The team should then decide which potential hazards should be addressed in the HACCP plan, and what control measures, if any, exist that can be applied for each hazard. More than one control measure may be required to control a specific hazard(s) and more than one hazard may be controlled by a specified control measure.

Sr. No.	Potential hazard (biological, chemical and physical	Severity of potential Hazard	Probability of their occurrence	Existing control measure	New control measure

4.9 CRITICAL LIMITS FOR CRITICAL CONTROL POINTS (CCP)

Following are the limits for critical control point.

Sr. No.	Potential hazard (biological, chemical and physical	Critical control point	Limit

4.10 MONITORING SYSTEM FOR EACH CCP

Sr. No.	Potential hazard (biological, chemical and physical	Critical control point	Monitoring system

Report No.:	LORDS PHARMACEUTICALS LIMITED	Page 180 of 222
	REPORT ON RISK ANALYSIS and RISK MANAGEMENT STUDY FOR **PURIFIED WATER PLANT**	Protocol Refn No:

4.11 CORRECTIVE ACTIONS

Sr. No.	Deviation /Non compliance observed	Corrective action	Responsibility

4.12 VERIFIATION PROCEDURES

Verify the effectiveness of HACCP system as per SOP No –
- Reviewed the HACCP system and its records;
- Reviewed deviations and product dispositions;
- Confirmed that CCPs are kept under control.

Enclosed test reports as annexure.

Verified by:
(Sign, Name and Date)

4.13 DOCUMENTATION AND RECORD KEEPING
As per annexure.

8.0 TRAINING
Topic:
Venue:
Trainer:
Evaluation reports enclosed

Sr. No.	Name	Designation	Sign

9.0 DEVIATIONS

Dev. No.	Deviation	Reason for deviation	Corrective action

Enclosed Deviation report.

Report No.:	LORDS PHARMACEUTICALS LIMITED	Page 181 of 222
	REPORT ON RISK ANALYSIS and RISK MANAGEMENT STUDY FOR **PURIFIED WATER PLANT**	Protocol Refn No:

10.0 CHANGE CONTROL

Change control No.	Existing system	Proposed change	Reason	Closed /Open

Change control forms enclosed.

11.0 LIST OF APPENDIX

Sr. No.	Appendix No.	Description

12.0 SUMMARY OF RISK ANALYSIS and RISK MANAGEMENT STUDY.

All the analysis, evaluation, tests are carried out as per protocol. Results are documented correctly. The entire potential hazard is analyzed scientifically, step to step and identification of control points to control the occurrence of hazards is successfully monitored and reported. . All the control points are working as expected, to control the potential hazards. All the results are within accepted limit, No failure is observed during evaluation and review. It is confirmed that all the potential hazards are analyzed correctly and control system is working effectively through out the process/product run.

"HENCE THE PROCESS /PRODUCT IS CERTIFIED AS *SAFE* FROM, PHISICAL, CHEMICAL and BILOGICAL POTENTIAL HAZARDS. "

Report No.:	LORDS PHARMACEUTICALS LIMITED	Page 182 of 222
	REPORT ON RISK ANALYSIS and RISK MANAGEMENT STUDY FOR **PURIFIED WATER PLANT**	Protocol Refn No:

13.0 CERTIFICATION OF REPORT:

Reviewed By:

HACCP Team	Name	Signature and Date
Production		
Engineering		
Quality Assurance		

Approved By:

HACCP Team	Name	Signature and Date
Team Leader		
Quality Assurance		

34. QUALTY STSTEM (GMP) DOCUMENTATION

Documents and records are the heart of quality management system. There are two types of documents: Quality Management Document and Technical Documents. Quality management documents such as SMF, Quality Manual are non confidential documents. These specify the objective of the organization, quality policy, organization charts, responsibility and authority and brief description about system. It doesn't include company's confidential information. Technical Documents are confidential documents, documents such as SOPs, manufacturing formulae, instructions, R and D procedures, specification are the technical documents. There are three levels of documents Level 1, Level 2 and level 3. In Level 1, Quality management system Documents e.g. Site Master File, Quality Manual, Quality Policy, In Level 2, All SOPs, STPs, SCPs, Specifications, MFR, and Instruction, In Level 3, All Forms and format when filled, becomes a record.

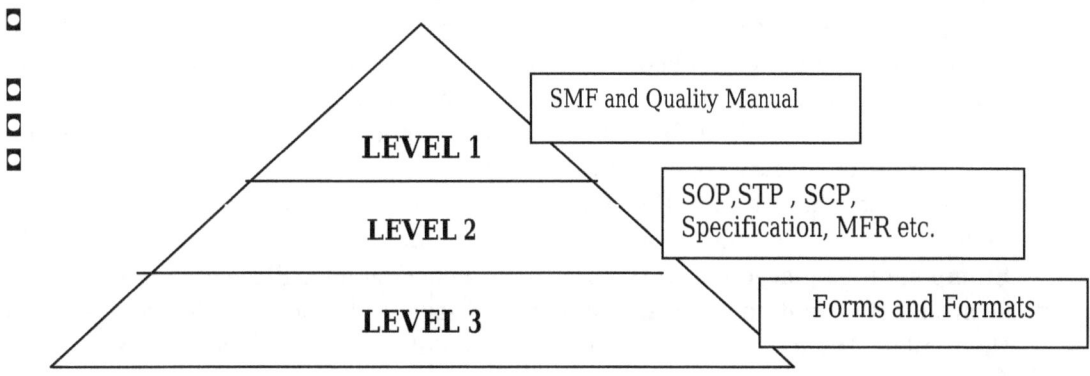

LEVELS OF DOCUMENTS

Documents: These are written procedures and instructions for the systems .These shall be authorised before implementation. Once approved, nothing can be written on these documents. *These are subjected for Updating and Revision.* E.g . SMF, QM, SOP, MFR etc.. These shall be controlled by stamping "Master", "Controlled", "Uncontrolled" and Obsolete" stamps.

Record: Records are the proof of action done as per the instruction given in documents. For example BMR and BPR the Record of Document MFR. *Record cannot be Revised or updated.* It is one time preparation. Records are repetitive and non repetitive type. Record cannot be controlled by stamping "Master", "Controlled", "Uncontrolled" and Obsolete". When forms and formats are filled it becomes a record.

TYPES OF DISTRIBUTION COPY:

1) **MASTER COPY:** This is original copy. "Master "or "Master copy "stamp shall be placed on every page of these documents. Place of stamp shall be such that it should not overlap any text and it should be viewed easily to the reader. QA or Management representative are the custodians of this copy. Use preferable blue colour stamp for stamping, or you can specify any ink but it should be specified in SOP. "Master, when in Blue" stamp can be more helpful to identify the type of copy. Master copy cannot be distributed as it is. There is only one master copy. No duplicate Master copy should be there. When some body makes photo copy of Master copy the Blue stamp becomes black and it will not be a master copy even though there is "Master" stamp , because it is Master when the stamp is in blue or in any specified colour ink. Obsolete copy of master shall be preserved for record by putting stamp of " OBSOLETE " in red ink.

2) **CONTROLLED COPY:** These are distribution copies to the related department and for display. These are called Controlled, because, there is control over these copies in case of revision. Record of distribution of these copies shall be maintained. After next revision of these documents, superseded (Obsolete/ old version)copy shall first be taken out from the copy holder and from display and new version copy shall be issued. These copies are prepared by making photocopies of Master copy or fresh printout can be taken. If the photocopy of Master is used for making Controlled copy then there will be two stamps, one is "MASTER" in black and other is "Controlled" or "Controlled Copy" in blue ink. Stamp shall be placed on every page of these documents. Place of stamp shall be such that it should not overlap any text and stamp . It should be viewed easily to the reader. Any concerned person (Departments) is the custodian of this copy. Use preferably blue colour stamp for stamping, or you can specify any ink. But it should be specified in SOP. "Controlled, when in Blue" stamp can be more helpful to identify the type of copy. There may one or more than one Controlled copy as per requirement. When some body makes photo copy of "Controlled" copy, the blue stamps of CONTROLLED becomes black and it will not be a Controlled copy even though there are "Master" and "Controlled" stamp on the pages, because it is controlled when the stamp is in blue or in any specified colour ink. Obsolete copies of controlled documents shall be collected to QA or MR. Obsolete Copy of Controlled copies shall be destroyed after putting Stamp of "OBSOLETE "in red ink. Record of Obsolete shall be maintained.

3) **UNCONTROLLED COPY:** These are distribution copies to the related personnel, Auditor or any external agency , training purpose applicable for particular period. These are called Uncontrolled, because, there is no control on these copies in case of revision. Record of distribution of these copies shall be maintained. After next revision of these documents; superseded (Obsolete/ old version)copy may *not* be taken out from the copy holder and new version copy need not to be issued. These copies are prepared by making photocopies of

Master copy or Controlled Copy or fresh printout can be taken. If the photocopy of Master is used for making uncontrolled copy then these will be two stamps, one is " MASTER " in black and other is "Uncontrolled "or "Uncontrolled Copy " in Blue ink. Stamp shall be placed on every page of these documents. Place of stamp shall be such that it should not overlap any text and stamp. It should be viewed easily to the reader. Use preferably blue colour stamp for stamping, or you can specify any ink but it should be specified in SOP. "Uncontrolled, when in Blue" stamp can be more helpful to identify the type of copy. There may be one or more than one uncontrolled copy as per requirement. When some body makes photo copy of "Uncontrolled" copy the blue stamps of UNCONTROLLED becomes black and it will not be a Uncontrolled copy even though these are "Master " and or" Controlled " and or "Uncontrolled "stamp are on the pages, because it is Uncontrolled when the stamp is in Blue or in any specified colour ink. Obsolete copies of uncontrolled documents cannot be collected to QA or MR. Obsolete Copy of Uncontrolled copies shall be destroyed by the user

4) **OBSOLETE:** These are the non current versions of the documents. Following are the some important quality system documents. Obsolete copies shall not be found at the user place. All the obsolete versions of the documents shall be taken back to QA or MR and "Obsolete" stamp shall be on every page of document in red ink. Obsolete Master copy of document shall be preserved for record and all other copies shall be destroyed.

Following are the Important Quality System Documents :

Site Master File

Validation master plan

Document and Data Control

Annual Product review

Complaints

Deviations and failure investigations

Change Control

Returned and Rejected goods handling

Self inspection,

Training

CAPA

Product Recall

OOS

Site master file: Iit is level 1 document, it is accessible to all. Similar to the quality manual Site Master File represents the type and status of the facility and systems in the organisation. Site Master File shall be as per the Regulatory guideline. Site Master File is mandatory documents for the pharmaceutical organization. Guidelines are published in Schedule M of Drugs and Cosmetics Rules, MHRA, PICs and other guidelines.

Detail guideline for SMF is given in IInd section of this book.

Validation master plan (VMP)

Facility and Process validation master plan for the plant is another Quality system document.

VMP is also given in the Section II of this book.

Document and Data Control:

There should be SOP for Document and Data control. This is First SOP in the Quality system, We can call it as "SOP for SOP ". Following points shall be incorporated in this Document.

1) Guideline about "Standard format of SOP" for the Organization.
2) Specimen of SOP Format.
3) Content titles in the SOP: Purpose, Scope, Responsibility, Definition and Abbreviations, Procedures, Risk and Safety Precautions, Equipments required, Supporting documents and attachments and References if any and Change History.
4) Header contents and Footer content.

   Logo, SOP title, originating department, SOP No, page No, revision No, revision date, supersedes No, next date of revision, effective date, guideline reference No, under which SOP is required or prepared, change control No, copy distribution list and status, type of copy that is master, controlled, uncontrolled, draft etc, signatures of the preparing, reviewing and authorizing authorities with dates.
5) Fonts specification
6) Font size.
7) Ink colour used for printing of SOP.
8) Paper colour and size used for printing of SOP.
9) It should be mentioned in the SOP that who will prepare the SOP, who will review and who will authorise the documents depending on their levels,
10) Distribution and retrieval guideline,
11) Implementation guideline,
12) Review of documents,
13) Electronic document and data control system,(password protection, restricted entry etc),

There should be distribution and retrieval record

Annual Product Quality Review (APQR):

APQR is the document which gives the history of the product. In addition to APQR, CPQR is also a helpful document as per the current industrial GMP trends. CPQR is Continuous Product Quality Review. After completion of every batch we have to have review on all previously manufactured batches instead of having review at the end of the year. In APQR we will come to know all abnormal observations at the end of the year, but in CPQR we will have this information online and we can revise the process and controls. Based on CPQR at the end of year APQR can be prepared. Following information should be incorporated in the APQR and CPQR. Trend Analysis (Retrospective Validation) is part of APQR and CPQR.

1) Product Details: Detailed information about product such as, product name, pharmacopoeial reference, strength, dosage form, dosage, unit composition formula, therapeutic category, license No, licensing schedule, shelf life, pack size, storage conditions etc.
2) Batches details: Batch numbers of batches manufactured in that year, batch sizes, shelf life and status of batch released or rejected.
3) Trend Analysis (Finished Goods): Comparison of analytical data of all batches.
4) Trend Analysis (In process Goods): Comparison of analytical data of all batches
5) Yield statistics: Study of yield of different batches at different stages.
6) Stability studies: Results of stability data.
7) Complaints and investigation: Total number of market complaints, adverse reactions, market recall, market withdrawal etc.
8) Validation: Total validation on this product in the review year.
9) Change control history
10) Control sample study
11) Raw material and packing material details, and any change.
12) Regulatory status
13) Compliance to last review recommendations.
14) Recommendation and conclusion.
15) Certification.

Complaints (Refer Section 2: Highlights in new Sch.M and its implementation)

Deviations and Failure Investigation:

Quality systems tells that "Write – what you want to do" "Do – Whatever is written" "Record – What ever is done" means we must follow the written down and authorised procedures and specification and facility; doing other than authorised is deviation. Deviations are not permitted in regular practices. But for the improvement in quality, safety and efficacy of product and in case of accidental and unpredictable failure, deviations are allowed by following a system. Based on situation there are two categories of the deviation, that is planned deviation and unplanned deviations. Deviation which are decided prior to happening, the deviation for the improvement in quality, safety and efficacy of product is planned deviation and unplanned deviations are deviation happened in case of accidental and unpredictable failure of facility. These deviations are of three types : Critical, Major and Minor. Deviations that affect the quality parameters, safety and efficacy of the product directly are the critical. In major deviation is the deviation due to which quality of the product is affected but not critical and there is less risk compared to critical deviation. In minor deviations quality of the product is not affected directly, there is no risk in this deviation. Deviations shall be raised by the originated department, once the deviation form is filled the department head will write his comments, then it should be logged in the deviation log. After logging the deviation, approval from concerned department shall be completed and at last QA head will approve the deviation. Deviation shall be closed within the specified period. At the time of closure, compliance of all recommendations from the various departments shall be verified. Necessary supporting documents shall be enclosed to the deviation report.

All the failures shall be investigated by root cause analysis. First investigation report shall be prepared by the originating department. Then based on these reports QA and regulatory investigations shall be completed. Failure investigation SOP shall be prepared and authorized. Corrective and preventive actions shall be reviewed and verified for any failure.

Change Controls:

Change Control is a very important record for the regulatory point of view. Every change in the system shall be documented and authorised through a system of change control. For making any change or modification in the existing system, document and facility; change control shall be filed. Originating department will raise the change control in change control form. Existing system and proposed system with reason for change or modification shall be mentioned. Put the reference to the documents wherever is applicable. After HODs remark, change controls are logged in change control log. After logging change control, concerned departments comments including QA, Change control is approved by QA head. Change control can be refused if it is not acceptable to any related department. Then reason for refusal shall be mentioned. After approval of change control, changes and modifications shall be initiated. All other documents and systems shall be revised where these changes are reflected. After verification and review of all the necessary changes as per requirement and revision of concerned system and document, change controls shall be closed. Closer of change control shall be within a defined time period. Changes shall be communicated to customers and related personnel though a proper communication system. Record of communication shall be maintained. Closed change controls shall be filed with necessary enclosures such , as draft SOP, drawing, photographs, revised documents etc.

Return and Rejected goods handling:

There shall be SOP for handling of rejected and returned goods. At the arrival of market return goods in the factory, check the required documents such as invoice, DC, octroi papers, sender's letters and details. Returned goods shall be stored in "Market return and Recalled goods area". After receipt give the intimation to QA and to the regulatory authority. Quarantine the goods securely. Make the entries in the return goods registers. QA will analyse the goods depending on situations. Then QA will take the decision of reprocess (Product affected by natural disasters, flood, earthquakes, and accidents during transport) or rejection. Once the fate of product is decided the goods are transferred for reprocess or destroy as per SOP in presence of regulatory authority if required. The destruction of reprocessing is recorded.

Shelf Inspection:

Shelf inspection is also called as Internal Quality Audits. Shelf inspection is mandatory for all types of pharmaceutical organization. Sop and record shall be made available at the time of inspection. The entire departments shall be included in the shelf inspection plan. Shelf inspection is audit carried out by organization itself to verify the effectiveness of the quality system and to ensure that all systems are at place and working satisfactorily. SOP for shelf inspection shall include the frequency of shelf inspection, for example every two months or every 3 months. Team of auditors shall be made. All the auditors shall be trained for inspection; record of their training shall be available. One qualified, experienced and sufficient field knowledge persons shall be selected for inspector team. Auditors shall be selected from different disciplines such as R and D, Production, QA, QC, P and A, Stores, and Engineering and Safety etc. Check list as per regulatory guidelines shall be prepared before going for inspection. Following points shall be covered in the audits:

(a) Personnel.
(b) Premises including personnel facilities.
(c) Maintenance of building and equipment.
(d) Storage of starting materials and finished products.
(e) Equipment.
(f) Production and in-process controls.
(g) Quality control.

- (h) Documentation.
- (i) Sanitation and hygiene.
- (j) Validation and revalidation programmes.
- (k) Calibration of instruments or measurement systems.
- (l) Recall procedures.
- (m) Complaints management.
- (n) Labels control.
- (o) Results of previous self-inspections and any corrective steps taken.

Self inspection plan for year and schedule for particular audit shall be prepared including the date and time of inspection, name of the inspectors and name of the auditee. The procedures for self-inspection shall be documented indicating self-inspection results, evaluation, conclusions and recommended corrective actions with effective follow up programme. Auditor's observations and recommendation shall be discussed in the management review meeting. All the non conformities and recommendations shall be complied within the time period given. Inspection record shall be maintained for external inspection. Quality systems can be audited based on different GMP guidelines from external experts and consultants which is also part of internal quality audit.

Training:

Training is the catalyst for effective implementation of quality systems. SOP and record shall be available for the training. Every person shall under go GMP and other related trainings.

Training can be categorised as below based on situation:
1) Schedules training
    a. Calendar training
    b. SOP or On Job training.
2) Need based training
    a. Induction training for new joining
    b. General training

Types of training based on information
1) Technical trainings
2) General trainings

Types of training based on Levels:
1) Bottom level training (Shop floor training from workmen to executive)
2) Middle level training (Manager level)
3) Top level training (Higher management training such GM,VP,Directors and MD)

Different trainings are applicable to different personnel; operational training may not be required for top level. Managerial training may not be applicable to the operator.

At the beginning of the year, training schedule shall be finalised and distributed to all concerned departments. Training such as GMP, first aid, safety, personnel hygiene, cleaning and sanitations, pest control, emergency, fire fighting, calibration, validations, environmental control can be incorporated in the calendar. Regular SOP revision and operation training shall be done as per the due dates of SOP.

In need based training; Training is given when the need arises. For example if there is accident while operating the blister machine, then there is need to train the operator. New SOP, new validations, new machine installations and external training are considered in this category.

Following the steps taken during the training:
1) Training need identification
2) Identification of resource person (verify the suitability and training of training)
3) Intimation of training (Agenda , date , time , topic, venue, trainer , duration etc)
4) Actual training session.
5) Verification of effectiveness of training and feed back report(Written test).
6) Record and data compilation(filing) ,
7) Retraining.

Corrective Action and Preventive action (CAPA):

CAPA is decision and action oriented. It is applicable in case of any nonconformity (rejection) and accidents. Corrective actions are the act, process or action taken to correct the nonconformity so that the nonconformity will conform to the acceptable standards. It may include correction of wrong printing on packing material, reprocess and rework of rejected goods. Preventive action is the action taken to avoid the occurrence of such nonconformity in future or to prevent the repeated nonconformity. If any non conformity is observed, then stop the further processing and quarantine the non conformed product and keep it under hold in restricted area. Carry out the detailed investigation, know the cause, root because analysis shall be done. If the nonconformity is major and will affect the product quality, safety or efficacy and any violation to the regulation, then plan the corrective actions as applicable so that product will comply with specification. If the non conformity is not as above then deviation can be filed as per procedure and policy of the company to release the product. Based on the root cause, preventive action shall be taken so that recurrence of such events will not occur in future. Any deviation filed shall be closed immediately. If required, revise the SOP and give the training to the operation and concerned personnel. Record the investigation, root cause, deviation, training, corrective and preventive action. There shall be time limit for closing the non conformity. After completion of time period, QA should verify the effectiveness of corrective and preventive action and closing of non conformance.

Following points shall be incorporated in the non conformity and CAPA report.
1) Description of non conformity,
2) Reference to the clause or document No under which non conformity is established.
3) Reason for non conformity.
4) Nonconformity observed by.
5) Responsibility for nonconformance.
6) Proposed corrective action,
7) Time limit for completion of corrective action.
8) Proposed preventive action,
9) Time limit for completion of preventive action
10) Remark of AQ for Review on Closing of non conformity and effectiveness verification.
11) Enclose the Annexure of investigation report, OOS report, deviation report, incident report etc which ever is applicable.

Product Recall (See Section I)

OOS (See Section 3)

❖ ❖ ❖

35. SOLUBILITY : DEFINITIONS AS PER IP 2007

Definitions And Types:

Solubility is defined as, "The number of grams of the substance which will dissolve in 100 grams of the solvent at a stated temperature".

Solute: The substance which is dissolved in solvent is called solute.

Solvent: The substance in which solute is dissolved.

The solubility of solid substance in a given solvent depends strongly on the temperature and slightly on the pressure. The solubility of most of the solids substances increases with increase in temperature.

Sr. No.	Types of Solubility	Approximate volume of solvent in milliliters per gram of solute at 20 to 30 °C temp.
1.	Very Soluble	Less than 1
2.	Freely Soluble	From 1 to 10
3.	Soluble	From 10 to 30
4.	Sparingly Soluble	From 30 to 100
5.	Slightly Soluble	From 100 to 1000
6.	Very Slightly Soluble	From 1000 to 10,000
7.	Insoluble or Practically Insoluble	More than 10,000

Example: Very soluble means 1 gm of solute substance will require less than 1 ml of solvent.

❖❖❖

36. MICRO-ORGANISMS AND NUTRIENT MEDIAS

Micro-organisms	Culture medias	Remark.
1) For Total Aerobic Microbial Count - Test:		
1) Plate count for Bacteria:	Soybean Casein Digest Medium	Incubate for 30 to 35°C for 5 days.
2) For Fungi.	Sabouraud Chloramphenicol Agar. (or Saubouraud dextrose digest agar with antibiotic).	Incubate for 20 to 25°C for 5 days.
2) Test for Specified Micro-Organism: (Pathogens)		
1) *Escherichia coli*	Nutrient Broth, MacConkey Broth, MacConkey Agar.	Incubate for 36 to 38°C for 48 hours.
2) *Salmonella*	Nutrient broth, Selenite F broth, Tetrathionate-bile brilliant green broth, Bismuth Sulphite agar, Brilliant Green Agar. Urea Both.	for streaking
3) *Pseudomonas aeruginos:*	Nutrient Broth, Soyabean-Casein digest, Cetrimide Agar Medium, Pseudomonas Agar.	For streaking.
4) *Pseudomonas aureus*	Nutrient Broth, Soyabean-casein digest, Cetrimide agar medium, Pseudomonas Agar.	For streaking.
5) *Sterility testing*		
(a) *Bacillus subtilis, Candida albicans, Bacteroides vulgatus.*	Fluid Thioglycollate Medium.	
(b) *Bacteroides vulgatus.*	Alternative Fluid Thioglycollate Medium.	
(c) *Bacillus subtilis, Candida albicans.*	Soyabean Casein Digest Medium	

❖❖❖

37. VALIDATION OF AIR SAMPLER USED IN MICROBIOLOGY

1. **Introduction**

This chapter provides guidance and describes techniques for the evaluation and qualification of the efficiency of air samplers used for measuring aerobic contamination. Usually, this will be performed by manufacturers of air samplers or third-party test organizations.

The overall efficiency of microbial air samplers is a product of two different actions:
a) the physical efficiency;
b) the biological efficiency.

The physical efficiency of impacting samplers depends upon the physical characteristics of the particles, including their size, shape and density. The biological efficiency is dependent on a number of factors such as:
a) type of viable particles collected;
b) growth characteristics of viable particle(s);
c) metabolic activities of the viable particle(s);
d) previous treatment of air;
e) the composition of the atmosphere (including humidity and temperature);
f) type and age of the aerosol;
g) the mechanism of capture and sampling time;

It is therefore important to have information and characteristic data of both efficiency factors before a microbial aerosol sampler is used, so that the sampler is qualified for its purpose and the contamination results obtained from the samples can be related to the potential.

2. **Principle of Qualification**

To qualify a device, characterisation of both physical and biological efficiency of a bioaerosol sample shall be carried out, taking into consideration:

a) The physical efficiency of collection of aerosol panicles over 2 range of particles likely to be encountered in appropriate rooms;
b) The biological efficiency of Gram-positive bacteria, Gram-negative bacteria and spores. When qualification of the sampler is necessary for the detection of fungal contamination in zones at risk, the collection of a yeast bioaerosol sample shall be included:
- in an environmentally controlled area;
- with a standard bioaerosol;
- with a standard method for generating and maintaining the airborne state of the bioaerosol; at defined environmental parameters.

NOTE: Some airborne micro-organisms, particularly vegetative metabolically active forms, are often inactivated by the collection process.

3. Sampling apparatus and test conditions

3.1 Experimentation area

The experimental area should be supplied with HEPA filtered air outlets and extracts and should be run at negative pressure.

The temperature should be maintained at (22 ± 2) °C and the relative humidity at (50 ± 10) %. The apparatus within the experimentation area must be manipulated without personnel entering the lest area.

3.2 Bio aerosol

To facilitate the measurements, the trial aerosol should be of a non-pathogenic nature and should have good survival and storage properties i.e., genetically stable.

The aerosol is made from a liquid suspension of an appropriate test organism grown in a culture medium meeting the nutritional requirements of this organism.

3.2.2 Test strain for testing physical efficiency

The test strain used should be *Bacillus subtilis var. niger* NCTC 10073 (= DSM 2277) prepared as a washed spore suspension. The washed spores should be centrifuged and suspended in a 80% solution of ethanol at a concentration of between 10^6 and 10^7/ml with different concentrations of suspended solids to give a range of particle sizes when aerosolized. The concentrations of solids required can be calculated as described below.

3.2.3 Biological efficiency

For biological efficiency testing, a mixture of viable spores (10^9 VU/ml) and vegetative cells (50: 50) should be used.

3.2.3.1 Test strain, Gram-positive

Lactobacillus acidophilus ATCC 4556 (= DSM 20079; = NCIB 8690) is recommended as an appropriate test strain, representing Gram positive bacteria.

The organism should be grown at (36 ± 1) °C in Elliker Broth or validated equivalent medium for (18 ± 2)h.

As a suitable solid collection media, Elliker Agar or validated equivalent medium recommended and should be incubated at (36 ± 1) °C.

3.2.3.2 Test strain, Gram-negative

Escherichia coli ATCC 10536 (= DSM 682; = NCIB 8879) is recommended as an appropriate test strain representing Gram-negative bacteria.

The organism should be grown at (36 ± 1) °C and 5 ml of this culture should be inoculated into a 45 ml of fresh Tryptone Soy Broth or validated equivalent medium and grown for 4 hours. The broth should then be used as the spray solution in a 50: 50 mix with a 10^9 spores per ml *Bacillus subtilis* var. *niger* suspension.

The solid collection media used should be Casein-Peptone Soy meal-Peptone Agar or validated equivalent medium and incubated at a temperature of (36 ± 1) °C.

3.2.3.3 Yeast test strain

NOTE: If required, *Saccharomyces cerevisiae* ATCC 9804 (= DSM 70478; = NCYC 91; = CBS 4000) a yeast not necessarily normally found in clean rooms, is recommended as an appropriate test strain to represent fungi.

The organism should be grown at (30 ± 1) °C for (18 ± 2)h in Malt Extract Broth or validated equivalent medium. The broth should then be used as the spray solution in a 50: 50 mix with a 10^9 spores/ml *Bacillus subtilis* var. *niger* suspension.

The collection media used should be Malt Extract Agar or validated equivalent medium and incubated at a temperature of (30 ± 1) °C.

3.3 Qualification

3.3.1 Physical efficiency testing

The aerosolizer used should allow the production of an aerosol of controlled particles size such as by the spinning top aerosol generator (STAG) device [28]. The initial particle size produced is given by equation:

$$d = K \sqrt{\frac{g}{w^2 \times r \times D}} \qquad \ldots (1)$$

where,
- d = initial wet particle diameter (m);
- K = a constant of value 5.0;
- γ = surface tension (J × m^{-2});
- ω = rotation speed (s^{-1});
- ρ = density (kg × m^{-3})
- D = diameter of spinning disc (m).

After formation, the particle will reduce by evaporation to a size related to the solid content calculated as follows:

$$V_i = \frac{4}{3} \pi d^3 \qquad \ldots (2)$$

where,

V_i is the original volume (m^3) and d is the original radius formed from the spinning top aerosol generator prior to evaporation. The volume of this original particle should be less than 10^{-7} m^3 to ensure that only one spore is present in each particle. The amount of solids in this particle W (g) is the product of the particle volume and the concentration of the solid $C_{(conc\ solid)}$ (g*m^3) in the original solution as given below:

$$W = V_i \times C_{(conc\ solid)} \qquad \ldots (3)$$

The volume of the particle after total evaporation of the solvent (V_p) will be made up of the solids and one monodisperse spore only, and so be the solids content in the original particle divided by the density I of the solid as calculated by equation (4):

$$V_p = \frac{W}{r} \qquad \ldots (4)$$

Therefore, the particle radius can be calculated according to equation (5).

$$R = \left[\left(\frac{3}{4}\right)\left(\frac{V_p}{p}\right)\right]^{\frac{1}{3}} \qquad \ldots (5)$$

The radius of a particle containing a spore (r_s) will be:

$$r_s = \left[\left(\frac{3}{4}\right)\left(\frac{V_p + V_p}{p}\right)\right]^{\frac{1}{3}} \qquad \ldots (6)$$

where,

V_s is the volume of a spore (approx.: 4.9×10^{-10} m^3).

Since the density of solid is different from that of the spore, the equivalent particle diameter (EPD) is calculated by equation (7):

$$EPD = \sqrt{\frac{I\,(d_s)}{r_{H_2O}}} \qquad \ldots (7)$$

where,

d_s = diameter of spore;
ρ_{H_2O} = density of water.

Five solutions should be prepared to give particle sizes over the range 0.8 µm to 15 µm diameter. The 0.8 µm particle will be the naked spore suspended in distilled water.

3.3.1 Testing

3.3.1.1 Physical efficiency

The spinning top aerosol generator (STAG) should be supplied with oil-free filtered (0.01 µm) compressed air and supplied with the spray solution by a peristaltic pump at a flow rate of approximately 1 ml/min.

The experiments should take place in the experimental area as described previously. The sampler to be tested and a membrane filter of 0.45 µm, operating at flow rate of about 5 L/min., are placed approximately 1 m apart from the STAG and at the same level of the spinning disc to give a 100% recovery of the *Bacillus subtilis* spores. At each panicle size selected at least 10 comparative experiments should be carried out.

The collection media used should be Casein-Peptone Soymeal-Peptone Agar or validated equivalent medium.

3.3.1.2 Biological efficiency

The mixed suspensions should be aerosolized in the experimental area, described previously, containing the sampling device for testing. The nebulizer used should produce a poly disperse aerosol as, for example, produced by a disposable hand-held therapeutic device. The aerosol should be produced continuously for approximately one minute with the sampling device being run for the same time or whichever time is required to avoid overloading of the media.

4. Enumeration of colonies

After the appropriate incubation period, visible colonies are counted either visually or using an automated device. The number of colonies are counted and expressed in viable units (VU) related to 1 m^3.

5. Evaluation and interpretation of results

5.1 Physical efficiency testing

The VU yield from the test sampler (TS) divided by the concentration of micro-organisms (VU) obtained by the filter sampler (MS) multiplied by 100 gives the physical efficiency factor (P_e) for the collection device and may be calculated according to equation (8). The results may be plotted as: particle size against percentage of efficiency, with all points plotted as means ± standard deviations.

$$P_e = \frac{VU_{(mean\ TS)}}{VU_{(mean\ MS)}} \times 100 \qquad \ldots (8)$$

It is preferable to take the physical efficiency factor of air samples within the boundaries from 0.5 to 0.7 as calculated by equation (8). It is recommended to use the physical efficiency factor for interpretation of results of aerobiocontamination assessment by the following equation.

$$C = \frac{C_{ts}}{P_e} \qquad \ldots (9)$$

where, C = True concentration of aerosol.
C_{ts} = Test sampler obtained concentration of aerosol
P_e = Physical efficiency factor calculated by equation (8)

Biological efficiency testing

The ratio between the test strain and the spore tracer (*Bacillus subtilis* spores) should be evaluated for the aerosol by dilution and by counting the number of the spore colonies and colonies of the test strain on the surface of the sampling containers.

The ratio found in the sample divided by the spray solution ratio multiplied by 100 gives the percentage of bioefficiency for the strain and sampler.

The ratio of the colonies of test strains to spore tracer:

$$\frac{VU_{(GN)}/VU_{(GP)}}{VU_{(spores)}} \qquad \ldots (10)$$

is determined after sampling and should be calculated for each dilution and divided by the initial VU count of the micro-organism/spore suspension and multiplied by 100 to give the biology efficiency factor B in equation (11):

$$B_e = \frac{VU_{t(GN/GP)}}{VU_{t(spores)}} \times 100 \qquad \ldots (11)$$

38. ANALYTICAL METHOD TECHNOLOGIES

Quality of drug should meet the standards related to safety, efficacy and potency. Hence, for the evaluation of quality of drugs, various quality control methods are used. These methods are used alone or in combination as per requirements. Following are the types:

1) **Chemical methods:**
   a) Volumetric analysis
      - Neutralisation titrations
      - Precipitation titrations
      - Non aqueous titrations
      - Complexometic titrations
      - Oxidation reduction titration
   b) Gravimetric method
      By weight method
   c) Gasometric method
      (measurement of volume of gases)

2) **Instrumental or physicochemical methods:**
   1) Potentiometry - (electric potential)
   2) Conductometry – (electric conductometry)
   3) Polarography, voltametery – (electric current)
   4) Spectrophotometry, colorimetry, atomic absorption spectroscopy – absorption of radiation.
   5) Emition spectroscopy, flame photometry, fluorimetry – emission of radiation
   6) Turbidometry, Nephelometry – Scattering of radiation
   7) Refractometry – Refraction of radiation
   8) Polarimetry, optical rotatory dispersion – Rotation of plane polarized light
   9) Thermal method – Thermal properties
   10) Mass spectroscopy – Mass to charge ratio
   11) Chromatography – separation technique

3) **Microbiological method:**
   Zone of inhibition, zone of growth, radio immunoassay.
   Biological method:
   Bio assay, animal testing, pyrogen, test.

39. IMPORTANT TERMS USED IN MICROBIOLOGICAL TESTING

1. **Aerobe:** An organism that requires oxygen for growth and can grow under an air atmosphere (21% O_2).

2. **Anaerobe:** An organisms that dose not use O_2 to obtain energy, cannot grow under an air atmosphere and for which O_2 is toxic.

3. **Angstrom:** A unit of length equal to 10^{-8} cm. ($10A° = 1$ nm, 1 μm $= 1000$ nm)

4. **Autolysis:** The disintegration of cells by the action of their own tissues.

5. **Bactericide:** An agent which destroys bacteria.

6. **Bacteriostatic:** Inhibiting the growth of bacteria without killing them.

7. **BOD:** Biochemical Oxygen Demand. Quantity of oxygen required to degrade the organic matters which are degradable by bacteria in water.

8. **Clone:** A population of cell descended from a single cell.

9. **Colony:** A macroscopically visible growth of micro-organisms on solid culture medium.

10. **CFU:** Colony forming units. The cells or aggregate of cells which give rise to a single colony in the plate count technique.

11. **Culture:** A population of micro-organism cultivated in a medium.

12. **Decimal reduction time:** The amount of time at a particular temp sufficient to reduce available microbial population by 90%.

13. **Detergent:** A synthetic cleaning material containing surface active agents which do not precipitate in hard water.

14. **Dialysis:** The separation of soluble substances from a colloid by diffusion through a semipermeable membrane.

15. **Dilution (serial):** Successive dilution of a specimen e.g. a 1: 10 dilution equals 1 ml of specimen plus 9 ml of diluent, a 1: 100 dilution equals 1 ml of a 1: 10 dilution plus 9 ml of diluent.

16. **Disinfectant:** An agent that frees from infection by killing the vegetative cells of micro-organisms.

17. **Effluent:** The liquid waste of sewage and industrial processing.

18. **Endotoxin:** A heat stable toxin which consists a lipopolysaccharide, it is located in the outer membrane of gram negative bacteria and is liberated only when the bacteria disintegrate.
19. **Gram negative bacteria:** Bacteria that do not retain the crystal violet – iodine complex when subjected to Gram staining and thus acquire the colour of the dye.
20. **Gram positive bacteria:** Bacteria that retain the crystal violet iodine complex stain when subjected to Gram staining technique and thus appear dark blue or violet.
21. **Habitat:** The natural environment of organism.
22. **Incubation:** In microbiology, the subjecting of cultures of micro-organism to conditions favourable to their growth.
23. **Inoculation:** The artificial introduction of micro-organism or other substances into the body or into a culture media.
24. **Inoculum:** The substance, containing, micro-organisms other material, that is introduced in inoculation.
25. **In-situ:** In the original or natural location.
26. **In-vitro:** In glass, in test tube or in laboratory.
27. **In-vivo:** Within the living organism.
28. **Medium:** A substance used to provide nutrition for the growth and multiplication of micro-organisms.
29. **Mold:** A fungus characterized by filamentous structure.
30. **Mutant:** An organism with a changed or new gene.
31. **Oncology:** The study of the causes, development, characteristics and treatment of tumors.
32. **Phenol coefficient:** The ratio between the greatest dilution of a test germicide capable of killing a test organism in 10 min but not in 5 min and the greatest dilution of phenol giving the same result.
33. **Phycology:** The study of algae.
34. **Pure culture:** A culture containing only one species of organism.
35. **Pyrogen:** A chemical which affects the hypothalamus which regulates body temperature.

36. **Sanitizer:** An agent that reduces, to levels judged safe by public health authorities, the microbial flora in materials or on such articles as eating, utensils.

37. **Sludge:** The semisolid part of sewage that has been sedimented or acted upon by bacteria.

38. **Smear:** Thin layer of material, e.g. a bacterial culture spread on a glass slide for microscopic examination.

39. **Spore:** A resistant body formed by certain micro-organisms.

40. **Stem cell:** Formative cells in the bone marrow from which specialized cells, such as lymphocytes arise.

41. **Stock culture:** Known species of micro organism maintained in the laboratory for various tests and studies.

42. **Strain:** All the descendents of a pure culture usually a succession of cultures derived from an initial colony.

43. **Symbiosis:** The living together of two or more organism in microbial association.

44. **Thermal death point:** The lowest temperature at which micro-organism are killed in given time.

45. **Type species:** The species that is permanent reference examples of the genus.

46. **Type strain:** The strain that is the permanent reference stain of the species. It is the strain to which all others strains must be compared in order to be molecule in the species.

40. FREQUENTLY USED ABBREVIATIONS IN PHARMACEUTICALS

BOPP	-	Biaxially oriented Polypropylene.
CF boxes	-	Corrugated Fiber Board.
DFC	-	Duplex Fiber Corrugation.
HVAC	-	Heating Ventilation and Air conditioning.
FDV	-	Forced Draught Ventilation.
AHU	-	Air handling Unit.
EHS	-	Environment, Heath and Safety.
GMP	-	Good Manufacturing Practices.
cGMP	-	current Good Manufacturing Practices.
BPR	-	Batch Packing Record.
BMR	-	Batch Manufacturing Record.
MFR	-	Master Formula Record
GRN	-	Goods Receipt Note.
MRN	-	Material Receipt Note.
PLA	-	Personal Ledger Account.
RG 1	-	Register 1.
RT 12	-	Written 12 (months).
AR No.	-	Analytical Report Number.
PPM	-	Planned Preventive Maintenance, Parts Per Million.
ETP	-	Effluent Treatment Plant.
ECC No	-	Excise Control Code Number.
DMF	-	Drug Master File.
SMF	-	Site Master File.
LAF	-	Laminar Air Flow.
RLAF	-	Reverse Laminar Air Flow
GLP	-	Good Laboratories Practices.
GALP	-	Good Automated Laboratories Practices.
HEPA filters	-	High Efficiency Particulate Air Filters.
ULPA Filters	-	Ultra Low penetration Air filters.
SULPA filters	-	Super Ultra Low penetration Air filters
GSM	-	Grams per square meter.

ROPP	-	Roll On Pilfer Proof.
RAG	-	Return Air Grills.
SAG	-	Supply Air Grills.
RH	-	Relative humidity.
DBT	-	Dry Bulb Temperature.
WBD	-	Wet Bulb temperature.
ETO	-	Ethylene Oxide.
DT	-	Disintegration Time.
HT	-	Heigh Tension.
RMG	-	Rapid Mixer Granulator .
FBD	-	Fluidized Bed Drier.
NFD	-	Non-filled Detection.
DM	-	De Mineralized
WFI	-	Water For Injection.
EU	-	Endotoxin Unit, European Union. ;
NTU	-	Nephelometry Tubidity Unit.
RO	-	Reverse Osmosis.
EDR	-	Electro Deionization Reversal.
MOC	-	Material of Construction.
PET	-	Preservative Efficacy Test
GPT	-	Growth Promotion Test.
BIS	-	Bureau of Indian Standard.
ISO	-	International Organization Standardization.
ACPH	-	Air Changes Per Hour.
FPM	-	Feet Per Minute.
RPM	-	Revolutions/Rotations Per Minute.
MCC	-	Microcrystalline Cellulose.
HPMC	-	Hydroxypropyle Methyle Cellulose.
CCPC	-	Conversion Cost Packing Cost.
CMC	-	Carboxy Methyle Cellulose, Critical Micelles Concentration
HLB	-	Hydrophilic Liphophilic Balance.
OOS	-	Out Of Specification.
NC	-	Non-Conformance
NDA	-	New Drug Applications.
ANDA	-	Abbreviated New Drug Applications.

NDA	-	New Drug application.
Sch.	-	Schedule
SOP	-	Standard Operating Procedure
STP	-	Standard Testing Procedure
SCP	-	Standard Cleaning procedure.
GTM	-	General Test Methods.
AQL	-	Acceptance Quality Level.
SQC	-	Statistical Quality Control.
FG	-	Finished Goods.
RM	-	Raw Material.
PM	-	Packing Material
FDA	-	Food and Drugs Administration
FIFO	-	First In First Out
FP	-	Finished Products
GMP	-	Good Manufacturing Practices
HDPE	-	High Density Poly Ethylene
MLT	-	Microbial Limit Test
MRM	-	Management Review Meeting
PPC	-	Production Planning and Control
PVC	-	Polyvinyl Chloride
PVDC	-	Polyvinyl Dichloride
QA	-	Quality Assurance
QC	-	Quality Control
QMS	-	Quality Management System
TQM	-	Total Quality Management
PET	-	Polyethylene Terapthalate.
QU	-	Quality Unit
IP	-	Indian Pharmacopoeia
BP	-	British Pharmacopoeia
EP (Ph.Eur.)	-	European Pharmacopoeia
USP	-	United States Pharmacopoeia.
NF	-	National Formulary.
WEF	-	With Effect From.
ORS	-	Oral Redydration Salts.
MDI	-	Metered Dose Inhaler.

LD	-	Lethal Dose.
COD	-	Chemical Oxygen Demand.
BOD	-	Bio-chemical Oxygen Demand.
DR	-	Double Rotary
SR	-	Single Rotary.
KFR	-	Karl Fishers Reagents
PO	-	Purchase Order.
DO	-	Dispatch Order.
VRS	-	Voluntary Retirement Scheme.
SVP	-	Small Volume Parentarels.
LVP	-	Large Volume Parenterals
RT	-	Retention Time.
RRT	-	Relative Retention Time.
SD	-	Standard Deviation.
RDS	-	Relative Standard Deviation.
STN	-	Signal To Noise.
ACE	-	Angiotensin Converting Enzyme
ACTH	-	Adrenocorticotrophic Hormone
ADH	-	Antidiuretic hormone
ADHD	-	Attention Deficit Hypersensitivity Disorder
AF	-	Atrial Fibrillatiorn
AIDS	-	Acquired Immunodeficiency Syndrome
ALL	-	Acute Lymphoblastic Leukemia
ALT	-	Alanine Transaminase
AML	-	Acute Myeloid Leukenia
ANF	-	Antinuclear Factor
ASD	-	Atrial Septal Defect
AST	-	Aspartate Transaminase
ATN	-	Acutetubular Necrosis
BBB	-	Bundle Branch Block
BMT	-	Bone Marrow Transplant
CABG	-	Coronary Artery Bypass Graft
CAPD	-	Chronic Ambulatory Peritoneal Dialysis
CCF	-	Congestive Cardiac Failure
CCU	-	Coronary Care Unit.

CEA	-	Carcino Embryonic Antigen
CLL	-	Chronic Lymphoblastic Leukemia
CML	-	Chronic Myeloid Leukemia
CMV	-	Cytomegalovirus
COLD	-	Chronic Obstructive Lung Disease
CRF	-	Chronic Renal Failure
CSF	-	Cerebrospinal Fluid
CT	-	Computed Tomography
CVA	-	Cerebrovascular Accident
CVP	-	Central Venous Pressure
CXR	-	Chest X-ray
DIC	-	Disseminated Intravascular Coagulation
DM	-	Diabetes Mellitus
DU	-	Duodenal Ulcer
DVT	-	Deep Venous Thrombosis
EBV	-	Esptein Barr Virus
ELISA	-	Enzyme-Linked Immuno Sorbent Assay
EMG	-	Electromyography
ESR	-	Erythrocyte sedimentation rate
FFP	-	Fresh Frozen Plasma
FTA	-	Flouroscent Treponemal Antibody test
FVC	-	Forced Vital Capacity
GABA	-	Gamma Amino Butyric Acid
GFR	-	Glomerular Filtration Rate
HBV	-	Hepatitis B Virus
HIV	-	Human Immuno deficiency Virus
HOCM	-	Hypertrophic Obstruction Cardio myopathy
HSV	-	Herpes Simplex Virus
IBD	-	Inflammatory Bowel Disease
ICP	-	Intracranial Pressure
IDL	-	Intermediate Density Lipoprotein
IHD	-	Ischemic Heart Disease
INR	-	International Normalized Ratio
ITP	-	Idiopathic Thrombocytic Purpura
IVC	-	Inferior Venacava

IVU	-	Intravenous Urography
JVP	-	Jugular Venous Pressure
LA	-	Left Atrium
LBBB	-	Left Bundle Branch Block
LDH	-	Lactate Dehydrogenase
LDL	-	Low Density Lipoprotein
LFT	-	Liver Function Test
LH	-	Lutenizing Hormone
LVF	-	Left Ventricular Failure
MCV	-	Mean cell Volume
MI	-	Myocardial Infarction
MSU	-	Midstream Urine
MTP	-	Metatarsophalangeal
NSAID	-	Non-steroidal Anti-inflammatory Drug
OCP	-	Oral Contraceptive Pill
OGTT	-	Oral Glucose Tolerance Test
PA	-	Pulmonary Artery
PABA	-	Para-Amino Benzoic Acid
PAS	-	Para-Aminosalicylic Acid
PCP	-	Pneumocystis carini pneamonia
PCV	-	Packed Cell Volume
PEEP	-	Positive-End Expiratory Pressure
PEFR	-	Peak Expiratory Flow Rate
PPD	-	Purified Protein Derivative
PTH	-	Parathyroid Hormone
PT	-	Prothrombin Tune
PTT	-	Partial Thromboplastin Time
PUO	-	Pyrescia of Unknown Origin
RA	-	Rheumatoid Arthritis
RAD	-	Right Anis Deviarion
RAG	-	R antigen
RAST	-	Radioallerglosorbent Test
RVF	-	Right Ventricular Failure
SBE	-	Subacute Bacterial Endocarditis
SLE	-	Systemic Lupus Erythrematosus

SVT	-	Supraventricular Tachycardia
TIA	-	Transient Ischemic Attack
SVC	-	Superior Venacava
TPHA	-	Treponema pallidum Hemagglutination Assay
TPN	-	Total Parenteral Nutrition
TRH	-	Thyroid Releasing Hormone
TSH	-	Thyroid Stimulating Hormone
TURP	-	Transurethral Resection of Prostate
UandE	-	Urea and Electrolyte
UC	-	Ulcerative Colitis
URTI	-	Upper Respiratory Tract Infection
UTI	-	Urinary Tract Infection
US	-	Ultrasound
VDRL	-	Venereal Disease Research Laboratory
VF	-	Ventricular Fibrillation
VLDL	-	Very Low Density Lipoprotein
VSD	-	Ventricular Septal Defect
VT	-	Ventricular Tachycardia
WPW	-	Wolf – Parkinson – White
AAS	-	Atomic Absorption Spectrometery
A/C	-	Asbestos – Centre
ADA	-	Amplicillin Dexciln Agar
ADI	-	Acceptable Daily Intake
a.i.	-	Active ingredient
AIDS	-	Acquired Immunodeficiency Syndrome
ALAD	-	Aminolacyulinic Acid Dehydratase
ALAT	-	Alanine Aminotransferase
AOC	-	Assimilable Organic Carbon
APHA	-	American Public Health Association
BOD	-	Biochemical Oxygen Demand
Bq	-	Bequerel
BSP	-	Bromosulfophthalein
BUN	-	Blood Urea nitrogen
bw	-	Body weight
CAS	-	Chemical Abstracts Service

CFU	-	Colony forming units
CHO	-	Chinese Hamster Overay
CMC	-	Carboxymethyl Cellulose
DENA	-	Diethylnitrosamine
DMAA	-	Dimethylarsinic acid
DNA	-	Deoxyribonucleic acid
ECG	-	Electrocardiogram
EDTA	-	edetic acid(Ethylene Diamine Tetra Acetic Acid)
EEG	-	Electroencephalogram
EP	-	Erythrocyte Protoporphyrin
EPA	-	Environmental Protection Agency (USA)
ETEC	-	Entero Toxigenic *E.Coli*.
FAO	-	Food and Agriculture Organization in the United Nations
FPD	-	Flame photometric detection
GC	-	Gas Chromatography
GCI	-	General Cognitive Index
GEMS	-	Global Environment Monitoring System
GOT	-	Glutamic – oxaloacetic transaminase
GPT	-	Glutamic – pyruvic transaminase
h	-	hour
HD	-	Hodgkin's disease
HDL	-	High-density lipoprotein
HPLC	-	High performance liquid chromatography
UPLC	-	Ultra High performance liquid chromatography
IARC	-	International Agency for Research on Cancer
ICRP	-	International Commission on Radiological Protection
ID	-	Infective Dose
Ig	-	Immunoglobulin
IgG	-	Immunoglobulin G
IgM	-	Immunoglobulin M
ILO	-	International Labour Organization
IPCS	-	International Program on Chemistry Safety
IQ	-	Intelligence Quotient
ISO	-	International Organization for Standardization.
JECFA	-	Joint (FAO/WHO) Expert Committee on Food Additives

JMPR	-	Joint (FAO/WHO) Meeting on Pesticide Residues
LC_{50}	-	Lethal Concentration, median
LD_{50}	-	Lethal Dose, median
LH	-	Luteinizing hormone
LOAEL	-	Lowest observed adverse effect level
LT	-	Heat labile Entero toxin
MAC	-	Mycobacterium Avium Complex
MAIS	-	*Mycobacterium Avium, M. intracellulare, M. scrofulaceum* complex
MDI	-	Mental Development Index, metered dose inhaler.
MFI	-	Million Fibers per liter
MIB	-	2-Methyl Isoborneol
MMAA	-	Monomethylarsonic Acid
MNCV	-	Motor Nerve Conduction Velocity
MS	-	Mass Spectrometry
MSCA	-	McCarthy Scales of Children's Abilities
MTD	-	Maximum Tolerated Dose
NADPH	-	Nicotinamide Adenine Dinucleotide Phosphate (reduced)
NAG	-	Neon Agglatinable
NHANES	-	US National Health and Nutrition Examination Survey
NHL	-	Non-Hodgkin Lymphoma
NOAEL	-	No-observed Adverse Effect Level
NTP	-	National Toxicology Program (USA)]
NTU	-	Nephelometric Tubidity Unit
Pa	-	Pascal
PDI	-	Psychomotor Development Index
Pka	-	log Acid Dissociation Constant
PMTDI	-	Provisional Maximum Tolerable Daily Intake
PTWI	-	Provisional Tolerable Weekly Intake
PVC	-	Polyvinyl Chloride
RNA	-	Ribonucleic Acid
SAED	-	Selected Area Electron Diffraction
SAP	-	Serum Alkaline Phosphatase
SGOT	-	Serum Glutamic Oxaloacetic Transaminase
CGPT	-	Serum Glutamic Pyruvic Transaminase

SMR	-	Standardized Mortality Ratio
ST	-	Ireat Stable Cuterotoxin
T$_4$	-	Thyroxine
TCU	-	True Colour Unit
TDI	-	Tolerable Daily Intake
TDS	-	Total Dissolved Solids
TEM	-	Transmission Electron Microscopy
TOC	-	Total Organic Carbon
TPA	-	Tetradecanoyl Phorbol Acetate
UNEP	-	United Nations Environment Program
UV	-	Ultraviolet
WHA	-	World Health Assembly
WHO	-	World Health Organization
CEN	-	Committee European de Normalization.
IEC	-	International Electrotechnical Commission.
DIS	-	Draft International standard
TC	-	Technical committee.
RTV	-	Room temperature Vulcanizes
RTD	-	Resistance Temperature Detector.
TSE	-	Transmissible Spongiform Encephalopathy.
BSE	-	Bovine Spongiform Encephalopathy
PMS	-	Post Marketing Surveillance.
PDA	-	Parenteral Drug Association.
ISPE	-	International Society for Pharmaceutical Engineering.
OPPI	-	Organization of Pharmaceutical Producers of India
IPA	-	Indian Pharmaceutical Association.
IDMA	-	Indian Drugs Manufacturers Association.
DIN	-	Deutsches Institut Fur Normung. (German institute for standardization.)
PIC	-	Pharmaceutical Inspection Convention.
CBER	-	Center for Biological Evaluation and Research.
CDER	-	Center for Drug Evaluation and Research.

❖❖❖

41. LIGHT ILLUMINATION (LUX) FOR PHARMACEUTICAL PLANT

Requirements and Measurements:

Adequate lighting in pharmaceutical unit is necessary. Without adequate lighting nobody can carry out their work satisfactorily and correctly. If the work area has too little light it will cause eye strain and fatigue particularly when detailed work is to be performed. Too much light is also not desirable as it can cause glare and dazzle. For adequate lighting, following points shall be kept in mind:

(1) Position of source of light.

(2) Selection of tubes or bulbs.

(3) Intensity of light.

The minimum recommended intensity of lights is 500 Lux.

For detailed work like inspection, an intensity of 1000 Lux is recommended. For ampoules and vials inspection 1800 to 2200 Lux is recommended.

The unit of intensity of illumination is the intensity of illumination produced by a standard candle on the inside white surface of a sphere of unit radius when placed at it's centre, if the radius of sphere is one meter, then intensity of illumination is 1 lumen per square meter and known as meter candle or LUX.

LUX meters are used to measure the illumination of light and Intensity meters are used to measure the intensity of UV radiations.

42. CLEAN ROOM LIGHTING

Sterile (Clean) Rooms:

Several lighting options are provided to meet your clean room needs. Several clean room design companies have designed various types of lighting fixtures. Following are some of them:

1) **Versa-Clean:** These are square sided fixtures with Neoprene gasketing, and cold rolled steel.

2) **Super Seal Lay in Fluorescent Light Fixtures:** Meeting and exceeding the stringent demands of various clean room applications, the super seal lighting fixtures housing is totally sealed to prevent infiltration of contaminants.

3) **Tear Drop Light Fixtures:** Offers a tear drop-shaped fluorescent lighting fixture designed to eliminate particulate and vapour contamination in clean environment. The aerodynamic design minimizes air flow disruption in laminar flow areas.

4) **Free Flow Light Fixtures:** An innovative lighting fixture that has the ability to provide lighting under a HEPA filter without disturbing the Laminar Flow.

For applications that do not require 100 % FFU ceiling coverage, 2' x 4' illuminators can be positioned in unused ceiling grids.

For applications that require total or near-total FFU ceiling coverage, tear drop and flow- through lighting modules are available in market. Tear drop fluorescent lights mount to the ceiling grid below the FFU. Their aerodynamic design does not interfere with the laminar airflow. Each of these single tube lights requires 6" of vertical clearance below the FFU Filter face.

As an alternative to tear drop lights, one can select 2' x 4' flow through lights, which are stacked below the FFU. Flow through lights requires no vertical clearance below the filter face, making them ideal for low ceiling clean rooms.

Guideline to select the appropriate number of lighting modules:

Light Level	Viewing Requirements	Foot - Candles per Sq. Ft.
Dim	Large Particle Sizes, High contrast.	20 – 50
Average	Small Particle Sizes, Medium contrast.	100 – 200
Bright	Small Particle Size, Low contrast.	200 – 500

Number of fixtures:

= Desired foot candles per sq. ft x Room area/4560 (for 2' x 4 ' lights)

= Desired foot candles per sq. ft x Room area/1260 (for Teardrop lights)

= Desired foot candles per sq. ft x Room area/3150 (for Flow through lights)

Lighting fixtures should be recessed flush with the ceiling. Since most lighting fixtures are not tightly sealed, the diffusers should be sealed internally with the ceiling and the lamp changed from outside clean room. Special "Wash down" fixtures are well sealed, but protrude obtrusively into the room and have clips and sealing lips which are difficult to sanitize.

Areas having a full HEPA ceiling obviously cannot accommodate recessed lighting fixtures. In these areas fixtures are of a special "Tear drop" shape which minimises disruption too the laminar air flow pattern.

43. COLOUR CODING FOR PIPELINES AND GASLINES

Colour coding is a shortest numbering, colouring and marking system for identification and traceability. Coding system should be defined on paper before coding on item. Colours or stainless steel or aluminium embossed or engraved arrows can be used to show the direction of rotation or direction of flow on moving parts and on pipe lines respectively or wherever necessary.

Advantages of Coding and Colour Coding Systems:
1. Easy identification and traceability.
2. GMP, ISO requirement.
3. To avoid mistake.
4. To avoid mix-ups.
5. To avoid time loss in searching.
6. To avoid missing and to know location.
7. To avoid stealing (Theft).
8. To avoid duplication in market.
9. Easy documentation.
10. Easy and accurate communication.
11. To develop standard.
12. Computer data coding and programming.
13. Colour coding helpful for illiterates.
14. To avoid accidents and improve safety.

TABLE 1: GENERAL SERVICES

Contents	Ground Colour	First Colour Band	Second Colour Band
Water:			
Cooling 8-25 degree C	Sea Green	French Blue	—
Boiler Feed	Sea Green	—	—
Condensate (distilled)	Sea Green	Light Brown	—
Drinking	Sea Green	French Blue	Signal Red
Treated (DM)	Sea Green	Light Orange	—
Central Heating Below 60 degree C	Sea Green	Canary Yellow	—

Contd..

Central Heating 60 - 100 degree C	Sea Green	Dark Violet	—
Central Heating above 100 degree C	Sea Green	Dark Violet	Signal Red
Cold Water down service 2-8 degree C from Storage Tanks	Sea Green	French Blue	Canary Yellow
Domestic, Hot	Sea Green	Light Gray	—
Hydraulic Power	Sea Green	Black	—
Sea, River, Untreated	Sea Green	White	—
Air:			
Compressed, upto and Including 15 kg/cm^2	Sky Blue	—	—
Compressed to over 15 kg/cm^2	Sky Blue	Signal Red	—
Vacuum	Sky Blue	Black	—
Steam	Silver Gray	—	—
Drainage	Black	—	—
Town Gas	Canary Yellow	—	—
Oils:			
Diesel Fuel	Light Brown	Brilliant Green	—
Furnace Fuel	Light Brown	French Blue	—
Lubricating Oil	Light Brown	Light Gray	—
Hydraulic Power	Light Brown	Dark Violet	—
Transformer Oil	Light Brown	Light Orange	—
Fire Service	Fire Red	—	—

COLOUR CODE FOR INDUSTRIAL GASES

Gas	Ground Colour	First Colour Band	Second Colour Band
Ammonia	Dark Violet	—	—
Chlorine	Dark Violet	Signal Red	—
Hydrocyanic Acid	Dark Violet	French Blue	—
Phenol	Dark Violet	Canary Yellow	—

Contd..

Sulphur dioxide	Dark Violet	Brilliant Green	—
Acetylene	Canary Yellow	Dark Violet	—
Argon	Canary Yellow	French Blue	—
Benzole	Canary Yellow	Dark Violet	French Blue
Blast Furnace Gas	Canary Yellow	Signal Red	Light Grey
Butane	Canary Yellow	Signal Red	—
Coal Gas	Canary Yellow	Signal Red	Brilliant Green
Carbon Dioxide (temperature)	Canary Yellow	Light Grey	—
Carbon monoxide	Canary Yellow	Signal Red	White
Coke Over Gas	Canary Yellow	Signal Red	Dark Violet
Ethylchloride (inflammable)	Canary Yellow	Light Gray	Signal Red
Ethylchoride (non-inflammable)	Canary Yellow	Light Gray	White
Ethylene	Canary Yellow	Dark Violet	Signal Red
Ethylene Oxide	Canary Yellow	Dark Violet	Brilliant Green
Freon (Chlorofluoro derivative of Methane and Ethane)	Canary Yellow	Light Gray	Dark Violet
Hellum	Canary Yellow	Light Brown	—
Hydrogen	Canary Yellow	Signal Red	French Blue
Methane	Canary Yellow	Signal Red	Light Brown
Methyl Bromide	Canary Yellow	French Blue	Black
Methylchloride (inflammable)	Canary Yellow	Brilliant Green	Signal Red
Methyl Chloride (non-inflammable)	Canary Yellow	Brilliant Green	French Blue
Neon	Canary Yellow	Light Brown	Black
Nitrogen	Canary Yellow	Black	—
Oxygen	Canary Yellow	White	—
Propane	Canary Yellow	Signal Red	Black
Phosgene	Canary Yellow	Black	White

❖❖❖

44. PURE STEAM QUALITY

In pharmaceutical industries, steam is used on large scale as source of heat and for killing of microorganisms. It is used in jackets as well as in a direct contact of product, components and product contact surfaces. The purity of steam is very important for all the purpose, specifically in sterilization areas. Steam should be checked for the quality before addition in to the sterilizer.

Steam provides moisture that allows the coagulation of cell wall protein and supplies the energy that heats the components and maintains their temperature. Steam system should be designed to ensure that the steam delivered to the sterilizer is saturated steam having steam quality of **97 to 100 %**. Steam of poor quality can contribute to wet packs and to sub-optimal steam sterilization cycles that might not be identified by biological monitoring.

Steam quality can be monitored as per the European standard EN 285 and HTM 2010.

Wet steam:

The correct steam quality combined with proper packing and sterilizer loading technique, should ensure that dry loads are consistently achieved. When items are processed, steam condenses and gives up latent heat, should surplus condensate settle on the item either as result of water entrained in the steam or by condensate dripping from another item, it may not dry. In practice, as steam condenses, much of the water generated will drain and reduce the need for the latent heat contribution from the item. The drying time will be dependent up on the location of the condensate, it's surface contact surface area and specific heat of the item. Large quantities of condensate in contact with a small surface area of an item will be slow to evaporate and insulators will dry more slowly than good conductor of heat. To test for wet steam, we can weight a towel pack before and after sterilization and cooling. These should be no more than a 3% increase in the weight of the pack and no visible evidence of excessive moisture.

Superheated steam:

Superheated steam is that is at an elevated temperature for it's saturation pressure and is usually generated as the result of pressure drops through either pressure – reducing valve or orifices. The impact of the pressure drop is to modify the pressure of the steam while its' energy content remains same. The excess energy for the pressure present will result in any excess moisture turning to steam. If the steam is already dry saturated, or if excess energy is still present after converting moisture to steam, an increase in temperature will be evident. Once steam is dry saturated only a small amount of energy is needed to create high temperatures. Superheated steam acts as hot air and at the temperature present will have little or no sterilizing effect. The excessive temperature can also cause damage to items and packaging. To test for super heated steam, a small load test is performed where a thermocouple is placed 2 inches above a standard linen pack. According to European standard EN 285, the temperature measured by the thermocouple at the start of the sterilization stage should not exceed by more than 5°C and should reduce to less 2°C in one minute.

Non condensable gases:

Non condensable gases(NCG) are gases liberated by steam when it condenses. The sources of such gases is usually the steam generator feed water, and the impact of such gases is that they modify the steam from being pure water vapour to a mixture of steam and gas, So that they are an unwanted contaminant. If the steam is from a hollow or porous source these gases will be forced to the center and can prevent direct contact or insulate the item. Such condition are identical to inadequate air removal, where small amount of air remains.

Following are specification as per EN 285 for pure steam.:

1) **Non condensable gases:**

   Using the SQ1 portable steam quality test Kit, The amount of gas collected per 100ml of condensate should not exceed 3.5 ml, that is should not be more that 3.5%. It should be noted that 100ml of water will generate 169.4 liter of steam at atmospheric pressure and while referring the result is expressed as a percentage, by volume of gas: steam the actual value is 0.00206 %, a very small value.

2) **Dryness Value:**

   The dryness value of the steam should be equal to or grater than 0.9 for porous loads or 0.95 where metal loads are processed. Invariably this means the latter limit is applicable. In any event, in plant steam terms, steam containing 5% of moisture would be seen to be poor quality and a dryness value of 0.99 would be more commonly seen to be acceptable.

3) **Degree of super heat:**

   When steam is reduced from line to atmosphere using the pilot and expansion tube shown, the temperature measured should not exceed 25°C above boiling temperature for the atmospheric pressure at the test point(typically measured value should not exceed 125 °C). It is stressed that the limit describes the maximum temperature and that no minimum to value applies to this test.

❖ ❖ ❖

45. WATER PIPELINE – SLOPE MEASUREMENT AND LIMIT

Following procedure can be used to measure the slope of the pharmaceutical water distribution pipe line slope.

1. Form the segments of the water pipeline with the help of marker. Length of the segment shall be not too long and not too short. It should be easy to measure.
2. Take the water filled the level silicon tube and place one tip of tube at point A and another tip on B1, exactly above the another end of pipe segment where the both the levels of liquid in tubes are equal. Mark the level point.
3. Measure the distance between B to B1. as C in mm (Slope).
4. Measure the distance between A to B1 as D in mm (Length of Pipe).

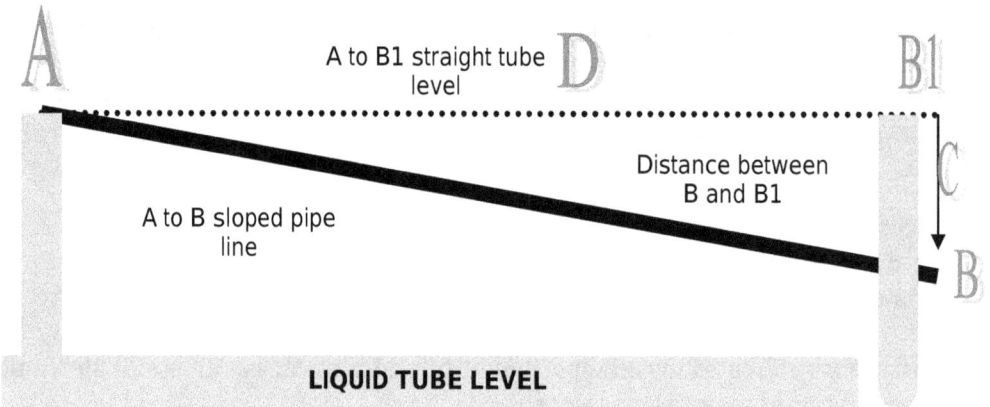

Acceptance criteria: As per the ISPE base line guide the Water distribution system process pipes or tubing should be a minimum slope of 1/146 inch/Ft or 0.52 cm /m. That is if the D in above figure is 1 meter the c shall be at least 0.52 cm or 52 mm.

BIBLIOGRAPHY

1. Merck and Co. Incorporation The Merck Index of Chemical and Drugs, Rahway, New Jersey, U.S.A.
2. C. C. Chattergee, Physiology Volume -I, 11th edition.
3. Good Laboratories Practices and Current Good Manufacturing Practices; Ludwig Huber.
4. Instrumental Methods of Chemical Analysis; Gurdeep Chatwal and Sham Anand, Seventh Edition.
5. Marketing Authorization of Pharmaceutical Products with special referance to multisource (Generic) Products : A Manual for Drug Rulatory Authorities; WHO/DMP/RGS/98.5.
6. 32nd Report, WHO expert committee on specifications for Pharmaceutical Preparation.
7. WHO GMP for Pharmaceutical Products. Technical Report Series No. 823, Geneva 1992.
8. Rules and guidelines for Pharmaceutical manufacturers and distributors, Medicine Control Agency, Department of Health, London U.K.
9. Clean Rooms and associated controlled environmments; ISO 14644-1:1999(E), ISO 14644-2: 2000(E); ISO /DIS 16644-3; ISO14644 - 4 : 2001(E); ISO /DIS 4644 - 5, International Standard, First edition.
10. Review of Federal Standard 209E by Gerry Greiner.
11. Cole-Parmer Incorporation U.S.A. Directory.
12. ISO 9001 : Quality management system requirements, International Standard, 3rd edition.
13. Principles of Chromatography; K. R. Mahadik and K. G. Bothara.
14. Pharmaceutical Chemistry Part II; Dr. A. V. Kasture, S. G. Wadodkar, K. M. Gikhale, 6th edition, 1991-92.
15. Opportunities in Pharmacy Careers; Fred B. Gable, First edition.
16. Analytical Chemistry; Dr. Subhash - Satish, Seventh edition.
17. Viva in Biochemistry; Dr. Varunkumar Malhotra, 4th edition.
18. The Theory and Practice of Industrial Pharmacy; Leon Lachman, Liberman and Kanig, 3rd edition "Recombinant DNA Technologies : Refined Boundaries" PharmaBioworld, Vol. I, Issue-2
19. Pharmaceutical Dosage Forms - Parenteral Vol. III; Herbert A. Lieberman, Leon Lachman.
20. Pharmaceutics-I; S. B. Gokhale, P. V. Kasture, S. R. Parakh, S. A. Hasan. 8th edition.
21. Pharmaceutics-II; P. V. Kasture, S. R. Parakh, S. B. Gokhale and A. R. Paradkar
22. Good Manufacturing Practices for Pharmaceuticals : A plan for total Quality Control. Second edition; Sidney H. Willig, Murray M. Tuckerman, William S. Hitchings. Marcel Dekker, Inc. New York and Basel.

23. Vijay Malik, Drugs and Cosmetics Act,; 18th edition, EBC publishing (P) Ltd., LUCKNOW, 1940.
24. Pharmacognosy; C. K. Kokate, A. P Purohit and S. B. Gokhale, 22nd edition.
25. Microbiology; Michael J. Pelczar, Jr. E. C. S. Chan, Noel R. Krieg, 5th edition.
26. Essentials of Pharmacotheraputics; FSK Barar, 2nd edition.
27. Principles of Biochemistry; Albert L. Lehninger, Worth Publishers Inc. New York, USA.
28. How to Practice GMPs; P. P. Sharma.
29. United States Pharmacopoeia, USP XIX, United States Pharmacopoeial Convention Inc., Rockville, Md. USA.
30. Organization Pharmaceutical Producers of India Guide; 2nd edition.
31. Internation Conference on Harmonization : ICH M2 EWG – eCTD.
32. European Union Guideline.
33. Air Born Particulate Cleanliness Classes in Clean rooms and Clean Zones - Federal Standard 209 E; The Institute of Environmental Science USA.
34. "Validation of Manufacturing Processes"; WHO GMP, manufacturing Principles for Pharmaceutical Products; Essential Drugs and Medicinal Policy.
35. ICH – Q1A R – Stability Testing of New drugs substances and Products.
36. "Sterile Pharmaceutical Products" WHO GMP : Specific Pharmaceutical Products; Essential Drugs and Medicines Policy.
37. ICH – Q1B – Photostability testing : Photostability testing of new drug substances and drug products.
38. Guidelines of "The European Agency for the Evaluation of medicinal Products" Committee for Proprietary medicinal Products (CPMP), Committee for Veterinary NNP medicinal Products (CVMP).
39. Journal of Parenteral Science and Technology, Princeton, NJ USA, 1992.
40. Guidelines on General Principles of Process Validations May 1987, Center for Drugds and Biologics and Food and Drug Administration, Rockville, Maryland USA.
41. Guideline on Sterile drug products produced by Aseptic Processing, JUNE, 1987, Center for Drugs and Biologics and Food and Drug Administration, Rockville, Maryland USA.
42. Guidelinees for submitting samples and analytical data for methods validation, Feb. 1987 Center for Drug Evolution and Research, Center for Biologic Evolution and Research, Center for Drugs and Biologics and Food and Drug Administration, Rockville.
43. TGA -Theraputic Goods Administration, Modue -1, NTA, Volume 2B, CTD, TGA Edition OCT. 2002.
44. Guidelines of "International Conference on Harmonization".
45. Drug Master Files; Center for Drug Evolution and Research, Department of health and Human Services, Food and Drug Administration, Rockville, Maryland USA.
46. Guideline for submitting document for the stability of human drugs and Biologics,

Guideline for Industry, Center for Drug Evolution and Research, Department of Health and Human Services, FDA, RockVille, Maryland, USA.

47. 21 Code of Fderal Standard Parts 210 and 211 : cGMP in manufacturing, processing, Packaging or holding of Drugs. US FDA, U.S.A.
48. Interviews; Rjinder S. Dhillon, and Surgeet Rajinder Dhillon 3rd edition.
49. Drugs Formulation Manual, D. P. S. Kohali, 1st edition.
50. FUMIGATION "Training Manual for the Commercial pesticide Applications" Univercity of Nebraska Lincoln.
51. Pharmaceutics - The science of Dosage Form Design, Aulton Michael E. First Edition.
52. Cooper and Gunns Tutorial Pharmacy; S. J. Carter, CBS Publishers Delhi.
53. Dispensing for Pharmaceutical Students; S. J. Carter and Gunn, Pitman London.
54. New Schedule "M" to the Drug and Cosmetic Act 1940. Part II - Section 3, subsection - (i) 11/12/2001, No.- 617, Ministry of Health and Family Affairs, Govt. of India, New Delhi.
55. Verious Volumes of Pharma Search, Express Pharma Pulse, and Other Perodicalsa and Journals, Magazins.
56. Marketing Literatures of Products and Information/Operation mauals of verious Products, Machine and Equipments.
57. Indian Pharmacopoeia, Vol. I, II and III, 5th edition, **2007**, & Vol. I and II, 4th edition, 1996, Ministry of Health, Govt. of India, New Delhi.
58. Remington's Pharmaceutical Sciences, Alfonsa R. Gennro, Mack Pub. Co. USA.
59. Introduction to Chemical Engineering, Badger. W. L and Banchero J. T. McGraw-Hill Book Company Singapore.
60. Points to Consider Cleaning Validation. TR No. 29, PDA. Volume 12, No. 6 Nov. Dec. 98
61. Validations of analytical procedure : Methodology, ICH, Q2B, CDER Rock ville, MD 20857.
62. International standards ISO/DIS 14698 – I (draft).
63. "Cleanrooms and associated controlled environments biocontamination control" part I, general Annexure – C and F.
64. "Cleanrooms and associated controlled environments part 5, operation. Anex-F- international standard ISO/DIS 14644-5.
65. "Guide line for drinking water quality" IInd edition volume–2. World Health Organisation General 1999. & IIIrd current edition.
66. "Indian standard – drinking water Specification" 1st revision. Oct 96 BIS New Delhi.
67. "Environmental management systems – specifications with guidance for use" IS/ISO 14001 – 1996.
68. "Estern pharmacist" Jan. 1994. Vo –XXX VII, No. – 433.
69. "Pharma Times" Vol. 35, Aug. 2003.
70. OIML Recommendations No. R III. Revised in 2002.

71. "Current drinking water standards" US EPA. EPA 816 – F – 02 –13. Jul 2002.
72. "Explanatory Notes for industry on the preparation of a site muster file".
73. Pharmaceutical inspection convetion, PE 008 – 1 1- annex – 1 Nov. 2002.
74. "A review of the US FDF guideline on aseptic processing" Journal of pharmaceutical science technology, Vol. 46, No. 3/May Jun – 1992.
75. Various Volumes of Chronicle pharmabiz, Express Pharmapluse, Internet Websites and Literatures from manufacturers of material & machines.
76. "General requirements for the competence of testing and calibration laboratories." ISO/IES – 17028; 1999, ISI4874; 2000.
77. "Engineer's handbook" Associated consuting of engineers.
78. "Guidance document" Good manufacturing pactice for medicines in S. Africa, MCC 2003.
79. B.S Bahl, GD Tuli, Arun Bahl," Essentials of Physical Chemistry" S.Chand & CO. Ltd, New Delhi, 2004.
80. U.B Hadkar, Text book of physical pharmacy" 3 rd Edition, Nirali Prakashan, Pune- 2003.
81. Robert A.Nash, " Pharmaceutical Process Validation "Third Edition, Marcel Dekker, Inc. 1993.
82. Frederick J.Carlton, James P.Agalloco," Validation of Pharmaceutical Processes, Sterile product, 2nd edition, Marcel Dekker, Inc, Newyork.
83. GSR -517, Ministry of Health & Family welfare, Department of health,New Delhi -2003.
84. GSR -431(E), Drugs and Cosmetics (5th Amendment) Rules 2005, Ministry of Health & Family welfare, Department of health, New Delhi – Jun, 2005.
85. Pharma Times, Vol.37, No. 5, Indian Pharmaceutical Assocoan, Mumbai,2005.
86. European standard 285 & GAMP 4 guide, Version 4, Dec.2001, ISPE.
87. Pharmaceutical Engineering – July/August 2002. ISPE.
88. World Health Organization, Technical Report Series NO 902, 2003, Annexure -1.
89. World Health Organization, Technical Report Series NO 937, 2006, Annexure -2.
90. LCGPTI, " Journal of GMP & Industrial Pharmacy" June 2008, Vol-2, Issue –II.

www.ingramcontent.com/pod-product-compliance
Lightning Source LLC
Chambersburg PA
CBHW081415230426

43668CB00016B/2240